INTERNATIONAL ORGANIZATIONS AND CIVIL WARS

INTERNATIONAL ORGANIZATIONS AND CIVIL WARS

HILAIRE McCOUBREY
Senior Lecturer in Law, Director, Centre for International Defence Law Studies, University of Nottingham

NIGEL D. WHITE
Lecturer in Law, Secretary, Centre for International Defence Law Studies, University of Nottingham

Dartmouth
Aldershot • Brookfield USA • Singapore • Sydney

Published by
Dartmouth Publishing Company Limited
Gower House
Croft Road
Aldershot
Hants GU11 3HR
England

Dartmouth Publishing Company
Old Post Road
Brookfield
Vermont 15036
USA

British Library Cataloguing in Publication Data
McCoubrey, H.
　International Organizations and Civil
　Wars
　I. Title　II. White, N. D.
　341.68

Library of Congress Cataloging-in-Publication Data
McCoubrey, H., 1953–
　International organizations and civil wars / Hilaire McCoubrey,
　Nigel D. White.
　　　p.　cm.
　Includes bibliographical references and index.
　ISBN 1-85521-468-7
　1. Civil war.　2. United Nations—Armed Forces.　3. International
agencies.　I. White, Nigel D., 1961–　.　II. Title.
JX4541.M36 1994
341.5'23—dc20　　　　　　　　　　　　　　　　　　　94-21208
　　　　　　　　　　　　　　　　　　　　　　　　　　　　CIP

ISBN 1 85521 468 7
Printed and bound in Great Britain by
Hartnolls Limited, Bodmin, Cornwall

Contents

Preface

In the context of the 1990–91 Gulf conflict, a 'new world order' of efficacy in the maintenance of international law and international peace and security was confidently predicted. Unfortunately, although the work of the United Nations and the functioning of the UN Charter have undoubtedly been somewhat facilitated by the end of the northern hemisphere Cold War confrontation, the world order thereafter seems to have retained a depressing number of 'old' features and problems.

This has nowhere been more the case than in the context of non-international armed conflicts or civil wars. After 1991 the appalling crises in Somalia, Sudan and former Yugoslavia either erupted or continued; in other countries, too, internal violence at a variety of levels of intensity continued uninterrupted. Indeed, the end of the Cold War itself had negative as well as positive features in this context. On the credit balance the danger of superpower military, and possibly nuclear, conflict was alleviated and with it the various conflicts subsidiary to the ideological confrontation of the northern hemisphere superpowers. On the debit side of the equation, however, nationalist and regional tensions, going back in some cases to the 1930s and even into the period before 1914, were, so to speak, unfrozen by the end of the Cold War. The classic case was the violent dissolution of former Yugoslavia in the early 1990s into new, or – rather – old, units which had their roots in the historic position of the territory as the fulcrum of confrontation between the Russian (taking on the mantle of the East Roman), Holy Roman (later Austro-Hungarian) and Ottoman Empires. Whatever the complex historical, credal and ideological roots of the conflict(s), the hostilities waged over the territory of Bosnia-Herzegovina demonstrated with stark clarity both the terrible consequences of non-international armed conflict and the difficulties of the international community in responding to it.

The international institutions which are called upon to tackle the problems of non-international armed conflict face both legal and practical difficulties. The two are to some degree distinct but also intermesh since the problems of legal prescription, proscription and implementation are inevitably shaped by the practical context(s) of application.

The problems of legal prescription are largely set by the very fact of the *non-international* nature of the armed conflicts in question. There are problems of definition, largely founded upon considerations of levels of intensity. Somewhere between international armed conflict and sporadic criminal violence (such as a bank robbery) there lies the sector of 'non-international armed conflict'. Both upper and lower criteria of identification require to be set, not least in order to determine what minimum legal norms are applicable. Modern international law provision seeks to do this, but questions still remain to be resolved. The post-colonial development of the right to self-determination and its implications in the context of the 'internationalization' of certain *prima facie* non-international armed conflicts by reference to 1977 Protocol I Additional to the 1949 Geneva Conventions is one matter of considerable potential significance. At the other end of the scale is the continuing problem of terrorism. Terrorist violence is not something that readily submits to regulation by norms which are within or analogous to the laws of armed conflict. But at the same time the international response to, and even conception of, terrorism is both patchy and inconsistent, a situation which can hardly be considered satisfactory.

In the central context of this work – those episodes of violent confrontation within the territory of an existing state which may firmly be categorized as non-international armed conflicts – there remain serious legal difficulties. These largely turn upon issues of inevitable sovereign sensitivity. Non-international armed conflicts may clearly pose a threat to international peace and security within the meaning of Chapter VII of the UN Charter. The conflict(s) in former Yugoslavia in the early 1990s, with both their devastation and humanitarian crises (especially in Bosnia-Herzegovina), and the danger of regional confrontations thus posed were a striking example.

The various peacemaking efforts on the part of the UN and the European Union enjoyed very little immediate success. The ultimate placement of United Nations Forces, UNPROFOR, initially to guard relief convoys and increasingly in an active enforcement and peacemaking role, highlighted many problems in the mandating and functioning of UN Forces, not least the fact that the relevant provisions of Chapter VII of the UN Charter have, largely by reason of the 'Cold War', never quite functioned as originally intended. The difficulties faced by UNPROFOR in former Yugoslavia and UNOSOM in Somalia raise important issues for the future conduct of peacekeeping and peacemaking operations. The same is true of the involvement in UN-approved operations by regional defence alliances such as NATO, which was called upon to operate enforcement air strikes in former Yugoslavia.

The practicalities of humanitarian relief for victims of non-international armed conflicts are not, of course, new. The work of the International Red Cross, the UN High Commissioner for Refugees and other variously focused organizations (such as *Médecins sans Frontières*, OXFAM or Amnesty International) continues to be both difficult and vitally important. One obvious problem is getting relief supplies through to beleaguered populations in the face of armed opposition. This inevitably raises questions of the degree and form of cooperation possible between UN Forces and humanitarian agencies. In both Somalia and former Yugoslavia these arrangements were at times problematic, although it must be said that, without some forceful backing, much less aid would have reached intended destinations.

So far as the conduct of hostilities in non-international armed conflicts is concerned, even more intractable conceptual and practical difficulties arise. The idea that the internal conduct of a state, as compared with its external relations with other states, is a proper concern of public international law is of relatively recent development. It derives in large part from the experience of certain aspects of modern totalitarianism in the 1930s and 1940s, and has found primary expression in the development of the modern law of Human Rights. The relation between human rights and international humanitarian laws of armed conflict, in both the narrow and the broader sense, is highly controversial. However, it is essentially in that context that the laws of armed conflict governing the conduct of hostilities have, since the Second World War, begun to extend into non-international armed conflicts. The minimum 'Geneva' provision, essentially concerned with the protection of victims of armed conflict made by common article 3 of the four 1949 Geneva Conventions, has been considerably expanded by the provision of 1977 Protocol II Additional to the 1949 Geneva Conventions. States are of course inevitably reluctant to concede any 'legitimate' status to dissident forces fighting within their established territory. It is this which marks the most fundamental distinction between the provision for international and non-international armed conflicts. 'Hague' provision governing methods and means of warfare is extremely limited in the context of non-international armed conflicts for the same broad reasons of sovereign sensitivity. However some provision does now exist, both explicitly and by implication. International reaction to the use of chemical weapons against the Kurds in northern Iraq and to actions taken against the Shi-ite Marsh Arabs in the south of that country in the 1990s, for instance, may be significant in that regard. Concern over some of the methods and means of warfare used in former Yugoslavia found, potentially, a yet more pointed response in the contemplation of international criminal proceedings.

In any legal context, 'enforcement' is to some degree a symptom of failure. The purpose of legal prescription, or proscription, is to set norms of conduct in the society concerned with a view to their being observed. Before questions of enforcement arise there has, by definition, been a failure in the pursuit of that primary objective; this is nowhere more pointedly the case than in the context of armed conflict. Nonetheless, the necessity for enforcement by way of immediate response, reaffirmation and future deterrence may clearly arise. Trials for violations of law – municipal and international – in civil wars have an extended and not wholly reputable history. The shock caused to the international community by the brutality of the hostilities in former Yugoslavia led to the setting up of an International Tribunal, pursuant to UN Security Council Resolution 808 of 22 February 1993 with a view to the trial of those suspected of major crimes. The issue posed many questions, not least that of the law to be applied in view of a network of agreements between the parties, honoured sadly more in the breach than in the observance, that much of the law relating to the conduct of *international* armed conflicts should be applicable to the hostilities in former Yugoslavia. At the time of writing the outcome of these processes still remains to be seen, but their potential effects, positive or otherwise, seem very considerable.

The incidence of non-international armed conflict at this latter end of the 20th century, whether the world order be 'new' or 'old', shows little if any sign of abating. The issues addressed in this book – the response of international institutions to such conflicts and their legal context – are now and seem set to remain high on the agenda of international concern. It is for this reason that these issues must be considered worthy of consideration and debate.

Abbreviations

ADF	Arab Deterrent Force
AJIL	*American Journal of International Law*
All E.R.	All England Reports
ANC	African National Congress
BFSP	British and Foreign State Papers
Bull. EC	*Bulletin of the European Community*
BYIL	*British Yearbook of International Law*
CIA	Central Intelligence Agency
CIS	Commonwealth of Independent States
CMF	Commonwealth Monitoring Force
COG	Commonwealth Observer Group
CSCE	Conference on Security and Cooperation in Europe
EC	European Community
ECOMOG	Economic Community of West African States Military Observer Group
ECOSCOC	United Nations Economic and Social Council
ECOWAS	Economic Community of West African States
EJIL	*European Journal of International Law*
EPC	European Political Cooperation
EPLF	Eritrean Peoples Liberation Front
EU	European Union
FLN	National Liberation Front
FMLN	Farabundo Marti National Liberation Front (El Salvador)
FUNCINPEC	United Front for an Independent Cambodia
GAOR	United Nations General Assembly Official Records
ICJ Rep.	Reports of the International Court of Justice
ICLQ	*International and Comparative Law Quarterly*
ICRC	International Committee of the Red Cross
IJIL	*Indian Journal of International Law*
ILM	*International Legal Materials*
IRA	Irish Republican Army
IRO	International Refugee Organization
JNA	Yugoslav National Army

KB	Law Reports of the King's Bench Division
Keesing's	*Keesing's Record of World Events*
M&S	Maule and Selwyn's Reports
MFO	Multinational Force in Sinai
MINURSO	United Nations Mission for the Referendum in Western Sahara
MPLA	Popular Movement for the Liberation of Angola
NATO	North Atlantic Treaty Organization
NILR	*Netherlands International Law Review*
OAS	Organization of American States
OAU	Organization of African Unity
OECS	Organization of Eastern Caribbean States
OJ	*Official Journal of the European Community*
ONUC	United Nations Operation in the Congo
ONUCA	United Nations Observation Group in Central America
ONUMOZ	United Nations Operation in Mozambique
ONUSAL	United Nations Observer Mission in El Salvador
ONUVEH	United Nations Observer Group for the Verification of Elections in Haiti
ONUVEN	United Nations Observer Mission to Verify the Electoral Process in Nicaragua
PLO	Palestine Liberation Organization
POLISARIO	Popular Front for the Liberation of the Sanguia el-Harura and the Rio de Oro
RPF	Rwandese Patriotic Front
SCOR	United Nations Security Council Official Records
SCR	Southern Cape Reports
SWAPO	South West Africa Peoples Organization
UAR	United Arab Republic
UDI	Unilateral Declaration of Independence
UKTS	United Kingdom Treaty Series
UN A/PV	United Nations Provisional Records (General Assembly)
UN Doc. A/	United Nations Document (General Assembly)
UN Doc. S/	United Nations Document (Security Council)
UN S/PV	United Nations Provisional Records (Security Council)
UNAMIC	United Nations Advance Mission in Cambodia
UNAMIR	United Nations Assistance Mission to Rwanda
UNAVEM	United Nations Angola Verification Mission
UNCIP	United Nations Commission on India and Pakistan
UNEF	United Nations Emergency Force
UNFICYP	United Nations Force in Cyprus

UNGOMAP	United Nations Good Offices Mission in Afghanistan and Pakistan
UNHCR	United Nations High Commissioner for Refugees
UNIFIL	United Nations Interim Force in the Lebanon
UNITA	National Union for the Total Independence of Angola
UNITAF	Unified Task Force
UNMIH	United Nations Mission in Haiti
UNMOT	United Nations Mission of Observers in Tajikistan
UNOGIL	United Nations Observer Group to the Lebanon
UNOMIG	United Nations Observer Mission in Georgia
UNOMIL	United Nations Observer Mission for Liberia
UNOMSA	United Nations Observer Mission in South Africa
UNOSOM	United Nations Operation in Somalia
UNOVER	United Nations Observer Mission to Verify the Referendum in Eritrea
UNPROFOR	United Nations Protection Force in Yugoslavia
UNRRA	United Nations Relief and Rehabilitation Administration
UNSF	United Nations Security Force
UNTAC	United Nations Transition Assistance Authority in Cambodia
UNTAG	United Nations Transition Assistance Group
UNTEA	United Nations Temporary Executive Authority
UNTS	United Nations Treaty Series
UNYOM	United Nations Yemen Observer Mission
WEU	Western European Union
ZANU	Zimbabwe African National Union

PART I
THE INSTITUTIONAL AND
LEGAL FRAMEWORK

1 Principles of International Law Governing Civil Wars

The aim of this chapter is to describe the wider legal framework within which international organizations operate in internal conflicts. This will involve looking at the general legal principles governing the law prohibiting intervention in internal armed conflicts (the *jus ad bellum*) and the law regulating and mitigating the conduct of hostilities in such conflicts (the *jus in bello*). The analysis will be mainly concerned with the obligations of the parties to the conflict and of outside states rather than the rights, duties and role of international organizations. However, it is necessary to paint the wider legal picture before the reader can begin to understand the role and operation of international organizations.

The *jus ad bellum*

By taking a general overview of the history of the *jus ad bellum*, it can be seen that the international community has taken faltering steps towards the control of the occasions when war can lawfully be launched.[1] This development culminated in the outright prohibition of war, or more generally the use of armed force, in the UN Charter of 1945, article 2(4), which reads as follows:

> All Members shall refrain in their international relations from the threat or use of force against the territorial integrity or political independence of any State, or in any other manner inconsistent with the purposes of the United Nations.

The only exceptions to this are, on the one hand, the rights of individual or collective self-defence 'if an armed attack occurs' against a member state embodied in article 51; and, on the other hand, the option possessed by the Security Council of the UN to take 'such action by air, sea, or land forces as may be necessary to maintain or restore international peace and security' after determining that there exists 'any threat to the peace, breach of the peace, or act of aggression' according to articles 42 and 39 of Chapter VII of the Charter.

These rules appear relatively straightforward[2] and can be readily applied to modern-day situations in which one state attacks or commits an aggression against another state. In August 1990, Iraq breached article 2(4) when it invaded and occupied Kuwait,[3] so entitling Kuwait and it allies to prepare to act in collective self-defence, and also prompting a recently revitalized Security Council to authorize the use of force to remove Iraq from Kuwait.[4] Although academic legal debate raged as to whether the Coalition military action between January and March 1991 properly came under either the exception contained in article 51 allowing for self-defence or under the provisions of Chapter VII of the Charter defining the Security Council's powers,[5] the military response to Iraqi aggression was in fact justifiable under international law.

The Iraqi invasion of Kuwait was a case of the direct use of force by one state against another; in other words, it was an inter-state conflict involving two or more states directly confronting each other by force of arms. There have been other examples of such conflicts in the post-1945 world order, such as the Falklands War of 1982, but by far the most frequent type of conflict is internal or intra-state which takes place between factions within a state, with or without the involvement of outside states. These are what have been traditionally labelled civil wars. Third states can be involved either indirectly (by supplying arms for example) or directly (by supplying troops) on behalf of the factions.

During the Cold War period 1945–90, the two world superpowers, the United States and the Soviet Union, used both methods of intervention, although they did not confront each other directly. For example in Afghanistan after the Soviet invasion of 1979, the Soviet Union propped up its puppet government with Soviet troops until the Geneva Accords of 1988,[6] whilst the United States supported the *mujahedin* in the form of arms and supplies. Although the levels of support varied in each conflict, this pattern was mirrored or repeated in many of the internecine conflicts around the world – in Angola, El Salvador, Nicaragua, Cambodia and Yemen to name but a few. Sometimes the conflict would appear a curious hybrid between inter-state and intra-state use of force when conflict broke out between two halves of a divided state such as in Korea in 1950 and in Vietnam in the 1960s.

Any hopes that such conflicts would be reduced with the end of the Cold War and the collapse of the Soviet Union in 1991 have proved to be very naive. Although the change in the world order enabled steps to be taken to end some of the conflicts that had been raging for many years, a new crop of internal disputes broke out as the repression of the Cold War period was removed and the simmering ethnic and religious tensions in many countries gave way to bloody conflicts, for example in Yugoslavia and Somalia, as well as within several of the new states emerging from the former Soviet Union.

What becomes apparent after considering these civil wars is that article 2(4) containing the ban on force, and articles 51, 39 and 42 enumerating the exceptions to that ban, do not seem readily applicable to such conflicts. To start with, in considering the obligations of the parties to the conflict to use or not to use force against each other, the Charter provisions seem wholly inapplicable since they apply only to members of the UN (i.e. states) *in their relations with each other*, although, as shall be seen in Chapter 2, the Security Council has developed the concept of a 'threat to the peace' within the meaning of article 39 to cover internal situations. Even in the cases of Korea, when there appeared to be a clear-cut attack by the North against the South in 1950, it was not possible to state that this was a clear breach of article 2(4) entitling the South Koreans to act in self-defence, since neither North Korea nor South Korea was a member of the UN or a state in the full sense of the word in international law. Thus it was possible to argue that the war was a civil conflict between the two Korean factions.[7] Having said that, the international community in general treated it as an inter-state conflict.

Is it possible to apply the norms of the UN Charter to a civil conflict when two factions within a state are fighting for supremacy? A layman might argue that to rebel against the established government of a state must be unlawful, and that rebellion in some sense represents illegal use of force against the government, entitling it to defend itself. Whether this perception is correct will be discussed below, as will the obligations of outside states *vis-à-vis* the warring factions within a state. Following from our layman's perception, can a government invite in outside states' troops to help it defend itself from rebels, or does it have to prove that the rebels are themselves supported by outside powers before it can appeal for help? The problem becomes increasingly complicated when one considers the varying levels of support each faction may receive – from basic medical aid and clothing to the provisions of arms or indeed of troops. How can the rather simple rules of the UN Charter be applied to such complex situations?[8]

Before examining the obligations of the parties to an internal conflict in terms of the *jus ad bellum*, it is necessary to say a few words about the old doctrines of insurgency and belligerency which formerly purported to govern civil conflicts, both for the parties themselves and for outside states. This doctrine has been outmoded since 1945 for reasons that will become clear, but is sometimes found in the literature[9] and was discussed in relation to conflicts as late as the Spanish Civil War (1936–39).[10]

Insurgency and Belligerency

Professor Padelford has examined the rules and principles of international law accepted and acted upon during the Spanish civil war when the Nationalist forces of General Franco, supported by Germany and Italy, rebelled against the established Republican government, aided to a far lesser extent by the Soviet Union as well as by International Brigades of up to 60,000 volunteers.[11]

Under this traditional doctrine, a state that experienced a revolt, insurrection, rebellion, revolution or civil war was essentially beyond the purview of international law. It was seen basically as an internal situation. Revolution was not unlawful under international law though, 'by the municipal law of all countries, the taking up of arms against the state or its duly established government is a supreme crime, treason'. However, when the insurrection became so widespread that it could not be contained by the state's civil administration, then it was customary, according to this doctrine, for the government and foreign states 'to make an admission of insurgency'. This 'was an acknowledgement of the fact that an organized uprising for political ends involving the use of armed force and temporarily beyond the control of the civil authorities' was taking place. Admission of insurgency did not alter the legal status of the rebels either as regards the government or foreign states, although it did relieve the government of responsibility for the acts of the insurgents, whilst permitting foreign states to enter into informal relations with them.

If the civil conflict continued and the rebels effectively established a state within a state, in other words they occupied, controlled and administered a substantial area of the state, then according to the traditional doctrine, the time was right for outside states to recognize the existence of the status of belligerency. However, there was no duty on outside states to grant belligerent rights to the parties to the conflict; thus 'the granting of belligerent rights by one state is not binding or compulsory upon other states'. One of the results of an acceptance of belligerency was that the recognizing state had to adopt a legal status of neutrality according to the rules of the *jus in bello*.[12]

The problem with this rather formalistic set of rules was its inherently discretionary nature: recognition of insurgency and belligerency were not duties imposed on states when a civil conflict reached a certain level, but were often politically motivated acts. In addition, there have been very few formal declarations of recognition of belligerency as regards civil wars. Indeed, the last appears to be the British recognition of belligerency of the Confederate States in the American Civil War in 1861. It was possible to imply recognition of belligerency by examining the conduct of states to see if they were adopting a policy equivalent to the granting of belligerent rights but, as Oppenheim has warned us, 'care must be taken ... not to treat as recognition of belligerency what has properly been described as recognition of insurgency'. On top of this confusion there was the added difficulty that the recognition of insurgency and belligerency were not options available to states when the conflict in question lost the character of a civil war. Oppenheim gives the example of the Spanish Civil War:

> During the Spanish Civil War of 1936–39 recognition of belligerency was correctly refused for the reason that the accepted rules of recognition of belligerency did not apply to a situation in which as a result of the illegal intervention of foreign States the hostilities had lost the character of a civil war in the accepted meaning of the term.[13]

What the traditional doctrines failed to deal with adequately was the problem of when a civil war becomes internationalized, with the 'illegal' involvement of outside powers. The fact that so many conflicts are internationalized in one way or another and the uncertainty as to the application of the doctrines of insurgency and belligerency have led to the desuetude of the traditional doctrine, to be replaced by rules derived from the UN Charter and customary international law as developed since 1945.

The Use of Armed Force in Internal Conflicts

One surviving aspect of the traditional approach to civil conflicts is that there is still no norm of international law prohibiting the use of armed force in rebellion against an established government. It follows that, in general terms, governments are permitted to attempt to suppress rebellions by force of arms. However, although there is no *jus ante bellum* governing the conflict, other norms of international law do operate in an attempt to control some of the worse excesses of war. The *jus in bello* reviewed below is probably the most important, although there is a developing panoply of international human rights standards, such as those prohibiting genocide and torture (which may be of some import in a civil conflict) as well as a complex web of human rights treaties, both regional and international, which may allow for some international review of internal conflicts occurring within the borders of states party to these treaties.

It can be seen that, apart from the development of human rights norms, which may be applicable to internal conflicts, and the further development of the *jus in bello*, the situation as regards norms which attempt to prohibit the launching of war within a state has not changed in many respects since the American Civil War of 1861–65. However, there is a limited and ambiguous exception to this general proposition – the 1970 Declaration on Principles of International Law concerning Friendly Relations and Cooperation among States in Accordance with the Charter of the United Nations (known as the 1970 'Declaration on Friendly Relations'),[14] adopted by the UN General Assembly by consensus states that: '[e]very State has the duty to refrain from any forcible action which deprives peoples of [their] right to self-determination and freedom and independence'.

In the important *Case Concerning Military and Paramilitary Activities in and Against Nicaragua*, the International Court of Justice seemed to indicate that military action by a state to suppress the right of self-determination constituted an unlawful use of force contrary to article 2(4) of the UN Charter, but was not of sufficient gravity to amount to an armed aggression or armed attack entitling people to act in self-defence.[15]

The development of the legal principle of self-determination must be viewed in terms of the change in the composition of the world community since 1945. In that year, 51 states were members of the UN. By the end of the Cold War, in 1990, this number had leapt to 159, the increase being mainly composed of newly independent states who formed the Non-Aligned Movement (sometimes known as the Group of 77). The end of the Cold War produced another batch of new members with the break-up of the Soviet Union, Yugoslavia and Czechoslovakia; the admission of the separate Korean states; the independence of Namibia from South Africa and Eritrea from Ethiopia; and the admission of several so-called micro states – Micronesia, Liechtenstein, the Marshall Islands, San Marino, Andorra and Monaco, bringing the number in September 1993 to 184.

The development of the principle of self-determination was really a product of pressure from the Non-Aligned Movement in the late 1950s and 1960s. It was natural that this new majority in the UN would wish all colonies to become independent, a desire that quickly became embodied in the principle that all colonial peoples had a right to self-determination.[16] Indeed, it is not difficult to interpret colonialism as the illegal use of force against a people in a situation where the colonizing state is physically distant from the colonial territory and maintains its control by occupation (similar to military occupation following invasion by another state). This is recognized by the 1970 Declaration on Friendly Relations which states that 'the territory of a colony … has under the [UN] Charter a status separate and distinct from the territory of the state administering it'. However, a distinction must be drawn between the administering state maintaining its presence by force, which is a breach of the principle of self-determination, and merely maintaining law and order whilst encouraging the people towards independence, which is not.[17]

Further, it would be wrong to argue that the suppressed people have a right of self-defence against the colonial power[18] because self-defence is a right reserved to states, a right that the majority of states are unlikely to want to lose or to grant to other alleged subjects of international law. For this reason, the use of force to suppress a colonial people is not an armed attack or aggression, but is an illegal use of force by the colonial power which 'disentitles' it to seek outside support in the form of military aid from other states. It is also possible to say that this illegal use of force gives suppressed peoples the right to rebel in pursuit of self-determination. This means that wars of national liberation are justified, but are not equivalent to inter-state wars in which the victim can rely on collective self-defence. Indeed, it will be contended below that peoples struggling for self-determination are not allowed to receive military aid from outside states, and that the only 'advantage' they have over other rebellious groups is that the state or government denying them the right of self-determination is itself disentitled to receive military aid.[19]

Normally international law is neutral as regards rebellions seeing them as essentially internal matters, although the rules do favour the established government when the issue of self-determination is not involved. However, when considering a people struggling for self-determination, the 1974 Definition of Aggression and the 1987 Declaration on the Non Use of Force,[20] both adopted by the General Assembly by consensus, recognize 'the *right* of peoples to struggle to that end'. This necessarily implies that the colonial states should not have the advantage of outside help and also raised the possibility of assistance to the colonial people, discussed below. However, if one considers the right of self-determination to have spread beyond the colonial situation to include peoples subject to 'alien subjugation'[21] or governed by 'racist regimes',[22] which are concepts intended to cover past and present situations in the Israeli Occupied Territories and in South Africa,[23] it becomes more difficult to accept these as situations involving the use of force by a *state* against a people. Rather it appears to be an internal matter between a *government* and its people although, in the case of the Palestinians in the Occupied Territories, strong aspects of neo-colonialism by Israel seem apparent. However, apart from these limited, and rather selective, extensions of the right of self-determination, state practice has rarely suggested that the right to self-determination extends to the majority within an already established state.[24] Having said that, the break-up of the Soviet Union and Yugoslavia has led to suggestions that units within a *federal* (as opposed to *unitary*)

state have the right to self-determination if they meet the requirements of statehood.[25]

Intervention by Outside States in Internal Conflicts

The term 'intervention' in the context of armed conflicts is usually
applied to outside interference in a civil war. The difficulty with the
concept of outside intervention in an internal conflict is that it can
assume many forms and may be given either to the government or to
the rebels or to both.

The landmark judgment of the International Court of Justice delivered on 27 June 1986 in the *Nicaragua Case* identified four levels of
support for the insurgents or guerrillas. The case itself concerned
two covert operations. On the one hand there was the alleged support given to the FMLN (Farabundo Marti National Liberation Front)
rebels in El Salvador by the Sandinista government in Nicaragua; on
the other hand was alleged US support for the Contra rebels in
Nicaragua whose aim, until the electoral defeat of the Sandinistas in
February 1990, was the overthrow of the legitimate government of
Nicaragua.

The Court determined the level of intensity of each covert operation by examining the facts before it.[26] The Court found that although
the US had neither created nor sent the Contra force, it had financed,
supplied, equipped, armed, trained and provided strategic guidance
to the rebels in the years 1981–84 through its agency – the CIA
(Central Intelligence Agency). There could be no doubt that these
acts were attributable to the US government. The CIA, in fact, built
up the Contras from a poorly armed and poorly disciplined group of
1,000, to a force of over 12,000 heavily armed insurgents who operated from bases in Honduras and Nicaragua itself. Although the
Contra force was very closely linked to the government of the US, it
could not be viewed as an appendage of that government. Nevertheless, the level of outside involvement in the Contra force strongly
suggests that it did not represent a widely supported indigenous
armed movement. The level of US support to the Contras did fall off
after 1984, with the Court finding that the Contras thereafter received only humanitarian assistance, namely the provision of food,
clothing and medical supplies.[27]

The US alleged that it had taken this action in 1981 in response to
the Nicaraguan government's support for left-wing rebels in El Salvador which allegedly was of at last equal intensity as the support
instigated by the US for the Contras.[28] Judge Schwebel, in his dissenting opinion, agreed with the American argument. He stated that
'the Salvadoran rebels, vitally supported by Nicaragua, conduct a
rebellion in El Salvador; in collective self-defence, the United States

symmetrically supports rebels who conduct a rebellion in Nicaragua'.[29] However, the Court found that, although there were arms flowing from Nicaragua to the FMLN in El Salvador between 1979–81, no evidence emerged of greater Nicaraguan involvement in those years or thereafter. The FMLN certainly appeared to be a more indigenous revolt than that undertaken by the Contras. Having said that, the US did seem to be responding to an unlawful intervention and possibly an indirect use of force by Nicaragua. The question remains whether the unlawful intervention by Nicaragua justified the counter-intervention by the US.

In the course of its judgment, the Court identified four different levels of support for an armed rebellion within another state, relying principally on General Assembly resolutions. Based on the General Assembly's 1974 Definition of Aggression, it identified the highest level of involvement as equivalent to an indirect aggression or armed attack. Article 3(g) of that Definition stated that 'the sending by or on behalf of a state of armed bands, groups, irregulars or mercenaries, which carry out acts of armed force against another state ... or its substantial involvement therein' shall constitute an armed aggression by the supporting state. The World Court added the proviso that the activities of armed bands could qualify as aggression only if they had 'scale and effects'.[30] There is a problem with the phrase 'substantial involvement' which appears imprecise,[31] but the Court interpreted it quite strictly to mean that the outside state must virtually create or control the insurgency for it to constitute an armed attack by means other than using the outside state's regular army.[32]

The Court did not find that US support for the Contras nor Nicaraguan support for the FMLN fell within this category; instead it found that both came within the next level of outside involvement, namely an indirect use of force. This level is best encapsulated in the phrases 'assisted' and 'participated' in rebellion, as found in the 1970 Declaration on Friendly Relations which was relied upon by the Court. This could involve what would appear to be 'substantial involvement' in the insurgency, such as US support for the Contras; at the other extreme, it could be simply the *arming* of insurgents, as occurred between the Nicaraguan government and the FMLN.[33] The Court made it clear that there was a sharp difference between the *arming* of the rebels, which it indicated was an unlawful use of force by the supporting state, and mere *funding* of the rebels, which it regarded as unlawful intervention. It derived the latter principle from the 1970 Declaration on Friendly Relations and the earlier 1965 Declaration on Non Intervention which, read together, categorized the 'financing' of armed activities directed at the violent overthrow of the regime of another state as unlawful intervention, but not as an unlawful use of force by the supporting state.[34] Finally, the Court found that there did exist a legitimate type of aid to insurgents, namely humanitarian assistance such as that given by the US to the Contras after 1984.[35]

After the Court had identified the acts of Nicaragua and the US as being *prima facie* unlawful breaches of the norms of the non-use of force and non-intervention, it dismissed the US contention that it was entitled to support the Contras because the Nicaraguans had supported the FMLN. It found that since the Nicaraguan support had amounted, at most, to only an indirect use of force against El Salvador (and therefore did not constitute an 'armed attack' within the meaning of article 51) the US was not entitled to act in collective self-defence of El Salvador.[36] Judge Schwebel, in his dissenting opinion, heavily criticized this aspect of the Court's judgment because it allows a state enjoying the support of a powerful political ally to intervene in a victim state, without permitting the victim state's allies to 'intervene effectively to preserve' that victim state.[37]

Judge Schwebel appeared to be alluding to the Cuban and Soviet support for Nicaragua by supplying it with arms and matériel. However, it is a well-established principle of international law that, whilst states may not arm rebels, they may lawfully arm established governments. Indeed, Judge Schwebel appears to be ignoring the fact that the US was supplying the government in El Salvador with proportionately larger quantities of arms than the Soviets or the Cubans were supplying to the Sandinista government in Nicaragua. It follows from this that a victim state's allies can come to its assistance in the form of military hardware and advice on how to use such equipment. Furthermore, the Court clearly suggests that the victim state can lawfully respond to an intervention by taking counter-measures in the form of internal police action against rebels and their arms supply routes.[38] In the light of such protection afforded to the victim state, it is incorrect to assert that the Court's judgement is a 'prescription for the overthrow of weaker governments by predatory governments'.[39]

One final issue was not resolved in considering this case because the World Court decided that it was not raised by the facts,[40] namely that of an outside state supporting a people fighting for self-determination. The 1970 Declaration on Friendly Relations, the 1974 Definition of Aggression, and the 1987 Declaration on the Non Use of Force, all contain a paragraph which superficially seems to suggest that the rules on intervention change if the support being given is directed at a people fighting for self-determination. For instance, article 7 of the 1974 Definition states the following:

> Nothing in this Definition ... could in any way prejudice the right to self-determination, freedom and independence, as derived from the Charter, of peoples forcibly deprived of that right ..., particularly

peoples under colonial and racist regimes or other forms of alien domination; nor the right of these peoples to struggle to that end and to seek and receive support, in accordance with the principles of the Charter ... .

The General Assembly's declarations do not in themselves suggest that support for people struggling for self-determination can be greater than that allowed for any rebellious people.[41] The resolutions explicitly state that 'support' must be consistent with the principles of the UN Charter; as has been seen, the central principles of that instrument are contained in articles 2(4) and 51. Support for peoples fighting for self-determination cannot breach the principle outlawing the use of force,[42] but providing funds might not be unlawful since that is not a use of force but only an otherwise unlawful intervention. On balance it appears that Judge Schwebel correctly ascertained the law in his dissenting opinion when he stated that 'it is lawful for a foreign state ... to give to a people struggling for self-determination moral, political and humanitarian assistance, but it is not lawful for a foreign state ... to intervene in that struggle with force or to provide arms, supplies and other logistical support in the prosecution of armed rebellion'.[43] This still leaves open the prospect of the funding of such people being lawful, although the relationship between the norm prohibiting intervention (which normally forbids such funding) and the principle of self-determination is still far from clear.

It must also be remembered that the rules as to what support a *government* can receive change once it is established that the people it is suppressing are fighting for self-determination. As outlined above, if a government or another state uses force against such a people, then it is breaching the principle prohibiting the use of force, thus disentitling it to receive military assistance of any kind, including the provision of arms.

Humanitarian Intervention and the Protection of Nationals

There are two somewhat different justifications that states occasionally put forward for intervening within another country which is in some kind of civil turmoil; both involve military intervention in another state to protect the most basic human right – that of life. A few states and writers propound the right to intervene to protect the lives of their nationals which are being threatened, either directly by the government of another state or as a result of civil unrest within that country. Whilst there is some support for this right, very little support exists for the wider right of humanitarian intervention to protect the lives of the population (or part of it) in another state. It is our contention that neither of these alleged rights is accepted as a rule of customary international law.

It has been argued that both the protection of nationals abroad and humanitarian intervention can be justified as exceptions to the ban on force in that they are designed to protect human rights.[44] However, whilst accepting the importance of human rights, objectively speaking, the ban on the use of force is *the* primary rule in the international legal system, a rule of *jus cogens* that cannot be overridden by other concerns. The only possible breach of international law which may justify military intervention, apart from self-defence, is when another peremptory rule of international law has been broken. Of the two claims being discussed, such an argument can be raised only in support of the alleged right of humanitarian intervention. This assumes that the abuse of the human rights of the population has reached the level of genocide.

Genocide is defined in article 2 of the Genocide Convention 1948[45] as one of a list of acts committed with the intention to 'destroy, in whole or in part, a national, ethnical, racial or religious group'. The acts listed include killing members of that group and deliberately inflicting on the group conditions designed to bring about its physical destruction in whole or in part. The Convention embodies a rule of customary international law, which could be said to be as important as the ban on the use of force. This is not only evidenced by the fact that the Convention has 103 state party signatories, but more importantly because the UN Charter emerged after a war fought against a regime that had committed acts of genocide against the Jews and other groups within Germany and German-occupied territories. At Nuremberg, German leaders were charged and in many cases convicted of crimes against humanity, which included acts equivalent to genocide.[46] In such circumstances, it could be argued that when the abuse of human rights reaches such an atrocious level, the ban on force no longer operates.

Indeed, article 1 of the Convention obliges state parties to 'prevent and punish' the international crime of genocide. However, jurisdiction over state officials and leaders guilty of such crimes is granted only to the tribunals of 'the state in the territory of which the act was committed, or by such international penal tribunal as may have jurisdiction with respect to those Contracting Parties which shall have accepted its jurisdiction' in article 6. In addition, subsequent state practice has not indicated support for a right of humanitarian intervention.

Sadly, there have been several modern instances of a state killing or attempting to kill large numbers of particular groups within its own frontiers, actions which on occasion have led to military intervention. At other times, no state has been prepared to intervene militarily, even when large numbers of citizens were clearly being massacred. In May 1967, Biafra declared its independence from Nigeria. In the ensuing civil war many thousands of the Ibo tribe which inhabited Biafra died, due in part to the brutality with which the insurrection was put down, brutality directed at the whole of the Ibo tribe, not just the combatants. However, whilst a mere five states were willing to recognize Biafra, none was prepared to intervene to protect the Ibos, preferring instead to leave attempts to solve the crisis to the OAU which had a clear policy against secession.[47]

Other instances of alleged genocide have prompted a military response, but neither the intervening nor other states has sought to justify the action solely as a humanitarian intervention, thus reflecting the fact that little *opinio juris* exists amongst states for such a right. Examples of actions which would appear to constitute humanitarian interventions by outside states include the Indian military intervention of 1971 following the Pakistani army's brutal repression of the rebellion in East Pakistan, the Vietnamese invasion of Cambodia in 1978 to remove the genocidal regime of the Khmer Rouge, and the Tanzanian invasion of Uganda in 1979 to help rebels overthrow the brutal regime of Idi Amin. However, neither India nor Vietnam nor Tanzania attempted to justify these military actions as legitimate instances of humanitarian intervention.

If the UN authorizes intervention for humanitarian purposes, then of course the action is lawful. In April 1991, the Security Council adopted a resolution categorizing Iraq's repression of the Kurds as a threat to international peace and security.[48] The resolution did not specify express measures, although sanctions imposed as a result of the Iraqi invasion of Kuwait were maintained. Western states at least appeared to think that the resolution justified the despatch of up to 20,000 troops to occupy a large part of northern Iraq to prevent further repression and to protect the distribution of humanitarian aid. Even if the Western operation was not considered to be authorized by the UN, it could still be accepted as lawful in that it was not full-blown humanitarian intervention – it did not seek to overthrow the brutal regime of Saddam Hussein. Indeed, it appeared to be an action somewhere between the well accepted right of states to provide humanitarian aid and the generally unacceptable right of humanitarian intervention. Given that very few states objected to the operation, this may be a significant putative right to be developed in the future.

Whilst humanitarian intervention cannot be justified within the terms of the UN Charter, except as a collective right authorized by the Security Council, strong arguments are put forward by jurists[49] and some states that the terms of articles 2(4) and 51 can be reconciled with the alleged right to protect nationals whose lives are at risk in a foreign country. It is argued that such a limited action does not breach the 'territorial integrity or political independence' of the victim state within the meaning of article 2(4), ignoring the fact that these are not words of limitation but should be read as signifying territorial inviolability or sovereignty. Alongside this contention, it is stated that rescue missions are compatible with the doctrine of self-defence. This position must lean heavily on the contention that pre-existing Charter law on self-defence survives article 51. Nineteenth- and twentieth-century practice by a few powerful states in an era when a loose doctrine of self-help was accepted is no reason for condoning the claim today when a ban on force is paramount.

The right of self-defence as embodied in article 51 is stated in terms of a UN member responding to an armed attack; in other words, an armed attack against a *state*. It appears to follow that, where conditions within a state threaten the lives of foreign nationals, there is no armed attack by that state against the state of nationality. Furthermore, the General Assembly's 1974 Definition of Aggression, which specifies with some accuracy what constitutes an armed attack, refers to the 'territory' of a state, and at one point to its 'land, sea or air forces, or marine and air fleets' as being targets of aggression. It does not mention a state's nationals.

Other arguments put forward to support an autonomous right to protect nationals are based on the theory that views article 2(4) as just one component of the total collective security system; if the system as a whole is not working, then article 2(4) cannot be invoked to prevent acts of self-help. Such an argument ignores the fact that the vast majority of states and analysts treat article 2(4) as an absolute prohibition, independent of the workings of the security system established elsewhere in the Charter. The fact is that the international system as a whole would not work if article 2(4) contained a very flexible rule that could be ignored when a state felt that it was being unjustly treated. In addition, there is an in-built safety valve in article 51 which allows a state the right of self-defence if unjust treatment amounts to an armed attack against it.

Similarly, the theory that allows for military intervention to protect human rights was dismissed when discussing the claim to humanitarian intervention. It must be the case that if unilateral intervention to prevent genocide is an unlawful use of force, then so is intervention to protect nationals. However, as with the claim to humanitarian intervention, there are strong moral grounds in favour of the protection of nationals so that condemnation of such actions is often muted. Nevertheless, only a handful of states, almost exclusively Western, assert the right to intervene to protect their nationals, principally the US, Britain, France, Belgium and Israel, either as an aspect of self-defence or an autonomous right of customary international law. However, such limited practice cannot be deemed sufficient for such a right to exist.

Examples of limited operations designed to free endangered nationals include: the American operation to free the US merchant ship *Mayaguez* and its crew seized by Cambodia in 1975; the Israeli operation to free airline passengers held by terrorists at Entebbe airport in Uganda in 1976; the aborted American attempt to free its diplomats held hostage by revolutionaries in Iran in 1980; the American action to evacuate its and other Western states' citizens from strife-torn Liberia in August 1990; and similar operations by French and Belgian troops in October 1990 in Rwanda following an attack on that country by Ugandan-based rebels, as well as in Zaire, in September and October 1991, during unrest there.

Small states are justifiably worried, not only about powerful states using such a right to intervene directly in their internal affairs, but also about the repercussions of even limited rescue operations. From a small state's perspective, even a limited operation in Western terms is likely to embroil the political situation in the country. Powerful Western states, with large numbers of nationals working in developing countries or travelling on business, see it as their duty to protect them, particularly when the local government is unwilling or unable to do so. However, the balance of world opinion indicates that the *majority* of states see such actions as unlawful. Nevertheless, the lack of overwhelming, and in particular institutional, condemnation perhaps indicates that, while such actions are unlawful uses of force contrary to article 2(4), they do not constitute an armed attack or an aggression against the victim state. Thus the latter has what is essentially a sovereign right to attempt to rebuff the trespassing state by force if it so wishes and if it is able (given that rescue attempts often occur when a state is factionalized); however, its counter-measures cannot be extra-territorial or collective.

The *jus in bello*

The *jus in bello*, the law *in* war, represents in some respects the outer limits of legal regulation. It seeks to impose some degree of essential constraint upon conduct, not in the 'open-textured' context of lawful international relations, but when 'normal' international relations ultimately break down in times of war. The regulation of hostilities in international armed conflicts between established states presents sufficient difficulties, but where armed conflict arises *within* a state, the problems are compounded. Where groups are in military contention for control of the domestic government or seeking the separation of some part of a state to constitute a new entity, the bitterness inherent in armed conflict tends to be greatly exacerbated. A soldier from a foreign enemy power may not be liked but can still be recognized as an individual performing his/her duty. An opponent in a 'civil war' tends all too often to be branded a traitor, with the consequent drastic diminution of any humanitarian inclinations. The evils of civil wars are no new phenomenon. Referring to his experience of the 17th-century English Civil War, Thomas Hobbes wrote in 1651 that,

> the greatest [incommodity], that in any forme of Government can possibly happen to the people in general, is scarce sensible, in respect of the miseries, and horrible calamities, that accompany a Civill Warre; or that dissolute condition of masterlesse men, without subjection to Lawes, and a coercive Power to tye their hands from rapine and revenge... .[50]

Some of Hobbes's political and constitutional arguments clearly represent a reaction to just such extreme conditions, while others may (from a modern point of view) require very considerable modification, but his picture of 'civil war' remains as cogent in the late 20th century as it was in his day. Indeed, one of the more alarming features of late 20th-century non-international armed conflicts is the resurgence of religious division as a causal factor. Such attitudes actually run contrary to the teaching of virtually all of the major religions which, however much their doctrines are distorted, on the whole counsel moderation in both resort to and use of armed force. However, the practice of branding opponents not only as 'traitors' or 'oppressors' but also as 'enemies of God' has obvious and horrifying anti-humanitarian implications. The consequences have been displayed in some aspects of the late 1990's conflicts in former Yugoslavia, in the Sudan, in Iraq and elsewhere.

The Difficulty of Establishing Legal Principles

In seeking legal principles to mitigate at least the worst horrors of civil wars, difficult issues of both principle and practice must be addressed. In particular, politically sensitive definitions both of the conflict and the parties thereto are required to establish a basis for constraint upon the conduct of hostilities, without implying political or constitutional concessions unacceptable to either side. As a result of such political considerations, the *jus in bello* regime applied to civil wars is significantly reduced and modified in comparison with that applicable to international conflicts. It is nonetheless based upon the same essential principles and can only properly be understood as a derivative from the provisions of the former.

The *jus in bello*, as applied to international armed conflicts, is conventionally divided into two broad sectors. These are 'Hague' and 'Geneva' (international humanitarian) law. The former governs methods and means of warfare, such matters as weapons restrictions and tactical battlefield constraints,[51] whereas the latter is concerned with the protection of the victims of armed conflict – for this purpose defined as the wounded, sick and/or shipwrecked, prisoners of war and civilians.[52] The division between 'Hague' and 'Geneva' sectors is, admittedly, somewhat artificial in so far as the fundamental concern of each is a 'humanitarian' endeavour to limit the suffering caused by warfare. Some matters, such as the definition of 'legitimate' targets, find a place in both 'Hague' and 'Geneva' provisions. Nonetheless, the distinction is one of practical convenience in separating the 'method'-centred 'Hague' provisions from the 'victim'-centred 'Geneva' principles. For this reason the distinction is adhered to here, though a significant degree of overlap obviously exists between the two sectors.

The precise *jus in bello* regime to be applied in a non-international armed conflict will depend to some extent upon the nature of the conflict in question. In determining this there are some delicate issues of definition which require consideration.

The Categorization of Non-international Armed Conflicts

In the context of international armed conflicts, controversies surrounding the criteria for applying the *jus in bello* to hostilities have largely been avoided in modern legal practice. A considerable and technical jurisprudence has developed around the meaning of the term 'war' for this purpose, which proves less than helpful in determining how the law applies to actual military crises.[53] In modern practice the term 'armed conflict' is generally preferred,[54] referring simply to the factual occurrence of military hostilities between states.

In the case of non-international armed conflicts between different factions within a state, no such simple solution is immediately available. Amongst other factors, the question of scale is of obvious significance. In some ways a confrontation between the police and a gang of armed bank robbers might be considered a 'non-international' armed conflict. However, as a criterion for the application of the *jus in bello* at any level, this would be manifestly absurd. Some minimum threshold, in terms of the extent of military confrontation between organized forces, is clearly required. At the 'international' end of the scale, controversy arises over conflicts waged in pursuit of the right to national self-determination, some of which tend to be described as 'internationalized'. In other words, the full *jus in bello* tends to be applied 'as if' the conflict were between states, although it is in fact between a state and an entity which desires independence but has not yet succeeded in achieving it.

The clearest attempts to establish these definitional distinctions are found in the 'Geneva' humanitarian provisions. Common article 3 of the four 1949 Geneva Conventions, which makes a minimum humanitarian provision for non-international armed conflicts, refers simply to cases of 'armed conflict not of an international character occurring in the territory of one of the High Contracting Parties'. This is of course a 'maximum' criterion separating 'international' conflicts, with which the rest of the Conventions deal, from the 'non-international' conflicts covered by common article 3. The expanded humanitarian provision for such conflicts made by 1977 Protocol II Additional to the 1949 Geneva Conventions sets out far more detailed criteria of application. Article 1(1) of the 1977 Additional Protocol II refers to conflicts which

> take place in the territory of a High Contracting Party between its armed forces and dissident armed forces or other organized armed groups which, under responsible command, exercise such control over a part of its territory as to enable them to carry out sustained and concerted military operations and to implement this Protocol.

This sets out a number of requirements which a conflict must satisfy to attain the status of a non-international armed conflict, subject to reduced *jus in bello* regulation. Some of these present significant practical difficulties, but the concept at least is clear enough. Article 1(2) then adds the necessary 'minimum' limit:

> This Protocol shall not apply to situations of internal disturbances and tensions, such as riots, isolated and sporadic acts of violence and other acts of a similar nature, as not being armed conflicts.

Mere disorders, and bank robberies, are thus clearly excluded. For the avoidance of doubt, the Protocol adds, by article 3(1) that,

> Nothing in this Protocol shall be invoked for the purpose of affecting the sovereignty of a State or the responsibility of the government, by all legitimate means, to maintain or re-establish law and order in the State or to defend the national unity and territorial integrity of the State.

This unequivocal statement makes clear that the humanitarian provision of the Protocol is unrelated to the question of the legitimacy or otherwise of the claims of dissident forces or groups.

The advantages, and difficulties, of these definitions are best considered in the light of practical instances. Article 1(1) clearly excludes terrorist action as such, though the meaning of 'sustained and concerted military operations' is debatable. The International Committee of the Red Cross Commentary upon 1977 Additional Protocol II emphasizes 'continuity and persistence', leading to the important conclusion that we are talking about military operations conceived and planned by organized armed groups; ... the criterion whether military operations are sustained and concerted, while implying the element of continuity and intensity, complies with an objective assessment of the situation.[55]

It must also be remembered that territorial control and a willingness and ability to implement the Protocol are demanded. Apart from the question of ratification of the Protocol, these various criteria would serve effectively to exclude bodies such as the IRA in Northern Ireland or ETA in the Basque region of Spain. In the case of the IRA, sporadic acts of terrorist violence, with neither willingness nor ability to comply with any level of the *jus in bello*, from a body which (even at the time of the so-called 'no go areas' in parts of Belfast) has never exercised the quasi-governmental control demanded by the Protocol, could not lay claim to the application of such law. This of course is the real point. The dissident forces covered by the Protocol would be recognizably 'military' in organization and conduct, and would be responsible to an 'authority' which had succeeded in taking on significant characteristics of a *de facto* government. It is important to note, however, that one is speaking of a pragmatic *de facto* position which can be observed objectively; no implication of *legitimacy* is made by such criteria.

This position has been subjected to mild criticism, or at least to suggestions that more radical provision is required. R.C. Hingorani suggests that the

> *Protocol* says that it will be applied only in cases of armed conflicts and not in cases of ... riots or sporadic ... violence. Unfortunately, internal wars start like this. ... [P]eople suffer in initial stages when the activities have not achieved momentum ... . Once the dissident activities have secured momentum, the rebel group can get better treatment on [the] basis of reciprocity... . It is, therefore, suggested that some protection may be provided in initial stages. ...[56]

The humanitarian motivation of this suggestion is evident. However, as Hingorani earlier concedes, securing the assent of states in such a delicate area is far from easy, while such a move would, perhaps wrongly (since the Protocol in its present structure by no means imports this), raise some fears of a move towards legitimation of terrorism. People in the early stages of conflict described by Hingorani would not of course be left wholly without guarantees even under present provision. There are, for example, certain human rights and 'due process' expectations which would apply in any event.

The controversial complicating factor of the 'internationalization' of certain *prima facie* non-international armed conflicts also arises. 1977 Protocol I Additional to the 1949 Geneva Conventions (article

1(4)) makes supplementary humanitarian provision for international armed conflicts by including

> armed conflicts in which peoples are fighting against colonial domination and alien occupation and against racist regimes in the exercise of their right of national self-determination, as enshrined in the Charter of the United Nations. ...

This, course, begs the difficult question of the precise nature of the right to national self-determination.[57] From the point of view of *jus in bello* application, this question has become especially pointed in the closing years of the 20th century as the concept of national self-determination enters a new phase in its evolution. The de-colonizing concept of the right has for some time been implicit in UN practice, although not expressly in the Charter, and is made explicit in the present context by 1977 Protocol I Additional to the 1949 Geneva Conventions, article 1(4). This concept has very nearly become *functus officio*. Thus, as the process of de-colonization moves towards completion, the new problem might be termed one of 'secondary self-determination', a phrase suggested here for convenience rather than for its technical value. That is to say that some states which emerged in terms of the 1919 and 1945 concepts of self-determination continue to present 'unfinished business' as groups within their boundaries campaign to exercise the right further. The matter has become controversial in Europe in the 1990s. The peaceful dissolution of former Czechoslovakia into Czech and Slovak states and the disastrously violent dissolution of former Yugoslavia both raise this question. Neither state was in any sense a colonial entity so that their break-ups could not be described as 'de-colonization'. In Yugoslavia, claims of 'self-determinatory' struggle have been made by some factions, although perhaps without valid foundation. The issue of self-determination in the post-colonial age, involving most particularly a reconsideration of who constitutes a 'people' for this purpose, is forcing itself upon the international agenda with increasing urgency. In the context of the *jus in bello* and in the light of article 1(4) of 1977 Additional Protocol I, the matter is of special importance, since ambiguity in determining the law to be applied is more dangerous in armed conflict than in almost any other situation.

The Jus in Bello *and Internal Disturbances*

Situations falling below the threshold of non-international armed conflict may loosely be categorized as 'internal disturbances'. This is of course a potentially vast sub-category, even if implicitly limited by reference to confrontations between the state and its opponents. In considering this issue Hans-Peter Gasser remarks that,

> from time to time, States are affected by outbreaks of internal violence. Such upheavals are usually referred to as internal disturbances or tensions, disorders, states of emergency, revolutions or insurrections. These ... refer to situations that appear contrary to justice, order, stability and internal peace.[58]

Clearly such 'disturbances' do not descend to the level of an armed bank robbery, but definitions of context are nonetheless so problematic as to render resolution a matter of grave doubt. Partly for these reasons, as well as the inevitable and extreme sensitivity of the political issues potentially involved, such states of internal unrest are not currently covered by the *jus in bello*. 1977 Protocol II Additional to the 1949 Geneva Conventions expressly provides by article 1(2) that '[t]his Protocol shall not apply to situations of internal disturbances and tensions ...'. This does not mean, however, that such situations are wholly outside the scope of international legal regulation. A number of basic Human Rights provisions continue to apply. Thus the 1966 International Covenant on Civil and Political Rights provides by article 7 that '[n]o-one shall be subjected to torture or to cruel, inhuman or degrading treatment or punishment'. Article 4(2) further forbids any derogation from, *inter alia*, this requirement even '[i]n time of public emergency which threatens the life of the nation and the existence of which is officially proclaimed ...'. Similar provision is found in article 3 of the 1950 European Convention on Human Rights and article 5(2) of the 1969 American Convention on Human Rights. The use of torture at any time, whether as a means of securing information or of degradation, may thus be considered a violation of these provisions. Hans-Peter Gasser in the article referred to above has proposed a code of conduct for internal disturbances, identifying many of the essential human rights and 'due process' requirements. At present, however, the conduct of the state in circumstances of internal disturbance is bound only by certain basic requirements of the Human Rights treaties, bearing in mind, however, that some provisions are derogable in circumstances of declared national emergency.

This is perhaps as far as the process can now reasonably be expected to be taken. Any extension even of the full 'non-international' conflict *jus in bello* regime into the large and ambiguous sphere of internal disturbances seems likely to be defeated by, amongst many other considerations, these very basic problems of definition.

The Patterns of Jus in Bello *Obligations*

Where a *prima facie* non-international armed conflict is held to have been 'internationalized' by reference to article 1(4) of 1977 Additional Protocol I,[59] the full 'international' Geneva humanitarian regime should be applied. Whether this principle would also include the 'Hague' prescription in relation to technical methods and means of warfare may be debatable.[60] However, granted the inclusion of many well-established 'Hague' principles within 1977 Additional Protocol I itself, this matter is perhaps less important in practice than in theory. In general it seems reasonable to conclude that 'Hague' limitations would be applicable in such a context.

Where an armed conflict within a state is clearly non-international, the limited principles of a *jus in bello interno* are applied. The details of this are set out below,[61] although certain matters of principle are of immediate importance. The 'Geneva' provision, found in common article 3 of the 1949 Geneva Conventions and 1977 Additional Protocol II, is most clearly defined. These provisions set out a humanitarian regime which is in part focused on 'human rights' and in part incorporating at least some of the most basic requirements of the 'international' regime. The transition from 'international' to 'non-international' conflicts is, however, made only with considerable difficulty.

The relation of international humanitarian law to human rights has always been a matter for debate. The two prescriptions are undoubtedly closely analogous in broad function, even though the context of application of international humanitarian law is so specialized and extreme as to justify distinct technical categorization. Some commentators, such as Geza Herczeg, have argued in effect that international humanitarian law cannot be part of any 'human rights' provision on the basis that armed conflict is itself a violation of human rights.[62] Igor P. Blishchenko, in contrast, has argued that

> the fundamental objective of what is known as the laws of war is the protection of human rights.... For this reason it seems ... appropriate to establish a closer relationship between the norms and principles which prohibit and limit ... methods for the conduct of war on the one hand, and the international norms concerning human rights ... on the other.[63]

There seems much to commend in this argument. If 'human rights' are not to be protected in circumstances where, *ex hypothesi*, they are threatened as seriously as in armed conflict, and especially in civil war, a major lacuna in the 'human rights' spectrum is revealed. Nonetheless a narrower distinction from 'human rights' may be accepted. It has been commented elsewhere that,

It seems reasonable … to conclude that humanitarian provisions in the laws of armed conflict are best regarded as a specialist application of human rights principles in peculiarly extreme circumstances. … [T]he nature of the relevant circumstances [however] … entails so distinctive a set of characteristics as to make their assignment to a distinct … sub-category inevitable.[64]

This is a matter of some conceptual importance but, naturally, it does not seriously affect the application of the relevant rules and principles on the ground. In the 'Geneva' sector these rules and principles are, for the most part, clearly set out. The difficulties lie in securing due implementation.

The application of 'Hague' law, in so far as it is not reiterated in a relevant 'Geneva' provision, presents considerable difficulties in the context of non-international armed conflicts. Much of the 'Hague' law originated at a time when the conduct of non-international armed conflict was, like the treatment of citizens in general by their government, considered a purely internal matter, subject at most to external expressions of moral outrage. Since 1945 this absolute 'sovereignty' has been much weakened, *inter alia* by the development of the law of human rights. The application of 'Hague' principles to methods and means of combat in non-international armed conflicts nevertheless remains somewhat problematic. Antonio Cassese remarks that

The bulk of [the rules concerning internal armed conflicts] … has an exclusively humanitarian scope and purpose. It aims at protecting all civilians who do not take part in hostilities …, or the wounded and sick who, having taken part in armed violence, are no longer in a position to fight. Methods of combat are not regulated, except to the extent that this serves to spare civilians.[65]

As Cassese concedes, there are some exceptions to this. Thus article 1(4) of 1977 Additional Protocol II repeats the well-established ban upon orders of 'no quarter', i.e. 'It is prohibited to order that there shall be no survivors'. There thus arises the important question of use of weapons in non-international conflicts. For example, would it be legitimate for a government to use chemical or biological weapons against an insurgent force? Iraq, for example, is known to have used chemical weapons against Kurdish dissidents in northern Iraq. A case may be made that such use is illegal on grounds exceeding the *jus in bello*,[66] but many grey areas remain. It is interesting that article 2(10)(d) of the 1992 UN Convention on the Prohibition of the Development, Production, Stockpiling and Use of Chemical Weapons and on their Destruction includes amongst purposes not prohibited by the Convention, '[l]aw enforcement including domestic riot control purposes'. One might argue that the level of this exception is set by the reference to 'riot control', which anyway would fall into the area of 'human rights' *stricto sensu* rather than of the *jus in bello*. The potential ambiguity of a phrase such as 'law enforcement' nonetheless points, again, to the basic dichotomy in the *jus in bello interno*. The claim of a government to be maintaining its 'legitimate' authority as against insurgents claiming to establish a new 'authority' underlies many of the most difficult questions in this area of law.

This is not the true root of the difficulties encountered in adapting the rules and principles of the *jus in bello* to non-international armed conflicts. Theodor Meron goes to the heart of the issue in commenting that

> States are prone to consider violent acts committed with political objectives as crimes regulated by domestic penal law, even when the violence has escalated into a non-international armed conflict. ... It is rare that even in major conflicts, governments are willing ... to extend to dissidents combatants' privilege ... .[67]

The point may be illustrated in the context of 1977 Protocol II Additional to the 1949 Geneva Conventions. In an international armed conflict, under 1949 Geneva Convention III, a recognized combatant who is captured by the enemy is entitled to 'prisoner of war' status and, whilst subject to internment, cannot be otherwise prosecuted or punished. However, no provision for 'prisoner of war' status is made by either common article 3 of the 1949 Geneva Conventions or 1977 Additional Protocol II. The latter, by article 6, makes provision for due process in any prosecutions, while article 6(5) adds that,

> at the end of hostilities, the authorities in power shall endeavour to grant the broadest possible amnesty to persons who have participated in the armed conflict, ...

The International Committee of the Red Cross Commentary upon 1977 Additional Protocol II made the following observations on this paragraph:

> Amnesty is a matter within the competence of the authorities. It is an act by the legislative power which eliminates the consequences of certain punishable offences, stops prosecutions and quashes convictions. ... The object [here] ... is to encourage gestures of reconciliation which can contribute to reestablishing normal relations in the life of a nation which has been divided.[68]

The provision is, of course, exhortatory rather than mandatory. A captured fighter in a non-international armed conflict might be prosecuted, e.g. for treason, simply by virtue of having been involved.

Enemy soldiers captured in an international conflict cannot be prosecuted for participation in the conflict, although they may be for other acts, such as complicity in war crimes.[69] This most important distinction symbolizes the difference between the two levels of conflict and the provisions relating to each.

Further Jus in Bello *Protection*

The provisions of common article 3 of the 1949 Geneva Conventions and of 1977 Additional Protocol I are set out as a *minimum* for humanitarian regulation of non-international armed conflicts. This is expressly stated by common article 3, which then adds, in its penultimate paragraph, that

> the Parties to the conflict should further endeavour to bring into force, by means of special agreements, all or part of the other provisions of the present Convention.

Such agreements are sometimes entered into. The parties in the armed conflict(s) in Bosnia-Herzegovina agreed at a conference in Geneva that the majority of the humanitarian provisions for 'international' armed conflicts should apply to themselves, This hardly had an ameliorating effect upon the savage conduct of hostilities, but it did establish a criterion by reference to which the international community could respond to developments there.

Conclusions

The application of the *jus in bello* to non-international armed conflicts admittedly remains problematic. Granted the political sensitivity and the inherent ambiguity of the situations under consideration, this can hardly be thought surprising. Nevertheless, a number of important principles have been established which as a prerequisite to any meaningful implementation, must be considered a positive advance. That said, a brief perusal of the all too many non-international armed conflicts which have occurred in the closing years of the 20th century demonstrates incontrovertibly that much yet remains to be done.

Notes

1   See generally H. McCoubrey and N.D. White, *International Law and Armed Conflict* (Dartmouth, 1992), chapter 2.
2   But appearances can be deceptive; see McCoubrey and White, *Armed Conflict,*

28   *International Organizations and Civil Wars*

chapters 3–7 and 10, and A.C. Arend and R.J. Beck, *International Law and the Use of Force* (Routledge, 1993), chapters 3–10.

3   See SC Res 660, 662, 45 UN SCOR (1990).

4   SC Res 678, 45 UN SCOR (1990).

5   See for example O. Schachter, 'United Nations Law in the Gulf Conflict' (1991) 85 *AJIL* p.425; J. Quigley, 'The United States and the United Nations in the Persian Gulf War: New Order or Disorder' (1992) 25 *Cornell International Law Journal* p.1.

6   (1988) 27 *ILM* p.577.

7   See arguments of the Soviet Union SC.496 mtg, 5 UN SCOR (1950).

8   Discussion of possible responses that the Security Council may take to civil wars, either by way of military action, economic sanctions or peacekeeping forces, will be left to later chapters since these are really institutional responses to civil conflicts.

9   R. Jennings and A. Watts, *Oppenheim's International Law, Volume 1: Peace* (Longman, 1991), part 1, pp.165–9.

10   See for example J.W. Garner, 'Recognition of Belligerency' (1938) 31 *AJIL* p.398.

11   N.J. Padelford, *International Law and Diplomacy in the Spanish Civil Strife* (Macmillan, 1939).

12   *Ibid*, pp.1–2, 196–200.

13   L. Oppenheim, *International Law Vol. II: Disputes, War and Neutrality*, 6th edn, H. Lauterpacht (ed.), (Longmans, 1940), p.199.

14   GA Res. 2625, 25 UN GAOR (1970).

15   ICJ Rep. 1986, p.14 at pp.101–3.

16   See Declaration of the Granting of Independence to Colonial Territories and Peoples, GA Res 1514, 15 UN GAOR (1960). Also the *Western Sahara Case*, ICJ Rep. 1975, p.12.

17   A. Tanca, 'The Prohibition of Force in the UN Declaration on Friendly Relations' in A. Cassese (ed.), *The Current Legal Regulation on the Use of Force* (Martinus Nijhoff, 1986), pp.404–8.

18   As advocated by some developing states; see UN doc. A/5746, p.42.

19   J. Faundez, 'International Law and Wars of National Liberation' (1989) 1 *African Journal of International and Comparative Law* p.85 at p.96.

20   GA Res. 3314, 29 UN GAOR (1974); GA Res. 42/22, 42 UN GAOR (1987).

21   See GA Res. 1514 above n.16.

22   See Article 1(4) of 1977 Protocol I Additional to the Geneva Conventions.

23   See GA Res. 3236, 29 UN GAOR (1974) re Palestine; GA Res. 2878, 27 UN GAOR (1972) re South Africa.

24   See generally M. Pomerance, *Self-Determination in Law and in Practice* (Martinus Nijhoff, 1982).

25   EC Arbitration Commission on Yugoslavia, 1992, 31 *ILM* p.1485.

26   The US had withdrawn from the case. See *Judgement on Jurisdiction and Admissibility*, ICJ Rep. 1984, p.392 and *Nicaragua Case* ICJ Rep. 1986, pp.23–6. Judge Schwebel, in his dissenting judgment, produced a different set of facts; ICJ Rep. 1986, p.249.

27   ICJ Rep. 1986, pp.53–62.

28   *Ibid.*, pp.70–73.

29   *Ibid.*, p.270.

30   *Ibid.*, pp.103–4. See also article 2 of the 1974 Definition of Aggression. But see Y. Dinstein, *War, Aggression and Self-Defence* (Grotius, 1988), pp.181–3.

31   Judge Schwebel (dissenting), *ibid.*, p.346. But see P.L. Zanardi, 'Indirect Military Aggression' in A. Cassese (ed.), *The Current Regulation on the Use of Force* p.111 at p.115.

32   *Ibid.*, pp.103–4.

33   *Ibid.*, pp.118–27.
34   *Ibid.*, pp.107–8, 118–19.
35   *Ibid.*, pp.124–5.
36   *Ibid.*, p.119.
37   *Ibid.*, p.350.
38   *Ibid.*, p.127.
39   *Ibid.*, p.350 (Judge Schwebel).
40   *Ibid.*, p.108.
41   In voting for both the 1970 Declaration and the 1974 Definition, Western states explicitly gave their votes on the understanding that the paragraph did not diminish the principle of the non-use of force. See, for example, New Zealand, 25 UN GAOR 1181 mtg 6th Committee, p.21 (1970); Portugal, 25 UN GAOR 1182 mtg 6th Committee, p.27 (1970). For the more ambiguous attitude of the Socialist and Non-Aligned states see, for example, Poland, 25 UN GAOR 1178 mtg 6th Committee p.7 (1970); Senegal, 25 UN GAOR 1180 mtg 6th Committee p.17 (1970).
42   L. Henkin in Henkin *et al.*, *Right v Might: International Law and the Use of Force* (Council of Foreign Relations Press, 1989), pp.42–4.
43   ICJ Rep. 1986, p.351. See D.W. Bowett, 'The Interrelation of Theories of Intervention and Self-Defence' in J.N. Moore (ed.), *Law and Civil War in the Modern World* (Johns Hopkins University Press, 1974), p.43.
44   See summary in N. Ronzitti, *Rescuing Nationals Abroad through Military Coercion and Intervention on Grounds of Humanity* (Martinus Nijhoff, 1985), pp.5–7.
45   78 UNTS 277.
46   (1947) 42 *AJIL* p.172.
47   M. Reisman and M.S. McDougal, 'Humanitarian Intervention to Protect the Ibos' in R. Lillich (ed.), *Humanitarian Intervention and the United Nations* (University Press of Virginia, 1973), pp.167 and 194.
48   SC Res. 688, 46 UN SCOR (1991).
49   For example D.W. Bowett, 'The Use of Force for the Protection of Nationals Abroad' in Cassese (ed.), *The Current Regulation on the Use of Force*, p.39.
50   T. Hobbes, *Leviathan*, 1651, Ch. XVIII (Pelican, edited by C.B. Macpherson, 1968), p.238.
51   See Chapter 5.
52   See Chapter 6.
53   For an English example of this, see the arguments in *Kawasaki Kisen Kabushiki Kaisha v Bantham S.S. Co.* [1939] 2 KB, 544.
54   See C. Greenwood, 'The Concept of War in Modern International Law' (1987) 36 *ICLO* p.283 and Rao, 'When does War Begin?' (1972) *IJIL* p.368.
55   Y. Sandoz, C. Swinarski and B. Zimmerman (eds) in collaboration with J. Pictet (writer on Protocol II, S-S. Junod), *Commentary on the Additional Protocols of 8 June 1977 to the Geneva Conventions of 12 August 1949,* (International Committee of the Red Cross with Martinus Nijhoff, 1967), p.1353.
56   R.C. Hingorani, 'Need for Humanitarianism in Internal Strifes' in C. Swinarski (ed.), *Studies and Essays on International Humanitarian Law and Red Cross Principles in Honour of Jean Pictet* (International Committee of the Red Cross with Martinus Nijhoff, 1984), p.343 at pp.347–8.
57   See above, pp.8–10 *ante*.
58   Hans-Peter Gasser, 'A Measure of Humanity in Internal Disturbances and Tensions: Proposal for a Code of Conduct', (1988) January-February, *International Review of the Red Cross*, pp.38–58, at p.38.
59   Both the 1977 Additional Protocols are of course treaties which, except in so far as they embody prior principle, are binding only as between states which are Party to them. Dissident forces are by definition not party to either common

article 3 of the 1949 Conventions or 1977 Additional Protocol II. The obligations thus assumed might be pursued by some interested state or organization but, so far as the dissident forces are concerned, the matter ultimately rests upon the unilateral assumption of obligation by the state, with (by clear implication from article 1(1) of the Protocol) some expectation of reciprocity.

60   See below, p.25.
61   See Chapters 5 and 6.
62   See G. Herczeg, *Development of International Humanitarian Law*, trans. Sandas Simon and Lajos Czante (Akedemiai Kiado, Budapest, 1984).
63   I.P. Blishchenko, 'Humanitarian Norms and Human Rights' in M. Bedjaoui (ed.), *Modern Wars* (Zed Books, 1986), p.143.
64   H. McCoubrey, *International Humanitarian Law* (Dartmouth, 1990), p.5.
65   A. Cassese, 'Respect of Humanitarian Norms in Non International Armed Conflict' in M. Bedjaoui (ed.), *op.cit.*, p.86 at p.87.
66   See below, p.109.
67   T. Meron, *Human Rights in Internal Strife: Their International Protection* (Grotius, 1987), p.73.
68   ICRC *Commentary on the Additional Protocols of 8 June 1977* (note 54), p.1402.
69   See 1977 Geneva Convention III, article 85. For discussion see H. McCoubrey, *op.cit.*, pp.103–5. Also M.A. Meyer, 'Liability of Prisoners of War for Offences Committed prior to Capture: The Astiz Affair' (1983) 32 *ICLQ* p.948 (not concerning war crimes).

2 The Involvement of International Organizations in Civil Wars

After reviewing the general legal principles governing internal conflicts, it is now pertinent to concentrate on the powers of international organizations, particularly in their dealings with internal conflicts. An examination of how international organizations function in this area will be left until Part II of this book, although some illustrations will be used in this chapter. But first it is necessary to say something about the status of international organizations in the international legal system, an issue usually discussed under the concept of 'international personality'.

The Personality of Public International Organizations

Sovereign states are clearly legal persons or legal actors in the international legal system. They create the law through treaties and custom, and therefore possess most of the rights and duties that exist in international law. Other subjects of international law are far less significant: international institutions, individuals and multinational corporations are generally cited as having some degree of personality on the international stage.[1] Within this second tier of international actors, international organizations are probably by far the most significant, at least in terms of their impact on international legal and political systems.

Of course the major public international organizations such as the United Nations are composed of states which generally do not wish to see their sovereignty eroded by those organizations, but instead wish to use them to further their own interests. In this way international organizations can be seen as simply reflecting the dominance of the modern sovereign state. This was certainly reflected in the voting structures of the League of Nations, based as it was on unanimity. The sovereignty concept was continued in the United Nations, with article 2(1) of the Charter stating that '[t]he Organization is based on the principle of the sovereign equality of all its Members'. As will be seen, the issue of sovereignty is still dominant in the fields of humanitarian assistance, fact finding and peacekeeping by international organizations, where such activities are dependent upon the consent of the countries concerned.

However, in other areas, the sovereignty of members has been worn down. In voting, for instance, neither the Security Council nor the General Assembly is based on the traditional sovereignty requirement. Article 18(1) reflects the principle of sovereign equality by embodying the 'one state one vote' principle, but this is limited by article 18(2) which provides that '[d]ecisions of the General Assembly on important questions shall be made by a two-thirds majority of those present and voting'. This has allowed the General Assembly to adopt resolutions which are contrary to the interests of a significant minority of states. During the 1970s and 1980s, when the Non-Aligned and Socialist majority dominated the Assembly, the economically and politically powerful Western states tended to be in a minority on many issues.

Nevertheless, although the Assembly can adopt resolutions or 'recommendations' against the wishes of a significant number of states, it cannot fundamentally affect the sovereignty of states. The Security Council on the other hand can adopt mandatory decisions. Article 25 states that '[t]he Members of the United Nations agree to accept and carry out the decisions of the Security Council in accordance with the present Charter'. Simply by becoming members of the UN, states consent to the binding nature of certain Security Council resolutions; in this sense, therefore, the overriding principle of sovereignty remains intact. However, considering that membership of the UN is now almost universal and also essential for many smaller states, it can be argued that the element of consent is missing and that what in fact exists is a hierarchical relationship, with the Security Council as the paramount executive and (in some senses) legislative organ. Looking at the voting rules in the Security Council, it can be seen that power lies with the permanent members. Whereas article 27(2) provides that decisions on 'procedural matters' (such as inclusions or removal of items from the agenda) are to be taken by a positive vote of 9 out of 15 members, article 27(3) provides that '[d]ecisions of the Security Council on all other matters shall be made by an affirmative vote of nine members including the concurring votes of the permanent members'. During the Cold War, the power of the Security Council seemed a figment of the drafters' imagination. However, the end of the Cold War has seen the Security Council flexing its muscles, with the three Western permanent members – France, the UK and the US (sometimes known as the 'permanent three' or 'P3') – dominating the economically and politically vulnerable Chinese and Russians.

The powers of the Security Council in relation to internal conflicts will be reviewed below, whilst its practice will be left to Part II. What is clear from the above discussion, however, is that the UN has a significant degree of international personality. To use the rather conservative words of the International Court in the *Reparation Case*:

> In the opinion of the Court, the Organisation was intended to exercise and enjoy, and is in fact exercising and enjoying, functions and rights which can only be explained on the basis of the possession of a large measure of international personality and the capacity to operate upon an international plane. It is at present the supreme type of international organisation, and it could not carry out the intentions of its founders if it was devoid of international personality. It must be acknowledged that its Members, by entrusting certain functions to it, with the attendant duties and responsibilities, have clothed it with a competence required to enable those functions to be effectively discharged. Accordingly, the Court has come to the conclusion that the Organisation is an international person. This is not the same thing as saying that it is a State, which it certainly is not, or that its legal personality and rights and duties are the same as those of the State. Still less is it the same thing as saying that it is a 'super-State', whatever that expression may mean.[2]

According to this functionalist approach, different organizations will have different types of personality on the international plane. It would be fruitless to identify these types given that, as shown by the rather equivocal language of the World Court, the concept of personality is not too helpful in a practical examination of the work of international organizations. With this in mind, we will now investigate the powers of the various types of international organizations that work in the field of civil conflicts.

The United Nations System

Non-Intervention by the United Nations

An attempt was made in the UN Charter to reassert the principles of sovereignty and exclusivity of domestic jurisdiction in the following provision:

> Nothing contained in the present Charter shall authorize the United
> Nations to intervene in matters which are essentially within the do-
> mestic jurisdiction of any State or shall require the Members to submit
> such matters to settlement under the present Charter; but this princi-
> ple shall not prejudice the application of enforcement measures under
> Chapter VII.[3]

A very narrow reading of this provision would mean that all internal
matters would be beyond the purview of the Security Council, the
General Assembly or the Secretary General, unless the Security Council was utilizing its enforcement powers (i.e. economic or military
measures) under Chapter VII.[4]

However, in practice all three 'organs' of the UN concerned with
international peace and security have interpreted this provision as
concentrating on what is and what is not 'essentially within the
domestic jurisdiction of any State'. As international law has developed since 1945, a number of *prima facie* domestic matters have now
been deemed of international concern and thus susceptible to Security Council recommendations under Chapter VI or to similar General Assembly resolutions, as well as to the 'good offices' of the
Secretary General; alternatively, they have been deemed to constitute
threats to the peace within Chapter VII. It will be seen in the sections
below that civil wars, the denial of the right to self-determination
and the widespread abuse of human rights are amongst the major
issues that the UN has addressed in recent times.

However, this is not to say that the UN has concerned itself with
every instance of internal conflict. It did not intervene in the civil war
in Nigeria in 1967 when the Biafrans tried to secede, in contrast to its
involvement in the Congo in 1960–64 when Katanga took the same
course. The different UN actions in these two conflicts can be ration-
alized in both legal and political terms. Essentially the difference was
one of the danger or threat to international peace. The involvement
of Belgian troops, foreign mercenaries and the interest of UN permanent members in the Congo civil war meant that, both for legal and
political reasons, it was deemed a threat to international peace. On
the other hand, the secession in Biafra was not considered sufficiently internationalized nor of interest to the permanent members
for it to be similarly characterized.

Another example concerned the Security Council's initial response
to the rebellion in Iraq following that country's defeat by the Coalition in Kuwait in March and April 1991. The Security Council determined that the suppression of the Kurds in the north and the Shias in
the south, and also the consequences in terms of the massive flow of
refugees to neighbouring Turkey and Iran, constituted a threat to
international peace. In contrast the Security Council initially refused

to allow the issue of Haiti onto its agenda in September 1991 after the elected government of that country had been overthrown by a military dictatorship. The ambassador of Haiti, a representative of the deposed government, had requested a meeting of the Security Council under article 35 of the Charter. Members of the Council decided that the Haiti coup was an internal affair in which the Council should not become involved.[5] Despite the fact that thousands of Haitian refugees fled the new regime, the initial response was that the situation was not a danger or a threat to international peace and so could not justify Council involvement.

In contrast, the General Assembly judged that the situation was of international concern when it adopted by consensus a resolution which strongly condemned 'both the attempted illegal replacement of the constitutional President of Haiti and the use of violence, military coercion and the violation of human rights in that country'.[6] Finally in 1993, with a change of Administration in the US, there came a change in attitude from the Security Council when on 17 June 1993, it imposed a mandatory oil and arms embargo against Haiti, determining that the 'unique and exceptional circumstances', the continuation of the crisis in Haiti, 'threatens international peace and security in the region'.[7] Some members' feared that this involved an extension of authority into states' internal affairs following a denial of democracy; such fears were allayed to some extent by a Presidential statement reinforcing the fact that the resolution was unique and therefore could not be seen as a precedent.[8] Nevertheless, what the episode in Haiti shows is that the Security Council can become involved with internal situations if there is sufficient political consensus to obtain the necessary substantive vote.

The Security Council and the Pacific Settlement of Disputes

The Security Council is the organ of the UN that has 'primary responsibility' for the maintenance of international peace and security'.[9] In order to fulfil this responsibility, the Charter confers on the Security Council an impressive array of powers in Chapters VI and VII. Chapter VI contains mainly recommendatory powers enabling the Security Council to encourage the pacific settlement of disputes, whereas Chapter VII contains a mixture of recommendatory and mandatory enforcement powers to enable the Council to take action with respect to threats to the peace, breaches of the peace or acts of aggression.

An examination of the provisions of Chapters VI and VII reveals that, whilst the Security Council is concerned with disputes or situations which are 'likely to endanger the maintenance of international peace and security'[10] in Chapter VI, or constitute threats to international peace, breaches of international peace or acts of aggression between two or more states within the meaning of Chapter VII, the Council is not solely concerned with clear inter-state disputes. Rather it has the capacity to deal with internal conflicts if they either endanger international peace (so allowing the Council to act under Chapter VI) or threaten international peace (so that it can take enforcement action under Chapter VII).[11]

The Council has consistently used the concept of a danger to international peace in relation to internal conflicts or situations which have international repercussions. A sub-committee of the Security Council in 1946 found that the remaining European Fascist regime of General Franco in Spain constituted a danger to international peace within the meaning of Chapter VI, but was not yet a threat to the peace in terms of Chapter VII.[12] Between 1963 and 1977, the Security Council dealt with the internecine conflict in South Africa under Chapter VI;[13] indeed, numerous other examples occurred during the Cold War of the Council attempting to deal with internal situations using the powers of Chapter VI.

Those provisions of Chapter VI which appear to be suitable for dealing with internal 'situations' as well as international 'disputes' and have been used as such are articles 34 and 36. Article 34 provides that '[t]he Security Council may investigate any dispute, or any situation which might lead to international friction or give rise to a dispute, in order to determine whether the continuance of the dispute or situation is likely to endanger the maintenance of international peace and security'. Examples of fact-finding missions being authorized to report on essentially internal situations or internal conflicts include those despatched to report on the Greek civil war in 1946, on the Nicaraguan conflict in 1988, to several of the former Soviet Republics and new states in 1992 (including Azerbaijan, Georgia, Moldova and Tajikistan), and to Haiti in 1993. These will be reviewed more thoroughly in Chapter 4.

Article 36(1) provides that the 'Security Council may, at any stage of the dispute', the continuance of which is likely to endanger international peace and security, 'or of a situation of like nature, recommend appropriate procedures or methods of adjustment'. The Council has used this provision to suggest methods of settlement or to support plans proposed by the parties to an internal conflict, sometimes with the good offices of the Secretary General and quite often with the utilization of a peacekeeping force. These will be reviewed in Part II of the book; it is sufficient here to note just some of the relevant conflicts – Indonesia, Cyprus, South Africa, Namibia, Afghanistan, Nicaragua, Cambodia, El Salvador, Yugoslavia, Somalia and Mozambique.

The Security Council and Threats to the Peace

Whereas under Chapter VI the Security Council deals with disputes that may endanger international peace, under Chapter VII the jurisdictional threshold is whether the internal situation under consideration actually constitutes a 'threat to the peace' under article 39 of the Charter. Article 39 also authorizes the Security Council to take action if there is a 'breach of the peace' or 'act of aggression', but these are terms that the Security Council has used primarily in relation to major breaches of inter-state peace – the Korean War, the Falklands conflict and the Iraqi invasion of Kuwait.[14]

It is the concept of a 'threat to the peace' within article 39 that the Security Council has had to develop because of the growth of internecine conflicts in the post-Second World War era, including civil wars and internationalized civil wars. The most extensive use of the term 'threat to the peace' undoubtedly occurred during meetings of the Security Council between 1965 and 1968, although very few speakers explained why the internal situation in Southern Rhodesia constituted such a threat. The meeting of 16 December 1966, at which the first mandatory resolution of a more general nature was adopted, revealed that at least some of those in attendance had considered the issue. The representative of Jordan stated that the Unilateral Declaration of Independence from the UK by the white minority regime amounted to 'an invasion of the rights of the majority. It is an act of aggression that cannot be condoned. The answer to such invasion and aggression is Chapter VII.'[15] Although he appeared to be referring to an inter-state conflict rather than an internal situation, the 'invasion of the rights of the majority' clearly shows that the primary reason for the situation being a threat to the peace was the denial of the right to self-determination of the people of Southern Rhodesia and their consequent struggle to achieve that right. Of course another element in a threat to the peace is the potential spillover effect, from internal to international violence. Perhaps the spillover element is overplayed, however, because any situation which denies people self-determination or significantly deprives them of human rights has the potential to ignite international violence, for example through misconceived or misapplied unilateral humanitarian intervention.

Although all-race elections now mark a new beginning, the fact remains that the denial of the right to self-determination to the majority of South Africans resulted in a low-intensity civil conflict which for many years constituted a 'threat to the peace'. The Council did not express such a finding in general terms, although resolutions passed in condemnation of the system of apartheid implied as much. For example, resolution 473 of 13 June 1978 reaffirmed that 'the policy of apartheid is a crime against the conscience and dignity of mankind and is incompatible with the rights and dignity of man, the Charter of the United Nations and the Universal Declaration of Human Rights and seriously disturbs international peace'. Designating apartheid as a 'crime against humanity'[16] must surely have subsumed the whole situation (and not just the acquisition of arms by South Africa)[17] within the concept of a 'threat to the peace'. The decision to deal with the situation within the terms of Chapter VI was a political one on behalf of the Western permanent members who were not willing to subject the regime to a more comprehensive embargo.[18]

It appears that a 'threat to the peace' is the term the Council has evolved for situations of non-traditional violence in which the main danger to international peace is not a conflict between two or more states; instead it arises primarily from an internal struggle which may, as in South Africa, manifest itself in the form of attacks upon other states.[19] Whereas South Africa and Rhodesia epitomized the denial of self-determination by racist regimes, the crisis in the Congo was primarily a civil war situation. The problems of civil strife and human suffering were in themselves sufficient to warrant a finding of a threat to the peace, although the Council tended to consider this compounded by the menace of Belgian and mercenary military intervention.[20]

In other conflicts the question of civil strife is often overshadowed by foreign intervention. In 1974 a Greek-backed coup against Archbishop Makarios, followed by the Turkish invasion of the northern part of Cyprus, led the Council to adopt resolution 353, which stated that there was a 'serious threat to international peace and security' and demanded 'an end to foreign military intervention' in Cyprus. The threat to international peace was inherent in the civil strife between the Greek and Turkish Cypriots, a fact recognized by resolution 186, adopted in 1964, which described the violent eruptions on the island as 'likely to threaten international peace'. The Turkish invasion in 1974 was a manifestation and realization of this threat.

The term 'threat to the peace' was thus being applied increasingly by the Security Council to internal situations. In 1969, Ireland requested a meeting of the Security Council to consider the situation in Northern Ireland, with a view to sending a UN peacekeeping force to the province to contain the serious disturbances caused by the alleged denial of civil rights to the Catholic community.[21] Although the question was not even put on the agenda, it is interesting to note that Lord Caradon, the British representative on the Council, was sufficiently perturbed by Irish references to southern Africa that he not only relied on article 2(7), as would be expected, but also denied that the situation in Northern Ireland was in any sense a threat to international peace.[22]

The Northern Ireland situation illustrates that the concept of a 'threat to the peace' is restricted to denials of self-determination or civil wars (which is not the case in Northern Ireland), with the additional requirement that the situation must have consequences for international peace in terms of destabilizing neighbouring states or drawing in outside powers. Recent post-Cold War practice, when the Council has been more willing to embrace Chapter VII, illustrates this point. The civil wars in Iraq, Yugoslavia and Somalia were all designated threats to the peace in 1991–92, not only because of the massive scale of destruction inflicted in each of these conflicts, but also because of their adverse effects on neighbouring states.

The extension of the concept of a 'threat to the peace' into what are essentially internal situations has not been without controversy. It is interesting to note that resolution 688 of 5 April 1991 – which found that the consequences of the Iraqi repression of the Kurds (which mainly took the form of a 'massive flow of refugees' towards and over the Iranian and Turkish frontiers) threatened international peace – was the least supported of all the Council's resolutions on the Gulf Crisis. It received only ten votes in favour, with three against (Cuba, Yemen, Zimbabwe) and two abstentions (China and India). Many states who chose not support the resolution expressed alarm at the intrusion it condoned into another state's internal affairs.[23] On the other hand the resolutions on Yugoslavia, which found that the continuation of the fighting 'constituted a threat to international peace and security',[24] and on Somalia, which determined that the civil conflict had 'consequences on the stability and peace in the region', the continuation of which 'constitutes ... a threat to international peace and security',[25] received unanimous votes. The difference appeared to be that resolution 688 concerned the suppression of a minority population group by the legitimate government of Iraq, a move that would clearly disturb members of the Council who were themselves guilty of suppression, whilst the other states, Yugoslavia and Somalia, were completely factionalized by the time the Council determined that they represented a threat to the peace. These resolutions were not directed against an established government and therefore could be supported by all members.[26]

It can be seen from the above discussion that the Security Council has moulded the concept of a 'threat to the peace' in article 39 to cover civil conflicts, but only if members can be persuaded that such conflicts have international repercussions, either in the form of a spillover of refugees or, more straightforwardly, in terms of regional or international peace. The latter qualification is so flexible as to make the concept of a threat to *international* peace a political decision rather than a legal requirement.[27]

The importance of a finding of a 'threat to the peace' is that it is the gateway into Chapter VII and the enforcement provisions of the Charter. The powers and practice of the Security Council in the use of economic and military enforcement measures as regards internal conflicts will be reviewed in Chapter 10.

The General Assembly's Powers

In 1945, when the UN Charter was drafted, there was a split between the Great Powers and the smaller states at the San Francisco conference as to the role and powers of the General Assembly. The Great Powers wanted it simply as a discussion chamber for the world community without granting it any real power, whereas the smaller states insisted that it be given more extensive authority. The result, in the best tradition of treaty drafting, was a compromise between those provisions which grant the Assembly wide powers and those that attempt to restrict it.

Article 10 allows the Assembly to 'discuss any questions or any matters within the scope of the present Charter' and 'make recommendations to the Members of the United Nations or to the Security Council or both on any such questions or matters'. Article 14 states that the Assembly 'may recommend measures for the peaceful adjustment of any situation, regardless of origin, which it deems likely to impair the general welfare or friendly relations among nations, including situations resulting from a violation of the provisions of the present Charter, setting forth the Purposes and Principles of the United Nations'. Both these very wide *recommendatory* powers are explicitly stated to be subject to article 12(1) which provides that '[w]hile the Security Council is exercising in respect of any dispute or situation the functions assigned to it in the present Charter, the General Assembly shall not make any recommendation with regard to that dispute or situation unless the Security Council so requests'. This provision has, in practice, been ignored, mainly because of the uncertainty as to what is meant by the Security Council performing its 'functions'.

The only other provision in Chapter IV of the UN Charter which attempts to restrict the General Assembly's powers is article 11(2) which provides, in part, that any question 'on which action is necessary, shall be referred to the Security Council'. In the *Expenses Case*, the World Court seemed to favour the view that the word 'action' in this provision referred to mandatory enforcement action which only the Security Council could order under Chapter VII and did not in any way restrict the recommendatory power of the Assembly.[28] This interpretation is reinforced by article 11(4) which states that the provisions of article 11 do not limit the Assembly's recommendatory powers contained in article 10.

Whatever the legal niceties of Chapter IV, the practice of the Assembly during the period of Western domination (1945–55), through the years in which the Non-Aligned and Socialist majority were dominant, to the rather subdued post-Cold War era in which North-South issues have surfaced as the major concern, shows that the Assembly has developed its competence to deal with issue of peace and security. Apart from its development of principles governing disarmament amongst nations, it has developed a wide competence in recommending peaceful solutions (reviewed in Chapter 9), a subsidiary competence in peacekeeping matters (reviewed in Chapter 8), as well as a quasi-judicial capacity under which it condemns breaches of international law, all of which it has utilized extensively as regards internal conflicts.

In addition there was an early attempt to recognize that the Assembly had competence in the field of enforcement. The ideal of a 'concert of Great Powers' collapsed in the first few months of the UN's life, with the Soviet Union's use of the veto seriously debilitating the Security Council. Wanting to use its dominant position within the organization[29] and realizing that the Security Council's action in Korea had only been possible because of the Soviet absence at the time, the US proposed the Uniting for Peace Resolution, which was duly adopted by the pro-Western majority in the General Assembly in November 1950.[30] The resolution stated that, although the initiative for the creation of a collective security system rested with the Security Council, the General Assembly desired that in the meantime the UN should have the means for maintaining international peace and security. The Assembly then resolved

> that if the Security Council, because of lack of unanimity of the permanent members, fails to exercise its primary responsibility for the maintenance of international peace and security ... the General Assembly shall consider the matter immediately with a view to making appropriate recommendations to members for collective measures, including in the case of a breach of the peace or act of aggression the use of armed force when necessary. ...

The Soviet Union stated that the resolution was *ultra vires*, arguing that collective action was solely within the province of the Security Council.[31] However, the resolution recognized the primary responsibility of the Security Council, and only granted the Assembly the power to *recommend* collective measures. Given that the Charter does appear to grant the Assembly wide recommendatory powers as regards peace and security, in addition to the fact that the World Court in the *Expenses Case* recognized that the Assembly possessed significant subsidiary powers,[32] it can be argued that the resolution is indeed *intra vires* and that the only powers exclusively within the domain of the Security Council are the *mandatory* ones granted by articles 40, 41 and 42.

Paradoxically, the Uniting for Peace Resolution, whilst being accepted in practice as a procedure of transferring items from the Security Council's agenda to the General Assembly's (meeting in Emergency Special Session), has failed to make its intended impact in the realm of collective security. No UN enforcement action has been sanctioned by it, although it was used to authorize the first UN peacekeeping force, the United Nations Emergency Force (UNEF I) in the Sinai in 1956, and it did take over as the mandating body for the UN operation in the Congo (ONUC) in 1960 which, as we shall see in Chapter 8, came close to being an enforcement action.

Despite the fact that it has failed to develop a recommendatory power in the field of military action, the General Assembly has developed an ability to call for sanctions against member states. It must be stressed, however, that these are *voluntary* sanctions, not *mandatory* ones. In relation to internal situations, the Assembly has in the past called for voluntary sanctions against South Africa and Southern Rhodesia, against Portugal for persevering with its colonial policy until 1975 and against Israel for its continued occupation of territories originally seized in the Six Day War of 1967.[33]

The Secretary General

From the relatively narrow provisions of the UN Charter concerning the office of Secretary General, the various holders of this post have developed an impressive set of powers to call on in the peaceful settlement of disputes. Article 97 states that the Secretary General 'shall be the chief administrative officer of the Organization'. However, unlike the Secretary General of the League of Nations who was simply a 'civil servant', the UN Secretary General is granted somewhat wider powers in the Charter. Article 98 provides that the Secretary General 'shall perform such other functions as are entrusted to him' by the Security Council, General Assembly, Economic and Social Council and the Trusteeship Council. Under this provision the Secretary General carries out whatever mandates are granted to him. These may range from sending a fact-finding mission to offering his good offices to organizing and putting in place a peacekeeping force.

The only autonomous power granted to him in the Charter is contained in article 99 which provides that '[t]he Secretary General may bring to the attention of the Security Council any matter which in his opinion may threaten international peace and security'. Given the importance of the concept of a 'threat to the peace' in the workings of the Security Council, particularly as regards internal conflicts, this is potentially a very important provision. However, it has been little used by office holders, although one notable exception occurred when Secretary General Hammarskjold, explicitly relying on article 99, brought the deteriorating situation in the Congo to the attention of the Security Council in 1960.

Nevertheless, despite this single autonomous power – to bring to the attention of the Security Council threats to international peace – over the years incumbents have developed some significant inherent powers, such as good offices, mediation, even arbitration and fact finding, all of which have been used as regards internal conflicts (examples follow in later chapters). These powers have developed either with the acquiescence of the Security Council and General Assembly, or sometimes with their active encouragement, in recognition of the fact that the Secretary General is not dependent on a specific mandate from one of the other principal organs of the UN.[35]

Using his autonomous powers, the Secretary General was initially allowed to use his own authority to send a fact-finding mission to a conflict, but not to authorize an observer force or a peacekeeping force, which still had to be mandated by the Security Council.[36] However, as UN activity grew in the late 1980s as the Cold War came to an end, so did the Secretary General's powers, at least to negotiate and put in place an observer force. Under a General Assembly mandate of 1980,[37] the representative of the Secretary General helped negotiate the Geneva Accords of 1988 which, *inter alia*, provided for the withdrawal of Soviet troops from Afghanistan under UN supervision. The 50-strong observer team was quickly drawn from other UN operations and despatched by the Secretary General, with Perez de Cuellar simply informing the Security Council by letter.[38] Strangely, it was not until the end of October 1988 that the Security Council formally confirmed its agreement to the measures envisaged and already executed by the Secretary General, 'in particular the temporary dispatch to Afghanistan and Pakistan of military officers'.[39] No explanation was given in the Security Council. It appears that the Secretary General had the consent of the Security Council to redeploy existing UN observers to Afghanistan and Pakistan without formal authorization. Given the exigencies of the situation, and the fact that both superpowers wanted a UN presence, the need for a prior mandate from the Security Council was ignored; UNGOMAP (the United Nations Good Offices Mission in Afghanistan and Pakistan) was thus established under the inherent powers of the Secretary General.

The United Nations High Commissioner for Refugees

Of all the agencies and bodies operating within the UN framework, the UN High Commissioner for Refugees is one of the most important as regards internal conflicts. As the recent upheavals in Afghanistan, Iraq, Somalia, Haiti and Yugoslavia illustrate, the flows of refugees displaced by internecine conflict pose an increasing problem. The UNHCR's roots can be traced back to the High Commissioner for Refugees established by the League of Nations in 1921. This body was first replaced by the United Nations Relief and Rehabilitation Commission set up before the UN proper in 1943 to deal with the millions of persons displaced by the fighting during the Second World War; then by the International Refugee Organization in 1946, and finally by the UNHCR in 1951. The General Assembly resolution establishing the UNHCR contained its Statute, the first paragraph of which reads as follows:

> The United Nations High Commissioner for Refugees, acting under the authority of the General Assembly, shall assume the function of providing international protection, under the auspices of the United Nations, to refugees who fall within the scope of the present Statute and of seeking permanent solutions for the problems of refugees by assisting governments and, subject to the approval of the governments concerned, private organisations to facilitate the voluntary repatriation of such refugees, to their assimilation within new national communities.

The resolution goes on to state that the work of the UNHCR 'shall be of an entirely non-political character; it shall be humanitarian and social and shall relate ... to groups and categories of refugees'. The Statute then proceeds to list the functions of the UNHCR.[40] These, together with the 1951 Convention on Refugees and the 1967 Protocol on Refugees, will be reviewed in Chapter 7, as will the work of the UNHCR and other agencies in this field.

Unlike the so-called specialized agencies of the UN which in many ways are quite independent of the World body, the UNHCR is clearly a subsidiary entity established by the General Assembly under article 22 of the UN Charter (which permits the Assembly to establish 'such subsidiary organs as it deems necessary for the performance of its functions'). The General Assembly has been recognized as possessing competence in the field of human rights and humanitarian relief, derived from article 13(1)(a) of the UN Charter under which it is responsible for promoting 'international cooperation in the economic, social, cultural and educational, and health fields, and assisting in the realization of human rights and fundamental freedoms without distinction as to race, sex, language or religion'. The UNHCR's mandate is renewed every five years by the General Assembly, to which it must submit annual reports. The UNHCR depends entirely on voluntary contributions from governments and from private sources.

Regional and Defence Organizations and Internal Conflicts

The purpose of this section is not to review all the regional and defence organizations which exist, but to provide an overview as to what constitutes such bodies, what the difference is between regional organizations and defence pacts and what their relationships are with the UN; also to examine what powers such organizations may legitimately possess as regards internal conflicts. The main example used here of a regional organization is the oldest, namely the Organization of American States (OAS)), whilst the main defence organization examined is the most prominent, namely the North Atlantic Treaty Organization (NATO). Other organizations and bodies will be mentioned in Chapter 10, but it must be noted from the outset that organizations may claim a range of differing powers according to their constituting treaties. Whether or not they sometimes act beyond their powers in dealing with specific internal situations will be reviewed in Chapter 10. At the moment the concern is to examine those powers that may reasonably be claimed by a regional organization and a self-defence pact, using the OAS and NATO as illustrations.

When negotiations over the UN were taking place in the years and months preceding the adoption of its Charter, a disagreement emerged between the two principal allies as to the form that the new post-war collective security system should take. Churchill favoured a regional security system on the grounds that positive action to combat aggression or threats to the peace would only be taken by states close to the source, whereas Roosevelt favoured a global trusteeship system whereby the Great Powers in the Security Council would act as the world's policemen, protecting and policing the smaller, and disarmed, states.[41]

The compromise achieved in Chapter VIII of the Charter favoured the global approach of Roosevelt rather than the regional one of Churchill. It did this by making regional organizations subservient to the UN in the most significant area – that of enforcement action. Article 53(1) states:

> The Security Council shall, where appropriate, utilize such regional arrangements or agencies for enforcement action under its authority. But no enforcement action shall be taken under regional arrangements or by regional agencies without the authorization of the Security Council. ...

Although regional organizations have autonomy in terms of the peaceful settlement of disputes,[42] article 53(1) states clearly that when it comes to enforcement action (which is normally interpreted to signify the possible use of military force and perhaps also mandatory sanctions), the Security Council must 'authorize' any such measures undertaken by regional organizations. Any doubts as to the supremacy of the Security Council in this area appear to be removed by article 103 of the UN Charter which states that 'in the event of a conflict between the obligations of the Members of the United Nations under the present Charter and their obligations under any other international agreement, their obligations under the present Charter shall prevail'.

However, the fear that article 53(1), which effectively gives each permanent member of the Security Council a veto over proposed action by a regional body, 'might cripple the functioning of regional arrangements' led to the insertion of article 51 in the UN Charter.[43] This provides that:

> Nothing in the present Charter shall impair the inherent right of individual or collective self-defence if an armed attack occurs against a Member of the United Nations, until the Security Council has taken measures necessary to maintain international peace and security. Measures taken by members in the exercise of this right of self-defence shall be immediately reported to the Security Council and shall not in any way affect the authority and responsibility of the Security Council under the present Charter to take at any time such action as it deems necessary in order to maintain or restore international peace and security.

This provision apparently reverses the process envisaged in article 53(1) in that it allows states – whether in regional organizations, collective self-defence pacts or on an *ad hoc* basis – to act in collective self-defence as long as they report such action to the Security Council; they are also subject to the Council then taking necessary measures. In other words, the veto cannot operate to block action in collective self-defence. However, article 51 does not reverse article 53(1). Article 51 is confined to responses to 'armed attacks' which (as has been seen in Chapter 1) are rare in internal conflicts, so that article 51 would seldom operate in such situations. Article 53(1) is concerned with 'enforcement' actions which is a much wider concept, dealing not only with armed attacks, but with any threats to or breaches of the peace.

Writers have tended to concentrate on the difference between regional bodies as collective self-defence pacts under article 51 and regional organizations as 'arrangements' and 'agencies' under Chapter VIII, rather than determining whether specific actions taken are of a defensive or enforcement nature.[44] The approach taken here is that organizations such as NATO and the former Warsaw Pact are not, *prima facie*, regional arrangements under Chapter VIII. Indeed, as shall be seen, the treaties establishing these bodies seem clearly to be based on article 51. Such arrangements are probably confined to those which have similar functions and powers to the UN as regards international peace and perhaps as regards economic and social co-operation, except that these powers are operated on a more limited regional basis. Organizations designed primarily to enhance the defence and military capabilities of power blocs do not fit this concept. This does not mean that such 'collective self-defence' pacts do not undertake enforcement action, but if they do, it should be authorized by the Security Council under article 53(1). On the other hand, if a regional organization, which primarily appears to come within Chapter VIII, operates on occasion solely in collective self-defence, it should not require such authorization since it is acting under article 51. Designating that a regional organization or body comes within article 51 or Chapter VIII is only a *prima facie* presumption that its actions will be based on those provisions. It does not prevent that organization from taking collective self-defence action under article 51, even if this is a regional arrangement under Chapter VIII; nor does it prevent a *prima facie* collective self-defence pact from taking enforcement action under article 53(1) as long as it is authorized by the Security Council.

Nevertheless, although this appears to be the position under the UN Charter, an examination of the constituent treaties of these bodies is required to see whether or not their members envisage both types of action – self-defence and enforcement.

The North Atlantic Treaty came into force on 24 August 1949. The treaty has 16 parties drawn principally from Western Europe and North America.[45] Unlike regional organizations such as the Organization of American States, which have a defensive pact built in, NATO has no economic or social trappings. The defensive right is contained in article 5:

> The parties agree that an armed attack against one or more of them in Europe or North America shall be considered an attack against them all; and consequently they agree that, if such an armed attack occurs, each of them, in exercise of the right of individual or collective self-defence recognized by article 51 of the Charter of the United Nations, will assist the party or parties so attacked by taking forthwith, individually, and in concert with the other parties, such action as it deems necessary, including the use of armed force, to restore and maintain the security of the North Atlantic area.
>
> Any such armed attack and all measures taken as a result thereof shall immediately be reported to the Security Council. Such measures shall be terminated when the Security Council has taken the measures necessary to restore and maintain international peace and security.

This provision follows article 51 quite closely: its requirements of an armed attack, its duty to report to the Security Council, and the temporary nature of defensive action in advance of Security Council measures. The subservience of NATO to the UN is reinforced by article 7, which reaffirms the primary responsibility of the Security Council for the maintenance of international peace and security.

It has been stated that NATO is based entirely on article 51 of the Charter, so that there is no question of its taking more than defensive action.[46] Article 5 appears to be based on this premise in that it embodies the right of a collection of states to take *defensive* action before the Security Council possibly takes *enforcement* action. If the treaty's intention was to give NATO enforcement powers – the right to take offensive measures to remove threats to the peace arising from events within the NATO area, or indeed from outside it, including internal conflicts which threaten regional or international peace – then the obligation would have been stated in terms of the Security Council authorizing such action within article 53 of the UN Charter.

However, article 5 appears to blur the distinction between collective self-defence and collective security when it implies that NATO members, if faced with an armed attack, shall take measures, not merely to repel the attack, but 'to restore the security of the North Atlantic area'. This suggests the possibility of NATO undertaking enforcement action, but only in response to an armed attack and not to a threat to the peace. Collective self-defence does not allow states to exceed the constraints that operate to define the extent of a legitimate response to any armed attack – in other words it must be proportionate and immediate. This usually means that self-defence, whether individual or collective, must be limited to repelling an initial attack. It follows that article 5 should be interpreted as permitting action only in collective self-defence. The sole exception is the possibility of the Security Council authorizing NATO to take enforcement action (if it deems NATO the most suitable body to do so and if NATO members accept such a flexible interpretation of the treaty); however, NATO clearly cannot take such action without that authority.

The Charter of the OAS of 1948 (the Bogota Charter) also contains the concept of a defensive pact,[47] but encompasses wider rights as well. Article 28 provides that:

If the inviolability or the integrity of the territory or the sovereignty or political independence of any American State should be affected by an armed attack or by an act of aggression that is not an armed attack, or by an extracontinental conflict, or by a conflict between two or more American States, or by any other fact or situation that might endanger the peace in America, the American States, in furtherance of the principles of continental solidarity or collective self-defence, shall apply the measures and procedures established in the special treaties on the subject.

The provision clearly anticipates some sort of action regarding internal conflicts that may endanger peace in the region. Indications of the type of action envisaged can be found in the special treaties that form part of the inter-American collective security network, mainly the Inter-American Treaty of Reciprocal Assistance (Rio Treaty) of 1947.[48]

Article 1 condemns the 'threat or use of force'. Article 2 obliges state parties to undertake peaceful settlement of their disputes. Articles 3–4 detail the collective self-defence system, explicitly referring to article 51 of the UN Charter. Article 5 then states that the parties 'shall immediately send to the Security Council of the United Nations, in conformity with articles 51 and 54 of the Charter of the United Nations, complete information concerning the activities undertaken or in contemplation in the exercise of the right of self-defence or for the purpose of maintaining international peace and security'. This clearly envisages enforcement action as regards threats to the peace, possibly in the form of internal conflicts. Article 6 then repeats article 5 of the Bogota Charter, adding that the Meeting of Consultation of Foreign Ministers of the OAS 'shall meet immediately in order to agree on the measures which must be taken in the case of aggression to assist the victim of the aggression or, in any case, the measures which should be taken for the common defense and for the maintenance of peace and security of the Continent'. Article 8 was revised in 1975 explicitly to enumerate the types of measures that can be taken by the OAS:

> For the purposes of this Treaty, the measures on which the [Meeting] of Consultation may agree will comprise one or more of the following: recall of chiefs of diplomatic missions; breaking of diplomatic relations; breaking of consular relations; partial or complete interruption of economic relations or of rail, sea, air, postal, telegraphic, telephonic … communications; and the use of armed force.

Article 17 provides that the Meeting of Consultation shall take its decisions by a vote of two-thirds of the states which have ratified the treaty, and article 20 provides that 'decisions which require the application of measures specified in article 8 shall be binding' upon all the state parties 'with the sole exception that no state shall be required to use armed force without its consent'. Although there is no elaborate procedure for a standing army as there is in the UN Charter (see Chapter 10), it is clear that the OAS has a collective security capability very similar to the UN's, so that it has the power, subject to the provisions of Chapter VIII and article 103 of the UN Charter, not only to attempt pacific settlements, but also to take economic and military measures as regards internal conflicts which endanger inter-American peace. The actual practice of the OAS in this regard will be reviewed in Chapter 10.

Humanitarian and Relief Agencies

The threat to international peace and security not uncommonly posed by non-international armed conflict almost invariably runs in parallel with humanitarian disasters. The UN is seriously involved in providing humanitarian assistance in such cases, the endeavours of the UN Commissioner for Refugees being an obvious example.[49] United Nations Forces may also play a very significant part in humanitarian relief, the function of UNPROFOR in escorting food and medical supply relief convoys to beleaguered populations in former Yugoslavia in the early 1990s being an important instance. There are also a considerable number of institutions and organizations of varying scale and focus outside the UN framework whose humanitarian work may impinge upon situations of non-international armed conflict. These range from large organizations such as the International Red Cross through to quite small bodies operating in a fairly local milieu. The sum total of their endeavours, and their sometimes complex interactions, play an important part in mitigating the effects of non-international armed conflicts.

The International Red Cross

A detailed review of the structure and functions of the International Red Cross organization and its constituent elements in the context of non-international armed conflict is set out below.[50] Certain facts about the distinctive structure and constitution of the International Red Cross, however, require emphasis.

The International Red Cross organization comprises recognized national Red Cross and Red Crescent Societies,[51] the Federation of Red Cross and Red Crescent Societies and the International Committee of the Red Cross, together with the International Red Cross Conference as a 'supreme deliberative body'.[52] Detailed provision has been made concerning the roles of national societies, the Federation and the International Committee (ICRC) in armed conflict,[53] but the working of the ICRC and the Federation require particular comment.

The International Committee of the Red Cross   The International Committee of the Red Cross is a private Swiss organization. Its Statutes provide, by article 2, that

> as an association governed by Article 60 and following the Swiss Civil Code, the ICRC shall have legal personality.[54]

That is, the ICRC functions as a person in Swiss municipal law rather than in public international law. No principle exists which would necessarily debar the ICRC from assuming an international legal personality, but such status has not been thought conducive to the effective performance of its functions. To anticipate discussion in Chapter 6 (below), the ICRC's performance of humanitarian work in armed conflict, whether international or non-international, depends *inter alia* upon the maintenance of impartiality as between the Parties in conflict and independence. These, indeed, are among the *fundamental principles* of the Red Cross. As formally stated by the XXth International Conference of the Red Cross in Vienna in 1965, the principle of *impartiality* means that

> it makes no discrimination as to nationality, race, religious beliefs, class or political opinions. It endeavours to relieve the suffering of individuals, being guided solely by their needs, and to give priority to the most urgent cases of distress.[55]

In the same manner *independence* means that

> the Red Cross is independent. The National Societies, while auxiliaries in the humanitarian services of their Governments and subject to the laws of their respective countries, must always maintain their autonomy so that they may be able at all times to act in accordance with Red Cross principles.[56]

The ability of the Red Cross to render humanitarian relief and to endeavour to secure the humane treatment of victims of armed conflict, in compliance with the relevant provisions of international humanitarian law,[57] rests upon the trust of the Parties in conflict and upon persuasion rather than public confrontation. The requirements of impartiality and independence are fundamental to this methodology and could conceivably be compromised by international legal personality. The essential point of legal personality is the ability to act independently, to sue and be sued, on an international plane;[58] this could involve entanglement in controversies which might dangerously compromise Red Cross endeavours.[59]

Not only is the ICRC itself a Swiss organization, but its personnel too is Swiss. This again is founded upon the need for neutrality in humanitarian action, but resulted originally from historical accident. The origins of not only the Red Cross organization, but modern 'Geneva' law itself, lie in the humanitarian work of Henry Dunant among the wounded on the battlefield of Solferino in 1859 and his subsequent proposals for ameliorating the condition of battlefield wounded.[60] Henry Dunant was Swiss and from this, essentially, has derived the Swiss identity of the ICRC. The constitutional neutrality of Switzerland also renders that country an ideal base for this impartial humanitarian organization. Of course it must be emphasized that, in accordance with the fundamental principle of *independence*, the ICRC is autonomous of any government, including that of Switzerland.

The ICRC is thus strictly not an 'international' organization in terms of institutional substance or membership. It is 'international' in its functions, however, which in the present context is much the most important criterion of identification.

The basic humanitarian role of the ICRC and the whole Red Cross organization has always essentially been conceived in terms of international armed conflicts. However, provision is also made for involvement in non-international armed conflicts, an aspect which has become very significant in the ICRC's work.[61]

The International Conference of the Red Cross   The International Conference of the Red Cross (the Conference) represents the essential interface between institutional elements of the Red Cross organization – the National Societies, the Federation of National Red Cross and Red Crescent Societies and the ICRC – and the states party to the Geneva Conventions. The members of the Conference with participatory and voting rights are stated by the Rules of Procedure of the International Conference of the Red Cross, article 1, to be,

> (a) the delegates of National Red Cross Societies recognized in accordance with … the Statutes of the International Red Cross;
> (b) the delegates of the States parties to the Geneva Convention for the Amelioration of the Condition of the Wounded and Sick in Armed Forces in the Field (1864, 1906, 1929 or 1949);
> (c) the delegates of the International Committee of the Red Cross and those of the [Federation] of Red Cross Societies.[62]

Other persons or representatives of organizations may be invited to attend the Conference as observers, with the right to speak if authorized by the Chair.[63]

The Conference normally meets quadrennially, but this date may be advanced at the request of the ICRC, the Federation, one-third of recognized National Societies or the Standing Commission[64] 'as an exceptional measure'.[65] During the meeting of the Conference, there will also be meetings of the Council of Delegates, comprising representatives of National Societies, the ICRC and the Federation, and of the General Assembly of the Federation.[66] Apart from an important role in making recommendations for the appointment of Conference offices, the Council of Delegates will determine the order of the Conference agenda and render opinions upon such matter as may be referred to it by the Conference or the Standing Commission[67] The provisional programme and agenda for the Conference are prepared by the Standing Commission, but National Societies, the ICRC and the Federation may propose items of concern for inclusion to the Standing Commission.[68]

The Standing Commission is constituted under article IX of the Statutes of the International Red Cross. It comprises five members in a personal capacity elected by the Conference and holding office until the close of the following Conference, with any vacancies being filled by the Standing Commission; two representatives of the ICRC, including normally its President; and two representatives of the Federation, including normally the Chair of its General Assembly. At least one year before the meeting of the Conference, the Commission may also invite a member of the National Red Cross or Red Crescent Society which is to be the next Conference host to attend in an advisory capacity.[69]

The matters considered by International Red Cross Conferences are very various in nature and in ultimate significance. They may include, *inter alia*, possible additional treaty provision where experience of armed conflict suggests this. Thus the process which ultimately led to the two 1977 Protocols Additional to the 1949 Geneva Conventions was initiated by a resolution adopted by the XXI International Conference of the Red Cross in Istanbul in 1969. The resolution requested the ICRC to propose additional rules for the affirmation and development of international humanitarian law for the consideration of various government experts. The Protocols emerged from a long process of discussion and negotiation between 1971 and 1977, and in particular from the work from 1974 onwards of a Diplomatic Conference on the Reaffirmation and Development of International Humanitarian Law Applicable in Armed Conflicts. This development was of very great significance in developing the *jus in bello* in relation to non-international armed conflicts. The prior provision of common article 3 of the 1949 Geneva Conventions was, and is, minimalist in nature, although inviting a much broader application of the humanitarian *jus in bello* where and to the extent that this may be agreed. 1977 Protocol II Additional to the 1949 Geneva Conventions, greatly supplementing common article 3 of the 1949 Conventions, is a much more substantial and detailed provision.

Powers of the International Red Cross

The detailed provisions governing the conduct and involvement of the International Red Cross in non-international armed conflicts are considered below.[70] However, it may be noted in passing that the primary duty of humanitarian relief for the victims of non-international armed conflict will fall upon the National Red Cross or Red Crescent Society of the country concerned.[71] However, common article 3 of the 1949 Geneva Conventions permits the ICRC to *offer* its humanitarian services in a context of non-international armed conflict, although these services need not be accepted.[72]

Other Humanitarian and Relief Organizations

Although the International Red Cross organization has a primary role in humanitarian relief in armed conflict, it is not unique in humanitarian endeavour in such situations. Other organizations vary widely in type and concern. Charities such as OXFAM engage in general relief and assistance, the forms and possibilities naturally varying considerably from situation to situation. Specifically medical assistance is emphasized by, e.g., the French organization *Médecins sans Frontières*. A very different endeavour is represented by Amnesty International. This organization is concerned with the problems of political prisoners, their treatment and release, which are clearly not issues confined to 'civil wars' but which have a manifest relevance in such situations.

The variety of these organizations and initiatives, which are almost all 'international' in scope if not in institutional composition, may sometimes conceal their collective weight and significance. It is thus worth noting, as Paul Sieghart remarks, that

> the greatest pressures on states [in a human rights context] still come from the non-governmental organizations ... which are active in this field. Without the unremitting efforts of voluntary societies ... human rights all over the world would be respected far less than they now are.[73]

Notes

1 M.N. Shaw, *International Law*, 3rd edn (Grotius, 1991), chapter 5.
2 *Reparation for Injuries Suffered in the Service of the United Nations Case*, ICJ Rep. 1949, p.174, at pp.178–79.

3　Article 2(7) of the UN Charter.
4　D.R. Gilmour, 'The Meaning of "Intervene" within Article 2(7) of the United Nations Charter' (1967) 16 *ICLQ* p.330 at p.349.
5　SC 3011 mtg, 46 UN SCOR (1991).
6　GA Res. 46/7, 46 UN GAOR (1991).
7　SC Res. 841, 48 UN S/PV (1993).
8　SC 3238 mtg, 48 UN S/PV (1993).
9　Article 24(1) of the UN Charter.
10　Article 34 of the UN Charter.
11　On the difference between 'danger' and 'threat', see N.D. White, *Keeping the Peace: The United Nations and the Maintenance of International Peace and Security*, 2nd edn (Manchester University Press, 1993), pp.38–48.
12　Report of the Sub-Committee on the Spanish question, 1 UN SCOR Special Supp. (No. 2) 4–5 (1946).
13　See for example SC Res. 181, 18 UN SCOR (1963).
14　SC Res. 82, 5 UN SCOR (1950); SC Res. 502, 37 UN SCOR (1982); SC Res. 660, 46 UN SCOR (1991).
15　SC 1340 mtg, 21 UN SCOR (1966).
16　SC Res. 556, 39 UN SCOR (1984).
17　SC Res 418, 32 UN SCOR (1977).
18　See for example UN doc. S/18087 (1986), vetoed at SC 2686 mtg, 41 UN SCOR (1986).
19　See SC Res. 567, 571, 574, 40 UN SCOR (1985).
20　SC Res. 161, 16 UN SCOR (1961).
21　UN doc. S/9394 (1969).
22　SC 1503 mtg, 24 UN SCOR (1969).
23　SC 2982 mtg, 46 UN SCOR (1991).
24　SC Res 713, 46 UN SCOR (1991).
25　SC Res. 733, 47 UN SCOR (1992).
26　SC 3009 mtg, 46 UN S/PV (1991); SC 3039 mtg, 47 UN S/PV (1992).
27　For the extension of the concept to cover state support of terrorism in the case of Libya, see White, *Keeping the Peace*, pp.47–9.
28　*Certain Expenses of the United Nations Case*, ICJ Rep. 1962, p.151 at p.163.
29　See generally E. Luard, *A History of the United Nations: The Years of Western Domination 1945–1955*, Vol. 1 (Macmillan, 1982).
30　GA Res. 377, 5 UN GAOR (1950).
31　GA 299 mtg, 5 UN GAOR (1950). See articles 11(2) and 12 of the UN Charter.
32　ICJ Rep. 1962, pp.162–5.
33　GA Res. 1663, 16 UN GAOR (1961); GA Res. 2107, 20 UN GAOR (1965); GA Res. 2151, 21 UN GAOR (1966). See for example GA Res. 39/146, 39 UN GAOR 50 (1984).
34　SC 873 mtg, 15 UN SCOR (1960).
35　See the General Assembly's Declaration on the Prevention and Removal of Disputes and Situations which may Threaten International Peace and Security and the Role of the United Nations in this Field; GA Res. 43/51, 43 UN GAOR (1988).
36　See R. Lavalle, 'The "Inherent" Powers of the UN Secretary General in the Political Sphere: A Legal Analysis' (1990) 37 *NILR* p.22.
37　GA Res. ES-6/2, 6 UN GAOR ESS (1980).
38　UN docs S/19834, S/19835 (1988).
39　SC Res. 622, 43 UN SCOR (1988).
40　GA Res 428, 5 UN GAOR (1950).
41　R.M. Russell and J.E. Muther, *A History of the United Nations Charter* (Brookings Institute, 1958) p.105.

42   Article 52. The efforts of regional bodies in this area will be examined in the course of Chapter 9.

43   E. Berberg, 'Regional Organisations: A United Nations Problem' (1955) 49 *AJIL* p.166 at p.169.

44   See for example H. Kelsen, 'Is the North Atlantic Treaty a Regional Arrangement?' (1951) 45 *AJIL*, p.162.

45   34 UNTS 243. Parties: Belgium, Canada, Denmark, France, Germany, Greece, Iceland, Italy, Luxembourg, Netherlands, Norway, Portugal, Spain, Turkey, UK, US. In 1966 France unilaterally withdrew from its treaty commitments but without withdrawing from the Treaty itself.

46   W.E. Beckett, *The North Atlantic Treaty, the Brussels Treaty and the Charter of the United Nations* (Stevens, 1950), p.26, p.34; A.L. Goodhart, 'The North Atlantic Treaty of 1949' (1951) 79 *Hague Recueil* p.187 at pp.207–8, 220–21.

47   Article 27, 119 UNTS 4. There are 34 state parties to this treaty.

48   21 UNTS 77. There are 23 state parties to this treaty.

49   See above, pp.43–4; also Chapter 7 at pp.164–9.

50   See Chapter 6 at pp.141–3.

51   As to these emblems, see Chapter 6 at p.139.

52   Statutes of the International Red Cross, article I. The text is printed in the *International Red Cross Handbook*, 12th edn (International Committee of the Red Cross and the League (now Federation) of the Red Cross Societies in collaboration with the Henry Dunant Institute, 1983), p.407.

53   See pp.141–3, below.

54   The text is reproduced in the *International Red Cross Handbook*, 12th edn, at p.421.

55   Proclamation of the Fundamental Principles of the Red Cross, XX International Conference of the Red Cross, Vienna 1965, Resolution IX. The text is reproduced in the *International Red Cross Handbook*, 12th edn, at p.16.

56   *Ibid.*

57   See Chapter 6.

58   See also p.142, below.

59   On occasions the ICRC has made public statements, in suitably neutral terms, about serious violations of the laws of armed conflict in an effort to secure compliance; see Chapter 6 at pp.142–3.

60   See Chapter 6 at p.124.

61   See Chapter 6 at pp.124–6.

62   The text is set out in the *International Red Cross Handbook*, 12th edn, at p.414. The Convention referred to in paragraph (b) is 1949 Geneva Convention I and its precursors. The overwhelming proportion of States are party to this Convention, and to 1949 Geneva Conventions II, III and IV, the reference to predecessors ensuring that all which have adopted 'Geneva' principles are included. In the present context, common article 3 governing non-international armed conflicts forms part of 1949 Geneva Convention I. Membership of the Conference does not, however, require a State to be party to 1977 Additional Protocols I or II.

63   Rules of Procedure of the International Red Cross Conference, article 3.

64   For the Standing Commission, see below, p.53.

65   Statutes of the International Red Cross, article III.

66   *Ibid.*, article IV.

67   *Ibid.*

68   Rules of Procedure of the International Conference of the Red Cross, article 5.

69   Statutes of the International Red Cross, article IX(2).

70   See Chapter 6 at pp.141–3.

71 Xth International Red Cross Conference, Geneva 1921, Resolution XIV (ii); see also Chapter 6, pp.141–2.
72 See also Chapter 6, p.142.
73 P. Sieghart, *The Lawful Rights of Mankind* (Oxford University Press, 1986), p.104.

PART II
IMPLEMENTATION AND PRACTICE

3 The Status of Parties in Conflict

In international armed conflicts the existence of opposing parties, each of which enjoys international legal personality and thus the capacity to act upon the international plane, is not normally in doubt. This is not quite a universal proposition: in the 1990–91 Gulf conflict, Iraq sought to claim that Kuwait was its 'nineteenth province' and thus to cast doubt upon the applicable law. This claim, however, received scant if any acceptance outside Iraq. Kuwait enjoys general recognition as a state and, anyway, article 2(4) proscribes the enforcement of territorial claims by armed force, even where a hypothetical claim might be justified. Usually, therefore, an international armed conflict involves hostilities between two states which, whatever their differences over the legitimacy of involvement and conduct during the conflict, are not, either or each, denying the existence of the other or of the possibility of entitlements and liabilities arising between them. If there is any single criterion which distinguishes between the legal treatment of international and non-international armed conflicts, it is precisely this.

In hostilities waged between the armed forces of a state and separatist or insurgent forces taking place within the territory of the state, the status of the parties involved becomes, *ex hypothesi*, a matter of extreme political sensitivity. So much so that reference to the 'parties' in conflict in treaty provisions potentially constitutes an obstacle to implementation for fear that the opposing side(s) might be implicitly 'recognized'. Common article 3 of the 1949 Geneva Conventions, the basic minimum humanitarian *jus in bello* provision for non-international armed conflicts, concludes with the unequivocal statement that '[t]he application of the preceding provisions shall not affect the legal status of the Parties to the conflict'.

1977 Protocol II Additional to the 1949 Geneva Conventions, expanding upon the provision of common article 3 of the 1949 Conventions is, if anything, yet more cautious. The Protocol provides by article 3(1) that nothing in this Protocol shall be invoked for the purpose of affecting the sovereignty of a State or the responsibility of the government, by all legitimate means, to defend the national unity and territorial integrity of the State.

Thus the application of the humanitarian norms set out by the Protocol clearly does not legitimize dissident forces; indeed, it does not directly refer to them. Whether such forces are otherwise legitimized is, of course, a separate question. In relation to the generally cautious approach in the wording of 1977 Additional Protocol II, Frits Kalshoven remarks that

there is not a single reference to the 'parties to the conflict'. This utter silence reflects the fear of many governments that the mere reference to an adverse party might in concrete instances be interpreted as a form of recognition.[1]

It is especially significant in this context that neither common article 3 of the 1949 Geneva Conventions nor 1977 Additional Protocol II makes any reference to 'combatant' or 'prisoner of war' status. The implicit recognition entailed in any such provision might well seem a fatal obstacle to implementation in very many cases.

If sensitive issues are raised by questions of reference and definition in conflicts securely categorized as 'non-international', yet greater difficulties arise where involvement is less clear. This is especially the case for certain conflicts treated by 1977 Protocol I Additional to the 1949 Geneva Conventions (expanding the 1949 humanitarian provision for *international* armed conflicts) as 'internationalized'. These are 'national liberation' struggles in which people are exercising a right of national self-determination. In defining the scope of application of 1977 Additional Protocol I (in effect international armed conflicts), article 1(4) includes

armed conflicts in which peoples are fighting against colonial domination and alien occupation and against racist regimes in exercise of their right of self-determination... .

Such conflicts are not, yet, strictly 'international' but are treated by 1977 Additional Protocol I *as if* they were. The implications for 'recognition' and the sensitivities involved are both obvious and problematic in terms of implementation. The difficulties are compounded in the light of the developing interpretation of rights of 'self-determination' in the post-colonial era.[2] For the present purpose, three possible levels of conflict, below international armed conflict, require brief consideration in terms of the status of parties. These are (1) 'internationalized' armed conflicts within the meaning of article 1(4) of 1977

Additional Protocol I, (2) non-international armed conflicts and (3) internal disturbances. Each raises different, but equally sensitive, issues. Beyond the effects of categorization as such, there arises the question of the impact of any agreements between parties to non-international armed conflicts to apply some or all of the body of *jus in bello* rules and principles applicable to international conflicts.

'Internationalized' Armed Conflicts

Where a *prima facie* non-international armed conflict is deemed to be 'internationalized' pursuant to article 1(4) of 1977 Protocol I Additional to the 1949 Geneva Conventions, the potential impact upon the status of the parties is dramatic. Article 1(4) is so phrased that the situations referred to by common article 2 of the 1949 Geneva Conventions 'include' those added by the article. Common article 2 of the 1949 Conventions refers to their application in

> all cases of declared war or any other armed conflict which may arise between the High Contracting Parties [and] ... to all cases of partial or total occupation of the territory of a High Contracting Party... .

The customary status of the 1949 Conventions means that they will apply in any international armed conflict. It cannot, yet, be argued that article 1(4) of 1977 Additional Protocol I has attained such status.[3] However, where this provision is applicable, at least the 'Geneva' arm of the *jus in bello* relative to international armed conflicts must be considered to apply. This would include entitlement of captured fighters to prisoner-of-war status under article 4 of 1949 Geneva Convention III as long as they satisfied the requirements there stated, and under article 44 of 1977 Additional Protocol I. Such status implies legitimate combatancy under the 1949 Provision and is explicitly so stated by article 43 of 1977 Additional Protocol I.

All this turns upon the question of 'self-determination' in relation to any particular conflict. Protocol I does not seek to restrict the issue of claims to 'self-determination'. Indeed article 4 specifies that

> the application of the [1949] Conventions and of this Protocol, as well as the conclusion of the agreements provided for therein, shall not affect the legal status of the Parties to the conflict. ...

Nonetheless, it may reasonably be assumed that states will be exceedingly reluctant to concede either that the nature of a conflict waged against them within their borders is 'self-determinatory' or that the combatancy of the insurgent forces is legitimate.

This seemingly rather bleak prospect of debate and ambiguity in relation to the status of a conflict and the law to be applied (a problem which should be deplored in any attempt to regulate the conduct of armed conflict) may in reality be somewhat relieved. 1977 Additional Protocol I provides by article 96(3) that

> the authority representing a people engaged against a High Contracting Party in an armed conflict [as in] ... article 1(4), may undertake to apply the Conventions and this Protocol ... by means of a unilateral declaration addressed to the depositary. ...

The effects of such a unilateral declaration are then stated to include the assumption by the 'authority' of the same rights and obligations as those of a High Contracting Party[4] as well as the binding of all parties to the conflict to the 1949 Geneva Conventions and 1977 Additional Protocol I.[5] This does not, of course, mean that such an 'authority' could unilaterally declare itself to be engaged in a 'self-determination' struggle. The status of the struggle is, rather, a prerequisite for the making of such a declaration. The provision for declaration is nevertheless useful for determining the practical implications of article 1(4).

The establishment of status, which is a prerequisite for such a declaration, may also be resolvable in practice by means which avoid the technical debates which might otherwise obstruct humanitarian implementation. The primary relevant example here long predated the 1977 Protocol but may still be useful as an argument by analogy. That was the Algerian war of independence. In that conflict the FLN, the independence forces, announced its willingness to comply with the norms of the laws of armed conflict and set up prisoner-of-war camps. This in the end compelled the colonial power, France, to concede the *de facto* status of the FLN and then to apply the *jus in bello* norms thus enjoined. Although 1977 Additional Protocol I does not directly so specify, it would seem reasonable to argue that an 'authority' making a declaration under article 96(3) must be in a position practically to 'apply the [1949] Conventions and ... Protocol [I]'. If this were not the case, the declarations in question would have little or no value. It would follow that at least some level of success is necessary. An analogy with the requirements set out by article 1 of 1977 Additional Protocol II might be useful in this context.

When, and if, a separationist movement is recognized as fighting in an 'internationalized' self-determinatory struggle within the meaning of article 1(4) of 1977 Additional Protocol I, the conflict will cease to be governed by the norms applicable to non-international armed conflict. It will thereafter be governed by the full *jus in bello* regime applicable to international armed conflicts. Whether such a conflict then truly is an international armed conflict is open to some debate, especially granted the necessity for a final settlement of differences between the state and the separatists – including, potentially, such basic matters as frontiers. In any event the conflict will at that point not fall within the remit of the norms applicable to non-international armed conflicts *stricto sensu*, nor within the bounds of the present discussion.

Non-International Armed Conflicts

Parties to non-international armed conflicts, which may conveniently be taken as those governed by common article 3 of the 1949 Geneva Conventions and 1977 Additional Protocol II, almost always comprise the forces of a state and dissident forces within the territory of that state. The intensity which the conflict must have reached before being labelled 'non-international' has been considered above.[6] The criteria for application of the relevant *jus in bello* norms to dissident forces are set out by article 1 of 1977 Additional Protocol II, which refers to

> dissident armed forces which, under responsible command, exercise such control over a part of [the state's] ... territory as to enable them to carry out sustained and concerted military operations and to implement this Protocol.

The implications of this, amongst other requirements for the categorization of levels of armed conflict have been considered above.[7] The specific requirements set out in relation to 'dissident armed forces', however, merit particular examination here. The phrase does not necessarily mean mutinous members of the national armed forces, although such units could be included. Apart from the territorial control demanded of the authority to which they answer, three requirements are set down for the 'quasi-governmental' forces themselves. These are (1) responsible command, (2) capacity for sustained and concerted military action, and (3) capacity, and presumably willingness, to implement the norms set out in 1977 Additional Protocol II.

The International Committee of the Red Cross Commentary upon 1977 Additional Protocol II remarks that the requirement of 'responsible command'

> implies some degree of organization ..., but ... not necessarily ... a hierarchical system of military organization similar to that of regular armed forces. It means an organization capable of ... planning and

carrying out sustained and concerted military operations, and ... imposing discipline in the name of a *de facto* authority.[8]

Clearly one would not necessarily expect to find an elaborate hierarchy of military ranks and structures in a dissident armed force. However, a chain of authority, answerability and responsibility are clearly necessary for meaningful and verifiable implementation of *jus in bello* norms at any level of armed conflict. The point was well illustrated in the course of the armed conflict(s) in former Yugoslavia in the early 1990s. It has been suggested elsewhere that

> in several [instances in former Yugoslavia] ... the ... dubious status of the forces involved has been used by 'authorities' as a means of denying responsibility. ... If [an authority] ... genuinely *cannot* [discipline its operatives] ... its control over its own forces and its status as an authority must be doubted.[9]

This was not, of course, universally the case in former Yugoslavia, but such incidents illustrate the practical necessities which underpin the requirements of 'responsible command' in article 1 of 1977 Additional Protocol II.[10]

Capacity to mount 'sustained and concerted military operations' might in theory provoke complex debate. In practice the meaning seems clear enough: the operations in question should be significant in scale and duration and should be organized in character. Thus, sporadic acts of terrorism, which may be organized but are not 'sustained', would fall outwith the definition, as would extended rioting and disorder, which might be 'sustained' but rarely if ever 'concerted'. Interestingly, the ICRC Commentary upon 1977 Additional Protocol II suggests that,

> at the beginning of a [non-international] conflict military operations rarely have such a character; thus it is likely that only common article 3 [of the 1949 Geneva Conventions] will apply to the first stage of hostilities.[11]

Common article 3, indeed, refers only to 'armed conflict not of an international character', without identifying further criteria to be applied to the dissident forces involved. This is one of the ways in which 1977 Additional Protocol II may be said to progress well beyond the minimum provision set out in 1949 by common article 3.

The capacity to implement 1977 Additional Protocol II relates back in different ways to the other criteria – organizational and territorial – set out by article 1. Full implementation of the humanitarian requirements of the protocol in relation to victims of non-international armed conflict[12] manifestly requires a significant organizational structure and, in practice, some territorial base. This is not to suggest that the fluctuating exigencies of armed conflict would excuse serious derogations, merely to observe that the starting point involves certain practical suppositions about the parties in conflict. These suppositions all ultimately focus upon the scale and nature of organization of a dissident armed forced and its consequent ability to implement the norms in question.

The armed forces of the state do not pose the same problems of definition since they are generally recognizable as the armed forces. Rather, it is a question of whether they are meeting the obligations imposed by the relevant *jus in bello* provision. 1977 Additional Protocol II presumes that the armed forces of the state, meaning those remaining loyal to the state, will be a primary participant in a non-international armed conflict. Indeed, the Protocol in article 1(1) defines its material field of application in such terms.[13] What then if a non-international armed conflict occurs in which either two factions other than the government are in conflict or where various factions are contending after a collapse of established authority? The ICRC Commentary upon 1977 Additional Protocol II reveals that the ICRC draft provided for this contingency but that the Diplomatic Conference felt that it was a 'theoretical textbook example' which did not require coverage, despite past ICRC experience.[14] This was, however, precisely the situation in Somalia virtually from 1989–90. Following a period of brutal conflict between the government of President Siad Barre and numerous dissident forces (which arose partly from economic and political causes and partly from historic clan rivalries), the government collapsed completely in January 1991 and what remained of the government was driven out of the capital, Mogadishu. Somalia then descended into bloody anarchy which led initially to the US 'Operation Restore Hope' and ultimately to the establishment of the United Nations UNOSOM Force. The arrival of US and then UN forces raised other questions of *jus in bello* application,[15] but prior to this the relevant law would have been common article 3 of the 1949 Geneva Conventions. Somalia was not at the material times party to 1977 Additional Protocol II, but the general point of application is nonetheless made.

The applicability of humanitarian *jus in bello* norms, under 1977 Additional Protocol II or otherwise, in non-international armed conflicts is not a matter linked to the legitimacy of the insurgent forces or the insurgency. It is the identification of the relevant legal prescription in the given context which is of central concern for this purpose rather than the evaluation of the status of the parties in conflict.

Internal Disturbances

Internal strife or disturbances might be variously described but the International Committee of the Red Cross submitted a useful definition to the 1971 Conference of Government Experts on the Reaffirmation and Development of International Humanitarian Law Applicable in Armed Conflicts. It was suggested that internal disturbances are situations

> in which there is no non-international armed conflict as such, but there exists a confrontation within the country, which is characterised by a certain seriousness of duration and which involves acts of violence.[16]

As we have seen, internal disturbances do not fall specifically within the remit of the *jus in bello*,[17] although suggestions for a 'human rights' regime in relation to them have been strongly argued.[18] Those engaged in a wide range of confrontations, from riotous disturbance to individual crimes of violence, cannot fall within the provision of the *jus in bello*, although relevant human rights provisions will apply, e.g., in terms of trial and treatment. Of course the same basic principle would also apply in cases of terrorism.

Terrorist Violence

Since the 1937 draft League of Nations Convention for the Prevention and Punishment of Terrorism, which followed the assassination of King Alexander of Yugoslavia in Marseilles but was ratified by only one country, there have been many attempts to define 'terrorism'. None has achieved universal acceptance. This is partly because, while certain acts would almost universally be classified as 'terrorist' (such as leaving bombs in crowded shopping centres), there are areas of doubt at the fringes which continue to defy definitive classification. It must also be said that particular terrorist groups may attract the active or implicit sympathy of external powers, well removed from the effects of their actions, and this may also impede the drafting of adequate definitions. The sometimes stated paradox that a 'terrorist' from one point of view may be a 'liberation fighter' from another entirely misses the point. In the laws of armed conflict, violations are not, or should not be, defined by reference to sympathy with causes. It is what terrorists *do* that should be the criterion of evaluation, not what they *think*. Despite the various difficulties, the 'core' elements of indiscrimination, randomness and collective 'terror' which characterize most modern descriptions of terrorism may serve to clarify the basic concept.

In terms of the modern *jus in bello*, the considerable variety of modern terrorist organizations (such as the IRA operating in Northern Ireland and other parts of the UK, ETA operating in the Spanish Basque territories, the Maoist *Sindero Luminoso* (Shining Path) in Peru, the *Rote Armee Fraktion* (Red Army Faction) in Germany, the Red Brigades in Italy and *Action Directe* in France) would clearly not satisfy the requirements of article 1(1) of 1977 Additional Protocol II. Indeed, Protocol II forbids by article 4(2)(d) 'acts of terrorism' perpetrated against 'all persons who do not take a direct part or have ceased to take part in hostilities'. Such a ban would not permit 'terrorism' to be perpetrated against anyone else either. In most cases terrorists would not even meet the requirements set out by common article 3 of the 1949 Geneva Conventions since acts of sporadic terrorist violence hardly constitute 'armed conflict' for this purpose. Such a view may be supported by the reference of article 3(1) to 'armed forces' which, even without the organizational elaboration afforded by article 1(1) of 1977 Additional Protocol II, implies something well beyond the structure and conduct of most terrorists.

Arguments have nonetheless been made either for the *jus in bello* or some distinct laws of war regime to be made applicable to terrorists and to counter-action taken against them. The arguments generally advanced focus upon the possibility of limiting both terrorist action and response by bringing terrorism into the sphere of international legal norms. There are significant obstacles to any such proposals and certainly to the practical implementation of any extended *jus in bello* norms. The obstacles are legal and practical, relating both to issues of explicit or implicit 'legitimation' and to the actual phenomenology of terrorism. In this general context, Harry H. Almond has remarked that

> those who insist that terrorism is a form of 'warfare' are ... suggesting that the terrorist ... is entitled to the benefits and protection of [the law of war] ... in return for passing these on to those that the terrorist attack[s]. ... Terrorism as such is not permissible under the law of war, but is listed as a war crime. ...[19]

Certainly many, if not all, terrorist acts might well be considered war crimes if perpetrated by an 'armed force' engaged in armed conflict, particularly considering the covert nature of most terrorist activity and the indiscriminate nature of many terrorist attacks. The essential problem is well stated by Torsten Stein:

> The entire system of the laws of war is founded on the basic distinction between combatants and civilians, between lawful acts of combatancy and punishable war crimes. Without accepting these ba-

sic categories the whole system becomes unworkable. Consequently, the humanitarian law applicable in armed conflicts cannot apply, even by analogy, to peace-time terrorism.[20]

Terrorist 'methods and means' of attack are in a sense equated with unlawfulness; to bring them within the *jus in bello*, at any level, would in effect be a contradiction in terms.

The inclusion of terrorism within the *jus in bello* would also have considerable potential 'recognition' implications which most states which have been or are victims of terrorism would find unacceptable. Professor Almond advances a more moderate approach:

> we can conceive a kind of umbrella agreement among states laying down ... common objectives and goals ... . With such an agreement ..., they can cover, through annexes or supplements, a variety of specific acts that need attention. ... [Outstanding problems may be negotiated] until a network has been achieved of similar and effective instruments to deal with terrorism.[21]

Such a general provision to deal with the international dimensions of terrorism, including possibly matters of extradition and 'political' exceptions (which are currently vastly controversial in both substance and operation), might well have much to commend it. The benefits in terms of definition, both of 'terrorism' as such and the obligations of states in reaction to it, would be tangible. This might especially be the case where there is a tendency for an ill-informed and often 'romanticized' approbation of terrorist outrages as, for instance, in some appreciations of the IRA in the US. So far as the *jus in bello* is concerned, methods of attack falling within the general category of terrorism, including both its elements of indiscrimination and its calculated selection of 'soft' targets, are and would surely remain unlawful.

If terrorist organizations were to begin to conduct themselves, e.g., in accordance with article 1 of 1977 Additional Protocol II, they would by definition cease to be 'terrorists'. The same may also be said, for instance, of lawfully conducted resistance to a foreign military occupation.[22] In any situation, terrorist violence is not a matter which could or perhaps should be brought within a *jus in bello* shield. The matter is under active legal consideration in a variety of dimensions, and developments to constrain both terrorism and the external assistance it receives might be looked for. The international laws of armed conflict, applicable in international or non-international arenas, do not in present circumstances appear to be an appropriate context for progress.

It may also be noted that confrontations involving terrorism are not always insoluble. The long tragic confrontation between Israel and the Palestine Liberation Organization (PLO) commonly involved 'terrorist' acts both in and beyond Israel undertaken by extremist splinter groups. In 1993, after complex secret negotiations, the Israeli Government and the PLO reached an accord which set in train what may hopefully be a long-term peace process. Extremists on each side inevitably rejected the agreement and continued to perpetrate acts of terror, but the 'mainstream' parties persevered in a process of dispute resolution which not long before would have been deemed inconceivable.

Where terrorist violence is perpetrated, the *jus in bello* arguably does not provide an appropriate or workable normative framework. This is not to say that some humanitarian provisions cannot be applied in relation to terrorists and terrorist acts. Obviously human rights provisions, e.g. in relation to due process and modes of interrogation, will be applicable.[23] On occasion, also, humanitarian agencies may be admitted, by agreements falling outside *jus in bello* provision, to visit places of internment or imprisonment in which terrorist suspects or convicted terrorists are held. The Fundamental Red Cross Principle of *impartiality*, as stated by the XXth International Conference of the Red Cross (held in Vienna in 1965),[24] would also suggest that medical aid should be given to a suspected terrorist, even if injured by his or her own bomb, *in accordance with the priority of medical need*. Such a humanitarian principle does not, however, either condone terrorism or seek to hinder investigation and the processes of criminal prosecution in relation to its perpetrators.

The Conflicts under Consideration

The law applicable to non-international armed conflicts (under consideration here), is limited in its remit. To recap, the categories of 'internationalized' armed conflicts, whether in terms of exercising rights of self-determination, internal strife or crises of terrorist violence, fall either within different sectors of the *jus in bello* or outwith such provision altogether. Non-international armed conflicts, on the other hand, occur within the territory of a state; they have attained an extent and degree of intensity which places them organizationally and structurally beyond the level of civil strife, but without being 'internationalized' by reference to self-determination. In such conflicts, a number of particularly sensitive questions arise in relation to the status of the parties involved.

The Vexed Question of Belligerence

One of the central problems in international legal provision for non-international armed conflict is that of express or implied recognition and 'legitimation' of dissident organizations and forces. The *jus in bello* provision for non-international armed conflicts is extremely careful to avoid this issue. It is for this reason that the *de facto* status of dissident armed forces within, e.g., 1977 Additional Protocol II, is emphatically not to be taken as a comment upon the legitimacy or otherwise of dissident forces and their involvement in conflict. The only exception to this is the provision made by article 1(4) of 1977 Additional Protocol I in relation to armed struggles aimed at self-determination – in effect, 'wars of national liberation'. The question of the status of dissident organizations in non-international armed conflict is, however, wider than this, the legitimacy of involvement in armed conflict centring upon the concept of belligerency.

In a literal sense belligerency refers simply to engagement in hostilities or willingness so to be engaged. In the context of the laws of armed conflict, its meaning is significantly more restricted and carries, permanently or temporarily, at least some connotation of *legitimacy*. The question arises most importantly in relation to the position of states external to a state in which a condition of non-international armed conflict exists. The basic issue is well expressed by Schwarzenberger:

> It would have been too much to expect from third states to tolerate indefinitely a situation in which a recognised government involved in an internal war could claim the best of both worlds: non-responsibility for the acts of revolutionary authorities in areas over which it had lost control, and interdiction to third states of direct contact with the revolutionaries.[25]

The international response to this very real question has largely and inevitably been based on criteria of *de facto* control.

Much of the case law derives from wars of independence in South America and refers to situations which might now be regarded as 'internationalized' conflicts. This was not, however, the context of their original decision in which revolutionary 'authorities' were in large part recognized as 'belligerents'. In the *Murray Claim*, decided in 1862 by the Costa Rica–United States Claims Commission upon events arising from the separation of Nicaragua from Costa Rica, the issue turned upon whether acts of the Costa Rican armed forces, during which the claimant's property was destroyed, were undertaken in 'war'. The Arbitrator remarked of the status of the revolutionary Rivas-Walker authority in Nicaragua that the new government of Nicaragua, ... though illegitimate ... in its origin, was in fact and continued long to be the only government of that State.[26]

It was further pointed out that, by its own treatment of the conflict, the Costa Rican government had confirmed the state of belligerency existing between itself and the Rivas-Walker regime. The linkage between belligerency and *de facto* control in a non-international armed conflict was taken a little further in 1928 in *Oriental Navigation Company (USA)* v *United Mexican States*. It was there concluded that when a naval vessel of a government discovers a neutral ship in a port held by insurgent forces without government authorization papers, it may order the vessel to cease unloading its cargo and depart. In a persuasive dissenting opinion, the US Commissioner remarked that

it would not seem to be logical to attempt to make any distinction between the closure of a port held by insurrectionists who by some affirmative acts have been recognized as belligerents, and a port in the hands of revolutionists to whom such a status has not in this manner been accorded.[27]

In such cases, where no express or implicit recognition of belligerency seems to have been afforded by the 'legitimate' government of the state affected, the position of other states might be rendered exceedingly problematic. According to classical consensus, a foreign state might justify recognition of the belligerency of an insurgent force (a) where the insurgents are in fact exercising quasi-governmental powers over some part of the territory of the state affected, or (b) where the interests of the recognizing state are so affected by this shift of power that they must redefine their relations with the parties.[28] Such a decision is, by its nature, provisional. If the insurgents persevere and the insurrection achieves its objective, the question of recognition will advance from the context of belligerency to that of state and government. If the insurrection fails, then the factual basis of the 'belligerency' will dissolve with it.

In a post-1945 context this model is no longer wholly adequate. Quite apart from the question of rights to self-determination and a reinterpretation of that concept in a post-colonial context,[29] modern experience has shown that the questions of recognition of belligerency and of state or government cannot always be quite so easily decoupled as suggested by the classical view. The significance of the recognition of the parties to the conflict in former Yugoslavia in the early 1990s by member states of the European Union may be debated. The imminent break-up, which may not have been inevitable, was certainly not discouraged by such action which ignored any questions of belligerence *stricto sensu*. The present state of international law and practice in this area is thus far from satisfactory. Granted, however, the intense political sensitivities which the question has always and no doubt will continue to raise, a significant clarification of norms is perhaps a vain hope.

Even where belligerency is recognized or even conceded, it does not follow that foreign states are entitled to aid or assist the insurgents. Direct military assistance to insurgents by foreign states might in many cases contravene article 2(4) of the UN Charter. Less direct assistance may also be problematic. In the *Alabama Claims Arbitration*[30] in 1872, the question of British violation of neutrality during the American Civil War was considered. The C.S.S. *Alabama* was a Confederate commerce raider built in Liverpool by a British shipbuilder under a contract, the other party to which was unconvincingly disguised at various times as the imperial French Government and the Khedive of Egypt. The *Alabama* had a successful commerce-raiding career, destroying some 70 US merchant ships, until it was finally sunk by U.S.S. *Kearsarge* in 1864. Following protests to the British Government by the US, essentially based upon the former's failure to take adequate measures either to prevent the *Alabama* from being handed over to the Confederate authorities or, at least, to prevent it from sailing, the matter was considered by an Arbitral Tribunal. The central interest of this arbitration lies in its treatment of the general duties of a neutral state,[31] but it may also be noted that the UK had recognized the belligerency of the Confederacy during the Civil War and adopted a stance of neutrality. British assistance to the Confederate war effort, or more accurately connivance thereat, was then held to be an international wrong. The point retains value, although in cases where a non-international armed conflict is held by the UN Security Council to be a threat to international peace and security within the meaning of Chapter VII of the UN Charter, the matter of military supplies will tend to fall within the remit of UN-imposed sanctions. This was the case with former Yugoslavia in the early 1990s.

The Capacities of Dissident 'Authorities'

The type of non-international armed conflicts under consideration here will almost certainly involve some degree of territorial control by counter-governmental authorities.[32] From the viewpoint of the government of the threatened state, such an exercise of authority will certainly be illegal and, presumably, treasonable. If the dissident forces succeed in achieving their objective, their authority will become established and soon cease to be questioned.[33] If instead they are defeated or driven out of some part of the territory which they claim, the legitimacy of their acts of 'government' will be queried. Clearly some of their acts of a political or ideological character will be swept aside. Equally clearly during the period of their rule, they alone had authority to conduct day-to-day administration, including contracts for sale and purchase, which presumably could not be invalidated upon their departure.

The answer to this conundrum is, in principle, quite straightforward. As emphasized above, the status of a dissident authority in the process of establishing itself in a context of non-international armed conflict is essentially *de facto* and provisional. An analogy with the provisions made for an occupation regime in international armed conflict (developed from the Regulations Respecting the Laws and Customs of War on Land annexed to 1907 Hague Convention IV) has some validity. An 'occupation' regime is considered essentially one of necessity which may make certain administrative changes where that is unavoidable, but should otherwise maintain the law and as far as possible even incumbent officials. The *raison d'être* of dissident authority in a non-international armed conflict, in contrast, is profoundly to alter the existing administration and possibly also its laws. Should the territory be repossessed by government forces, routine administrative acts should be left undisturbed, though other more 'revolutionary' or radical changes have to be revoked.

The Problem of Combatant Status

The 'recognition' of dissident organizations and forces party to non-international armed conflicts poses a significant problem in applying *jus in bello* norms. A similar, and linked, problem arises in considering the status of individual members of such dissident forces. In the laws applicable to *international* armed conflicts, members of the armed forces of the warring state as well as certain civilian support staff are all entitled to 'combatant' status.[34] This concept would be highly problematic in the context of non-international armed conflict and has therefore been avoided.

Common article 3 of the 1949 Geneva Conventions avoids mentioning members of the dissident forces at all. The basic humanitarian requirements are applicable to 'members of armed forces who have laid down their arms', which clearly would apply to members of dissident forces, but their status is otherwise unresolved. Provision is made for requirements of due process by common article 3(1)(d) which would presumably include trial on such charges as treason or mutiny. 1977 Additional Protocol II goes rather further in urging by article 6(5) that at the end of hostilities the 'broadest possible amnesty to persons who have participated in the armed conflict' should be granted. This is carefully addressed to 'the authorities in power' and thus to a successful insurgent authority as well as to an existing government. However, the provision is exhortatory rather than mandatory. The ICRC Commentary upon 1977 Additional Protocol II states that

> the object of this sub-paragraph is to encourage gestures of reconciliation which can contribute to reestablishing normal relations in the life of a nation which has been divided.[35]

However laudable, this does not clarify the status of those engaged in conflict and in no way concedes legitimate combatancy status to members of dissident forces. To concede such status in non-international armed conflicts might in fact be to concede the legitimacy of the insurgency itself. In such circumstances, this dilemma cannot entirely be resolved.

Any *jus in bello* provision presupposes a certain convergence of forms and structures, at least in broad outline, as between the opposing parties to hostilities. Where, as in non-international armed conflicts, the division tends not to be between 'our' and 'their' armed forces but between 'the armed forces' and insurgents or rebels (or, from the opposing viewpoint, between 'freedom fighters' and 'oppressors'), achieving such a convergence is difficult. This, indeed, is one major reason why the *jus in bello* norms applicable to non-international armed conflicts are decidedly in a minor key in comparison with the equivalent provision for international armed conflicts. The best that can be done is to urge the greatest measure of humanitarianism in the conduct of both sides and then to exhort, as article 6(5) of 1977 Additional Protocol II does, the widest possible amnesty thereafter. The greater the observance of humanitarian norms the easier such an amnesty will be to grant; in any event, the term 'widest possible' in this context would exclude those convicted or facing trial in relation to gross breaches of the laws of armed conflict.

Conclusions

The status of parties to non-international armed conflicts is inevitably a matter of extreme political sensitivity, both from the point of view of established governments and from that of dissident 'authorities' seeking power. Such sensitivities have played a significant part in shaping and limiting the *jus in bello* provision applicable to non-international armed conflicts. The awkward processes of transition to statehood[36] of parts of a former unitary entity may also have a profound effect upon the shape of the conflict and the response of the international community to it. The dissolution of former Yugoslavia in the early 1990s afforded a particularly complex and appalling instance of this. Questions of status are at one level peripheral to attempts to regulate and diminish the horrors of non-international armed conflicts but, from another point of view, are issues of fundamental importance. Central to such armed conflicts is some questioning of the status of the parties involved, an uncertainty that inevitably influences the origins of the conflict, its conduct and ultimate resolution, satisfactory or otherwise.

Notes

1   F. Kalshoven, *Constraints on the Waging of War*, 2nd edn (International Committee of the Red Cross, 1991), p.139.
2   For discussion of this, see Chapter 1, p.22.
3   As to the customary status of provisions in 1977 Additional Protocol I, see C. Greenwood, 'Customary Law Status of the 1977 Additional Protocols' in A.J.M. Delissen and G.J. Tanja (eds), *Humanitarian Law of Armed Conflict: Challenges Ahead* (Martinus Nijhoff, 1991), pp.93–114.
4   Article 96(3)(b).
5   Article 96(3)(c).
6   See Chapter 1, pp.19–21.
7   See Chapter 1 at p.20.
8   Y. Sandoz, C. Swinarski and B. Zimmermann (eds), *Commentary on the Additional Protocols of 8 June 1977 to the Geneva Conventions of 12 August 1949* (International Committee of the Red Cross with Martinus Nijhoff, 1987), p.1352, paragraph 4463.
9   H. McCoubrey, 'Yugoslavia at War', *Solicitors Journal* (1992) Vol. 136, p.914 at p.916.
10 In the conflicts in former Yugoslavia there were in fact agreements amongst the parties that most of the *jus in bello* applicable to *international* armed conflict should be applied. This did not lead to significant practical implementation, but clearly had a strong influence upon discussion of liabilities for violations of legal norms. See Chapter 11 at pp.274–5.
11 *Op. cit.*, note 8, p.1353, paragraph 4469.
12 As to which see Chapter 6.
13 See Chapter 1, p.20.
14 *Op. cit.*, note 8, p.1351, paragraph 4461.
15 See Chapter 8, p.197.
16 Text set out by T. Meron, *Human Rights in Internal Strife: Their International Protection* (Grotius, 1987) at p. 76, citing Conference of Government Experts ... Geneva, 24 May – 12 June 1971; Documents submitted by the ICRC, Vol. V: *Protection of Victims of Non-International Armed Conflicts* 86 (1971).
17 So provided by 1977 Additional Protocol II, article 1(2); see Chapter 1, p.20.
18 See T. Meron, 'Internal Strife: Applicable Norms and a Proposed Instrument' in A.J.M. Delissen and G.J. Tanja (eds), *Humanitarian Law of Armed Conflict Challenges Ahead: Essays in Honour of Frits Kalshoven* (Martinus Nijhoff, 1991), pp.249–66.
19 Harry H. Almond Jr., 'Terrorism – Legal Control under the Law of War' in H.H.

Han (ed.), *Terrorism and Political Violence: Limits and Possibilities of Legal Control* (Oceana, 1993), p.355 at p.372.

20   T. Stein, 'How Much Humanity do Terrorists Deserve?' in A.J.M. Delissen and G.J. Tanja (eds), *Humanitarian Law of Armed Conflict Challenges Ahead: Essays in Honour of Frits Kalshoven* (Martinus Nijhoff, 1991), pp.567–81, at p.573.

21   *Ibid.*, at p.368.

22   In this context note in particular 1949 Geneva Convention III, articles 4A(2), recognizing 'organized resistance movements', and article 4A(6), recognizing subject to certain conditions a *levee en masse* in the context of international armed conflict.

23   See e.g. *Ireland v United Kingdom*, European Court of Human Rights, Series A, No.25.

24   Resolution IX.

25   G. Schwarzenberger, *International Law, Vol. II, Armed Conflict* (Stevens, 1968), pp.690–91.

26   J.B. Moore, *International Arbitrations to which the United States has been a Party* Volume II (US Government Printing Office, 1898), Ch. XXXIII, p.1551 at p.1561.

27   *Reports of International Arbitral Awards*, Vol. IV, p.341 at p.347.

28   For elucidation of this position, see J.B. Moore, *A Digest of International Law*, Volume I (US Government Printing Office, 1906), at pp.164–8.

29   See Chapter 1, p.22. In this context the provision of the *Declaration on the Granting of Independence to Colonial Territories and Peoples*, UN General Assembly Resolution 1514 (XV), 1960, paragraph 6 – 'Any attempt aimed at the partial or total disruption of the national unity and the territorial integrity of a country is incompatible with the Purposes and Principles of the Charter of the United Nations' – is of interest as a definition of the problem.

30   J.B. Moore, *International Arbitrations* ... (note 23), Vol. I, p.653.

31   For discussion see H. McCoubrey and N.D. White, *International Law and Armed Conflict* (Dartmouth, 1992), p.299.

32   See above, p.65.

33   For further discussion of this, see Chapter 11, pp.257–8.

34   See implicitly 1949 Geneva Convention III, article 4, and, expressly, 1977 Additional Protocol I, article 43. There is also a considerable body of case law upon the matter.

35   Y. Sandoz, C. Swinarski and B. Zimmermann, (eds), *Commentary on the Additional Protocols of 8 June 1977 to the Geneva Conventions of 12 August 1949* (International Committee of the Red Cross with Martinus Nijhoff, 1987), p.1402, paragraph 4618.

36   Discussions of this as a general matter of public international law will be found, *inter alia*, in I. Brownlie, *Principles of Public International Law*, 4th edn (Oxford University Press, 190), Chapters IV and V; M.N. Shaw, *International Law*, 3rd edn (Grotius, 1991), Chapter 5; and in D.J. Harris, *Cases and Materials on International Law*, 4th edn (Sweet and Maxwell, 1991), Chapter 4.

4 Observation and Fact Finding

Fact Finding and the *jus ad bellum*

The aim of this section is to examine the role of international organizations in sending fact-finding missions to civil wars. Fact finding is a preliminary step taken by an international organization prior to its possible involvement in a peace process or perhaps in the taking of enforcement measures. There is an overlap between the use of fact-finding missions and of military observers who normally have fact-finding and reporting functions. Although references to military observers will occur, the emphasis here is on civilian fact-finding missions which have become increasingly prevalent since the end of the Cold War. Military observers often have the added responsibility of overseeing provisional or interim measures agreed to by the parties to a conflict, and may then become involved in implementing a peaceful solution (for further discussion, see Chapters 8 and 9). In addition, fact finding by the UN can either be in the area of *jus ad bellum* or the *jus in bello* or both. Fact finding in the *jus in bello* is dealt with in a separate section in this chapter.

The United Nations

Development

As has been mentioned in Chapter 2, the Security Council, the General Assembly and the Secretary General of the UN all have a fact-finding capacity, although the only organ to be explicitly recognized in the UN Charter as having the power to dispatch fact-finding bodies is the Security Council (article 34):

> The Security Council may investigate any dispute, or any situation which might lead to international friction or give rise to a dispute, in

order to determine whether the continuance of the dispute or situation is likely to endanger the maintenance of international peace and security.

The establishment of a fact-finding *body* also derives from the power to create subsidiary bodies, found in article 29 of the UN Charter.

One problem which immediately becomes apparent is that article 34 does not empower the Security Council to establish bodies to ascertain the facts of the dispute or conflict, but only to determine whether the conflict is a 'danger to international peace' and so should be dealt with under Chapter VI. Thus its mission should be to decide whether the conflict is a 'threat to the peace' in the sense of article 39, Chapter VII, or simply a danger to be dealt with under Chapter VI. If the Council's express powers are limited in this way, then the General Assembly and the Secretary General, in their capacities as 'subsidiary' fact finders (as derived from implied and inherent powers), must be similarly restricted. For instance the Secretary General's powers to authorize fact finders could be said to derive from article 99 which allows him to bring to the attention of the Security Council 'any matter which in his opinion may threaten international peace and security'; his powers of investigation are thus arguably restricted to finding whether or not the conflict is a threat to the peace. Further, if the General Assembly's fact-finding capacity is considered to derive from article 14, which provides that it 'may recommend measures for the peaceful adjustment of any situation which it deems likely to impair the general welfare of friendly relations among nations:', then the Assembly's function is obviously restricted to such a determination.

Indeed, in the early years the Security Council did appear to follow the wording of article 34 literally. In April 1946 the representative of Poland at the UN invoked articles 2(6),[1] 34 and 35,[2] in requesting that the Security Council consider 'the situation arising from the existence and activities of the Franco regime in Spain', and further demanded the severance of diplomatic relations with that country in accordance with article 41.[3] Interestingly, in support of Poland, the Soviet representative stated that 'the Charter admits and provides for the necessity of taking definite measures with regard to States when their internal situation constitutes a threat to international peace and security'.[4] The Security Council then established a sub-committee of five of its members to determine whether the situation in Spain 'has led to international friction and does endanger international peace and security'.[5] The sub-committee reported that in its opinion no determination under article 39 could be made, but that there was a 'potential menace to international peace' and therefore a 'situation likely to endanger peace' within the meaning of article 34 of the UN

Charter.[6] In discussions of this report, the Australian representative on the Security Council stated that the provisions of article 2(7) of the UN Charter preventing UN intervention in the domestic jurisdiction of a state did not prohibit the Council from using its powers of recommendation under Chapter VI 'once a matter is recognised as one of international concern'. Nevertheless, a resolution could not be agreed upon, with the Soviet Union desiring action under Chapter VII.[7]

Expansion

However, since the Spanish question the UN organs have adopted a different approach: since they have the power to investigate whether a conflict constitutes a 'threat to the peace', which may in turn lead to the application of enforcement measures, they must implicitly have the 'lesser' power to ascertain the facts. Furthermore, while the sub-committee on the Spanish question simply examined the evidence from afar, subsequent UN fact-finding missions have usually been despatched to the country in question, with the consent of the government concerned. For instance when raiders from Pakistan threatened the rule of the Maharajah of Jammu and Kashmir, he acceded to India and asked for its military help. India protested to the Security Council about Pakistan's assistance to the invaders,[8] whereas Pakistan complained about massacres of Muslims perpetrated by Indian forces and asked for a plebiscite.[9] The Security Council adopted a resolution which stated that, as the Council had power to investigate the dispute 'which by its continuance, endangers international peace and security,' it would establish a UN Commission on India and Pakistan (UNCIP) in order 'to investigate the facts pursuant to Article 34' of the UN Charter.[10] Acting on UNCIP's subsequent report, the Security Council set out the modalities for conducting a referendum on the status of Kashmir under UNCIP auspices,[11] a resolution not complied with the demarcation of a cease-fire line between India and Pakistan in Kashmir.

Given that fact finding is often the first step in the UN's attempt at conflict resolution, it may, as in the case of UNCIP, use the fact-finding body for other purposes. The authorization of military observers in Indonesia between 1947–50, where the Indonesians were fighting for independence from the Netherlands, again illustrated how early on in its life the UN realized the necessity of having accurate, neutral information. Initially, following a call for a cease fire[12] and the establishment of successive cease fires and demarcation lines on the islands, the Security Council requested that career consuls in Batavia report on the observance of the cease fire called for in the earlier resolution.[13] The same resolution also established a Consular Commission to attempt peacemaking. The Consular Commission interpreted the functions of the military observers as follows: 'to observe any possible violations of the cease-fire; to investigate, where possible, allegations of violations of cease-fire orders; and to gather any other data that might be of value to the Commission and to the Security Council'.[14] These functions remained basically unaltered with the creation of the Good Offices Committee, which became the United Nations' Commission on Indonesia, although instead of observing temporary cease-fire lines, the team was required to observe the demilitarized zones created under the Renville Agreement. The resulting stability encouraged negotiations that led to an eventual resolution of the conflict.[15]

The use of observers in Indonesia illustrates that the roles of fact finder and observer are often blurred, as is the distinction between observation and peacekeeping. The dispatch of a UN Observer Group to the Lebanon (UNOGIL) in 1958 highlights this point as well. In response to a complaint by the government of Lebanon of intervention in its internal affairs by the United Arab Republic,[16] UNOGIL was established by Council resolution 128 of 11 June 1958. 'An observation group' was despatched to Lebanon 'to ensure that there is no illegal infiltration of personnel or supply of arms or other matériel across the Lebanese borders' from the United Arab Republic. Despite the use of the word 'ensure' in the enabling resolution, there was no suggestion that UNOGIL was being directed to forcibly prevent infiltration. Practically, such a mandate would have been impossible for an observation team numbering only 100. Indeed, the Secretary General's interpretation of UNOGIL's mandate, which was not contested in the Council, emphasized that its role was strictly limited to observing whether or not illegal infiltration occurred, and that it was present with the consent of the Lebanese government.[17]

Even after the US intervened in Lebanon in mid-July, UNOGIL's functions remained investigatory and observational, as envisaged by article 34. Although peacekeeping forces and observation teams are usually created to act in relation to provisional measures called for by the Assembly or the Council, UNOGIL's mandate was to ascertain the facts before the UN took any further action.

UNOGIL observed and reported that there was no significant infiltration of Lebanon from the United Arab Republic and that the conflict was mainly indigenous.[18] However, despite this finding, the US intervened in Lebanon. UNOGIL's continued presence, along with the American marines and the establishment of a new government under General Chehab, probably had the effect of stabilizing the situation.

Fact Finding and faits accomplis

Despite this encouraging use of article 34 in its early years, the Security Council relied on its fact-finding power less during the remainder of the Cold War, particularly in relation to internal conflicts. Occasionally fact finding was authorized, but only after the event. This was particularly so in relation to mercenary involvement in the internal affairs of states. For example, in February 1977, Benin complained of an 'armed attack' by mercenary forces aimed at overthrowing its government.[19] In response the Security Council sent a Special Mission to investigate. That Mission merely confirmed that an attack had taken place, that the attackers had pecuniary motives and that the financiers could not be found.[20] As a result, the Security Council strongly condemned the 'aggression' against Benin, calling on states not to assist mercenaries and to provide information about the attack on Benin.[21]

A smaller, ineffectual approach was taken in relation to the Seychelles in 1981. In this case, a group of about 50 mercenaries led by Michael Hoare was spotted carrying guns at the main airport. Prevented from carrying out their original plan, they took over the airport and eventually hijacked a plane to take them back to South Africa. The Security Council condemned this 'mercenary aggression' and sent a three-member commission to establish who was behind it.[22] The commission reported that it could unearth no conclusive evidence, but that it 'found it difficult to believe that the South African authorities did not at least have a knowledge of the preparations' for the attack.[23] The Council did not condemn South Africa directly but did refer to the fact that the mercenary aggression was 'prepared in and executed from South Africa'.[24]

The End of the Cold War

Although there were other examples of fact finding in internal conflicts during the Cold War, these can generally be characterized as selective and often ineffectual. However, on other occasions they did form the basis of a later peaceful settlement or at least some stabilization with the assistance of a UN peacekeeping force.[25] As early as 1988, with superpower relations beginning to thaw, there was an indication of greater fact-finding activity by the Security Council when a mission was sent to Nicaragua.[26] This was a foretaste of the regional settlement process started by the Guatemala Accords of 1987 and culminating in the UN supervision of peaceful elections in Nicaragua in 1990.

Nevertheless, fact finding by the Security Council is not undertaken as a matter of course; it often relies on a patchwork of sources including established peacekeeping or observation teams, the Secretary General and his staff, and the occasional formal fact-finding body mandated by Security Council resolution. Whatever the source, fact finding can be undertaken only with the consent of the state or states in dispute. The Security Council has not attempted to invoke mandatory power to despatch fact-finding missions, although in the Gulf crisis, after the conflict between Iraq and the Coalition forces ended in March 1991, Iraq was subjected to very intrusive missions. Although Iraq consented to them when it agreed to the permanent cease fire in Security Council resolution 687 on 3 April 1991, it really had little choice given the threat of further military actions against it.

Without mandatory power to order a state to accept a fact-finding mission, and in view of the fact that the Gulf crisis was exceptional in the sense that military action *preceded* the missions which normally should be a first step towards conciliation, fact finding cannot properly be institutionalized. If all its members were to agree that the Security Council had the power to oblige states to accept a fact-finding mission (by making it clear in the enabling resolution that it was binding under articles 34 and 25), there would not appear to be any legal limitation on this power. Article 34 itself is not restricted to recommendations although, if one accepts the Western view that binding decisions can only be made under Chapter VII, then such power would not appear to be *intra vires*.

It is questionable whether the effectiveness of fact finding will be improved as a result of a recent General Assembly resolution, supported by all member states, entitled the Declaration on Fact Finding by the United Nations in the Field of the Maintenance of Peace and Security, adopted without a vote on 17 January 1992. This followed a report of the Sixth Committee which in turn was based on work by the Special Committee on the Charter.[27] Although the resolution recognized 'that the ability of the United Nations to maintain international peace and security depends to a large extent on its acquiring detailed knowledge about the factual circumstances of any dispute or situation', and that the competent organs of the UN should endeavour to undertake fact-finding activities that are 'comprehensive, objective, impartial and timely', it still recognized that 'the sending of a United Nations fact finding mission to the territory of any State requires the prior consent of that State'. Although the Assembly encouraged states to adopt 'a policy of admitting ... fact finding missions to their territory', the UN's respect for the sovereignty of its members undermines the proper institutionalization of fact finding, whether it be by the Security Council, the General Assembly or the Secretary General. Even when states consent, however, such missions are often too late to help prevent a conflict breaking out or, if a conflict is already underway, can often achieve little towards its peaceful settlement.

Recent Developments

Despite the limitations inherent in the UN's fact-finding capability, as reflected in the above resolution of the General Assembly, there has been a recent plethora of fact-finding missions being sent by the UN to investigate internal conflicts, in particular to the former republics of the Soviet Union, now independent and often factionalized states.

Fact-finding missions have been dispatched to the disputed Armenian-dominated enclave of Nagorno Karabakh in Azerbaijan in May 1992 to report on the conflict there in which both Armenia and Azerbaijan are involved; also in July 1992 to investigate an Azeri complaint that Armenia had used chemical weapons. The team reported that it could find no evidence that chemical weapons had been used. The teams had been dispatched by the Secretary General, although their usefulness was subsequently recognized by the Security Council in spite of its own emphasis that peace efforts should be centred on Conference on Security and Cooperation in Europe (CSCE) initiatives.[28] The fact-finding missions' reports to the Secretary General were in turn relayed to the Security Council in April 1993.[29] The Secretary General stated that the fighting in Nagorno Karabakh seriously threatened the 'maintenance of international peace and security in the entire Transcaucasus region', and that it indicated the 'involvement of more than local ethnic forces'. In response the Security Council adopted a resolution on 30 April 1993 which expressed concern 'that this situation endangers international peace and security in the region', whilst reaffirming the 'territorial integrity of all States in the region'. This implicit condemnation of Armenia was reinforced by the demands that all occupying forces be withdrawn from Azerbaijan, and that a durable cease fire and unimpeded access for international humanitarian relief be established.[30] This demand was repeated in July and October 1993.[31]

The UN's fact-finding activities in the conflict in Nagorno Karabakh have enabled the Security Council to adopt resolutions which, while neutral in the sense of demanding the establishment of a cease fire, also identify the guilty party and thereby implicitly warn that party that further measures could be taken against it if the situation continues. This is in many ways an improvement on the over-sensitive neutralist approach adopted during the Cold War, when the Council was not prepared to identify the aggressor. However, despite these advantages in the UN's approach, the dispute over Nagorno Karabakh is a long-running one, leaving the UN open to accusations of crisis management and intervening too late to affect the situation. This is in some ways unfair, as the dispute only became internationalized with the break-up of the Soviet Union in December 1991. Only after this did the new states consent to the fact-finding activities of the UN.

The UN's fact-finding and related activities in Georgia have a greater chance of success because their response was more timely. A UN mission was sent by the Secretary General to study the conflict that had commenced on Georgia's independence between Georgian troops and Abkhaz separatist forces. This was after Abkhazia, an independent autonomous republic in Georgia, declared its independence.[32] The Secretary General's report of January 1993, based on the mission's observations, brought the Council's attention to the conflict and the 'serious humanitarian situation' it created, despite the cease fire agreed to by the parties under Russian good offices on 3 September 1992. That agreement had confirmed the territorial integrity of Georgia.[33] The Security Council called on the parties to implement this agreement,[34] as well as dispatching new missions to assess the continuing conflict and also the human rights situation. A cease fire agreed to by the parties on 14 May 1993 failed to hold. In July 1993, in response to the situation reported by the fact-finding missions and the Secretary General,[35] the Security Council called for another cease fire and agreed to the dispatch of 50 military observers once it had been implemented.[36] A cease fire was agreed upon on 17 July and a team was dispatched in August 1993.[37] The UN Observer Mission in Georgia (UNOMIG) was given the mandate of verifying and observing the cease fire as well as the task of reporting on any violations. In so authorizing UNOMIG, the Council considered that the conflict in Georgia threatened peace and stability in the region.[38] A breach of the cease fire by Abkhazian forces led to condemnation by the Security Council in October 1993, as well as confirmation of the sovereignty and territorial integrity of Georgia.[39] A new cease fire was established on 1 December 1993. This led to the Security Council expanding UNOMIG's to include contacts with both sides to the conflict, as well as with Russian forces still present in Georgia.[40] Further negotiations between the two parties led to a joint request for a UN peacekeeping force in January 1994.

It can be seen from this survey of UN fact finding and observation that the Organization's efforts have advanced much further in Georgia than in Nagorno Karabakh. Whilst fact finding is the only 'on the ground' activity of the UN in the latter conflict, in the former the UN has progressed from fact finding to the dispatch of military observers, to the possible emplacement of a UN peacekeeping force, as both parties inch towards a settlement.

It is also interesting to note that in both conflicts the Security Council has supported the maintenance of the territorial *status quo* in contrast to its approach to the conflict in the former Yugoslavia. After appearing to facilitate the break-up of the former Yugoslavia as well as having stood by during the collapse of another federal state, the Soviet Union. The world community, as represented by the UN, does not appear willing to sanction the further break-up of states after witnessing the instability caused by these two major collapses.

In other conflicts in the former Soviet Union, the UN has taken a lower-key approach, particularly when the internal conflict is not as destructive and does not threaten to spread to neighbouring states. A UN fact-finding mission was sent to Moldova in August 1992 by the Secretary General. The team reported that the conflict in the country's Transdniester region was receding following an agreement between the parties on 21 July 1993 which provided for the creation of a peacekeeping force from Russia and the two parties to the conflict.[41]

However, the danger of escalation seems more apparent in Tajikistan where a fact-finding mission was sent in September 1992 to report on the internal conflict between supporters of the former communist leader and the Islamic government.[42] The seriousness of this conflict led to the creation by the Secretary General of a UN Mission of Observers in Tajikistan (UNMOT) in January 1993. Reports from these observers led the Secretary General to state that the escalation in the conflict could affect neighbouring Afghanistan, itself still in a state of civil war.[43] Despite this report only limited further action has been taken by the UN so far: the appointment of a special envoy to Tajikistan.

This analysis of conflicts in the new nations in the Commonwealth of Independent States (CIS) reveals how civilian fact finding can lead to UN military personnel becoming involved, either in the form of a small observation team or of a larger peacekeeping force. Fact finding may also lead eventually to the supervision of elections, as happened in Nicaragua, or perhaps even to economic or military measures if the parties do not progress to a peaceful settlement. It must be remembered, however, that whereas fact finding, observation, peacekeeping and peaceful settlement are all based on consent, economic and military action is coercive – against the will of the target state or party within the state. This means that a move from fact finding to coercion requires the *Security Council* to use the powers it possesses under Chapter VII of the Charter (not Chapter VI which is the basis for fact finding and peaceful settlement).

Civilian observers were sent by the Secretary General to South Africa in November 1992. The UN Observer Mission in South Africa (UNOMSA) operated alongside observers from the Commonwealth, the European Union and the OAU. The emplacement of observers was endorsed by the General Assembly in December 1992 while calling for the peace process to continue and urging 'the representatives of the peoples of South Africa to resume, without further delay, broad based negotiations on transitional arrangements and basic principles for a process of reaching agreement on a new democratic and non-racial constitution and for its speedy entry into force'.[44] The UN's involvement developed to the extent that it was requested by the parties to the peace process in South Africa to observe the first all-race elections successfully held in April 1994.[45]

On the other hand, the UN's fact-finding mission to Haiti has not progressed towards peaceful supervision but has, due to the military dictatorship's intransigence, regressed into economic coercion. The General Assembly had approved a joint International Civilian Monitoring Mission to Haiti on 20 April 1993,[46] composed of personnel from the UN and the OAS. The mission discovered numerous human rights violations by the Haitian authorities, including torture and executions.[47] This led to increased international pressure on the dictatorship and the imposition of mandatory sanctions by the Security Council in June 1993.[48] An agreement to reinstate the deposed, democratically elected President Aristide was signed by the military dictatorship on 3 July 1993, largely as a result of international pressure in the form of UN and OAS sanctions. This agreement led to the suspension of sanctions and the dispatch of a military observer force known as the UN Mission in Haiti (UNMIH) to facilitate the transfer of power back to the democratically elected government and to train the Haitian police and military.[49] However, failure by the military dictatorship to abide by its agreement and its obstruction of UNMIH led to the reimposition of UN sanctions in October 1993.[50] Despite the UN's current failure to solve the crisis by this means and also its failure to emplace a military observer force, the Assembly's civilian monitoring mission is still in place, permitting the objective assessment of the facts and a continued UN presence in Haiti.

Regional Organizations

The recent expansion of the UN's fact-finding role reflects and has encouraged increased fact finding by regional and other organizations, often alongside the UN: the OAS in Haiti, the OAU in South Africa and the CSCE in the new states emerging from the former Soviet Union. This has built on traditions of fact finding already entrenched in the well-established regional organizations, some examples of which will be given here.

The League of Arab States has utilized fact finding in civil conflicts on several occasions. In 1948, when a conflict arose between two factions in the Yemen, the League was faced with the dilemma of which faction to recognize. Hassouna describes the League's action in the following terms:

... the ... crisis confronting the League reveals that it was neither in the nature of a dispute, nor an aggression between member states. It was an internal state of civil war between opposing factions seeking succession to the throne. Accordingly, the course of action followed by the League merely aimed at meeting the requirements of this situation. The organisation would not interfere in the civil strife, but would seek to determine its stand towards competing factions so as to decide which government was to represent Yemen in the League.

Pursuant to this mandate, the League's fact-finding mission, after visiting the Yemen and talking to both factions, recommended the League not to recognize either as the new government was in danger of being toppled. This prediction turned out to be correct, with recognition by the League eventually being conferred on the new stable monarchic government.[51]

In 1962 this regime was toppled by a coup d'état and a republican government established, which was recognized by the majority of League members (though the former royalist faction was still recognized by a minority of League members, namely those with monarchical governments). The crisis escalated; Saudi Arabia supported the royalist faction with weapons and men, whilst the United Arab Republic (UAR) similarly backed the republican faction. At this stage the UN negotiated a disengagement agreement between the UAR, Saudi Arabia and Yemen.[52] Besides disengagement, the parties agreed on a UN presence; they defined UNYOM's function to be observational – by about only 100 personnel – in the Saudi Arabian–Yemen area.[53]

The UN Security Council approved the Secretary General's reports in resolution 179, adopted on 11 June 1963, and requested that he 'establish the observation operation as defined'. The Secretary General further refined the functions of UNYOM in subsequent reports: these were limited to observing, reporting and certifying the disengagement between Saudi Arabia and Yemen, and to observe the departure of the United Arab Republic from Yemen. This constituted a limited observation mandate under which the UNYOM was not allowed to take any steps to resolve the conflict.[54]

UNYOM had a very limited purpose, namely the observation and certification of the disengagement agreement. 'The parties themselves' were 'totally responsible for fulfilling the terms of the disengagement'.[55] Nevertheless, UNYOM was to small to carry out even its limited mandate.[56] UNYOM not only failed in this respect but, after its departure in September 1964, several years elapsed before the conflict ended.

The League of Arab States also became involved when it sent a fact-finding and conciliation commission in September 1963 to investigate the dispute and to attempt to offer solutions. The mission did gain some assurances from Saudi Arabia and Egypt, but its neutral approach to the conflict, scrupulously observed in 1948, was now undermined because the League Council had already recognized the republican faction in March 1963 (though Saudi Arabia voted against). Although by article 7 of the Pact of the League of Arab States in 1945,[57] the resolution was not binding on those states voting against, the League Council's resolution represented an institutional decision in favour of the republican faction. The undermining of the League's neutrality meant that it was ineffectual for many years in bringing the conflict to an end. In fact the struggle continued until 1970.[58]

Although the 1945 Arab League Pact does not explicitly provide for fact finding, it does state in article 5 that

> the Council shall mediate in all differences which threaten to lead to war between two member states, or a member state and a third state, with a view to bringing about their reconciliation.

An explicit power to undertake mediation can be interpreted as tacit authority for lesser powers, such as dispatching fact-finding missions. However, the provision seems only to relate to inter-state wars, although it did extend to the intra-state Yemen conflict of 1962. Although not explicitly authorizing fact finding in purely civil conflicts, the League did dispatch a mission in the 1948 Yemen conflict, but under strictly neutral auspices. Besides, fact finding, being consensual, does not infringe the non-intervention requirements of the Arab League[59] nor, when undertaken by the UN, article 2(7) of the UN Charter.

Most other international organizations seem to possess an inherent or implied fact-finding capacity, and some have applied it to internal conflicts. For instance article 6 of the 1947 Inter-American Treaty of Reciprocal Assistance[60] permits the Foreign Ministers of the state parties, meeting as the Organ of Consultation, to take measures to deal with 'any fact or situation that might endanger the peace of America'. Fact-finding missions to investigate internal situations which threatened regional peace were sent to Nicaragua in 1959 to investigate mercenary activities against the Nicaraguan regime, and in 1960 to inquire into the Dominican-inspired attempt on the life of the Venezuelan Chief of State. As a result of the latter investigation, the Meeting of Consultation applied article 8 of the Rio Treaty, causing American state parties to break off diplomatic relations with the Dominican Republic, as well as imposing an arms embargo. The resolution authorized the Council of the OAS to extend the embargo if necessary and also to determine when it should end. To comply with this resolution, the OAS Council created a Special Committee to report on the activities and attitude of the Dominican Republic. The Committee's report of January 1961 led the Council to extend the embargo to cover petrol, petroleum products and trucks. This, in part, led to a change in attitude by the Dominican Republic, to the extent that by January 1962, the Special Committee was able to report that the Dominican Republic was no longer a danger to the peace. Accordingly, the OAS Council cancelled the embargo against it.[61]

A more modern example of institutional fact finding in an internal conflict relates to the activities of the European Community (EC)[62] and the CSCE[63] in the former Yugoslavia. The fact-finding powers of the EC appear to be contained in the Single European Act of 1987,[64] amending the Treaty of Rome 1957.[65]

Article 30 contains the treaty's provisions on European cooperation in the foreign policy sphere. 'The Ministers for Foreign Affairs [of the EC] ... shall meet at least four times a year within the framework of the European Political Cooperation' to 'ensure the swift adoption of common positions and the implementation of joint action'. Article 30 also provides for the coordination of the positions of member states 'more closely on the political and economic aspects of security'. Although not providing for specific powers such as fact finding, article 30 – representing a move towards a 'European foreign policy' – seems to imply them. If the Treaty of European Union (Maastricht Treaty) of 1992 eventually comes into force, then the concept of a common foreign policy will become even more deeply entrenched, as will the idea of the Council of Ministers being able to take joint action on security issues.[66]

A similar approach to the question of implied and inherent powers possessed by international bodies appears to be taken by the Conference on Security and Cooperation in Europe (CSCE), a process developed during the Cold War with the adoption of the Helsinki Final Act of 1975[67] by Eastern and Western European states as well as Canada, the Soviet Union (now Russia) and the US. This conference or process has rapidly expanded since the end of the Cold War; in creating various institutions and structures, it now appears to be virtually an international organization. However, the 1975 Final Act, not being a treaty, has raised questions as to the constitutional development of many of the powers now apparently possessed by the CSCE; indeed, it is perhaps true to say that the obligations created by the CSCE process are 'political rather than legal'.[68] In 1990, the states involved in he CSCE process, acting as the CSCE Council, invested the Consultative Committee and the Committee of Senior Officials with the authority to execute fact-finding and monitoring missions. This process was furthered in 1992 when the Council adopted a document which developed the CSCE's fact-finding capacity as well as its good offices, conciliation and dispute settlement powers. A further meeting laid down concrete peacekeeping (but not enforcement) provisions.[69] Again the legal basis of these powers can only be justified by the notion that, as individual states possess these consensual pacific settlement powers under customary international law, then so does the CSCE process. It simply enhances them by making them collective.

In July 1991, the Committee of Senior Officials of the CSCE dispatched a good offices mission to the former Yugoslavia to help facilitate dialogue between the various federal components and factions following the declaration of independence of Slovenia and Croatia in June 1991, whilst the EC dispatched observers to oversee cease fires. Despite the EC-brokered cease fires, the conflict spread to Croatia in September 1991, with the result that the EC and CSCE deployed more than 200 observers. The EC also put forward peace plans, although towards the end of 1991, with increasing UN involvement and the imminent deployment of UNPROFOR,[70] the peace initiative became a joint UN/EC one.

Despite greater UN involvement in the conflict, the EC and CSCE have maintained a presence. For example the CSCE sent a fact-finding mission to investigate detention camps in Bosnia as well as missions to other tense ethnic areas in Serbia and Montenegro, namely Vojvodna, Kosovo and Sandzak, in September 1992.[71] EC observers were also sent to Macedonia, although again the UN was the dominant organization, despatching an 800-strong element of UNPROFOR to the area in December 1992.[72] Finally, the EC continues with its joint mediation effort with the UN in trying to bring the three warring factions in Bosnia – the Serbs, Croats and Muslims – to a peaceful settlement and acceptable territorial division.[73]

Provision for Fact Finding in Relation to the *Jus in Bello*

Non-international armed conflict will commonly be accompanied, or followed, by investigations and judicial proceedings within the country affected. In many instances a primary focus of such processes will be on questions of treason, the substantive content of which will depend upon the outcome of the struggle.[74] Questions of repeated violations of the laws of armed conflict, and resulting liability, may also arise. The involvement of the international community in either investigating alleged unlawful acts (fact finding) or eventual trial processes inevitably raises very sensitive issues of national sovereignty. Such treaty provision as is made for investigation of alleged breaches of the laws of armed conflict always relates primarily to international rather than non-international disputes. Models of the

former may nevertheless be of value in some non-international contexts. The approach to fact finding during the armed conflict(s) in
former Yugoslavia in the early 1990s might be considered relevant
here.

The most significant provision for fact finding of this type is made
by article 90 of 1977 Protocol I Additional to the 1949 Geneva Conventions.[75] Article 90 makes provision for an International Fact-Finding Commission of 15 persons 'of high moral standing and acknow-
ledged impartiality'.[76] It was announced in April 1992 that such a
Commission had been set up, but that its future sphere of action
would depend upon whether states accepted its mandatory competence.[77] The formal competences of the Commission are set out by
article 90(2)(c)(d). Article 90(2)(c) provides that

> the Commission shall be competent to:
> (i) inquire into any facts alleged to be a grave breach as defined in the
> [1949 Geneva] Conventions and this Protocol or other serious viola-
> tions of the Conventions or this Protocol;
> (ii) facilitate, through its good offices, the restoration of an attitude of
> respect for the Conventions and this Protocol.

Article 90(2)(d) then adds that,

> in other situations, the Commission shall institute an enquiry at the
> request of a Party to the conflict only with the consent of the other
> Party or Parties concerned.

The practical utility of this procedure will inevitably depend largely
upon the circumstances of each given case. The willingness of states
to submit to investigation of this kind, perhaps especially in the
immediate aftermath of international armed conflict, may always
prove questionable. This is not to say that the provision of article 90
is to be considered *inutile* – merely to express some caution about its
ultimate prospects in present (1994) conditions.

Article 90 is not intended to apply to non-international armed
conflicts, which are probably not the 'other situations' referred to by
article 90(2)(d). The ICRC Commentary upon the Protocol indicates
that these 'situations' would be where either or both of the Parties
involved had not accepted the mandatory competence of the Commission.[78] The specific direction of 1977 Additional Protocol I to *international* armed conflicts would accentuate this view, although an
interesting question might arise in the unlikely event of parties to a
non-international armed conflict requesting investigation by the Commission. In practice it may reasonably be assumed that the requisite
consents would not be forthcoming, even if the end result of the
conflict was a division of the state.

Fact Finding in Former Yugoslavia

The armed conflicts which accompanied the disintegration of the former Federal Republic of Yugoslavia in the early 1990s involved many gross violations of the *jus in bello*. Response to these breaches was complicated by the diverse nature of the conflicts themselves. These matters are considered elsewhere;[79] in summary, the hostilities involved a combination of international and non-international elements. In so far as forces of new states emerging from former Yugoslavia were engaged, the conflict could be considered to be, or have become, 'international'. In so far as (and more usually) the conflict involved hostilities between Bosnian and dissident forces within Bosnia-Herzegovina, with a greater or lesser degree of external support, the conflict(s) must be considered as non-international. This was of relatively little substantive importance because the parties had agreed that the bulk of *jus in bello* principles for 'international' conflicts should be applicable.[80] This, unfortunately, was a useful criterion of liability rather than an indication of standards actually pursued.

International concern about the extent and gravity of breaches of the laws of armed conflict which became apparent in the course of the fighting found expression in the generation of a number of investigatory initiatives. The most significant were those of United Nations Commission of Experts and, rather differently conceived, of the Special Rapporteur to the United Nations Commission on Human Rights. Investigations and reports were also undertaken *ad hoc* by other bodies and organizations, including UNCIVPOL (the UN Civilian Police) and in some cases by UNPROFOR units as well as human rights organizations such as Amnesty International. Some of these investigations raised difficult questions of possible conflict with other roles primarily entrusted to the bodies concerned. These various investigations played an important part in the elucidation of relevant events.

The conduct of these programmes pointedly highlighted an inherent difficulty obstructing most attempts to investigate violations of the laws of armed conflict. Here, as in the case of judicial organization, the precedents of Nuremberg and Tokyo afford, at best, an uncertain guide. The point has often been made that a major difficulty of the investigations which preceded the proceedings before the International Military Tribunals at Nuremberg and Tokyo lay in the sheer volume of material to be processed. At the end of the Second World War, these investigations were hampered by the immediate post-war chaos and sometimes by the location and selection of relevant materials.

The United Nations Commission of Experts

The UN Commission of Experts was set up pursuant to a request made to the Secretary General by the UN Security Council in its Resolution 780, adopted unanimously on 6 October 1992. Its purpose was to report to the Secretary General upon grave breaches of international humanitarian law in the conflict(s) in former Yugoslavia. The specific remit requested by the Security Council was stated as follows:

> to examine and analyse the information submitted pursuant to resolution 171(1992) and the present resolution, together with such further information as the Commission of Experts may obtain through its own investigations or efforts ... with a view to providing the Secretary-General with its conclusions on the evidence of grave breaches of the Geneva Conventions and other violations of international humanitarian law committed in the territory of the former Yugoslavia.[81]

Resolution 780 also called upon states and, where appropriate, international humanitarian organizations and relevant UN bodies, to collate and submit to the Commission of Experts all substantiated information relating to such breaches.[82] The preamble to Resolution 780 (1992) referred generally to reports of 'widespread' violations, but laid particular emphasis upon mass killings and 'ethnic cleansing'.[83]

The Commission set up pursuant to this Security Council request had a membership of five, with Professor Frits Kalshoven as the first Chair, and met for the first time in New York in November 1992. It was faced with a considerable body of material for investigation, including concerns expressed by governments and a variety of UN and other non-governmental organizations. The UN bodies raising issues of concern included the United Nations High Commissioner for Refugees,[84] the United Nations Protection Force in Yugoslavia (UNPROFOR) and the Special Rapporteur to the Commission on Human Rights. Indications of events meriting investigation were also received from a broad range of non-governmental agencies involved in the crisis.[85] Inevitably, the volume of reports and allegations before the Commission seems to have required some degree of sifting; in its detailed investigations, special attention was accorded to events which might reveal unlawful patterns of behaviour rather than only isolated incidents.[86] A number of investigations of specific events were undertaken, including preliminary examination of alleged mass grave sites in various parts of the territory. Amongst these an initial inspection of a site near Vukovar was conducted on behalf of the Commission by an organization called Physicians for Human Rights.[87]

It may be remarked that Physicians for Human Rights is itself a fact-finding body, established in 1986 with special concern for problems of human rights abuses which directly affect health. Many human rights abuses do, of course, have a very severe impact upon the general and particular health of victims, as was notoriously the case in former Yugoslavia.

As its formal brief makes clear, the role of the Commission of Experts was investigatory and not formally prosecutorial, still less 'judicial'. Nonetheless, its investigations and conclusions were ultimately designed to be fed into a prosecutorial and judicial process. In this general context and bearing in mind the call by UN Security Council Resolution 780 (1992) for submission of substantiated information, *inter alia* by international humanitarian organizations, certain practical questions inevitably arise. In particular, the overriding requirements of neutrality and access to people in need must be borne in mind. This is a particular factor in relation to the work of the International Committee of the Red Cross,[88] but may also be an issue in relation to other organizations rendering humanitarian aid in situations of armed conflict, whether international or non-international.

Methodology of the Commission of Experts

The existence of widespread reports and general evidence of atrocities in the course of armed conflict may, as in former Yugoslavia, evince a *prima facie* case for investigation; it is not, however, sufficient in itself to comprise a case. Compiling conclusive evidence is a much slower and more difficult process. The problem is not new and was faced, if anything in a more severe form, in the aftermath of the Second World War. In relation to the historical background to the eventual trials of major war criminals at Nuremberg, John F. Murphy remarks that an early British view (supported by some in the US) was that

> an international trial would be too slow, its legality would be contested, it would give Nazi leaders an opportunity to engage in propaganda, and major Nazi leaders should be disposed of through political means (i.e., summary execution) ... since their guilt was taken for granted.[89]

In light of the proceedings ultimately conducted before the International Military Tribunal at Nuremberg and their considerable importance in modern international criminal jurisprudence,[90] it may be considered fortunate that this policy line was abandoned. Quite apart from anything else, no more efficient way of generating political martyrs could be imagined.

In the context of largely non-international armed conflict, as in former Yugoslavia, a careful investigation of reported violations was at last equally important. The Commission of Experts was largely established to meet the evident need for detailed substantiation. The Commission, which had only a small membership, was enpowered to summon witnesses and experts and also to visit the territory of states, in or beyond former Yugoslavia, subject to their consent.[91]

The Commission could cooperate with or seek the assistance of other appropriate bodies such as, for example, Physicians for Human Rights. The methodology of the Commission was developed in circumstances of considerable difficulty, but its design and parameters may at least be considered an appropriate model for such investigations in which the difficulties of location and access will always loom large. In contrast with the post-Second World war investigations, the Commission commenced its work whilst conflict was still in progress and had significantly less access to materials and personnel than was possible in 1945.

Other Investigations in Former Yugoslavia

The work of the United Nations Commission of Experts was the most focused on gathering prosecutorial evidence, but was by no means the only fact-finding investigation conducted in relation to the conflict(s) in former Yugoslavia. In 1992 Mr Tadeusz Mazowiecki, the former Prime Minister of Poland, was appointed Special Rapporteur to United Nations Commission on Human Rights to report on the situation in former Yugoslavia. This post was created under resolution 1992/S–1/1 of the UN Commission on Human Rights to investigate violations occurring and alleged to have occurred in former Yugoslavia. This was a reporting function. However, in so far as evidence or materials uncovered by Mr Mazowiecki related to matters falling within the remit of the UN Commission of Experts, the enjoined cooperation between the various bodies involved indicated that they should then pursue matters further where appropriate.

In terms of fact finding in former Yugoslavia other UN offices, such as the United Nations High Commissioner for Refugees, had a somewhat different role to play. UNPROFOR also contributed to fact finding to some extent, for example in relation to the mortar attack upon the marketplace in Sarajevo in February 1994. It was found that there was insufficient evidence precisely to pinpoint blame for this outrage, although its occurrence played a decisive role in initiatives to raise the siege of the city. The role of a UN force in fact finding, where evidence is before it, would seem unexceptionable so long as its approach is even-handed. Unfortunately, the problems encountered in interpreting mandates and the highly divergent demands made upon UN forces combine to exacerbate the already considerable difficulties of the task.

The Role of the Press

Before commenting upon press reports from former Yugoslavia a brief mention of the position of journalists in armed conflict is necessary. As reporters of information, journalists are manifestly vulnerable in any situation of armed conflict, whether international or non-international. The most extensive *jus in bello* provision for journalists is made by 1977 Protocol I Additional to the 1949 Geneva Conventions, article 79 (in respect of *international* armed conflicts). Article 79 classifies journalists who are gathering information in areas of armed conflict as 'civilians' and accords them protection under 'Geneva' law, provided that they do not act in a manner incompatible with that status, for example, by taking an active part in hostilities.[92] The exception to this, recognized by article 79(2), is the status of 'war correspondents'. The Third 1949 Geneva Convention recognizes 'war correspondents' accompanying and authorized by the armed forces and equipped with an appropriate identity card as entitled to 'prisoner of war' status upon capture.[93] In the modern media age, the idea of 'war correspondents' is almost obsolete, except in cases where a journalistic presence is otherwise totally impracticable.

In non-international armed conflicts the situation is much less clear. Neither common article 3 of the four 1949 Geneva Conventions nor 1977 Protocol II Additional to those Conventions, setting out international humanitarian provision for non-international armed conflicts, makes reference to journalists as such. In this context, however, Hans-Peter Gasser has remarked that

> the law applicable in [such] ... conflicts ... does not cover members of the press. This is no reason why journalists carrying out dangerous missions and who abstain from committing acts of hostility should not be granted the same protection as civilians.[94]

This is an interesting position and one that is certainly consistent with the treaty provision. A journalist could be considered a highly specialized 'civilian' whose job may demand deliberate entry into dangerous situations. A journalist reporting upon armed conflict might thus be thought to run a much higher risk of 'collateral' injury than most civilians. Provided that he or she does not engage in hostilities, however, there is no reason why a journalist should not, as a civilian, be legally protected from calculated attack. The issue of armed conflict reporting is also intimately bound up with questions of press freedom. However this is a matter within the general law of Human Rights rather than the laws of armed conflict *stricto sensu*.

Fact Finding and the Press in Former Yugoslavia

Significant evidence of abuses in the conflict(s) in former Yugoslavia were brought prominently to the attention of the international community by press reporting in August 1992. In particular, appalling revelations were made about conditions in a number of internment camps, including photographic evidence of gross malnutrition.[95] Other reports disclosed details of torture and brutal treatment inflicted on internees.[96] Descriptions of military brothels in which Bosnian Muslim women were interned and repeatedly raped were also reported in the press.[97] Some of these reports had a significantly beneficial effect in that local authorities, whether previously informed or not, were moved to act by the reports and the resulting international outrage. Inspection by representatives of the International Committee of the Red Cross of camps run by most of the parties in conflict was eventually admitted. In an unusual public statement, the ICRC was reported to have condemned the conditions it found as violating humanitarian norms.[98]

Even from a humanitarian point of view, newspaper coverage of armed conflicts can be a mixed blessing. As in former Yugoslavia, however, journalists can and not infrequently do play an important role in discovering and disseminating information which may be of vital importance. In 1983, Alain Modoux remarked significantly that

> public opinion, conditioned by the media, is an excellent means of bringing pressure to bear on belligerents and is capable of favourably modifying the attitude of combatants to victims protected by humanitarian law.[99]

This perception was well illustrated by the effect of some press revelations in relation to former Yugoslavia. The press cannot, strictly speaking, be considered part of the spectrum of international fact-finding organizations, but does play a role in uncovering facts which, treated with appropriate caution, can be of considerable importance in evaluating situations of armed conflict.

Notes

1   Article 2(6) provides: 'The Organization shall ensure that States which are not Members of the United Nations act in accordance with [the Principles of the UN] so far as may be necessary for the maintenance of international peace and

security'. At the time Spain was not a member of the UN and was not admitted until 1955.

2   Article 35(1) states: 'Any Member of the United Nations may bring any dispute, or any situation of the nature referred to in Article 34, to the attention of the Security Council or of the General Assembly'.

3   UN docs S/32, S/34 (1946).

4   SC mtg, 17 April 1946.

5   SC Res. 4, 1 UN SCOR (1946).

6   Report of the Sub-Committee on the Spanish Question, 1 UN SCOR Special Supp. (No. 2) (1946).

7   SC mtg, 6 June 1946, and SC 47 mtg, 1 UN SCOR (1946).

8   UN doc. S/628 (1948).

9   UN doc. S/646 (1948).

10   SC Res. 39, 3 UN SCOR (1948).

11   SC Res. 47, 3 UN SCOR (1948).

12   SC Res. 27, 2 UN SCOR (1947).

13   SC Res. 30, 2 UN SCOR (1947).

14   UN Doc. S/586 (1947).

15   SC Res. 31 2 UN SCOR (1947); SC Res. 67, 4 UN SCOR (1949).

16   UN doc. S/4007 (1958).

17   UN doc. S/4029 (1958).

18   UN doc. S/4040 (1958).

19   SC 1986 mtg, 32 UN SCOR (1977).

20   32 UN SCOR Special Supp. (No. 3) (1977).

21   SC Res. 405, 419, 32 UN SCOR (1977).

22   SC Res. 496, 36 UN SCOR (1981).

23   37 SCOR, Special Supp. (No. 2) (1982) p.45.

24   SC Res. 507, 37 UN SCOR (1982).

25   See SC Res. 377, 30 UN SCOR (1975), for the investigation which started the Western Saharan peace process.

26   SC 2802 mtg, 43 UN SCOR (1988).

27   GA Res. 46/59, 46 UN A/PV (1992).

28   (1992) 29(4) *UN Chronicle*, p.39.

29   UN doc. S/25600 (1993).

30   SC Res. 822, 48 UN S/PV (1993).

31   SC Res. 853, 874, 48 UN S/PV (1993). See also SC Res. 884, 48 UN S/PV (1993).

32   (1992) 29(4) *UN Chronicle*, p.39.

33   UN doc. S/25188 (1993).

34   UN doc. S/25198 (1993).

35   UN doc. S/26023 (1993).

36   SC Res. 849, 49 UN S/PV (1993).

37   SC Res. 854, 48 UN S/PV (1993).

38   SC Res. 876, 48 UN S/PV (1993).

39   SC Res. 876, 48 UN S/PV (1993).

40   SC Res. 892, 48 UN S/PV (1993).

41   UN Doc. A/47/1 (1992).

42   (1992) 29(4) *UN Chronicle*, p.39.

43   UN doc. S/25697 (1993).

44   GA Res. 47/116, 47 UN A/PV (1992).

45   SC Res. 894, 49 UN S/PV (1994).

46   GA Res. 47/20, 47 UN A/PV (1993).

47   UN doc. A/47/960 (1993).

48   SC Res. 841, 48 UN S/PV (1993).

49   SC Res. 861, 862, 867, 48 UN S/PV (1993).

50   SC Res. 873, 48 UN S/PV (1993).
51   H.A. Hassouna, *The League of Arab States and Regional Disputes* (Oceania, 1975), chapter 2.
52   UN doc. S/5298 (1963).
53   UN doc. S/5321 (1963).
54   UN docs S/5412, S/5447 (1963), S/5794 (1964).
55   UN doc. S/6142 (1964).
56   UN docs S/5927, S/6142 (1964).
57   70 UNTS 238.
58   Hassouna, *The League of Arab States*, chapter 9.
59   See Arab League Assembly Resolution, 280, 12th Session, 27 March 1950.
60   21 UNTS 77.
61   *The Inter American System: Its Development and Strengthening* (Inter American Institute of International Legal Studies, Oceania, 1966), pp.137–42.
62   See further G.F. Treverton, 'Elements of a new European Security Order' (1991) 45 *Journal of International Affairs*, p.91.
63   See further E.B. Schlager, 'Does CSCE spell stability for Europe?' (1991) 21 *Cornell International Law Journal*, p.503.
64   UKTS 31 (1988).
65   298 UNTS 11.
66   (1992) 31 *ILM* p.247.
67   (1975) 14 *ILM* p.1292.
68   D. McGoldrick, 'The Development of the Conference on Security and Cooperation in Europe – From Process to Institution' in B.S. Jackson and D. McGoldrick (eds), *Legal Visions of the New Europe* (Kluwer, 1993), p.176.
69   (1992) 31 *ILM* p.976, (1992) 31 *ILM* p.1390, (1993) 32 *ILM* p.551.
70   See below Chapter 8.
71   See also SC Res. 855, 48 UN S/PV (1993).
72   SC Res. 795, 47 UN S/PV (1992). See also SC Res. 842, 48 UN S/PV (1993).
73   *Keesing's* (1991) pp.38725, 38373, 38420, 38458, 38513, 38559, (1992) p.39012.
74   A specific if antique example may be seen in the trial of Charles I after the English Civil War. For discussion, see p.257, below.
75   As to the status of the Additional Protocol, see pp.125–7, below.
76   Article 90(1)(a).
77   International Committee of the Red Cross, Bulletin, No. 195, April 1992.
78   Y. Sandoz, C. Swinarski and B. Zimmermann (eds), *Commentary on the Additional Protocols of 8 June 1977 to the Geneva Conventions of 12 August 1949* (ICRC/Martinus Nijhoff, 1987), p.1046, paragraph 3628.
79   See pp.275–6.
80   International Committee of the Red Cross, Bulletin, *Yugoslavia* (ICRC, 1992).
81   SC Res. 780, 47 UN SCOR (1992), paragraph 2.
82   *Ibid.*, paragraph 1, reaffirming the call for information previously made in SC Res. 771, 47 UN SCOR (1992).
83   For analysis of the particular issue of 'ethnic cleansing' in the conflict(s) in former Yugoslavia, see pp.155–8, below.
84   As to the working of the UNHCR, see Chapter 7, p.164 ff.
85   Interim Report of the Commission of Experts, 26 January 1993, Annex I, paragraphs 11–16.
86   *Ibid.*, paragraph 31.
87   As to this investigation, see below, p.95.
88   See Chapter 6 at pp.142–3, below.
89   J.F. Murphy, 'Norms of Criminal Procedure at the International Military Tribunal' in G. Ginsburgs and V.N. Kudriavtsev (eds), *The Nuremberg Trial in International Law* (Martinus Nijhoff, 1990), p.61 at p.62.

90   See Chapter 11, at pp.271–3, below.

91   Rules of Procedure of the Commission of Experts, rule 8(1)(3).

92   Article 79(1)(2).

93   1949 Geneva Convention III, article 4A(4).

94   Hans-Peter Gasser, 'The Protection of Journalists engaged in Dangerous Professional Missions', delivered at the Round Table and Red Cross Symposium at the San Remo Institute of International Humanitarian Law in September 1982, *International Review of the Red Cross* (January–February 1983), Extract offprint, p.14.

95   *The Guardian* (London), 7 August 1992. See also pp.130–31, below.

96   *The Independent* (London), 7 August 1992.

97   *The Times* (London), 17 December 1992.

98   Reported in *The Times* (London), 14 August 1992.

99   Alain Modoux, 'International Humanitarian Law and the Journalists' Mission', delivered at the Round Table and Red Cross Symposium at the San Remo Institute of International Humanitarian Law in September 1982, *International Review of the Red Cross* (January–February, 1983), Extract offprint, p.19 at p.20.

5 Constraints upon the Conduct of Hostilities

The *jus in bello* sector of the laws of armed conflict, which makes provision for conduct during and in relation to hostilities, is traditionally subdivided into 'Hague' and 'Geneva' provision.[1] The former is that which primarily, but not exclusively, governs methods and means of warfare. In the context of *international* armed conflicts, the 'Hague' division of the *jus in bello* is well developed, but it is very much less so in the context of non-international disputes. This is partly because, during its early modern period of development (e.g. through the 1899 and 1907 Hague Conventions), it was not generally thought that the power of governments to suppress 'rebellion' or other armed dissent was subject to legal, as compared with moral, restraint. This view remained general until the period of the Second World War. The evidence for the abuses of government power which emerged from the time of Nazi rule in Germany, from 1933 to 1945, played a large part in inspiring the modern development of a law of Human Rights. It was this climate of opinion which also indirectly prompted the development of 'Geneva', or international humanitarian, provision for victims of non-international armed conflicts.[2] There is in practice some considerable overlap between the 'Hague' and 'Geneva' divisions of the *jus in bello*; in the present context, this does have some impact upon the question of methods and means of warfare in non-international armed conflicts. It must be admitted, however, that the 'Hague' division of the law in this regard is, at most, in an early stage of development.

Many non-international armed conflicts commence with anti-state activities which are, in their earliest stages, opposed by some form of 'police' action. At this level of 'internal disturbances and tensions' the *jus in bello* provision for non-international armed conflicts will not be applicable. Indeed, in the 'Geneva' sector, 1977 Protocol II Additional to the 1949 Geneva Conventions expressly excludes such situations from its 'material field of application'.[3] At this level of 'disturbance' the methods and means of suppression will be constrained by 'human rights' provision rather than the *jus in bello* as the law currently stands.[4] Where, however, internal strife reaches the level of non-international armed conflict or 'civil war', questions of constraint upon methods and means of warfare in the strict sense do begin to arise. Only relatively recently have such ideas been raised in the context of non-international armed conflict. Nonetheless in the post-1945 development of 'human rights' and related concerns, the argument that the 'rights of belligerents to adopt means of injuring the enemy is not unlimited' (to adopt the words of article 22 of the Regulations Respecting the Laws and Customs of War on Land annexed to 1907 Hague Convention IV), has begun to find expression in the law governing non-international armed conflict.

No direct reference to methods and means of warfare is made by common article 3 of the 1949 Geneva Conventions, although minor implications are to be found in some of its general humanitarian requirements.[5] 1977 Protocol II Additional to the 1949 Geneva Conventions[6] takes this development considerably further in spelling out the limitations upon methods and means adopted in the conduct of hostilities which are necessary in the furtherance of humanitarian protection.

The Structure of Constraint in 1977 Additional Protocol II

The Protocol does not contain a specific section devoted to methods and means of warfare *stricto sensu*. Within Part IV of the Protocol, headed 'Civilian Population', however, a number of provisions are set out which directly or indirectly define the modes of admissible military action.[7] As the heading indicates, the focus of concern is upon the greatest possible protection of civilians from the effects of hostilities. To this end, deliberate attacks upon civilians are forbidden;[8] objects essential to the survival of the civilian population are protected,[9] as are works and installations containing 'dangerous forces'.[10] Provision is also made for the protection of cultural objects and places of worship,[11] while the forced movement of civilians is proscribed.[12] These have all been serious issues in non-international armed conflicts in the late 20th century, with all too many painful illustrations of the need for effective persuasion in such matters.

General Protection of the Civilian Population

In modern international humanitarian law, civilians are considered as generically protected in armed conflict. In the context of non-international armed conflict, 1977 Additional Protocol II provides by article 13(1) that '[t]he civilian population and individual civilians shall enjoy general protection against the dangers arising from military operations ... '. As a general principle this may sound decidedly utopian; it is important to stress that the principle neither is, nor is intended to be, in any sense talismanic. A zone of conflict will by definition be dangerous, whether for military or civilian personnel. Anyone who has the misfortune to be in the wrong place at the wrong time will be at risk. What exactly is the 'wrong place' in this context raises the important question of 'collateral damage' which is considered further below.[13]

A more specific indication of the nature of this protection is given by article 13(2):

> The civilian population as such, as well as individual civilians, shall not be the object of attack. Acts or threats of violence the primary purpose of which is to spread terror among the civilian population are prohibited.

Calculated attacks upon civilian populations and/or individual civilians are thus proscribed; beyond this, to terrorize civilians by overt acts or 'threat' thereof is also forbidden. Several definitional questions arise from this provision. Most importantly, what is meant by an 'object of attack' and what constitutes a 'civilian population'?

The first question is fairly easily answered. The ICRC Commentary upon the Protocol remarks that

> this rule prohibits launching direct attacks against the civilian population. On the other hand, secondary effects of military operations directed against military objectives, which might incidentally affect the civilian population, are not specifically referred to here.[14]

It must again be stressed that the proscription of calculated attacks does not legitimate those launched without concern as to the presence or otherwise of civilians. Any practice of indiscriminate bombardment would seem to fall foul of the provision of article 13(1) for 'general protection against the dangers arising from military operations'.

The nature of a 'civilian population' is perhaps somewhat more problematic. The term is not defined by 1977 Additional Protocol II. However, in terms of international armed conflicts, additional Protocol I, by repeating the first sentence of article 13(2) in its article 51(1), does afford a definition. Article 50 of 1977 Additional Protocol I provides that,

> (1) A civilian is any person who does not belong to one of the categories of [armed forces or associated personnel entitled to prisoner of

war status upon capture]... . In case of doubt whether a person is a civilian, that person shall be considered to be a civilian.
(2) The civilian population comprises all persons who are civilians.
(3) The presence within the civilian population of individuals who do not come within the definition of civilians does not deprive the population of its civilian character.

In a non-international armed conflict, this distinction presents some difficulty in relation to the definition of the 'armed forces' involved. Across the broad range of conflicts, which are beyond mere 'internal tensions' but are not international or 'internationalized',[15] will usually (but not always)[16] be the state's national armed forces and various forms of insurgent forces. In this context, 'prisoner of war' status, which is an important focus in the full statement of article 50(1) of 1977 Additional Protocol I is severely problematic. In particular the implications of legitimation and recognition, if imported into Protocol II, might well prove an additional hindrance to humanitarian implementation. This said, the forces engaged in an armed conflict falling within the remit of 1977 Additional Protocol II are described by article 1(1) as

[the national] armed forces and dissident armed forces or other organized groups which, under responsible command, exercise such control over a part of its territory as to enable them to carry out sustained and concerned military operations and to implement this Protocol.

These requirements of military or, by implication, quasi-military discipline and commitment to specified, if reduced, *jus in bello* norms gives a reasonably clear indication of the nature of combatants in non-international armed conflict, as envisaged by 1977 Additional Protocol II. According to 1977 Additional Protocol I, article 50, civilians comprise the rest of the population. By analogy with article 50(3) of 1977 Additional Protocol I, it may then be taken that even if non-civilians, such as soldiers or other fighters on leave, are present, a population would retain its 'civilian' character. Finally it may be assumed, by analogy with article 50(2) of 1977 Additional Protocol I, that a 'civilian population' is an aggregation of individual civilians.

The matter of technical definition may not be unduly complex, but the record of practical implementation, both in general and in particular, has been far from encouraging. Civilians and civilian populations have been major victims, and by no means always accidentally, in a great many civil wars, irrespective of the strict applicability or otherwise of 1977 Additional Protocol II. In the late 20th century the conflicts in Angola, Cambodia (Kampuchea), Nicaragua, Sudan and former Yugoslavia all provide telling examples, a list which, sadly, is by no means comprehensive.

At one level there is the issue of simple terror attacks upon civilian populations. The armed conflict(s) in the early 1990s in former Yugoslavia were replete with examples of this, a telling point considering that the parties had, in theory, agreed to the general application of the stricter standards demanded by the *jus in bello* norms applicable in *international* armed conflicts.[17] One gross instance of terror bombardment occurred during the siege of Sarajevo. On 5 February 1994 a mortar bomb was fired from the surrounding area into the marketplace killing 68 people and injuring many others. Exactly who was responsible for the attack remained somewhat obscure. Ten days later an UNPROFOR investigation team reported that there was not sufficient physical evidence to determine conclusively who had been responsible[18] – not a surprising outcome considering the presumed mobility of the unit concerned and the nature of the terrain. Although, in the event, the brutal attack had positive political repercussions, this terror bombardment of civilians was manifestly unlawful under the rules applicable to *international* armed conflicts. Their applicability to former Yugoslavia is considered elsewhere,[19] but such attacks as this would clearly also fall foul of 1977 Additional Protocol II where its provisions are applicable.[20]

A second problem may arise in adequately distinguishing between hostile forces and the civilian population. This, however, is perhaps more difficult in theory than in reality. This has complicated the definition of 'combatant' status in the context of *jus in bello* rules applicable to *international* armed conflicts. Partly in the light of experience in the Vietnam war, 1977 Protocol I Additional to the 1949 Geneva Conventions provides by article 44(3) that,

> in order to promote the protection of the civilian population from the effects of hostilities, combatants are obliged to distinguish themselves from the civilian population while they are engaged in an attack or in a military operation preparatory to an attack. Recognizing, however, that there are situations in armed conflicts where, owing to the nature of the hostilities, an armed combatant cannot so distinguish himself, he shall retain his status as a combatant, provided that, in such situations, he carries his arms openly:
> (a) during each military engagement, and
> (b) during such time as he is visible to the adversary while he is engaged in a military deployment preceding the launching of an attack in which he is to participate. ...

This provision has been considered controversial because of the implications of the general need for combatants to be physically 'distinguished'. The question with which article 44(3) seeks to deal is a very real one. The provision is not repeated in 1977 Additional Protocol II or, of course, in common article 3 of the 1949 Geneva Conventions because of the urgent desire of both to avoid questions or legitimate combatancy. If such matters were permitted to intrude, there would undoubtedly be erected even further obstacles to humanitarian implementation. Thus, *prima facie*, article 44(3) will only affect non-international armed conflicts where the parties have agreed to apply it. Nevertheless, it is of special relevance since anti-government forces may be poorly organized or be using guerrilla tactics. Such problems were clearly illustrated in the context of hostilities in Bosnia-Herzegovina; it was remarked elsewhere that 'the status of many fighters [was] ... confused, ranging from members of "regular" forces, through "rebel" groups to mere bandits'.[21] It may be added that the rather variant nature of the forces involved may sometimes have been used to obscure what, if known, would have been embarrassing chains of responsibility.

In practice the answer is simple, if not particularly comforting. No provision of the laws of armed conflict requires a fighting force to submit supinely to attack. The question then essentially becomes one of 'collateral' risk to a surrounding civilian population, a question faced by UNOSOM in Somalia when their attackers were concealed by large civilian crowds.[22]

The issues of civilian protection merge to some extent into a different area of concern, that of constraint upon weapons types and usage. This is an important issue in the context of international armed conflict and, if anything, one which gains an additional controversial edge in the area of non-international armed conflicts.

Constraints upon Types and Uses of Weapons

The *jus in bello* as a whole contains a variety of proscriptions, both upon specific categories of weaponry and their use. Amongst prohibitions on particular weapon types relating to international armed conflict, there may be listed the 1868 Declaration of St Petersburg (Small calibre explosive projectiles); 1899 Hague Declaration 3 ('Dum Dum' bullets); 1907 Hague Convention VIII (in part, unanchored automatic submarine contact mines); 1925 Geneva Gas Protocol (asphyxiating, poisonous and other gases and bacteriological warfare); 1972 UN Convention on the Prohibition of the Development, Production and Stockpiling of Biological and Toxin Weapons and their Destruction; 1981 UN Convention on Prohibitions or Restrictions on the Use of Certain Conventional Weapons (non-detectable fragmentation weapons, booby traps, etc., and use of incendiary weapons against or in proximity to civilian populations); and the 1992 UN Convention on the Prohibition of the Development, Production, Stockpiling and Use of Chemical Weapons and their Destruction. Even so bare a recitation serves to indicate the piecemeal nature of this process of proscription. The absence of any reference to nuclear weapons is significant and relates directly to the 'Cold War' politics of the period between 1945 and the late 1980s. Such law as exists upon this matter is, at the time of writing, either regional in nature (e.g. the Treaties of Tlatelolco and Rarotonga) or derives from general principles of the *jus in bello* which were not originally framed with nuclear weapons in mind.

In addition the various weapons-specific proscriptions, there are a wide range of *jus in bello* provisions applicable in international armed conflicts which expressly or implicitly prohibit certain uses of weapons. This is by definition a much broader field of application than the type-specific prohibitions and includes such matters as indiscriminate bombardment and the infliction of 'unnecessary suffering'.[23] The weapons proscriptions derived from such provisions may be either absolute or conditional. The former will arise where any use of the weapon in question would lead to unlawful consequences; the latter where the outcome would be unlawful only in some cases. The question of lawfulness of possession, as compared with use, may arise, but in general these two categories are best considered as separate issues.

This is the general structure of the law of weapons control so far as *international* armed conflict is concerned. Almost all of the relevant provisions were not drafted with reference to non-international armed conflicts, however, and would not apply to them other than if an express agreement existed to the contrary. This leaves open a broad field for debate; indeed, serious questions of weapons type and usage do pertain to non-international armed conflicts. A particular issue arose in the period between the 1980–88 Gulf War and the 1990–91 Gulf conflict in relation to the use of chemical weapons against the Kurdish population in northern Iraq.

Chemical and Biological Weapons in Non-international Conflicts

So far as *international* armed conflicts are concerned, early attempts were made to ban the use of both chemical and biological weapons. 1899 Hague Declaration 2 banned 'the use of projectiles the sole object of which is the diffusion of asphyxiating or deleterious gases'. Whether the effects of gas attacks could be thus strictly defined may be debated,[24] but the horror occasioned by this form of warfare led ultimately to the 1925 Geneva Gas Protocol which prohibits the use 'in war' of poisonous, asphyxiating and other gases and analogous materials and extends this prohibition to 'bacteriological methods of warfare'. The implementation of this proscription has not been totally effective but, in international armed conflict, has enjoyed a very significant level of success.

Two types of situation may be advanced. The first arises where, as on the Western Front in the First World War and in the 1980–88 Gulf War, endeavours are made (almost certainly unsuccessfully) to break a vast infantry stalemate – a most unlikely situation in non-international disputes. The second, and more frequent, situation is where the imbalance of technological capacity between the parties in conflict implies immediate advantage and improbability of equivalent response. Instances include the 1935–36 Italo-Ethiopian War and the Sino-Japanese War commencing in 1937 and leading into the Second World War in the Far East.[25] The issues of technological imbalance and improbability of response no doubt also characterize the experience of chemical warfare in non-international armed conflicts.

A notorious modern instance of such use of chemical weapons was inflicted upon Kurdish settlements in the aftermath of the 1980–88 Gulf War. The Kurdish people straddle the frontiers of several states, notably, Iran, Iraq, Turkey and Syria, and the development of nationalist aspirations have led to serious border confrontations. The 1980–88 War was in considerable part fought over the frontier between Iran and Iraq which runs through Kurdish lands, resulting in the Kurds becoming variously enmeshed in the hostilities. In the closing days of the war, the Iraqi government was able to turn its forces upon those Kurds who may have used the conflict to advance their claims for independence. International outrage was caused by a gas attack by the Iraqi air force upon the Kurdish town of Halabjah in March 1988.[26] Patrick Brogan indicates that Western reports found a minimum of 100 dead, whilst Iran claimed that some 2,000 had died.[27]

It was also claimed that chemical attacks had been made upon other Kurdish settlements in October 1988, though the details remain obscure. The victims of such attacks in Kurdistan seem to have been trapped in a vicious interface between contemporaneous international and non-international conflicts, as Valerie Adams has commented:

> It is [hard] : to see the military and political rationale for the ... chemical attacks [upon] ... civilian targets ... in Iraq itself during 1987 and 1988. ... [I]t may ... have been connected to irritation at Iranian support for Kurdish rebels in Iraq. ... The use of chemicals at Hallabyah in March 1988 was presumably intended to terrorise and subjugate a dissident population.

Iraq is not party to 1977 Additional Protocol II, although the objections to chemical attacks upon civilians, or indeed insurgent fighters, are not restricted to that provision. For instance, chemical attacks upon civilian populations contravene the requirement of common article 3 of the 1949 Geneva Conventions that 'persons taking no active part in the hostilities … shall in all circumstances be treated humanely…'. In so far as chemical attacks took place during hostilities between Iraq and Iran, they of course breached the 1925 Geneva Gas Protocol.

The problems of non-international armed conflict have had a significant if implicit impact upon more recent treaty provision in this area. The use of lachrymatory agents (tear gas) was a cause of controversy in relation to the 1925 Geneva Gas Protocol because of its use by many states as an agent of police crowd control in riots and other disturbances. Even if the effects of such irritant gases are generally non-lethal, their proscription in the wording of the 1925 Protocol still applies. The Protocol refers simply to 'the use in war of asphyxiating, poisonous or other gases, and of all analogous liquids materials or other devices, …'. For instance, mustard gas (dichlorethyl sulphide), which was used in the First World War and which in part motivated the conclusion of the 1925 Geneva Gas Protocol, was in many cases severely disabling rather than fatal.[29] The 1992 UN Convention of the Prohibition of the Development, Production, Stockpiling and Use of Chemical Weapons and on their Destruction would seem to cover this matter in providing by article I(5) that '[e]ach state Party undertakes not to use riot control agents as a method of warfare'. This provision does not of course preclude the use of 'riot control agents' in riots.

The 1925 Geneva Gas Protocol proscribes the use of poison gases and bacteriological agents 'in war' which in context, must refer primarily to *international* armed conflicts. The 1992 UN Chemical Weapons Convention, however is, more broadly drafted. Article I(1) provides that,

> Each state Party to this Convention undertakes *never under any circumstances*:
> (a) To develop, produce, otherwise acquire, stockpile or retain chemical weapons, or transfer, directly or indirectly, chemical weapons to anyone;
> (b) *To use chemical weapons*;
> (c) To engage in any military preparedness to use chemical weapons;
> (d) To assist, encourage or induce, in any way, *anyone to engage in any activity prohibited to a state* Party under this Convention (emphases added).

The 1992 provision, unlike that of 1925, is both a proscription on use and a ban upon manufacture and possession of chemical weapons. The bans are phrased emphatically in absolute terms. Moreover, the aspirations stated by the preamble to the Convention and the fact that the 1992 Provision builds upon, as well as 'reaffirms', the provisions of the 1925 Geneva Gas Protocol, suggests that the former covers *any* military use of such agents – including in a non-international armed conflict. In so far as it goes beyond the requirements of the 1925 Geneva Gas Protocol, this 1992 Convention would create obligations only as between states party. However, it is interesting to note the ban on 'assisting anyone to engage in any activity prohibited to a state Party'. The term 'anyone' could be interpreted to mean non-state entities as well. This would, then, also preclude external powers from providing a chemical weapons capacity to insurgent forces.

The 1992 UN Chemical Weapons Convention was modelled directly upon the 1972 UN Convention on the Prohibition of the Development, Production and Stockpiling of Biological and Toxin Weapons and their Destruction. Although biological weapons have as old and disreputable a history as chemical weapons,[30] there is less evidence of their use in modern warfare at any level. Experiments were certainly conducted between the First and Second World Wars with biological weapons (including, e.g., anthrax weapons), but there is little suggestion of any actual use except, possibly, in the Second World War by Japanese forces in China.[31] The same general arguments advanced above for the application of the 1992 chemical weapons proscription in non-international armed conflicts may also be advanced for biological weapons.

Attacks upon Installations containing 'Dangerous Forces'

1977 Protocol II Additional to the 1949 Geneva Conventions provides by article 15 that,

> Works or installations containing dangerous forces, namely dams, dykes and nuclear generating stations, shall not be made the object of attack, even where these objects are military objectives, if such attack may cause the release of dangerous forces and consequent severe losses among the civilian population.

This provision is a somewhat shortened form of article 56 of the 1977 Additional Protocol I. The point of the proscription is obvious enough. An attack upon, e.g., a hydroelectric dam might well disrupt militarily significant industrial and other capacities of the enemy, but might also, through the ensuing flooding, occasion massive 'collateral' death and injury to the surrounding civilian population. The same considerations would apply, if anything yet more strongly, to an attack upon a nuclear power station.

Examples of problems associated with this type of action have arisen a number of times in the context of international armed conflict. One well-known instance was the 1943 'Dambusters' raid during the Second World War, undertaken by the RAF upon the Ruhr dams in Germany. Designed to deny electrical supplies to German military industrial plants, it had considerable success, as Albert Speer, the Reichsminister for Armaments, has conceded.[32] Whether in a modern armed conflict to which 1977 Additional Protocol I applied, such a raid would be lawful would depend upon the extent and location of ambient civilian habitation. There have also been attacks upon nuclear facilities, by Israel upon an Iraqi plant and by Iraq upon an Iranian facility, but in these cases, thankfully, the power stations were not yet commissioned and there were no radioactive materials on the sites.

The prohibition is not absolute. If the attack did not release a 'dangerous force' or, even so, if there were no 'consequent severe losses' amongst the civilian population, it would not seem to be proscribed by 1977 Additional Protocol II. The only possible area of ambiguity here lies in the concept of 'consequent severe losses'. The ICRC Commentary upon the Protocol remarks that,

> The term 'severe losses' is taken from military terminology, and clearly this must be judged in good faith on the basis of objective elements, such as the existence of densely populated areas of civilians (villages or towns) in the area which would be affected by the release of dangerous forces.[33]

The decision will ultimately turn upon an assessment of probabilities in relation, for instance, to patterns of settlement, likely flooding, the consequent extent of 'collateral' injury, etc. Such calculations are more feasible in the case of dams and dykes. The destruction of a functioning nuclear power station would, in the light of the Chernobyl experience, seem to have so great a potential for damage as to render the proscription set out by article 15 very nearly complete.

Starvation and 'Scorched Earth' Tactics

Scorched earth tactics – the reduction or destruction of the capacity of territory to support or sustain an advancing enemy – have a long history. The retreat of the Russian armies before Napoleon, thus denying the French forces supplies, and the ultimate burning of Moscow is but one significant example, Where one side 'scorches' the territory of another in international armed conflict, it would not contravene the provision of article 54 of 1977 Additional Protocol I in so far as it starved the civilian population or deprived it of objects indispensable to survival. This proscription is repeated, in somewhat abbreviated form, in the case of non-international armed conflicts by 1977 Additional Protocol II, article 14:

> Starvation of civilians as a method of combat is prohibited. It is there-fore prohibited to attack, destroy, remove or render useless, for that purpose, objects indispensable to the survival of the civilian popula-tion....

The article indicates that such indispensable objects include food, agricultural capacity and stocks, water supplies and associated works. To attack such vital supplies (calculated crop burning, destruction of water purification plants and so on) would therefore be an unlawful method of warfare.

On of the most prominent and distressing inflictions of the armed conflict(s) in former Yugoslavia involved the denial of basic food and medical supplies to beleaguered ethnic enclaves, the practical con-duct and consequences of which amounted to 'siege' warfare. A very large part of humanitarian relief endeavours was dedicated to get-ting essential supplies through to such beleaguered civilian populations. The attacks made upon supply flights and road con-voys, even when guarded by UNPROFOR units, highlighted the problem of starvation as a mode of warfare, closely linked as it was with the campaign of so-called 'ethnic cleansing'.[34]

Article 14 commences with the unequivocal statement that 'starva-tion of civilians as a method of combat is prohibited'. Thus, in a conflict to which 1977 Additional Protocol II applies, any means or method of warfare which inherently involves the starvation of the civilian population would seem to be unlawful. This view is con-firmed by the ICRC Commentary upon 1977 Additional Protocol II,[35] which also remarks that blockages and analogous actions directed against purely *military* targets would not contravene article 14, since this is only protective of civilians. In non-international armed con-flicts the question arises of whether a scorched earth policy adopted by an 'authority' within its own territory, in response to a hostile advance, would also contravene article 14. Probably not, since the aim would not be the starvation of civilians though, from other points of view, the legality of the action might depend upon the provision subsequently made for the local civilian population.

Forced Movement of Civilians

As typified by the 'ethnic cleansing' imposed in former Yugoslavia, the forced movement of civilians is a common problem in non-international armed conflicts. 1977 Protocol II Additional to the 1949 Geneva Conventions provides unequivocally by article 17(2) that '[c]ivilians shall not be compelled to leave their own territory for reasons connected with the conflict'. This would clearly proscribe actions falling within the category of 'ethnic cleansing', but would also apply to much smaller-scale inflictions on populations considered by another party in the conflict to be militarily or politically 'unreliable'. For this purpose the idea of 'own territory' clearly relates to community tradition and occupation. Modes of forced displacement may vary. At one level there is the simple application of coercive force but, separately or in combination, other modes are possible. The action taken against the Shi-ite Marsh Arab population in the Tigris–Euphrates Delta by Iraq in the aftermath of the 1990–91 Gulf conflict – by draining the marshlands, along with aerial bombardment – indicates other possibilities to which article 17 might apply.

As article 17(1) of the Protocol makes clear, the proscription does not mean that all movements of population are forbidden. Its initial statement, proscribing displacement of population for reasons related to a conflict, is more restrictive than that upon forced departure from 'own territory'. It then adds that such displacement is permissible where 'the security of the civilians involved or imperative military reasons so demand'. The reference to civilian security is more or less self-explanatory, the movement of the front line in hostilities towards a town or village presumably justifying such action. 'Imperative military reasons' are more problematic. They appear to be a virtual synonym for 'imperative military necessity', a controversial issue which is considered further below.[36] These 'reasons' probably refer to unavoidable exigencies of combat, such as where a settlement straddles a defensive line – which would anyway raise questions of the security of the population. In any event the reference to 'imperative military reasons' should not to be taken to justify a strategy or tactics which would necessitate forced displacement if another option were available. As suggested below, such provisions are a practical recognition of the real exigencies of warfare, not an invitation to callous inflictions dictated by military convenience.

Protection of Cultural Objects and Places of Worship

Provision for the protection of 'cultural objects and places of worship' might seem to be more appropriately considered as an issue associated with humanitarian protection in a narrow sense rather than with methods and means of warfare. In the context of non-international armed conflict, however, a good case may be advanced for sometimes considering this subject as a 'method of warfare' where warfare is between communities defined in whole or part by culture and/or faith, related buildings and other material objects may play a large part in civilian morale as well as in normal dally routines. Protection of such objects and places is set out in both 1977 Protocol II Additional to the 1949 Geneva Conventions and the 1954 Hague Convention for the Protection of Cultural Property in the Event of Armed Conflict.

1977 Additional Protocol II provides by article 16 that

> it is prohibited to commit any acts of hostility directed against historic monuments, works of art or places of worship which constitute the cultural or spiritual heritage of peoples, and to use them in support of the military effort.

The provision is expressly stated to be without prejudice to the provisions of the 1954 Convention. Clearly a monument or place of worship employed as a gun emplacement would lose any right to protection.

The 1954 provision is parallel in concern but somewhat more detailed. Although the Convention is drafted with primary reference to international armed conflicts, article 19(1) provides that in the event of internal conflict, 'each party' should, as a minimum, apply the provisions relating to 'respect for cultural property', i.e., article 4 of the Convention. Article 19(2), however encourages attempts to bring the remainder of the provision into application 'by means of special agreements'. The most important provision in the present context is made by article 4(1),

> The High Contracting Parties undertake to respect cultural property situated within their own territory as well as within the territory of other High Contracting Parties by refraining from any use of the property and its immediate surroundings or of the appliances in use for its protection for purposes which are likely to expose it to destruction or damage in the event of armed conflict and by refraining from any act of hostility directed against such property.

By reference to article 19(1), this obligation would apply equally to both, or all, parties to a non-international armed conflict.

Article 4(3) further requires the prohibition and, where necessary, stopping of theft, pillage, misappropriation or vandalism of cultural property and also the requisitioning of 'movable cultural property' in the territory of another party. Reprisals against cultural property are also forbidden by article 4(4).

During the armed conflict(s) in former Yugoslavia, there were many instances of attacks upon historic monuments and places of worship, no doubt often motivated by hostility to the religious and cultural heritage of the opposing community. Other aims – terrorizing the civilian population and damaging their morale – may also have played a part. It is significant that article 3(d) of the Statute of the International Tribunal, set up to conduct war crimes trials arising from the conflicts in former Yugoslavia,[37] included within its jurisdiction seizure, destruction or wilful damage to religious, charitable and educational institutions, historic monuments and scientific and artistic work and institutions.

The only exception to the duty to respect cultural property set out by article 4 of the 1954 Convention is stated by article 4(2) which refers to imperative 'military necessity', an idea of little significance in the *jus in bello* provision relative to non-international armed conflicts.[38] So far as basic humanitarian norms in relation to international hostilities are concerned, Jean Pictet has remarked that

> there is no express or implied clause in the law of war giving priority to military necessity ... [but] there is an implicit clause in any law to the effect that no-one is obliged to do what is impossible ... [meaning] only ... a genuine material impossibility ... .[39]

This would also be the case for the essential humanitarian norms of non-international armed conflict. So far as the protection of cultural property is concerned, however, the matter may not be so simply resolved. Property damage, even of an historic monument, must take secondary place to the protection of human lives, including soldiers' lives. In a more general context,

> property destruction is unlikely ever to be 'impossible' to avoid but it may more commonly not be reasonably avoidable in the light of overwhelming military exigencies. This is not ... to counsel a dangerous confusion of military necessity with mere military convenience. ... The general criterion which appears to emerge is one of 'unavoidability' rather than 'impossibility', subject to the much stricter criteria ... applied to fundamental humanitarian norms.[40]

In the present case the 1954 Convention itself supplies a clear criterion of assessment. Article 4(1) bans the hostile military use of cultural property since such use could render attacks upon that property 'necessary'. Obviously the decision would have to be weighed and a preliminary demand to desist might be appropriate. If, however, an ancient church tower is being used as a gun position, neither law nor sense suggests that it should be left untargeted. The same reasoning may be applied to article 16 of 1977 Protocol II Additional to the 1949 Geneva Conventions.

Application and Extension of Constraints

The constraints upon methods and means of warfare contained in the *jus in bello* provision strictly applicable to non-international armed conflicts are important but decidedly limited. This basic provision, however, always also enjoins a wider application to *jus in bello* norms wherever possible. Thus, common article 3 of the 1949 Geneva Conventions requires that

> the parties to the conflict should further endeavour to bring into force by means of special agreements, all or part of the other provisions of the present Convention.

Admittedly the 1949 Geneva Conventions contain little overt reference to methods and means of warfare, although some provisions imply detailed restrictions of that kind. However, the invitation to extended application of the *jus in bello*, including its 'Hague' sector, is plain enough.

This issue became a matter of substantial importance in former Yugoslavia. The status of the conflict(s) was a matter of some controversy,[41] but a network of agreements between the Parties themselves seemed to establish that the bulk of the *jus in bello* provision applicable to international conflicts should be applied. The International Tribunal set up pursuant to Resolution 808 (1993) of the Security Council in relation to the hostilities included within its jurisdiction, by article 3 of its Statute, a number of 'Hague' concerns. These included use of poison and other weapons calculated to inflict unnecessary suffering (i.e. in the 'St Petersburg' sense), wanton destruction of urban settlements unjustified by military necessity; bombardment of 'undefended' settlements and wilful damage to cultural property. The reference to 'undefended' towns and villages derives from article 25 of the Regulations Respecting the Laws and Customs of War on Land annexed to 1907 Hague Convention IV. It is possible that such 'undefended' localities (in the pre-1914 sense) might still actually exist. Generally, however, the major issue in this context is that of indiscriminate bombardment.[42]

Even in terms of internecine conflicts, the hostilities in former Yugoslavia were notable for the savagery of the methods and means adopted. This raises the question as to whether formal proscriptions applied to methods and means of warfare can be more than utopian in such cases. Although such rules and principles cannot offer any panacea for the cruelty of hostilities, they do set norms against which conduct may be judged and by reference to which the international community may respond. As Frits Kalshoven remarks,

> the strong injunctions against intervention in Article 3 of the Protocol notwithstanding, there ... remains the possibility for the international community, from the United Nations down to the media and public opinion, to call upon the parties to an internal armed conflict to respect their obligations under Protocol II.[43]

Although not specifically in the context of 1977 Additional Protocol I, this was what eventually happened in former Yugoslavia in terms of international response. Clearly, where the state under threat is endeavouring to retain international support and credibility and where 'insurgents' are seeking to gain and develop both, each side has a pragmatic incentive at least to appear to abide by basic norms in the conduct of hostilities. Indeed, few parties will openly flaunt their war criminality.

The methods and means of warfare adopted in civil wars touch upon a raw nerve in the context of national sovereignty, by arson of the 'policing' tradition from which the non-international *jus in bello* emerged and is seeking to liberate itself. Ultimately this is perhaps the most difficult interface between humanitarian law and human rights. If, as Theodor Meron remarks,

> The idea of humanity has become the common denominator of human rights law and of humanitarian law. ... Current trends point to an even greater reliance on the shared idea of humanity.[44]

Thus, in the 'Hague' sector of the non-international *jus in bello* there still remains some distance to be travelled.

Notes

1 See Chapter 1 at pp.18–19, above.
2 Specifically through common article 3 of the four 1949 Geneva Conventions and 1977 Protocol II Additional to the 1949 Geneva Conventions. For detailed discussion, see Chapter 6.
3 Article 1.
4 There is, however, a body of opinion which holds that conflicts at this lower level should also be the subject of a humanitarian instrument, beyond the general regulation of 'human rights'; see Theodor Meron, 'Internal Strife: Applicable Norms and a Proposed Instrument' in A.J.M. Delissen and G.J. Tanja,

(eds), *Humanitarian Law and Armed Conflict Challenges Ahead: Essays in Honour of Frits Kalshoven* (Martinus Nijhoff, 1991), pp.249–66. Also discussions by R. Abi-Saab, 'Humanitarian Law and Internal Conflicts: the Evolution of Legal Concern', in *ibid.*, at pp.209–23 and P.H. Koijmans, 'In the Shadowland between Civil War and Civil Strife: Some Reflections on the Standard-Setting Process', in *ibid.*, at pp.225–47. See also A. Eide, 'Respect for Humanitarian Norms in Internal Disturbances and Tensions' in Mohammed Bedjaoui (ed.), *Modern Wars: The Humanitarian Challenge* (Secretariat of the Independent Commission on International Humanitarian Issues, published by Zed Books, 1986), at pp.102–20.

5   Article 3(1) requiring humane treatment of 'persons taking no active part in the hostilities' might at least seem to impose some constraint upon calculated attack upon them.

6   This is, of course, a 'Geneva' provision but, like 1977 Additional Protocol I in relation to international armed conflicts, it does include significant 'Hague' elements in a proper humanitarian context.

7   In particular, articles 13–17.

8   Article 13(2).

9   Article 14.

10 Article 15.

11 Article 16.

12 Article 17.

13 See pp.108 and 112.

14 Y. Sandoz, C. Swinarski and B. Zimmermann (eds), *Commentary on the Additional Protocols of 8 June 1977 to the Geneva Conventions of 12 August 1949* (International Committee of the Red Cross with Martinus Nijhoff, 1987), p.1451, paragraph 4779.

15 For discussion see Chapter 1 at pp.19–20.

16 A divergent instance may be seen in the conflicts following the collapse of civil authority in Somalia in the early 1990s.

17 See above, p.94.

18 News Summary (United Nations Information Centre for the United Kingdom and Ireland, 17 February 1994).

19 See pp.94–5.

20 See pp.105–6.

21 H. McCoubrey, 'Yugoslavia at War: International Laws of Armed Conflict and the Yugoslav Crisis' (1992) 136 *Solicitors' Journal*, p.914 at p.915.

22 See p.197.

23 A phrase traceable to the 1868 Declaration of St Petersburg but which has attained a much wider currency.

24 See E.M. Spiers, *Chemical Warfare* (Macmillan, 1986), p.17.

25 For discussion of this point see H. McCoubrey, 'The Regulation of Chemical and Biological Weapons' in Hazel Fox and Michael A. Meyer (eds), *Armed Conflict and the New Law, Vol. II, Effecting Compliance* (British Institute of International and Comparative Law, 1993), p.123 at pp.134–6.

26 Reported in *The Guardian* (London), 24 March 1988.

27 P. Brogan, *World Conflicts*, 2nd edn (Bloomsbury Publishing, 1992), p.327.

28 V. Adams, *Chemical Warfare, Chemical Disarmament* (Macmillan, 1989), p.89.

29 H. McCoubrey, *op.cit.*, at p.125.

30 For examples of both chemical and biological attacks, see W. Moore, *Gas Attack* (Leo Cooper, 1987), Ch. 1.

31 V. Adams, *op.cit.*, at p.11, citing, Arthur H. Westing, 'The Threat of Biological Warfare', *BioScience*, Vol. 35, November 1985, No. 10, p.627.

32 A. Speer, *Inside the Third Reich* (Sphere Books, 1971: first published by the Macmillan Co., NY, 1970), pp.384–5.

33 Y. Sandoz, C. Swinarski and B. Zimmermann (eds), *Commentary on the Additional Protocols of 8 June 1977 to the Geneva Conventions of 12 August 1949* (International Committee of the Red Cross with Martinus Nijhoff, 1987), p.1463, paragraph 4821.

34 As to 'ethnic cleansing' see Chapter 7, pp.155–8, below.

35 Y. Sandoz, C. Swinarski and B. Zimmermann (eds), *op.cit*, pp.1456–7, paragraph 4795.

36 See p.277, below.

37 As to the organization of the Tribunal, see Chapter 11, pp.274–7, below.

38 As to the very limited doctrine of military necessity in relation to international armed conflicts, see H. McCoubrey, 'The Nature of the Modern Doctrine of Military Necessity', *Revue de Droit Militaire et de Droit de la Guerre* (1991) XXX, pp.217–42.

39 J. Pictet, *Development and Principles of International Humanitarian Law* (Martinus Nijhoff, 1985), p.88.

40 H. McCoubrey, 'The Idea of War Crimes and Crimes against Peace since 1945, (University of Nottingham Department of Law/Centre for International Defence Law Studies, *Research Papers in Law, No. 2*, June 1992), pp.22–3.

41 See Chapter 11 at pp.275–6.

42 Note, however, that in post-war Japanese judicial consideration of the nuclear attacks upon Hiroshima and Nagasaki in the *Shimoda case* (*Ryuichi Shimoda et al. v The state*), see (1984) *Japanese Annual of International Law*, 212; also R.A. Falk, 'The Shimoda case: A Legal Appraisal of the Atomic Attacks upon Hiroshima and Nagasaki' (1965) 59 *AJIL* , 759, some reliance was placed upon the concept of 'undefended' cities. Whether this is a useful extension of the 1907 'siege'-based concept might be debated.

43 F. Kalshoven, *Constraints on the Waging of War*, 2nd edn (International Committee of the Red Cross, 1991), p.145.

44 T. Meron, *Human Rights in Internal Strife: Their International Protection* (Grotius, 1987), p.14.

6 Humanitarian Assistance and Protection

The inherent difficulties which beset attempts to establish a scheme of humanitarian constraint and regulation in civil wars have been considered above.[1] However, a considerable body of humanitarian provision has developed in this sector which constitutes a 'diluted version of the corresponding provision for international armed conflicts. The substantive treaty provision is found primarily in common article 3 of the four 1949 Geneva Conventions, with extended supplementary provision in 1977 Protocol II Additional to the 1949 Geneva Conventions although, of course, relevant provisions exist in other instruments. The treaty provisions themselves may be clear, but in implementation there are, perhaps inevitably, all too many instances of ambiguity and doubt. Also, institutions with humanitarian concerns in non-international armed conflicts naturally vary in both their aims and methodology.

So far as international humanitarian law *stricto sensu* is concerned, the most important agencies are those of the International Committee of the Red Cross, the Federation of Red Cross and Red Crescent Societies[2] and the various National Red Cross or Red Crescent Societies. Each of these has a distinctive role, or roles, which may be of great importance in cases of civil strife. There are also a variety of other international and private bodies involved in humanitarian relief in non-international armed conflicts. These include the United Nations High Commissioner for Refugees,[3] the French medical charity *Médecins sans Frontières*, a variety of other charitable organizations such as OXFAM and Christian Aid and, in a rather different context, the human rights organization Amnesty International. The purposes and operations of these various bodies are highly diverse although, sharing a fundamental concern with the relief of suffering, they may all be termed 'humanitarian' in a general sense.

The substantive provision of international humanitarian law for non-international armed conflicts is clearly of fundamental importance in this context. In essence it may be considered a minimum 'human rights' derivative[4] from the humanitarian provision for international armed conflicts. However, the process of derivation in a situation which in some ways is radically different necessarily involves substantial amendments in both content and application.

The Development of Humanitarian Provision for Civil Strife

Ideas of constraint upon the freedom of governments in their response to rebellion or armed dissidence are older than might be imagined. The notion was canvassed by Emmer de Vattel as early as 1758:

> Civil war breaks all the bonds of society and of government, or at least suspends the ... effect of them; it gives rise, within the Nation, to two independent parties ... that being so, it is perfectly clear that the established laws of war ... should be observed on both sides in a civil war. ... [Without this] the war will become cruel, terrible and daily more destructive to the Nation.[5]

Such views remain a focus of argument at the end of the 20th century.[6] The present law certainly does not represent the total application of the international *jus in bello* which de Vattel advocated.

Approximately a century later a significant and remarkable development occurred during the American Civil War. After some initial thought that the rebel Confederacy was simply engaged in treason, the Federal Government determined to establish what rules might be applicable to the conflict. The result was the promulgation in 1863 of US Army General Order No 100, better known by the name of its principal author – Francis Lieber – as the *Lieber Code*. This document was to become a precedent for many subsequent attempts to codify the laws of war, but it is notable that it developed in response to a civil war.

The possibilities for action by the International Committee of the Red Cross in non-international armed conflicts were considered at a number of International Red Cross Conferences, in 1912, 1921, 1938, 1957 and 1963. Most notably, the XVIth International Red Cross Conference in London in 1938 resolved, *inter alia*, that

> [The Conference] pays tribute to the work spontaneously undertaken by the International Committee of the Red Cross in ... civil war and relies upon the Committee to continue its activity in this connection

with the co-operation of the National Societies... . [It] requests the International Committee ... to continue the general study of the problems raised by civil war as regards the Red Cross, and to submit the results of its study to the next International Red Cross Conference.[7]

The resolution specifically urged endeavours leading to the application of humanitarian legal principles to the wounded, sick and shipwrecked, to prisoners of war and to medical staff and equipment in civil wars. It also advocated humane treatment of 'political prisoners', protection of non-combatants, transmission of personal information and reuniting of families, and the effective protection of children.[8] These issues are still very much with us, as the painful experiences of 1992–93 in former Yugoslavia all too graphically demonstrated. The particular background to the 1938 resolution of the International Red Cross Conference lay in the disasters of the Spanish Civil War. The outbreak of the Second World War in 1939[9] brought an end to any hope of progress in extending humanitarian provision to civil wars but, with the drafting of the four 1949 post-war Geneva Conventions, the opportunity was taken to produce a brief provision for this type of conflict. This is common article 3 of the four 1949 Geneva Conventions. It is a greatly reduced statement of some of the fundamental principles applied to international armed conflicts, omitting certain important points such as provision for 'prisoner of war' status. This may in some ways be regarded as a miniature codification of minimum humanitarian provisions in civil wars taken from the body of provision for 'international' conflicts.

As a very brief provision, common article 3 of the 1949 Geneva Conventions inevitably leaves a number of matters open to debate. The continuing, and all too extensive, experience of non-international conflict since the Second World War led to the feeling that an extended provision was required, a feeling well expressed in 1974 by Richard R. Baxter:

> The difficulty with the ... Conventions of 1949 is thus that Article 3 does not afford enough protection, and the application of the Conventions as a whole tends to be politically unacceptable and unworkable.[10]

The matter was raised at the International Red Cross Conference in 1965 in Vienna. Following deliberations through the 1970s by a Conference of Government Experts, draft proposals were put forward and, finally, 1977 Protocol II Additional to the 1949 Geneva Conventions was adopted. It is a far more extensive, if still minimum, provision than common article 3 of the 1949 Geneva Conventions – with which it works in parallel rather than supersedes. Although not ideal, it probably does as much as is practically possible; it must always be borne in mind that, if it is to work at all, international humanitarian law must be severely practical. Thus considerable wisdom is contained in the comment made in the International Committee of the Red Cross Commentary upon the Protocol that

> Protocol II constitutes a body of minim rules developed and accepted by the international community as a whole. Although it was not possible to go as far as one might have wished, the consensus ..., apart from its intrinsic value, indicates an undeniable moral weight.[11]

This factor of moral weight should be borne in mind before decrying the seeming limitations of Protocol II. As in many areas of humanitarian provision, the key is perhaps first to secure the effective implementation of the provision that already exists, rather than attempting to draft more elaborate provision which might well not be practical to apply.

The Fundamental Humanitarian Requirements

Both common article 3 of the four 1949 Geneva Conventions and, with greater elaboration, 1977 Additional Protocol II set out a very basic humanitarian regime for the protection of victims of non-international armed conflicts. Common article 3 provides that persons taking no active part in hostilities, including members of armed forces who have laid down arms or been rendered *hors de combat* by sickness, wounds, capture or otherwise, must be treated humanely, 'without any adverse distinction founded on race, colour, religion or faith, sex, birth or wealth, or any other similar criteria'. This requirement of humanity and impartiality is, of course, basic to the whole provision of international humanitarian law, but assumes very particular significance in the fraught context of civil war.

This general requirement is the main substance of common article 3, which then adds certain specific instances of application. Persons protected by common article 3 may not be subjected to violence, including murder, mutilation, cruelty or torture. Hostage taking is prohibited, as is the infliction of humiliating and degrading treatment. In criminal cases sentences may not be passed or executions (and presumably other penalties) carried out without judicial determination in accordance with due process in 'a regularly constituted court, affording all the judicial guarantees which are recognized as indispensable by civilized peoples'. Finally, article 3(2) expressly requires that '[t]he wounded and sick shall be collected and cared for'. This is, of course, a *sine qua non* for their humane treatment and refers back to the historical roots of modern international humanitarian law in the *ad hoc* rescue and relief work of Henry Dunant in the aftermath of the battle of Solferino in 1859.

This rather basic provision, which is expressly stated to be 'minimum' in nature, sets out very simple requirements. It avoids the sensitive questions of 'combatant' status and belligerency, except in so far as it rules out summary executions and requires judicial due process before the imposition of penalties. As established,[12] common article 3 is not intended to be a comprehensive humanitarian provision; indeed, its penultimate paragraph states that other provisions, and if possible the whole of the *jus in bello* applicable to international armed conflicts, should be applied by agreement between the warring parties. A more detailed provision expressly directed to non-international armed conflicts is, however, made by 1977 Protocol II Additional to the 1949 Geneva Conventions.

1977 Additional Protocol II, according to article 1(1), 'develops and supplements' common article 3. Like it, the Protocol is required to be applied

> without any adverse distinction founded on race, colour, sex, language, religion or belief, political or other opinion, national or social origin, wealth, birth or other status, or any other similar criteria....[13]

It will be noticed that this categorization of unlawful 'adverse distinction' is rather more extensive than that set out in common article 3. It includes political and other opinion, as well as national or social origin, and substitutes 'belief' for 'faith' in its reference to religious discrimination. This expansion of terms no doubt reflects the scope of the social and personal divisions in many modern civil conflicts.

After re-establishing these ground rules, the Protocol goes on the make more detailed humanitarian provision. In this respect 1977 Additional Protocol II has a stronger claim to the position of a miniature 'Convention' than does common article 3 of the 1949 Geneva Conventions.

The Standard of Humanity

Structurally, 1977 Additional Protocol II does not follow the same pattern as that established collectively by the 1949 Geneva Conventions. This in part reflects the different juridical nature of international and non-international armed conflicts, not least in the absence of reference to 'prisoners of war' and the particular requirements of their internment. However, certain basic principles are common, and most explicitly so, in the general requirement of humane treatment set out by article 4. The general principle merits quotation. Article 4(1) provides that

> All persons who do not take a direct part or have ceased to take part in hostilities, whether or not their liberty has been restricted, are entitled to respect for their person, honour and convictions and religious practices. They shall in all circumstances be treated humanely, without any adverse distinction. It is prohibited to order that there shall be no survivors.

This paragraph includes several essential protections. Respect for person and honour is obviously basic. However, in a context of civil war, respect for 'convictions and religious practices' clearly takes on special significance. Theodor Meron points out, *inter alia*, that article 4 parallels the requirement of the 1966 UN Covenant on Civil and Political Rights in this respect.[14] Article 18(1) of that 1966 Covenant requires that

> Everyone shall have the right to freedom of thought, conscience and religion. This right shall include freedom to have or adopt a religion of his choice, and freedom ... in public or private, to manifest his religion or belief in worship, observance, practice and teaching.

This principle is also stated by article 18 of the 1948 Universal Declaration of Human Rights and was strongly affirmed by the UN General Assembly Declaration on the Elimination of All Forms of Discrimination Based on Religion or Belief, adopted on 25 November 1981.[15] This Declaration proclaims by article 1(2) that

> No-one shall be subject to coercion which would impair his freedom to have a religion or belief of his choice.

In very many countries not afflicted by civil strife, such guarantees remain much more in the realm of aspiration than reality. Where non-international conflict turns partly upon ideological or religious differences, as is commonly the case, sustaining respect for opposing opinions presents peculiar difficulties.[16]

   Amongst many possible examples, the civil conflict in the Sudan (between the government in the largely Muslim north and dissidents in the largely Christian south) affords an specially painful demonstration of this problem in the 1980s and 1990s. On a smaller, but still very dramatic, scale the repression of the Shi-ite Marsh Arab peoples in Southern Iraq (the Tigris/Euphrates delta) by the Sunni orientated Ba'ath government since 1991 provides further illustration. In that case some attempt was made by Western states to establish protective 'no flight' zones, although with limited effect. In fact, the confessional division here was not the main cause of conflict. In the late 1990s the conflict(s) in former Yugoslavia were also in part marked by confessional divisions within and beyond Bosnia-Herzegovina – between Eastern Orthodox Bosnian Serbs, Roman Catholic Bosnian Croats and Bosnian Muslims. Here the antagonisms were deep-rooted in the complex political and cultural history of south-eastern Europe, reflecting the respective former spheres of influence of the Russian Empire (in effect as a successor to the Byzantine Empire, although Russia never ruled Serbia), the Austro-Hungarian Empire and the Ottoman Empire. Undoubtedly these bitter historical divisions in part underlay the conflicts and certainly embittered their conduct.

Despite well-attested difficulties in implementing the right to freedom of religion or belief (in both peace and war), 1977 Additional Protocol II at least reaffirms this basic human rights requirement. Article 4(2) of the Protocol adds other specific requirements 'without prejudice to the generality' of the overall imperative of humane treatment. Persons protected by the Protocol[17] may not 'at any time and in any place whatsoever' be subjected to violence to life, health or physical well-being (including murder, torture, mutilation or corporal punishment); collective punishment; hostage-taking; terrorist acts; outrages to dignity (including humiliating or degrading treatment, rape, forced prostitution or indecent assault); any form of enslavement; pillage; or threats of any of these. Any such actions would manifestly violate basic humanitarian expectations in the treatment of any person *hors de combat*. Indeed, in many cases they would not be legitimate methods or means of warfare even against active combatants in the *jus in bello* governing international armed conflicts.[18]

The Need for Humanitarian Norms: the Case of Former Yugoslavia

From many points of view the armed conflicts which followed the break-up of the former Federal State of Yugoslavia presented very complex questions. An immediate difficulty arises in how to categorize the conflict and, consequently, how to identify the *jus in bello* norms to be applied. In so far as the conflict(s) involved hostilities between forces of successor-states, they may be considered 'international'. In so far as they involved combat between the Bosnian army and powerful dissident forces inside Bosnia-Herzegovina, with whatever external encouragement and/or material aid, the warfare must be categorized as 'non-international'.[19] In terms of legal technicalities, this issue was largely avoided: at a meeting in November 1991 held under the auspices of the International Committee of the Red Cross, the parties in conflict agreed that the preponderance of the *jus in bello* principles applicable to *international* armed conflicts should be applied.[20] Tragically this undertaking was in many cases of little assistance to the victims of the conflict. Whether 1977 Additional Protocol II or indeed Protocol I (in so far as provision for 'international' conflicts was activated) was applicable raises interesting questions of state succession. Yugoslavia ratified both Additional Protocols on 11 June 1979, subject to a reservation which ceased to have much meaning following the break-up of the state.[21] Whether a successor-state inherits treaty obligations assumed by its predecessor when these do not have customary status is open to discussion.[22] Again, however, this was not of great practical import since most of the gross violations of humanitarian requirements clearly contravened even the minimal provision of common article 3 of the 1949 Geneva Conventions.

Appalling scenes were discovered at internment camps during the conflict. In the course of August 1992 Western newspapers carried reports of terrible conditions in the camps maintained by the Bosnian Serbs at Omarska, Brcko and Trnoplje.[23] Brutality was not the prerogative of any one party: parallel allegations were made by the Bosnian Serbs about camps variously run by Bosnian Croats or Muslims at Sarajevo, Tuzla, Bihac and Zenica.[24] Setting aside the interplay of allegation and counter-allegation, it was the grossly inhumane treatment of internees which proved shocking. Photographs recorded by Western journalists at the camp at Omarska, for instance, indicated all too clearly gross malnutrition and physical maltreatment. At the same time reports were published of torture, beatings and subjection of internees to dog attacks.[25] In light of the international outrage which these revelations occasioned, ICRC delegates were admitted to a number of camps in order to interview those detained.[26] Following these visits the International Committee of the Red Cross, in a significant departure from its normal practice,[27] denounced the conditions in all the camps inspected as breaching the humanitarian requirements of the 1949 Geneva Conventions.[28]

The brutal treatment of internees manifestly violated even the requirements of common article 3 of the 1949 Geneva Conventions, not to mention 1977 Additional Protocol II and/or the 1949 Geneva Conventions in general.[29] Further revelations were subsequently made that interned Bosnian Muslim women had been held by Bosnian-Serb forces in what amounted to 'military brothels' and been repeatedly raped in order to produce 'Serb' children.[30] Such treatment contravened the proscription by the 1949 Geneva Conventions, common article 3, of 'outrages upon personal dignity, in particular humiliating and degrading treatment'. More specifically, of course, 1977 Additional protocol II, article 4(2)(e), expressly prohibits 'outrages upon personal dignity, in particular ... rape, enforced prostitution and any form of indecent assault'. In the context of international armed conflicts, it may be remarked that in relation to persons such as these, protected by 1949 Geneva Convention IV, the same provision is made by article 27 of that Convention.

These specific instances, quite apart from the general outrage of so-called 'ethnic cleansing',[31] painfully demonstrate the need for the most basic humanitarian guarantees in non-international conflicts. They also unfortunately show the difficulty in sustaining the standards thus set. Apart from the arrangements for international judicial investigation, there were some internal proceedings in relation to these violations. Two Bosnian Serb fighters captured by Bosnian government forces were tried in Sarajevo on charges of involvement in the massacre of civilians and of raping civilian internees. One confessed without retraction; the other claimed that he had been coerced into admission. On 30 March 1993 both were convicted and condemned to death, subject to automatic appeal.[32] On a more encouraging note, the very adverse international publicity which these outrages provoked, together with the condemnatory reaction of the International Committee of the Red Cross, did apparently produce improvements in the conditions in internment camps and the 'military brothels' were abandoned.

For the various international agencies committed to seek a resolution to the crisis or to supply humanitarian relief, this conflict presented many difficulties. The supply of humanitarian aid, in the shape of food and medication, to besieged areas under the protective escort of UNPROFOR forces was beset by obstructions. Even when the authorities of the various parties agreed to the passage of humanitarian aid, this permission was frequently not respected by local 'warlords'. At various times attacks reached such a level of intensity that aid supplies were suspended, causing aggravated suffering in the besieged enclaves. Doubts over the extent to which armed force was permissible in terms of the mandate under which UNPROFOR operated led to ill-feeling between UN forces and some of the relief agencies. *Médecins sans Frontières* published a highly critical report entitled *Life, Death and Aid* in November 1993 which went so far as to accuse UN forces in Bosnia of non-compliance with the principles of international humanitarian law and of bargaining with the parties in conflict in order to obtain access for relief convoys at the expense of impartiality.[33] The difficult implications of such bargaining are in principle obvious enough but, in the immediate circumstances, the practical alternatives might seem somewhat less clear.

The Wounded, Sick and/or Shipwrecked

This most basic element of humanitarian provision in warfare is covered briefly by common article 3 of the 1949 Geneva Conventions:

> (1) Persons taking no active part in hostilities, including ... those placed *hors de combat* by sickness, [or] wounds ... shall in all cases be treated humanely ... .
> (2) The wounded and sick shall be collected and cared for.

This bare provision is considerably expanded by articles 7 to 11 of 1977 Additional Protocol II.

A necessary prerequisite for the treatment of the ill or injured is their retrieval and conveyance to an appropriate medical facility. Article 8 of the Protocol requires that 'all possible measures' be taken 'without delay' for search and rescue and also for the protection of the wounded and sick against 'pillage and ill-treatment'. This requirement is essentially the same as that set down for international armed conflicts.[34] No reference is made by the Protocol to the implicit and practical distinctions between the conduct and requirements of search and rescue at sea as compared with those on land.[35] Moreover, since the requirement of article 8 applies 'whenever circumstances permit' to 'all possible measures', such practical exigencies of 'possibility' would be recognized in non-international as in international armed conflicts. Of course, 'impossibility' refers to actual circumstantial preclusion and not to mere disinclination.[36]

The standard of care required for the wounded and sick similarly replicates, in general terms, that set for international armed conflicts. Article 7(2) requires that

> In all circumstances [the wounded and sick] ... shall be treated humanely and shall receive, to the fullest practicable and with the least possible delay, the medical care and attention required by their condition. There shall be no distinction among them founded on any grounds other than medical ones.

Again the question of 'possibility' arises, perhaps more sharply in a civil conflict than in international hostilities. Military field hospitals will not have full facilities; if a country's infrastructure has been massively disrupted, even city hospitals may be operating on a very inadequate resource base. In former Yugoslavia, quite apart from actual bombardments of hospitals, the dearth of basic medical supplies in besieged areas led to such horrors as performing major surgery under local anaesthetic. This would not represent an unlawful act on the part of medical staff, any more than the practical impossibility of carrying out some procedures. The circumstances and causes of such deprivations inevitably raise somewhat different questions. Also, in many situations of internecine conflict, dissident forces are likely to be less well equipped medically than those of the government.

Questions of the availability of facilities apart, the basic provision for 'medical ethics' made by the Protocol rests upon a fundamental plank of international humanitarian law: the criterion for priority in treatment is that of medical need, not factors such as rank or allegiance. The treatment on offer will be determined by practical exigencies. If a patient cannot be saved through the available medical facilities, he or she should clearly be made comfortable. Thereafter neither law nor common sense would suggest that the hopeless case should be pursued whilst a patient who might be saved dies for lack of attention. The ICRC Commentary upon 1977 Additional Protocol II states, in relation to the phrase 'to the fullest extent practicable', that

> It is sometimes materially impossible to immediately provide the care and attention required. The obligation remains to provide it and do so as well and as quickly as possible, given the circumstances.[37]

This merely recognizes the inevitable facts of battlefield or any other medical practice. Of course, recognizing that the impossible cannot be achieved should never slide into wilful neglect. In addition, it is unwise to read the content of one treaty or practice, referring to a given type of situation, into another. The question of wilful neglect is not expressly addressed by 1977 Additional Protocol II; however, 1949 Geneva Convention I provides by article 12, in relation to international conflicts, that

> [the wounded and sick] shall not wilfully be left without medical assistance and care, nor shall conditions exposing them to contagion or infection be created.

The express provision of article 7(2) of 1977 Additional Protocol II would seem to imply a similar requirement, a point worth emphasizing in light of the great bitterness inherent in many civil conflicts.

The often serious problem of inadequate medical supplies and insufficient medical or auxiliary personnel raises slightly broader issues than standards of treatment as such. Here the issue is largely one of relief endeavours by a variety of external agencies in the particularly fraught political context of civil war and analogous conflicts. These questions are considered below.[38]

Protection of Medical Personnel

It is an important strand of 'Geneva' protection for the wounded and sick that medical personnel charged with their care must not themselves either be made an object of attack or be penalized for the professional care they offer their patients. The importance of this will be obvious since medical staff might well be implicated in some circumstances by appearing to 'help the enemy'. Indeed in his *ad hoc* relief endeavours on the battlefield of Solferino, Henry Dunant was fired upon as a suspected partisan whilst assisting the wounded, although his efforts were in fact explicitly impartial. In a non-international armed conflict any imputation of 'treason' – a common suspicion and charge in such circumstances – must be avoided. The point is made clearly by 1977 Additional Protocol II, article 10(1), which provides that

> Under no circumstances shall any person be punished for having carried out medical activities compatible with medical ethics, *regardless of the person benefiting therefrom.* (emphasis added).

Medical personnel could, of course, be punished for malpractice, whoever the patient might be.

A more difficult question is addressed by Protocol II in article 10(3)(4): the acquisition and supply of information about their patients by medical personnel. Clearly, medical personnel could acquire information from patients – whether voluntarily or involuntarily, e.g. whilst in a confused state or under anaesthetic – which might be politically sensitive or damaging to the patient. Paragraph (3) provides that in handling such knowledge, the 'professional obligations' of medics must be respected, i.e. in particular the obligation of confidentiality. Paragraph (4) then adds that refusal or failure to supply such information by medical personnel should not attract penalties. However, both these provisions are made 'subject to national law' which seems largely to undermine their value. Nevertheless, a doctor could not be required to apply improper pressure on a patient in order to extract information.

So far as medical ethics in general are concerned, the requirements already implicit in the standards set for the treatment of patients are made explicit by 1977 Additional Protocol II in articles 9(1)(2) and 10(2). In particular, article 9(2) confirms the exclusively medical criteria used in determining priority of treatment, while article 9(1) stresses that medical staff must be 'respected and protected' and so far as possible assisted in performing their duties.

Article 9(1) of the Protocol requires in its concluding sentence that '[medical and religious personnel] shall not be compelled to carry out tasks which are not compatible with their humanitarian mission'. So far as *medical* personnel are concerned,[39] the matter is emphasized and elaborated by article 10(2) of the Protocol. Medical personnel may neither be compelled to act or to refrain from action in a manner contrary to 'the rules of medical ethics or other rules designed for the benefit of the wounded and sick...'. A somewhat difficult question arises in the definition of 'medical ethics'. In a parallel context, the ICRC Commentary upon 1977 Additional Protocol I refers to the 1949 Declaration of Geneva (a modified form of the Hippocratic Oath), the 1949 International Code of Medical Ethics, the 1962 Rules of Medical Ethics in Time of War and the 1967 Rules to Ensure Aid and Medical Care for the Wounded and Sick Particularly in Time of Armed Conflict.[40] The 1949 Geneva Declaration, as amended at Sydney in 1968, requires a doctor, *inter alia*, to undertake that

> The health of my patient will be my first consideration ... [and] I will not permit considerations of religion, nationality, race, party politics or social standing to intervene between my duty and my patient; I will maintain the utmost respect for human life from the time of conception, even under threat. I will not use my medical knowledge contrary to the laws of humanity.

Such statements cannot be considered more than guidelines, but these requirements accord closely with those expressed in the Conventions and Additional Protocols. The requirements of general medical ethics would probably involve at least this minimum.

Medical Units and Transport

It is stated by article 11(1) of 1977 Additional Protocol II that medical units (meaning hospitals, medical field stations and other similar units) 'shall be respected and protected at all times and shall not be the object of attack'. As in international armed conflicts, protection will cease only in the event of such units being used 'to commit hostile acts, outside their humanitarian function'. Warning must first be given, allowing, 'whenever appropriate', a reasonable time limit before such protection ceases. If a military unit is being fired upon from a hospital or ambulance, the response would obviously be rapid. Attacks upon hospitals in a number of the siege actions in former Yugoslavia were clearly 'indiscriminate' (if not deliberate) bombardments, with no evidence of hostile action emanating from the buildings. Such attacks are unlawful in terms of 1977 Additional Protocol II, as well as under the general provision of 'Geneva' law for international conflicts (which arguably applied in former Yugoslavia).

A more difficult question arose in September 1993 in the context of the UN relief action in Somalia when response was made with automatic weapons to firing from the Benadir Hospital in Mogadishu. Three US servicemen were wounded whilst searching for weapons stocks at a militia stronghold near the hospital. The UN spokesperson, Major David Stockwell, was reported to have stated that the hospital became a target after the assailants had taken up position on its roof and began firing.[41] This action involved UN forces,[42] but the argument advanced by Major Stockwell accurately reflects the general position of Geneva law in such a situation. Obviously any 'collateral' damage to a hospital in such a case should be minimized, and calculated attacks upon patients and medical staff who refrain from hostile action could not be justified.

Protection of Religious Personnel and Freedom of Worship

Where non-international armed conflict, at any level, involves confessional division, intense bitterness may often, though not invariably, prevail. In the context of the 17th-century English civil war, which had a distinct sectarian element, G.M. Trevelyan has remarked, in what is now a somewhat antique text:

> It may perhaps be asked why this war of religion was not distinguished by the cruelty which is the hallmark of other such contests. But it was not a war between two definite creeds.[43]

Even so, as Trevelyan admits, there were sectarian outrages, e.g. at Bolton and Basing and the associated campaigns in Ireland which often involved extreme brutality. Sadly the abuse of religious doctrines or feelings has been at least as prominent in the second half of the 20th century. The armed conflict(s) in former Yugoslavia were, in part, defined by religious divisions, although these communal identities should not be over-emphasized as an origin of conflict. Serious damage was nevertheless inflicted, to some extent deliberately, upon a number of historic churches and mosques as visible symbols of their faith communities. In some non-international conflicts with a religious dimension, the question of freedom of worship becomes a dominant issue. The outrage of so-called 'ethnic cleansing' in former Yugoslavia displayed some element of this,[44] but not so sharply as in Sudan. Sudan comprises an Islamic north which looks culturally to the Middle East and a largely Christian south which looks to sub-Saharan Africa. The conflict has complex origins but is hugely embittered by the religious division and the determination of the northern government to impose Islamic Shari'at law upon the largely unwilling southern population. The combined effects of long-running civil strife and exacerbated famine have produced what Patrick Brogan has described as 'one of the greatest disasters of modern times, a holocaust in the ... heart of Africa which the outside world is powerless to stop'.[45] Religious division has also played some part in the repression of the southern Shi-ite population of Iraq and, at the level of internal disturbances, in the long 'troubles' in Northern Ireland.

Under the heading of 'fundamental guarantees', 1977 Additional Protocol II article 4(1) requires, *inter alia*, that all persons who are or have been rendered *hors de combat* 'are entitled to respect for their ... convictions and religious practices'. This would clearly outlaw religious repression. Religious personnel (a neutral term adopted by the 1977 Additional Protocols which avoids denominational implications) are protected – with medical personnel – by article 9(1) of the Protocol. They are to be respected and protected and to be afforded any available help in performing their duties. Nor can they be compelled to act in any manner incompatible with their humanitarian functions. This again raises the question of information received by such personnel, here most particularly in the context of the confessional. Even the limited provision made by the Protocol for confidential medical information is not extended to information received by religious personnel. Whether the seal of the confessional, applicable in particular to Roman Catholic priests, falls within the heading of matters protected by article 9(1) would seem ambiguous. If an analogy is drawn with the 'national law' exception set out by article 10(3)(4) in relation to information received by medical personnel, this seems unlikely. The validity of such an analogy is itself doubtful.

Attacks, *inter alia*, upon 'places of worship which constitute the cultural or spiritual heritage of peoples, and to use them in support of the military effort' is forbidden by 1977 Additional Protocol II, article 16. Any church, mosque, temple or other religious building must be presumed *ex hypothesi* to form part of the 'cultural or spiritual heritage' at least while 'in use', however disrupted that use may be by hostilities. In this context the destruction of places of worship such as occurred in former Yugoslavia is considered unlawful only when deliberate or indiscriminate. This provision is stated to be without prejudice to the 1954 Hague Convention for the Protection of Cultural Property in the Event of Armed Conflict. Article 19 of that Convention requires that, at the minimum in a non-international armed conflict, the provisions of the Convention relating to respect for 'cultural' property should be applied. Such property includes, by article 1(a), 'monuments of architecture, art or history, whether religious or secular...'. Under article 4(1), 'respect' therefore means neither using such places or objects for purposes likely to expose them to damage in armed conflict nor attacking them. 'Military necessity', e.g., if a church were being used as a base from which to mount attacks, would be an exception under article 4(2).

The protection of religion and religious activity is largely phrased in terms of non-interference with religious observance. In the context of current religious 'fundamentalism',[46] however, the question of freedom *not* to believe or worship must also arise. Although the matter is not addressed expressly, the reference of article 4(1) to respect for 'convictions and religious practices' may reasonably be taken to include protection for those of non-religious conviction.

Respect for the Dead

1977 Additional Protocol II provides by article 8, *inter alia*, that

> Whenever circumstances permit, and particularly after an engagement, all possible measures shall be taken, without delay, to … search for the dead, prevent their being despoiled, and decently dispose of them.

Both public health and respect clearly dictate that the dead should be located and disposed of, although the interpretation of the word 'decent' may vary. 'Geneva' provision for international armed conflicts considers this matter in some detail.[47] The provision of Protocol II is much briefer. It is, as ever, unwise to read too much from the provision for international conflicts into the non-international sphere. Useful guidance is given on this matter by the International Committee of the Red Cross Commentary upon the Protocol which states:

> [The dead] are entitled to be paid their last respects, i.e. they must be decently buried (apart from cases of disposal of the body at sea and cremation) after a religious service, if required.[48]

This interpretation reflects the more detailed provision made for international armed conflicts, but may be accepted as a reasonable view of the essential requirements. Interestingly, interment is assumed to be normal in the 'international' provision, although this is not the case in Hinduism, for instance. It may perhaps be taken that, so far as possible, the obsequies should follow the pattern dictated by the community to which the deceased belonged. This would again be a matter of considerable potential sensitivity in the context of some non-international armed conflicts.

The Protective Emblem and its Use in Non-international Conflict

The protective emblems of the red cross (normally but not necessarily equal armed) or red crescent on a white background is used under 'Geneva' law to indicate personnel, transport, and buildings or other establishments which are protected under the Geneva Conventions and/or Additional Protocols.[49] They refer essentially to medical installations, in particular military medical services. In this primary 'protective' role, the emblem does not confer any additional entitlement to protection. It is always unlawful knowingly to attack a hospital which has not forfeited its protected status. Display of the emblem merely highlights the fact of protected status and helps to preclude dangerous ambiguities or disastrous misunderstandings. In times of peace national Red Cross or Red Crescent Societies may use the emblem in an 'identificatory' role in relation to activities conforming with principles laid down by International Red Cross Conferences. The International Committee of the Red Cross may, of course, use the emblem at all times.

1977 Additional Protocol II provides by article 12 that,

> Under the direction of the competent authority concerned, the distinctive emblem ... shall be displayed by medical and religious personnel and medical units, and on medical transports. It shall be respected in all circumstances. It shall not be used improperly.

This carefully phrased provision seeks to skirt a particularly sensitive question – the use of the neutral term 'competent authority'.

In an international armed conflict, this authority will be 'the competent military authority' of the government in question.[50] In civil conflict, identifying the 'competent authority' may be very problematic in the case of dissident forces. The International Committee of the Red Cross Commentary upon 1977 Additional Protocol II remarks simply that '[t]he competent authority : [f]or those who are fighting against the legal government ... will be the *de facto* authority in charge..'.[51] Government medical services would no doubt render medical aid to injured rebels in their hands, but can hardly be expected to supply medical personnel and units to sustain dissident forces. Equally, the medical facilities controlled by the dissidents may not be adequate; nor will there a recognized 'national' Red Cross or Red Crescent Society be in place to supplement them. To recognize any such putative 'national' society could compromise the international Red Cross organization's neutrality. In conclusion, the emblem may be used for protection by the *de facto* authority, without conceding to it present or future political legitimacy.

Protection of Civilians

In any armed conflict, whether international or non-international, the civilian population will to some extent be at risk from the effects of hostilities. However, a distinction can be drawn between the tragic accidents of war known in the jargon as 'collateral damage' and deliberate attacks upon civilians. Common article 3 of the 1949 Geneva Conventions is silent upon this point, except for the requirement that 'persons taking no active part in the hostilities' are to be treated humanely. Rather more extensive provision is set out by 1977 Additional Protocol II in articles 11 to 18.

The humanitarian protection of civilians in armed conflict inevitably involves a large 'grey area' between the traditional 'Geneva' and 'Hague' sectors of the *jus in bello*. Such matters as constraints upon targeting clearly involve both 'Hague' and 'Geneva' stipulations. Thus, the provision of 1977 Additional Protocol II in relation to the actual conduct of hostilities is more appropriately considered in the context of methods and means of warfare.[52]

However, it may be noted that the protocol by article 13(1) requires that civilians 'shall enjoy general protection against the dangers arising from military operations'. This general requirement is then specifically applied in a number of 'Hague'-type provisions.

Articles 14 and 17 of the Protocol deal with the important questions of starvation of civilian populations and forced population movements – two tactics used extensively in a number of late 20th-century civil conflicts. Article 14 states that '[s]tarvation of civilians as a method of combat is prohibited'. Specifically, destruction (or other deprivation to that end) of foodstuffs, the means of their production including irrigation works, and of drinking water is prohibited. The denial of food to civilians in besieged enclaves in former Yugoslavia was commonplace. The safeguarding of endeavours to get relief supplies through to such areas was indeed a primary original aim of the UNPROFOR forces.[53] Starvation and significant frustration of relief efforts were also major elements in the crisis in the Sudan. Such disasters emphasize the need for such provision, but also raise the ultimate question of maintaining and enforcing the law in the face of determined violation. This is ultimately an issue which combines basic juridical and political questions which go to the heart of what an international legal order means.[54]

The forced movement of civilians in non-international armed conflicts, other than for their own security or for 'imperative military reasons', is prohibited by article 17 of 1977 Additional Protocol II. This has arisen most clearly in the context of 'ethnic cleansing' and is thus considered under that heading.[55]

Humanitarian Relief in Non-International Armed Conflicts

The variety of agencies engaged in different types of humanitarian relief endeavour in non-international, as in international, armed conflicts, are described elsewhere.[56] The work of these organizations is undertaken in a variety of contexts exhibiting markedly different issues and difficulties.

The International Committee of the Red Cross

The International Committee of the Red Cross (ICRC) and its constituent elements have also been described elsewhere.

During armed conflict national Red Cross and Red Crescent Societies are expected to provide humanitarian assistance in accordance with the 1949 Geneva Conventions and, subject to the questions of ratification and status, the 1977 Additional Protocols. Most particularly national Societies will supplement military medical services and resources, their primary function being humanitarian work for the alleviation of suffering in armed conflict. The Federation of Red Cross and Red Crescent Societies[57] acts as a coordinating body between the various national Red Cross and Red Crescent Societies. In armed conflict, however, the ICRC plays the central role in the coordination of international humanitarian relief action. Carl Vandekerckhove puts the point succinctly:

> Emergency assistance in situations of armed conflict mainly belongs to the domain of the ICRC, in the sense that it then, apart from its own activities, also coordinates and supervises possible activities of other Red Cross bodies such as the ... [Federation] or national societies.[58]

In practice, contributions are made by all the elements of the international Red Cross movement. Thus, in the conflicts in former Yugoslavia the ICRC played a considerable role (with others) in visiting internment camps, while the International Federation of Red Cross and Red Crescent Societies worked to coordinate and organize food and medical supplies to areas in overwhelming need. Red Cross statistics published in December 1992 list some 29 national Red Cross and Red Crescent Societies which organized major donations of aid for former Yugoslavia, amounting to more than 1500 truckloads up to that point.[59]

In considering humanitarian action in non-international armed conflicts, a distinction must be drawn between the position of the national Red Cross or Red Crescent Society in the country concerned and that of the International Committee. The 10th International Red Cross Conference in 1921 resolved by Resolution XIV (ii) that,

> In every country in which civil war breaks out, it is the National Red Cross Society of the country which, in the first place, is responsible for dealing ... with the relief needs of the victims; ...[60]

This remains the case. However, the ability and capacity of a national Red Cross or Red Crescent Society actually to assist dissident authorities in a civil war may be very doubtful, for reasons already considered.[61]

In view of the necessity for strict impartiality and neutrality as regards the parties in conflict, involvement in internal conflicts by the International Committee of the Red Cross raises a number of sensitive issues. Does the integrity of the original state still hold? Is the dissident challenge legitimate? The need for assistance may nevertheless be overwhelming, and the ICRC is authorized to 'offer' this. Paragraph 2 of common article 3 of the 1949 Geneva Conventions provides that

> an impartial humanitarian body, such as the International Committee of the Red Cross, may offer its services to the Parties to the conflict.

This, as Marion Harroff-Tavel remarks,

> does not oblige States to accept the ICRC's offer of services. However, they have a duty at least to examine it in good faith and to reply. They may not consider an offer of services as interference in their internal affairs.[62]

The last point, of course, goes to the root of the matter. The action of the ICRC in a country afflicted by civil war can only be consensual; it would be legally, politically and practically impossible to *impose* assistance, although significant moral and diplomatic pressure may be exerted on parties to accept aid. When admitted to an area of internal conflict, the ICRC does not make moral or political judgments as between the parties involved, and its humanitarian counsel will almost invariably remain confidential. The ICRC aims to encourage, facilitate and check upon observance of the 'Geneva' humanitarian principles. This endeavour rests largely upon establishing contact and confidence with all parties; only rarely will the ICRC make public pronouncements – i.e. in cases of flagrant, determined and continuing violations. Even so, it is *conduct* which is denounced; particular judgments may be implicit, but the door must be kept open for continuing humanitarian diplomacy. On 14 August 1992 the ICRC was reported to have publicly condemned the conditions in internment camps run by various parties to the Yugoslav conflict(s).[63] Though not a 'typical' instance, this does serve to illustrate both the discretion and the objective to relieve suffering which are central to the working of the ICRC in armed conflicts.

Once its role has been accepted in a non-international armed conflict, the ICRC may serve a variety of humanitarian functions. The most straightforward, but sometimes very perilous, is relief work in getting food and medical supplies through to beleaguered or otherwise severely deprived populations. The ICRC also seeks to gain admittance to internment camps and other places of detention to check on the treatment of internees. Through the practice of 'interview without witnesses', detainees are enabled to communicate problems and difficulties without fear of reprisal. Where problems of unlawful mistreatment are discovered, the detaining authorities can be pressed to make changes so as to comply with 'Geneva' requirements. Wherever possible the ICRC will also seek to trace missing persons and their fate. Finally, the ICRC will encourage and offer to assist in the dissemination of knowledge and understanding of the requirements of international humanitarian law.

It is a treaty obligation laid upon states under the 1949 Geneva Conventions to disseminate knowledge of the 'Geneva' humanitarian provisions especially, but not only, in courses of military education.[64] The duty of dissemination is general, though 1977 Additional Protocol II provides by article 19 that '[t]his Protocol shall be disseminated as widely as possible'. Dissemination depends on a number of factors, including the availability of trained personnel. Article 4(g) of the Statutes of the International Committee of the Red Cross[65] includes amongst the roles of the ICRC that of working for better understanding and dissemination of the Geneva Conventions. Direct involvement in a national dissemination programme would, of course, depend upon the consent of the state concerned, but this has happened. In 1980 the ICRC received authorization to participate in the instruction of the armed forces in El Salvador in the requirements of international humanitarian law. This was an important task in terms of the brutal confrontation between political left and right which beset El Salvador in a variety of phases from 1979 until 1992. There is some evidence that the dissemination programme did have a positive impact.[66]

Humanitarian Action by the United Nations

The UN has a considerable brief for involvement in circumstances of non-international armed conflict, in particular those which pose a threat to international peace and security. The role of the United

Nations and UN forces in peacekeeping and peacemaking in situations of civil conflict is considered in detail elsewhere.[67] So far as strictly humanitarian assistance is concerned, the UN Charter provides by article 1(3) that the purposes of the organization include '[t]o achieve international cooperation in solving international problems of [a] ... humanitarian character...'. In practice UN forces have been involved in the supply of humanitarian aid in a number of non-international armed conflicts, including supplies to the Kurdish population of Northern Iraq and the guarding by UNPROFOR forces of relief convoys coming under attack in former Yugoslavia. In the latter case, the necessity to use armed force in order to secure deliveries of relief aid, and even then on a far from sufficient scale, raised difficult questions for the direction of the UN forces themselves, which were present under a peacekeeping mandate.[68] Obviously the use of armed force to achieve humanitarian relief raises a further complex dimension in UN military involvement. Reference has already been made to criticism of UN operations in Bosnia in the *Médecins sans Frontières* report, *Life, Death and Aid*.[69] In response to this Lieutenant-Commander Jean Marcotte at UNPROFOR HQ in Zagreb was quoted as follows:

> All we do is try and get aid to the people. You have to work with people on the ground to do that. We are being criticised by everybody – for doing too much, for not doing enough – you name it. We are getting used to being criticised.[70]

Undoubtedly, the practicalities of ensuring aid supplies in such situations do not lend themselves to easy solution.

The potential difficulties were perhaps most clearly illustrated by operations in Somalia. To describe the situation there in 1993 as a non-international armed conflict would be a considerable over-simplification. The Somali government had in effect collapsed, leaving a number of armed factions in contention, with consequent disintegration of the social and economic infrastructure. 'Operation Restore Hope' was originally a US initiative designed to bring in and distribute relief supplies, but was put under UN aegis and inevitably became entangled in factional fighting. The fatal shooting of a number of members of the Pakistani contingent in Mogadishu both symbolized the confusion and deepened UN involvement far beyond anything originally contemplated. Although the humanitarian relief work in the countryside achieved considerable success,[71] the fraught situation in the capital painfully illustrated the danger of humanitarian assistance sliding into full-scale military involvement.

The 'New World Order' proclaimed in the 1990s in the aftermath of international cooperation in the 1990–91 Gulf War and the end of the Northern Hemisphere 'Cold War' has by no means brought an end to conflict, international or non-international. On the contrary, it may be argued that there has instead been a shift of conflict emphasis to new, or in many cases revived, regional and internal tensions. The conflict(s) in former Yugoslavia, deriving from tensions which were ancient in origin and familiar to the political order prior to 1914, could be taken as a particular example. The humanitarian crises engendered by such conflicts in terms of deprivation and displacement of populations are likely to place an increasing burden of humanitarian assistance upon UN agencies which present institutional structures were not designed to provide for. In particular, the rather different dynamics of peacemaking, peacekeeping and humanitarian relief may require more distinct address. This would certainly seem to be a lesson to be derived from both former Yugoslavia and Somalia.

Notes

1   See Chapter 1, pp.18–22.
2   Formerly known as the League of Red Cross and Red Crescent Societies.
3   As to the UNHCR see Chapter 7.
4   For discussion of the relation between human rights and international humanitarian law, see pp.24–5 *ante*.
5   E. de Vattel, *Le Droit des Gens ou Principles du Droit Naturel*, 1758, trans. George D. Gregory (Carnegie Institute, 1916), Book III, Ch. XVIII, p.338.
6   See Chapter 1, pp.18–19.
7   XVIth International Red Cross Conference, London 1938, Resolution XIV. *International Red Cross Handbook*, 12 edn (International Committee of the Red Cross/ League of Red Cross Societies, 1983), p.642.
8   *Ibid*.
9   This is given as the conventionally accepted date of the outbreak of war; in fact hostilities which later became subsumed in the global conflict commenced at least as early as 1937 in the Far East.
10   R.F. Baxter, 'The *Jus in Bello Interno*: The Present and Future Law' in J.N. Moore (ed.), *Law and Civil War in the Modern World* (The Johns Hopkins University Press, 1974), pp.518–36 at p.527.
11   Y. Sandoz, C. Swinarski and B. Zimmermann (eds) (Protocol II section written by S-S. Junod), *Commentary on the Additional Protocols of 8 June 1977 to the Geneva Conventions of 12 August 1949* (International Committee of the Red Cross with Martinus Nijhoff, 1987), p.1336.
12   See p.20 *ante*.
13   1977 Additional Protocol II, article 2(1).
14   T. Meron, *Human Rights in Internal Strife: Their International Protection* (Grotius, 1987), p.25.
15   GA Res. 36/55, 36 UN GAOR (1981).
16   For a general discussion of the problem of religious discrimination in armed conflict, see H. McCoubrey, 'Protection of Creed and Opinion in the Laws of Armed Conflict', *University of Nottingham Research Papers in Law*, No. 7 (February 1993).

17   The same persons as those specified by common article 3 of the four 1949 Geneva Conventions; see p.128 *ante*.
18   This is not to imply that they would be legitimate methods or means in non-international armed conflict. For the methods and means of warfare, see Chapter 5.
19   For discussion of this issue, see H. McCoubrey, 'The Armed Conflict in Bosnia and Proposed War Crimes Trials' (1993) XI *International Relations*, p.411 at pp.414–17.
20   International Committee of the Red Cross Bulletin, *Yugoslavia* (ICRC, 1992).
21   As to ratification and the reservation, see A. Roberts and R. Guelff, *Documents on the Laws of War*, 2nd edn (Oxford University Press, 1989), p.468.
22   As to the 1977 Additional Protocols in this context, see Chapter 1, p.20 *ante*. Useful discussion of the extent to which provisions of the Protocols can claim customary status will be found in C.J. Greenwood, 'Customary Status of the 1977 Additional Protocols' in A.J.M. Delissen and G.J. Tanja, *Humanitarian Law of Armed Conflict Challenges Ahead: Essays in Honour of Frits Kalshoven* (TCM Asser Instituut, Martinus Nijhoff, 1991), pp.93–114.
23   *The Guardian* (London), 7 August 1992.
24   *Ibid*.
25   *The Independent* (London), 7 August 1992.
26   As to the organizations of such 'interviews without witnesses', see below, p.143.
27   See below, p.142.
28   *The Times* (London), 14 August 1992.
29   The War Crimes Tribunal set up to consider breaches of the *jus in bello* in the conflict(s) accepted that the 1949 Conventions were applicable. See Chapter 11, p.275.
30   *The Times* (London), 11 December 1992.
31   See Chapter 7, pp.155–8.
32   *The Daily Telegraph* (London), 31 March 1993.
33   *The Independent* (London), 23 November 1993.
34   See 1949 Geneva Convention I, article 15; 1949 Geneva Convention II, article 18.
35   See H. McCoubrey, *International Humanitarian Law* (Dartmouth, 1990), pp.64–7.
36   For discussion of this in an 'international' context, see J. Pictet, *Development and Principles of International Humanitarian Law* (Martinus Nijhoff, 1985), pp.88–9.
37   Y. Sandoz, C. Swinarski and B. Zimmermann (eds), (S-S. Junod writing upon Protocol II), *Commentary on the Additional Protocols of 8 June 1977 to the Geneva Conventions of 12 August 1949* (International Committee of the Red Cross, with Martinus Nijhoff, 1987), p.1410.
38   See pp.143–4.
39   As to religious personnel, see pp.136–8, *post*.
40   Y. Sandoz, C. Swinarski and B. Zimmermann (eds), *Commentary on the Additional Protocols of 8 June 1977 to the Geneva Conventions of 12 August 1949* (International Committee of the Red Cross, with Martinus Nijhoff, 1987), p.
41   *The Daily Telegraph* (London), 14 September 1993.
42   As to the application of the laws of armed conflict to United Nations Forces, see pp.187–94.
43   G.M. Trevelyan, *England under the Stuarts*, 1904 (Methuen, University Paperbacks, 1965), p.220.
44   See pp.155–8.
45   P. Brogan, *World Conflicts*, 2nd edn (Bloomsbury, 1992), pp.115–16.
46   This term is here used in its general sense of an intolerant political creed being imposed rather than in the technical sense of a literal interpretation of a given

doctrine or texts.

47 See 1949 Geneva Convention I, article 17; 1949 Geneva Convention II, article 20; 1949 Geneva Convention III, article 120; 1949 Geneva Convention IV, article 130.

48 Y. Sandoz, C. Swinarski and B. Zimmermann (eds), (S-S. Junod writing upon Protocol II), *Commentary on the Additional Protocols of 8 June 1977 to the Geneva Conventions of 12 August 1949* (International Committee of the Red Cross, with Martinus Nijhoff, 1987), p.1415.

49 The symbol of the red lion and sun formerly used by the Iranian military medical services is also officially recognized, but this symbol was abandoned at the time of the Iranian Revolution and that country now uses the red crescent emblem. The red star of David emblem *de facto* used by the Israeli military medical services is not officially recognized but was in practice accepted by opposing forces in the various Arab–Israeli wars.

50 1949 Geneva Convention I, article 39.

51 Y. Sandoz, C. Swinarski and B. Zimmermann (eds), (S-S. Junod writing upon Protocol II), *Commentary on the Additional Protocols of 8 June 1977 to the Geneva Conventions of 12 August 1949* (International Committee of the Red Cross, with Martinus Nijhoff, 1987), p.1441.

52 See Chapter 5.

53 See below, pp.191–2.

54 For discussion see Chapter 11.

55 See Chapter 7.

56 See pp.43–4.

57 Formerly known as the League of Red Cross and Red Crescent Societies.

58 Carl Vandekerckhove, 'Cooperation in Assistance: A Red Cross View' in Frits Kalshoven (ed.), *Assisting the Victims of Armed Conflicts and Other Disasters* (Martinus Nijhoff, 1989), pp.167–70 at p.167.

59 'Working together in former Yugoslavia' (International Federation of Red Cross and Red Crescent Societies/International Committee of the Red Cross, December 1992).

60 Full text given in the *International Red Cross Handbook*, 12th edn ((international Committee of the Red Cross, 1983), p.641.

61 See above, p.61.

62 M. Harroff-Tavel, 'Action Taken by the International Committee of the Red Cross in Situations of Internal Violence', May–June 1993, *International Review of the Red Cross*, p.195 at p.202.

63 *The Times* (London), 14 August 1992. As to the news reports which emerged concerning these camps, see above, p.130.

64 See 1949 Geneva Convention I, article 47; 1949 Geneva Convention II, article 48; 1949 Geneva Convention III, article 127; 1949 Geneva Convention IV, article 144; 1977 Additional Protocol I, article 83. These provisions are not 'common', but the same general principle of dissemination is applied in each particular context.

65 The text is set out in the *International Red Cross Handbook*, 12th edn (International Committee of the Red Cross, 1983), at p.422.

66 See *Dissemination* (International Committee of the Red Cross), No. 6, April 1987, pp.3–4.

67 See pp.177–83.

68 For discussion of this in the particular context of Security Council Resolution 770 of 13 August 1992 in relation to humanitarian relief in Bosnia-Herzegovina, see N.D. White, *Keeping the Peace* (Manchester University Press, 1993), pp.254–5.

69 See p.131, *ante*.

70   *The Independent* (London), 23 November 1993.
71   See report in *The Daily Telegraph* (London), 9 October 1993.

7 Refugees and the Problem of 'Ethnic Cleansing'

Refugees, in the general sense of persons displaced by the direct or indirect effects of hostilities, have always been prominent amongst the victims of warfare. This has particularly been the case in civil wars, for the obvious reason that adherents of the defeated faction may have good cause to depart overseas to escape disapprobation or revenge. In the 17th-century English Civil War, first the Royalists led by Queen Henrietta Maria and the Prince of Wales (Charles II) fled from the victorious Commonwealth; then, after the 1660 Restoration, the more determined Commonwealth Republicans fled to sympathetic refuges. This pattern has been replicated many times.

Historically, in the European context, such movements have played an important part in the shaping of communities and identities, and were by no means always seen as unwelcome or 'threatening'. For instance, the Huguenot Protestant refugees who fled from France to England in the reign of Louis XIV played a significant role in the development of the English lace industry. More recently, for a variety of political and economic reasons, actual or potential refugee influxes have come to be regarded more as a 'burden'. Partly as a result of this, a need has been felt both for a finer definition of 'refugee' status and more adequate provision for the entitlements of refugees and their maintenance. In response to the exigencies of refugee crises in the 20th century, both legal definition and institutional provision, notably through the United Nations High Commissioner for Refugees, have been considerably developed.

Defining Refugee Status

Various attempts were made in the era of the League of Nations to define refugees in relation to particular crises. These included the

149

exodus from Russia after the October 1917 Bolshevik Revolution and 'emigration', in particular from the Third Reich prior to 1939 in the face of racially based persecution. These 'definitions' largely rested upon concepts of a lack, or deprivation, of protection by any national government. J.C. Hathaway has remarked on this period of development as follows:

> The purpose of refugee status [thus] conceived in juridical terms is to facilitate the international movement of persons who find themselves abroad and unable to resettle because no nation is prepared to assume responsibility for them.[1]

Such formulations were not, however, adequate as a basis for general criteria of identification required after the Second World War. In the early UN era, the very large numbers of displaced persons generated by the war itself, together with the effects of entrenched ideological divisions which characterized the 'Cold War', rendered the perceived need for definition urgent. From this came the modern and legally limiting concept of 'refugee' status.

The 1946 Constitution of the International Refugee Organization defined a refugee as a person who has left or is otherwise outside his or her homeland or habitual place of residence as a victim of fascist of Axis-allied or collaborationist regimes during the Second World War, Spanish republicans who had fled from the Nationalist regime, or others who had been considered 'refugees' prior to the Second World War for reasons of race, religion, nationality or political opinion.[2] Apart from the more general indicators of the third clause of this formula, the specificity of the definition obviously denies it much continuing importance. However, it is of interest as an indicator of a trend of thought which in due course led to more general definitions.

The primary definition of 'refugees' in modern law is found in the 1951 United Nations Convention Relating to the Status of Refugees. Article 1A(1) of the Convention includes as refugees persons so defined under prior law and Conventions, but then adds by article 1A(2) any person who,

> as a result of events occurring before 1 January 1951 and owing to well-founded fear of being persecuted for reasons of race, religion, nationality, membership of a particular social group or political opinion, is outside the country of his [or her] nationality and is unable or, owing to such fear, is unwilling to avail himself [or herself] of the protection of that country, or who, not having a nationality and being outside the country of his [or her] former habitual residence as a result of such events, is unable or, owing to such fear, is unwilling to return to it.

This definition emphasizes persecution, or the well-founded fear of persecution, as a primary characteristic of the refugee, rather than mere statelessness. However, it is severely limited in applying only to events arising prior to 1 January 1951. Sixteen years later, in the light of the rather obvious point that 'new refugee situations have arisen', a redefinition was set forth in the 1967 Protocol Relating to the Status of Refugees. Article 1(2) of the Protocol consequently provides that a 'refugee' shall for the purposes of the Protocol be defined as by article 1 of the 1951 Convention, but with the date restriction withdrawn.

The essential requirement of the 1951/1967 definition is absence or exclusion from one's country of habitual residence and unwillingness or inability to return to or receive protection from that country, these conditions being occasioned by a well-founded fear of persecution. Absence and/or exclusion from the 'refugee's' country or habitual residence occasions little or no conceptual difficulty, being based on fact. 'Well-founded' fear of 'persecution' is a more problematic criterion, since both aspects require some form of interpretation.

The 1951/1967 definition lists five relevant types of persecution, founded upon race, religion, nationality, membership of a given social group or political adherence. The events of the 1930s and 1940s, with particular reference to the Third Reich, are manifest in this formulation, but the spectrum is sufficiently broad to cover most likely victims of selective persecution. In terms of the so-called 'ethnic cleansing' in former Yugoslavia,[3] the 1951 definition of 'persecution' is still relevant, though the categories of persecution(s) inflicted may be inaccurate. The forced population movements were not 'ethnically' based since the people involved are all South Slavs. The divisions are not racial but cultural and historic, in part reflecting divergent confessional 'badges' which have ancient roots in the collision of empires and spheres of interest in the south Balkans over many centuries. That 'ethnic cleansing' here embodies religious, and probably national, persecution may be strongly disputed.

The problem of 'national' persecution, however, raises delicate questions in any context of non-international armed conflict, and especially in relation to claims to national self-determination. This concept is undergoing some revision as the post-1945 definitions founded upon decolonization become increasingly irrelevant. International instruments, including the UN Charter[4] and the 1966 International Covenants on Economic, Social and Cultural Rights and on Civil and Political Rights,[5] refer, rather unhelpfully, to 'all peoples' but with a clear emphasis upon decolonization. Indeed, the right to self-determination is hardly considered in other contexts, as M. Shaw explains:

an international law concept of what constitutes a people for these purposes has been evolved so that the 'self' in question must be determined within the accepted colonial territorial framework. Attempts to broaden this have not been successful and the U.N. has always strenuously opposed any attempt at the partial or total disruption of the ... territorial integrity of a country.[6]

Obviously, no-one wishes to see the international order collapse as states fragment. In current circumstances, however, the established emphasis on territorial integrity is of limited usefulness.

Still greater difficulty arises with the concept of persecution founded upon membership of a 'social group'. G.S. Goodwin-Gill remarks in this context that

A fully comprehensive definition is impracticable ..., but ... [i]n determining whether a particular group of people constitutes a 'social group' within the meaning of the [1951] Convention, attention should ... be given to ... uniting factors such as ethnic, cultural, and linguistic origin; education; family background; economic activity; shared values, outlook, and aspirations.[7]

The 'social group' category is, in short, something of a 'catch-all' listing; however, by implying a cohesive group identification, it is somewhat analogous with the more specific categories preceding it in the definition.

As to the nature of 'persecution' as such, its essence lies in sustained and severe detrimental action against victims founded upon the criteria enumerated above. The actual parameters of 'persecution' for this purpose are open to some debate. A restrictive view would limit the concept to significant threat to life or liberty, whereas more 'liberal' commentators might accept lesser, but sustained, forms of harassment. In the context of the Indo-Chinese 'Boat People', Chooi Fong has written that

Although there is general agreement that a threat to life or freedom on one of the grounds stated will always constitute persecution, over and above that there is no consensus. ... [T]he term has been left undefined in the Convention, and ... [a] flexible concept which might be applied to new circumstances as they arose is perhaps what was envisaged.[8]

Thus, in the practical jurisprudence of refugee status, significant definitional lacunae exist so far as 'lesser' forms of persecution are concerned. This inevitably means that states can choose from a broad range of options in the determination of refugee status, presumably not always in the intended spirit of the 1951 Convention and 1967 Protocol.

Beyond the question of 'persecution' lies that of 'well-founded fear' to which a claimant to refugee status under the 1951/1967 definition must suffer. The obvious question is whether this criterion can be judged objectively or only subjectively. The qualifying term 'well-founded' clearly suggests that the 'fear' in question must have a substantial basis. This question was considered in an important English case, *R v Secretary of State for the Home Department, ex parte Sivakumaran (UN High Commissioner for Refugees intervening)*[9] which concerned six Tamil nationals of Sri Lanka who sought asylum as refugees in the UK on the basis of fear of persecution if they returned home. The Secretary of State for the Home Office denied their application because the facts known to him appeared not to suggest a likelihood of persecution. The House of Lords held that the test was indeed objective and that the Secretary of State had been entitled to reach the decision he did; he was also entitled to consider circumstances unknown to the claimants where that was appropriate. This decision allowed an appeal from the conclusion of the Court of Appeal that a person who genuinely feared persecution fell within the 1951/1967 definition, as embodied in the United Kingdom Immigration Rules as amended in 1983, even if the fear was actually erroneous. In the House of Lords, Lord Keith of Kinkel stated in judgment that

> the question is what might happen if he [a person claiming refugee status] were to return to the country of his nationality. He fears that he might be persecuted there. Whether that might happen can only be determined by examining the actual state of affairs in that country. If that examination shows that persecution might indeed take place then the fear is well-founded. Otherwise it is not.[10]

This objective approach seems to accord with the language of the Convention. It may thus be suggested as a general conclusion, provided, of course, that the relevant state authorities themselves proceed objectively and in good faith.

The British *Sivakumaran* test, however, raises certain potential difficulties on other grounds. J.C. Hathaway points out the additionally restrictive implications of the further remark of Lord Keith of Kinkel – that the demonstration of relevant 'fear of persecution' rests upon 'a reasonable degree of likelihood'.[11]

In the same case, Lord Goff of Chieveley remarked that

> [t]he true object of the Convention is not just to assuage fear, however reasonably and plausibly entertained, but to provide a safe haven for those unfortunate people whose fear of persecution is in reality well founded. ... [In agreement with Lord Keith of Kinkel] there has to be demonstrated a reasonable degree of likelihood of ... persecution for a

> Convention reason; indeed I understand the submission ... that there
> must be a real and substantial risk of persecution, to be consistent
> with that interpretation.[12]

This in no way refutes the probability test, but does add a useful
gloss to the formulation. Other jurisdictions have not chosen to follow this line of analysis;[13] an undue emphasis upon assessments of
probable persecution could tend to frustrate the humanitarian objectives of the Convention. The answer perhaps lies in a combination of
probability (a fear which is entirely unrealistic is surely not 'well-
founded') with the substantiated nature of the fear of persecution,
which Lord Goff's judgment in the *Sivakumaran case* might reasonably be read to imply.

Refugee Status Arising from Non-international Armed Conflicts

A person fleeing from civil war who seeks to establish 'refugee'
status must satisfy the same broad criteria as any other claimant.
Needless to say, non-international armed conflict will not uncommonly generate outright persecution, as in the so-called 'ethnic cleansing' in former Yugoslavia.[14] In the context of extended unrest in Sri
Lanka in the 1980s and 1990s, Lord Keith of Kinkel in *R v Secretary of
State for the Home Department, ex parte Sivakumaran* made brief reference to the question of civil war and refugee status. He remarked in
particular that

> for a considerable period of time Sri Lanka, or at least certain parts of
> that country, have been in a serious state of civil disorder, amounting
> at times to civil war. The authorities have taken steps to suppress the
> disorders and ... [t]hese steps, together with the activities of the
> subversives, have naturally resulted in painful and distressing experi-
> ences for many [innocent] persons... . The Secretary of State has ...
> expressed the view that army activities aimed at discovering and
> dealing with Tamil extremists do not constitute evidence of persecu-
> tion of Tamils as such.[15]

The view stated by Lord Keith seems to be in line with the proposition that civil war may generate, but is not itself a guarantee of,
refugee status. It may be added that the most recent relevant legislation in the UK at the time of writing, the Asylum and Immigration
Appeals Act 1993, provides by section 2 that,

> Nothing in the immigration rules (within the meaning of the 1971 Act)
> shall lay down any practice which would be contrary to the Conven-
> tion.

The Convention referred to is, of course, by section 1, the 1951 Convention.

An example of the type of situation which generates claims to refugee status occurred in former Yugoslavia. As the *Sivakumaran* case implies, however, the situation in Sri Lanka raised other and in some ways yet more complex issues. In may cases 'refugee' status is denied to those who are fleeing from the consequences of armed conflict because they do not fit the model as victims of discriminatory persecution. Many of the so-called 'Boat People' leaving Vietnam (for a variety of reasons) in small boats, at great risk from piratical depredation in the South China Sea, were held not to be genuine refugees, but economic migrants. From Hong Kong, a major destination for many 'Boat People', small numbers were resettled in other countries, but many were eventually deported back to Viet Nam, having failed to prove their refugee status.[16]

Any application for 'refugee' status has to be considered on an individual basis in the light of relevant facts, although the burden of proof may seem easier to satisfy in some instances than in others. However, where members of a particular community are singled out for adverse treatment, as opposed to being placed at risk by the mere fact of hostilities, a claim to refugee status may indeed by founded upon the exigencies of non-international armed conflict.

The Problem of 'Ethnic Cleansing'

During the armed conflicts which accompanied the break-up of the former Federal Republic of Yugoslavia, international concern was generated by forced population movements which came to be known by the term 'ethnic cleansing'. The use of the term 'cleansing' in such a context is highly offensive: the use of the term 'ethnic' was simply inaccurate. The background to this horror merits brief examination. The Kingdom of Yugoslavia, which became a Republic after the Second World War, was a product of the settlement which concluded the First World War. It brought together around the nucleus of the Kingdom of Serbia a group of South Slav territories with vastly different histories and traditions, establishing the Serbian Karageorgevic monarchy over the whole enlarged area. Within a much more complex picture, three broad groupings may be discerned. These are largely defined by culture and religious or denominational persuasions, which themselves arose largely from the interaction of three powers whose spheres of influence met in South Eastern Europe. Eastern Orthodox Serbia derives its tradition ultimately from the East Roman (Byzantine) Empire and was later very much in the sphere of influence of the Russian Empire. Roman Catholic Croatia was influenced rather

by the Austro-Hungarian Empire (prior to 1805 officially the Holy
Roman Empire). Bosnia became an Islamic territory under the influence of the Ottoman Empire. Even prior to Islamic conversion, however, the Bosnians had a marked confessional identity in that they
tended to a Cathar persuasion which was condemned as heretical by
the Church.[17] The divisions in the area are thus of long historical
provenance. The pre-1939 crisis in Yugoslavia resulted, in part at
least, from the factionalism arising amongst the historic groupings in
the country. From 1921 to 1931 the Constitution was abolished whilst
King Alexander took on autocratic powers; a limited constitutional-
ism was resumed in 1931 but the King was assassinated whilst visiting Marseilles in 1935. The divisions of the country considerably
exacerbated the experience of occupation during the Second World
War, but peace and apparent stability were restored – at a price –
under the communist government of Marshal Tito. The recent re-
fragmentation of the country in many ways merely revived bitter
divisions which long pre-dated the state of Yugoslavia itself.

The divisions of former Yugoslavia thus lie, not in ethnicity, but in
a combination of divergent creeds and cultural traditions in a political context which exploded into warfare. In areas of culturally mixed
population, members of minority traditions became objects of suspicion to their neighbours. When that issue became tied to territorial
claims, the scene was set for forced population movement and other
forms of persecution, with the frontiers of the components of the
former Federal Republic being violently redrawn. The Muslim population of Bosnia-Herzegovina, the original scene of conflict, were the
principal but not the only victims of 'ethnic cleansing'. The expul-
sions were carried out by combinations of threatened and actual
physical brutality, with the property of those expelled invariably
seized.

There can be no doubt of the unlawfulness of 'ethnic cleansing' in
the Yugoslav context, the parties having agreed in November 1991, at
a meeting held under the aegis of the International Committee of the
Red Cross, that the broad legal principles applicable in international
armed conflicts should be applied.[18] They were not, of course, but
the undertaking nonetheless remained. 1949 Geneva Convention IV,
relative to the protection of civilians in armed conflict, provides by
article 49 that,

> Individual or mass forcible transfers, as well as deportations of pro-
> tected persons from occupied territory ... are prohibited, regardless of
> motive.

The only limited exception is made for cases involving 'the security
of the population or imperative military reasons'; even then, return

must be permitted as soon as possible. The practice of 'ethnic cleansing' in many cases constituted 'mass forcible transfer'. The question of genocide also arises. According to Article 11 of the 1948 UN Convention on the Prevention and Punishment of the Crime of Genocide, this is 'committed with intent to destroy in whole or part, a national, ethnical, racial or religious group'. The acts then listed include 'causing bodily or mental harm to members of the group'. Whether acts of 'ethnic cleansing' were calculated to 'destroy' rather than displace the victim population is not entirely certain in many cases. Nonetheless the Commission of Experts set up under Security Council Resolution 780 (1992) to consider violations of international law in former Yugoslavia stated in an interim report that 'such acts could also fall within the meaning of the Genocide Convention'.[19] There is considerable evidence that massacres of victim groups also took place,[20] the international legal response to which raises important and delicate questions.[21]

Common article 3 of the 1949 Geneva Conventions applicable to non-international armed conflicts is somewhat more equivocal than are the international norms. It does, however, state by paragraph (1) that

> persons taking no active part in the hostilities ... shall in all circumstances be treated humanely, without any adverse distinction founded on race, colour, religion or faith, sex, birth or wealth, or any other similar criteria.

It would seem hard to reconcile this provision with 'ethnic cleansing' as applied to militarily inactive civilians. It may usefully be added that the more extensive provision made for non-international armed conflicts by 1977 Protocol II Additional to the 1949 Geneva Conventions[22] includes provision by article 17(1) that

> the displacement of the civilian population shall not be ordered for reasons related to the conflict unless the security of the civilians involved or imperative military reasons so demand. ...

In neither the 'international' nor the non-international' provision could 'imperative military reasons' be taken to include a belligerent policy of land seizure.[23]

The unlawfulness of 'ethnic cleansing' as such leaves open the question of the potential refugee status of its victims. In terms of the legal definition of a refugee set out above, it may be doubted whether a person who had suffered 'ethnic cleansing' but had succeeded in reaching the territory of his or her government of allegiance would actually be a refugee. However, such a person would still be a victim of unlawful action. Refugee status might most likely arise in the case of someone who had become trapped in a territory where they were at risk of 'ethnic cleansing'. Here enormous difficulties emerge beyond the narrow context of refugee law. Some of the evacuation convoys in former Yugoslavia arranged under UN aegis involved the liberation of beleaguered populations who had become trapped in enclaves surrounded by hostile forces. The humanitarian necessity for such action must seem self-evident, but such issues are delicate in a context of 'ethnic cleansing'. In the application of *de jure* and *de facto* norms, humanitarian impulses must be the yardstick: to leave people to suffer persecution would patently be unacceptable.

The Status of 'Internal Refugees'

'Ethnic cleansing' leaves open the question of those who are displaced but trapped in territories where they remain at risk. The general definition of 'refugee' status outlined above requires, *inter alia*, that claimants should be outside their 'home territory. However displaced people may be unable to leave the national territory due to economic circumstances or external military factors. As J.C. Hathaway once remarked,

> While ... the world community had a legitimate right to set standards ..., it was unthinkable that refugee law would intervene in the territory of a state to protect citizens from their own government. The best that could be achieved ... was the sheltering of such persons as were able to liberate themselves from the territorial jurisdiction of a persecutory state.[24]

This statement refers to the 1950s when the modern definition of refugee status was developed; Hathaway suggests that it reflected less the inherent status of 'refugees' than the practicality of implementing international legal norms.[25] In terms of modern human rights law, it is theoretically possible to protect persons inside their own territory being persecuted by their own state. Practical interventions in such cases are rare, however, and will normally only occur in unusual and complex circumstances.

A significant instance might be seen in the fate of the Kurdish people of northern Iraq and the Shi-ite Marsh Arabs after the 1990–91 Gulf conflict. Long subject to repression, chemical attacks were made against the town of Malbja on the Iraq/Iran border in March 1988[26] and later upon the Hammar Marshes in the south.[27] In the early 1990s attempts were made under UN aegis to extend some protection to both the Kurdish and Marsh Arab populations. These included zones of protection and 'no-fly' zones which were of varying effectiveness.[28] Of course, such protection arose only in the context of Iraq's defeat in the *international* armed conflict following its invasion of Kuwait.

That said, the international community does take some account of 'internal refugees' in somewhat less 'exceptional' circumstances. The UN High Commissioner for Refugees has from time to time been enabled by the UN to provide relief and assistance for people who were not in the strictly legalistic sense 'refugees'.[29] In a statement made on 3 March 1993 the UN High Commissioner for Refugees, Sadako Ogata, stated significantly that,

> Like refugees, the internally displaced are in a very vulnerable situation. ... [T]hey need protection, assistance, and a solution to their plight. Although UNHCR does not have a general mandate for the internally displaced, the interrelationship between their situation and that of refugees has meant UNHCR is frequently called upon to assume responsibilities on their behalf, particularly ... where the need for humanitarian assistance is coupled with a need for protection... .[30]

Humanitarian relief may also be supplied by other agencies, such as the International Committee of the Red Cross, in appropriate circumstances irrespective of claims to refugee status.

Persons Not Entitled to Refugee Status

The 1951 Convention Relating to the Status of Refugees by article 2F excludes from the status of refugee,

> any person with respect to whom there are serious reasons for considering that:
> (a) he has committed a crime against peace, a war crime, or a crime against humanity, as defined in the international instruments drawn up to make provision in respect of such crimes;
> (b) he has committed a serious non-political crime outside the country of refuge prior to his admission to that country as a refugee;
> (c) he has been guilty of acts contrary to the purposes and principles of the United Nations.

This apparently clear provision actually disguises certain difficulties. The first exclusion, relating to 'war crimes' etc., is phrased somewhat ambiguously by reference to unspecified 'international instruments'. The matter could be considered politically sensitive in that the formulation adopted in point (a) is taken straight from article 6 of the 1945 Charter of the International Military Tribunal at Nuremberg. Article 6(b) defined such crimes as violations of the laws or customs of war. Such violations shall include, but not be limited to, murder, ill-treatment, or deportation to slave labour or for any other purpose of civilian population or in occupied territory, murder or ill-treatment of prisoners of war or persons on the seas, killing of hostages, plunder of public or private property, wanton destruction of cities, towns or villages, or devastation not justified by military necessity.

This list was compiled in reaction to the circumstances of the Second World War and, as the saving clause makes clear, was not intended to be either definitive or comprehensive. However serious the crimes listed in the article 6 formulation, they hardly represent an adequate definition. In particular it should be remembered that 'violations' in general might include the most detailed of technical minutiae which would sit very oddly as 'war crimes' in the present sense.

A better guide, although one not expressly taken up by the drafters of the 1951 Convention, might be the concept of 'grave breaches' set out in the four 1949 Geneva Conventions and supplemented (with much material of relevance to methods and means of warfare as well as to strictly 'humanitarian' provision) by 1977 Additional Protocol I. It has been remarked elsewhere that

> It seems reasonable to conclude that the modern concept of war crimes embraces a flexible grouping of 'serious' breaches of the laws and customs of warfare with the 'Geneva' (including major 'Hague' elements) category of 'grave breaches' as an irreducible core but not a comprehensive definition.[31]

This is, however, a view expressed primarily in relation to international armed conflicts. Neither common article 3 of the 1949 Geneva Conventions nor 1977 Additional Protocol II make reference either to 'war crimes' or to 'grave breaches'. Where the application of the norms of 'international' armed conflict has been agreed in principle (as in former Yugoslavia), this exclusion of war criminals would become more obviously useful, relating, for example, to potential defendants in any 'international' trials.

Crimes against humanity and such crimes as genocide may also arise in the context of non-international armed conflicts. Persons 'seriously' suspected of involvement in such crimes would, under the terms of the 1951 Convention, not be entitled to 'refugee' status, should they seek it.

The reference in article 2F(c) to the purposes of the UN might, in principle, be raised in connection with certain actions relating to civil conflict. The rather uncertain implications of this exclusion suggest, however, some considerable caution in its practical interpretation.

Other provisions are made for loss of refugee status, relating primarily to changes in the circumstances which generated the original claim.

The Right of Non-refoulement

Amongst the most vital protections needed by refugees is a guarantee that they will not be forced to return to the original threatening situation from which they fled. This guarantee is the essence of the principle of *non-refoulement* which G.S. Goodwin-Gill has defined thus:

> broadly, that no refugee should be returned to any country where he or she is likely to face persecution or danger to life or freedom.[32]

Article 33 of the 1951 Convention Relating to the Status of Refugees provides that,

> (1) No Contracting Party shall expel or return ... a refugee in any manner whatsoever to the frontiers of territories where his [or her] life or freedom would be threatened on account of his [or her] race, religion, nationality, membership of a particular social group or political opinion.
> (2) [This benefit is excluded for a refugee] whom there are reasonable grounds for regarding as a danger to the security of the country in which he [or she] is, or who, having been convicted by a final judgment of a particularly serious crime, constitutes a danger to the community of that country.

This provision has come to be regarded as an expression of customary principle. Goodwin-Gill comments further:

> Article 33 ... is of a 'fundamentally norm-creating character' in the sense used by the International Court of Justice in the *North Sea Continental Shelf* cases [ICJ Rep. 1969, p. 3 at p.42]. That *refoulement* may be permitted in exceptional circumstances does not deny this premiss; instead in indicates the boundaries of discretion.[33]

The established nature of the right of non-refoulement may now readily be accepted, subject to certain important formal and informal limitations. As to the former, the wording of article 33(2) of the 1951 Convention suggests that the 'danger to security' should emanate from the refugee him or herself, rather than from threats made by the state from which refuge is being sought. Another question is at what point the principle of non-refoulement actually becomes operative.

Many states take the view that the principle will only arise once a person claiming refugee status has been admitted to the country as a refugee. Even the meaning of 'presence in the country' may be debated, as in the case of a person at airport immigration who is physically in the territory but with no legal right to be there. As states increasingly try to restrict refugee admission, this is likely to be a growing issue of concern for the United Nations High Commissioner for Refugees. The question of non-refoulement, of course, arises at the point of determining to what territory the non-admitted claimant to refugee status should be returned.

Development of International Refugee Organizations

Institutional concern for refugees has developed very much in parallel with the general growth of the modern international institutional infrastructure, the two principal stages being the League of Nations era in the inter-war years and the UN era since 1945. The proximate impetus for development lay in the Russian Revolution of October 1917,[34] which produced many refugees fleeing to the west. To cope with this influx the Council of the League of Nations in 1921 appointed Dr Fridtjof Nansen to be High Commissioner for Russian Refugees, with the general duties of identification and coordination of relief and resettlement endeavours. Many more refugees in the League of Nations era emerged from the dismantling of the Ottoman Empire and the reshaping of its former territories. By 1929 the High Commissioner had responsibility for a broad range of refugee groupings. Later a proliferation of organizational offices followed. The coming to power of the Nazi Party in Germany in 1933 very soon began to produce refugees as a result of both ethnic and political persecution within the Reich[35] and a designated office was created in 1933 to deal with these people. Finally, immediately before the Second World War, the Evian Conference agreed to set up the Intergovernmental Committee on Refugees.

The massive disruptions of the Second World War and the political and racial persecution which occurred in many territories produced enormous numbers of displaced people. All of them needed to be identified, provided for and either repatriated or resettled as the case might demand. The immediate post-war chaos is in some ways instructive. Of the many displaced persons at the end of the Second World War, most were simply that; some, however, were actual suspected war criminals attempting to evade detection amongst the crowd. The problem received prominent media attention in 1987 when the former SS Officer Klaus Barbie was arrested and returned to France to trial in relation to serious charges arising from the Nazi occupation of Lyons during the Second World War. It seems that after the War he had left Germany under the false name of Klaus Altmann upon papers issued by the Allied Forces High Commission in Munich. Subsequently the International Committee of the Red Cross issued travel documents in this assumed name which he used to enter South America.[36] In response to criticism in 1987 the ICRC pointed out that in the context of the huge numbers of displaced persons seeking travel documentation at that time,

It was impossible ... to verify the statements of those applying for travel documents. The ICRC believes that certain risks had to be accepted in the interests of the vast majority.[37]

Other bodies, including the Vatican, issued travel documents to refugees. The Holy See issued two forms of such documentation: proper passports issued to citizens of the Vatican state and persons travelling on the Vatican's business, and travel documents issued by the Vatican's Refugee Office. It is clear that in this context, too, errors were made.

There were a number of senior Nazis who actually or very nearly escaped during the confusion. The most senior, perhaps, was the Reichsführer SS, Heinrich Himmler who, rather poorly disguised, attempted to slip through Allied lines. As Ann and John Tusa put it,

while he was trying to work through Allied lines into Bavaria on 3 May [1945] he was captured at a British control point. He remained at a British interrogation centre for several weeks without being recognized until he ... decided to announce his identity. Soon afterwards Himmler bit on the ... capsule in his mouth and died.[38]

Many other figures actually succeeded in escaping under the guise of 'refugees' or displaced persons, including Adolf Eichmann, Dr Josef Mengele and, a matter of endless debate, possibly Martin Borman.[39] Such people were certainly 'in fear' but hardly of 'persecution'[40] and thus could not be considered as 'refugees'. Certainly, there was no intention to harass genuine claimants to refugee status.

In the Second World War context, the problem of displacement of populations was initially addressed by the creation of a United Nations Relief and Rehabilitation Administration (UNRRA) and, in 1946, the more specifically focused International Refugee Organization to tackle specific problems of the mid-1940s. 'Refugees' were defined in terms of those qualifying for such status prior to the Second World War by reason of race, religion, nationality or political opinion, together with victims of Nazi, Fascist or collaborationist regimes as well as Spanish Republicans and other victims of the Falangist government in Spain.[41] The latter group was not required to satisfy the criteria for general international refugee status. It will be noticed that, apart from the final general pre-war category, this list was limited to victims of the former enemy regimes and the Spanish nationalist government. For political reasons, no reference was made to victims of Stalinism, for instance, unless they were 'refugees' prior to 1939.

In this context considerable controversy has arisen over the repatriation of Axis prisoners of war who had fought against the Communist authorities in the former Soviet Union or against Marshal Tito's Partisans in former Yugoslavia and who, in many cases, were executed upon arrival home. This is more a question of the law governing prisoners of war than refugee law *stricto sensu*, but one which merits brief attention. 1949 Geneva Convention III relative to Prisoners of War[42] provides by article 118 that '[p]risoners of war shall be released and repatriated without delay after the cessation of active hostilities'. Where a genuine fear of persecution exists and the criteria for 'refugee' status are met, the terseness of article 118 should not condemn anyone to automatic repatriation. Indeed, it has been remarked elsewhere that 'such a reading ... flies in the face of the tenor of all "Geneva" provisions'.[43] (Of course, prisoners specifically suspected of war crimes and equivalent crimes would raise rather different considerations.) It may be added that in the context of the 1990–01 Gulf conflict, where some Iraqi prisoners did apparently fear to return to their country, considerable sensitivity was shown by the Coalition Powers in dealing with this matter, taking into account the expressed wishes of the prisoners of war themselves.[44]

Finally in 1949 the General Assembly voted to establish the Office of the United Nations High Commissioner for Refugees (UNHCR).[45] The UNHCR Statute was approved in the following year.[46] It was originally set up for a three-year period but, in light of the continuing large numbers of refugees, it has since been perpetuated for a series of five-year periods, most recently by General Assembly Resolution 47/104 of 1992, continuing the office until 31 December 1998.

The United Nations High Commissioner for Refugees

The UNHCR is a subsidiary body of the UN established under article 22 of the UN Charter which provides that '[t]he General Assembly may establish such subsidiary organs as it deems necessary for the performance of its functions'. The general functions thus assigned are set out by the 1950 UNHCR Statute, paragraph 1. This states that

> The United Nations High Commissioner for Refugees, acting under the authority of the General Assembly, shall assume the function of

providing international protection, under the auspices of the United Nations, to refugees ... and of seeking permanent solutions for the problem or refugees by assisting Governments and, subject to the approval of the Governments concerned, private organisations to facilitate the voluntary repatriation of such refugees, or their assimilation within new national communities.

This is a broad remit for action, which sets out the general functions of the High Commissioner, but which manifestly requires more detailed specification.

This is supplied by paragraph 8 of the 1950 Statute which sets out nine specific ways in which the High Commissioner is required to make provision for the protection of refugees. These are (a) promotion of international covenants for refugee protection, (b) promotion of ameliorating measures through special agreements with governments, (c) assisting government and private efforts to promote voluntary repatriation or assimilation, (d) promoting admission of refugees, (e) securing permission for transfer of assets, (f) obtaining information from governments upon numbers of refugees and applicable laws, (g) liaising with governments and relevant inter-governmental agencies, (h) maintaining appropriate contact with private concerned organizations, and (i) facilitating coordination of the endeavours of such organizations. Paragraph 9 adds the inevitable general provision of such further activities, including repatriation and resettlement, as the UN General Assembly might determine within the resources available.

The High Commissioner him or herself is, pursuant to paragraph 13 of the 1950 Statute, nominated by the Secretary General and approved by the General Assembly. In the performance of his or her functions, the High Commissioner is subject to two particular forms of guidance and direction. Paragraph 1 of the 1950 Statute provides that,

in the exercise of his [or her] functions, more particularly when difficulties arise, and for instance with regard to any controversy concerning the international status of these persons, the High Commissioner shall request the opinion of the advisory committee on refugees if it is created.

Such a committee was in fact created in 1951, by reference to paragraph 4 of the Statute, and has passed through several stages of development. UN General Assembly Resolution 1166(XII) of 26 November 1957 established the Executive Committee of the High Commissioner's Programme, which normally meets annually to approve UNHCR's projected programmes and financial organization. Its membership is determined by the UN Economic and Social Council

(ECOSOC) and is intended to reflect geographical diversity amongst those states known to have an interest in refugee assistance programmes.

Paragraph 3 of the Statute also provides that '[t]he High Commissioner shall follow policy directives given him [or her] by the General Assembly or the Economic and Social Council'. In practice, the role of ECOSOC has been somewhat less dramatic. A report is made by the UNHCR through ECOSOC to the UN General Assembly, but in most cases ECOSOC does not actively deliberate upon it. Detailed programme advice is afforded by the Executive Committee of the High Commissioner's Programme as set out above. The general supervision of the UNHCR's administration and finance is vested in the UN Advisory Committee on Administrative and Budgetary Questions.[47]

It is contended that, as a body acting upon the international plane, the UNHCR possesses international legal personality – the capacity to act on its own behalf as an entity in public international law.[48] In any legal system, legal personality rests essentially upon recognition of the capacity by an entity to take action at law on its own behalf – basically the right (or liability) to sue or be sued. So far as Public International Law is concerned, the 'typical' legal person is a state which can act upon the international plane in the following ways: by entering into binding obligations, taking or being the object of legal action for the enforcement thereof, having the advantages and restrictions of the privileges and immunities accruing to statehood, and being subject to that body of principle comprising customary international law and binding upon all its subjects.

If the state is the 'typical person' of international law, it is possible for other bodies, such as international organizations, also to have such 'personality'. Whether they take up or are entitled to make such a claim will depend upon the particular circumstances and functions in question. Of relevance here is the *Reparation Case*[49] which arose from the assassination in Jerusalem of Count Bernadotte in 1948 when acting as Chief United Nations Truce Negotiator. The immediate question was whether the UN had the capacity to bring an international claim where one of its agents suffered injury in circumstances where the responsibility of a state was in question. The International Court concluded that the UN did have such capacity, having been set up with the clear intention of exercising rights and purposes which could only be accomplished through an appropriate measure of international legal personality. From this it would seem that an international organization may enjoy a personality 'of necessity', i.e. that level of legal personality necessary for the performance of its proper purposes. The International Committee of the Red Cross, on the other hand, has hitherto chosen not to assert international legal personality in case such a position might inhibit or damage its established mode of operation.[50]

Clearly the legal capacities of the UN itself would extend to activities arising from the work of the UNHCR, but a strong case may also be made that the UNHCR itself possesses an appropriate degree of legal personality. Thus, article 35(1) of the 1951 Convention Relating to the Status of Refugees provides that

> the Contracting states undertake to co-operate with the Office of the United Nations High Commissioner for Refugees, ... in the exercise of its functions, and shall in particular facilitate its duty of supervising the application of the provisions of this Convention.

This 'supervisory' role strongly suggests some measure of legal personality. The extent of the capacities which are thus rendered necessary is clearly considerable if the working of the UNHCR is to be rendered effective, even if some detailed minutiae are debatable.[51]

The refugees whom the UNHCR is authorized to assist are essentially (under paragraph 6 of the 1950 Statute) those so defined by article 1A(2) of the 1951 Convention Relating to the Status of Refugees as amended (to remove the temporal limitation) by the 1967 Protocol. By reference to paragraph 7 of the Statute, the protection of the High Commissioner is lost, *inter alia*, where a person has regained or gained the protection of the former or a new home country or where the circumstances by reference to which 'refugee' status was gained have ceased to exist. Paragraph 2 of the UNHCR Statute provides that

> the work of the High Commissioner shall be of an entirely non-political character; it shall be humanitarian and social and shall relate, as a rule, to groups and categories of refugees.

This is a wide-ranging mandate. In various situations the General Assembly and the UN Economic and Social Council have urged the High Commissioner to provide emergency aid to groups which would not otherwise strictly qualify as 'refugees',[52] including internally displaced persons and victims of natural disasters.

The Practical Work of the UNHCR

It follows from the nature of world refugee problems that the work of the UNHCR has both emergency and long-term dimensions. Where non-international armed conflict or internal strife bring about a large-scale flight of refugees, there is an obvious need for immediate relief aid. In the longer term, a sustained programme of settlement and, where necessary, integration is clearly necessary. The general scope of this work is described by the UNHCR as including

> emergency relief, assistance in voluntary repatriation or local integration, resettlement through migration to other countries, as well as counselling, education, and legal assistance.[53]

The first aspect of this work, emergency relief, is concerned with the supply of necessities – food, medical aid and shelter – to new refugees or newly displaced persons in the immediate exigencies of the crisis which has precipitated their plight. The longer-term work of the UNHCR involves the settlement or resettlement of refugees, including programmes of *voluntary* repatriation. The 1951 Convention Relating to the Status of Refugees provides by article 1C(4) that

> This Convention shall cease to apply to any person ... if:
> He [or she] has voluntarily re-established himself [or herself] in the country which he [or she] left or outside which he [or she] remained owing to fear of persecution; ....

The same point is made by paragraph 6A(a) of the 1950 UNHCR Statute. Where such re-establishment is achieved, refugee status and needs will thus terminate. The emphasis here is on the voluntary nature of the return and also some evidence of the intended permanence of return, granted the policy of the UNHCR to interpret the cancellation of status provisions to the benefit rather than the detriment of refugees. In the context of civil conflicts, many people may be forced into refugee status for a relatively short time as a result of the hostilities, with voluntary repatriation often reasonably anticipated in due course. In such cases their most vital requirement will be immediate emergency provision.

Where voluntary repatriation is not possible, the issues of local integration or resettlement in another territory will emerge. Where large numbers are involved, as in the case of those 'boat people' granted refugee status, this may be a major problem.

UNHCR Funding

As a subsidiary body of the UN, the administration of the UNHCR falls within the organization's general budget and is subject to the same pressures. The High Commissioner may, however, make appeals for refugee programmes by reference to the financial review adopted by the Executive Committee of the High Commissioner's

Programme. Voluntary fund-raising for refugee assistance is also undertaken by the Secretary General.[54] In times of international economic recession, such as the early 1990s, governmental and other contributions to refugee relief tend to be cut back, with an inevitable and unfortunate effect upon relief capacity.

The International Committee of the Red Cross

The humanitarian role of the International Committee of the Red Cross in non-international armed conflicts has been considered above.[55] The remit of the ICRC in the protection and assistance, *inter alia*, of civilian victims of armed conflicts may well involve many who would also fall within the category of refugees, although it is by no means limited to such people., A Statement of Policy in relation to International Red Cross Aid to Refugees adopted by the XXIV International Red Cross Conference at Manila in 1981 provides by paragraph 1 that

> The Red Cross should at all times be ready to assist and to protect refugees, displaced persons and returnees, when such victims are considered as protected persons under the Fourth Geneva Convention of 1949, or ... refugees under article 73 of the 1977 Protocol I Additional to the Geneva Conventions of 1949, or in conformity with the Statutes of the International Red Cross, especially when they cannot, in fact, benefit from any other protection or assistance, as in some cases of internally displaced persons.[56]

The latter reference is of special significance in a context of non-international armed conflict for reasons considered above.[57] The same statement requires, by paragraph 5, that a National Red Cross or Red Crescent Society should inform the Federation of Red Cross and Red Crescent Societies or the International Committee of the Red Cross of any negotiations likely to lead to a formal agreement with the UNHCR, and also that the Federation or ICRC should concur with its terms before any such agreement is finalized.[58] In terms of the relation of the Red Cross to UNHCR action for the relief of refugees, the XXIV Conference in 1981 also, by Resolution XXI, pledged

> unremitting support and collaboration of the Red Cross with the United Nations High Commissioner for Refugees in their respective activities in favour of refugees and displaced persons.... [59]

The point is also made that the humanitarian remit of the ICRC may extend to persons who do not fall within the UNHCR's formal area of concern. However, the UNHCR may also be authorized to assist some groups not technically classified as 'refugees'.[60]

1977 Protocol I Additional to the 1949 Geneva Conventions, which makes further provision for *international* armed conflicts, simply refers to

> persons who, before the beginning of hostilities, were considered as stateless persons or refugees under the relevant international instruments accepted by the Parties concerned. ...

The general category of civilian victims of armed conflict will normally include many who would qualify as refugees or displaced persons. Article 74 of the Additional Protocol also emphasizes the reunion of dispersed families. These provisions may be brought into operation in non-international armed conflicts where this is agreed. Even where this is not agreed the International Red Cross may offer and effect assistance. In many cases the ICRC has organized food relief and other essential supplies for the emergency needs of persons displaced in armed conflict. In reference, *inter alia*, to such people and their urgent needs, an ICRC publication comments that

> the ICRC's relief activities aim to cover the emergency needs of such victims, often in areas to which other organisations do not have access. In 1992 230,000 tonnes of relief supplies were distributed in 54 countries.[61]

In the course of 1993–94, the relief endeavours for beleaguered populations in former Yugoslavia were prominent in this area of the ICRC's work and are typical of the emergency relief it offers in such situations. It must be stressed that in many cases this work is carried out in parallel with that of the UNHCR, although the remits of the two organizations are, by their nature, not identical.

Notes

1 J.C. Hathaway, *The Law of Refugee Status* (Butterworths Toronto, 1991), p.3.
2 1946 IRO Constitution, Annex I, Part 1, Section A.
3 For a detailed consideration of this phenomenon see below, pp.155–8.
4 Article 1(2).
5 Article 1, common to both Conventions.
6 M. Shaw, *International Law*, 3rd edn (Grotius, 1991), p.177.
7 G.S. Goodwin-Gill, *The Refugee in International Law* (Oxford University Press, 1983), p.30.
8 Chooi Fong, 'Some Legal Aspects of the Search for Admission into Other States of Persons leaving the Indo-Chinese Peninsula in Small Boats' (1981) 52 *British Yearbook of International Law*, p.53 at p.92.

9   In the House of Lords [1988] 1 All ER p.193.
10 *Ibid.*, at p.197.
11 J.C. Hathaway, *op. cit.*, p.78., ref. [1988] 1 All ER pp.197–8.
12 [1988] 1 All ER p.193 at p.202.
13 Hathaway cites trends in the US and Canada to this effect; see *op. cit.*, pp.78–80.
14 The term 'ethnic cleansing' is both offensive and inaccurate. However, this terminology represents the usage which became established. For discussion of this phenomenon see below, pp.155–8.
15 [1988] 1 All ER p.193 at p.198.
16 For discussion of the 'Boat People' and their situation see Chooi Fong, *op. cit.*, *ante.*
17 The Albigensian Heresy in Western Europe was of this form.
18 ICRC Bulletin, *Yugoslavia* (International Committee of the Red Cross, 1992).
19 UN doc. S/25274, p.16.
20 The organization, Physicians for Human Rights, acting on behalf of the Commission of Experts, investigated a mass grave near Vukovar and in a report of 19 January 1993 concluded that the 200 bodies found represented a mass 'execution' site. See UN doc. S/25274, Annex II, p.27.
21 For discussion, see Chapter 11.
22 As to the status of 1977 Additional Protocol II, see pp.20–2 *ante.*
23 'Military necessity' is an important but limited concept which does not provide an 'opt out' clause from the application of basic humanitarian norms. See H. McCoubrey, 'The Nature of the Modern Doctrine of Military Necessity', *Revue de Droit Militaire et de Droit de la Guerre* (1991) Vol. XXX, pp.217–40.
24 J.C. Hathaway, *op.cit.*, p.31.
25 *Ibid.*
26 *The Guardian* (London), 24 March 1988.
27 *The Guardian* (London), 8 November 1993.
28 SC Res. 688, 46 UN SCOR (1991) did not expressly authorize no-fly zones, although it did find that the repression in Iraq which caused the refugee problems was a threat to international peace and security.
29 See below, p.167 ff.
30 Reported in *Human Rights and Refugees*, No. 92, April 1993, p.11.
31 H. McCoubrey, *The Ideas of War Crimes and Crimes Against Peace since 1945*, Department of Law/University of Nottingham Centre for International Defence Law Studies Research Paper No. 2 (June 1992), p.18.
32 G.S. Goodwin-Gill, *The Refugee in International Law* (Oxford University Press, 1983, paperback 1985), p.69.
33 *Ibid.*, p.98.
34 There were two Russian Revolutions in 1917, that of February 1917 in which the social-democratic *Mensheviks* seized power following the collapse of the Tsarist monarchy and that of October in which the *Bolsheviks* seized power. It was the latter which prompted the major egress of refugees from Russia.
35 Some interesting English legal background to this refugee crisis can be gleaned from reading *Oppenheimer* v *Cattermole* [1975] 1 All ER 538. For discussion see H. McCoubrey, *The Development of Naturalist Legal Theory* (Croom Helm, 1987), pp.136–41.
36 As to settlement work by the UNHCR, see below p.168.
37 International Committee of the Red Cross Press Release 1539 (5 May 1987).
38 A. Tusa and J. Tusa, *The Nuremberg Trial* (Atheneum, 1986), p.34.
39 For an interesting and controversial discussion of this question, see L. Farago, *Aftermath: Martin Borman and the Fourth Reich* (Simon and Schuster, 1974).
40 For discussion of controversial aspects of international or transnational criminal jurisdictions, see Chapter 11.

41   International Refugee Organization Constitution 1946, Annex I, Part 1A, article 1.
42   This Convention applies to international armed conflicts. It may, however, under common article 3 of the four 1949 Conventions, be brought into application in a non-international conflict. The point is raised here to illustrate a more general issue.
43   H. McCoubrey, *International Humanitarian Law* (Dartmouth, 1990), p.108.
44   See G. Risius, 'Prisoners of War in the United Kingdom' in P. Rowe (ed.), *The Gulf War 1990–91 in International and English Law* (Routledge/Sweet and Maxwell, 1993) p.289 at pp.300–301.
45   GA Res. 319 A(IV), 4 UN GAOR (1949).
46   GA Res. 428(V), 5 UN GAOR (1950).
47   United Nations High Commissioner for Refugees Information Paper (UNHCR, 193), p.13.
48   For extended argument upon this, see G.S. Goodwin-Gill, *op.cit.*, pp.133–4.
49   ICJ Rep., 1949, p.174.
50   See above, pp.51–2.
51   For a strongly expressed argument concerning the legal personality of the UNHCR, see G.S. Goodwin-Gill, *op.cit.*, at pp.132–4.
52   See above, pp.158–9.
53   UNHCR Information Paper (March 1993), p.10, paragraph 32.
54   Such contributions are funnelled through an Annual Conference held pursuant to GA Res. 1729 (XVII), 17 UN GAOR (1961).
55   See pp.141–3.
56   This text is reproduced in the *International Red Cross Handbook*, 12th edn (ICRC, 1983) at p.495.
57   See pp.18–19.
58   As to the structure and relationship of the Federation and the ICRC, see above, p.50.
59   The text of this Resolution is reproduced by the *International Red Cross Handbook*, 12th edn (ICRC, 1983), at pp.665–6.
60   See p.167.
61   *Panorama 93* (ICRC, 1993), p.23.

8 The Emplacement and Status of Peacekeeping Forces

The United Nations

UN peacekeeping, in the sense of establishing a team of 'blue helmets', has come a long way from its origins – the few observer forces emplaced in the immediate post-war era as a result of the emergence of new states and zones of influence. Those small unarmed observation teams in the Middle East, Indonesia and in Kashmir established the nature of UN peacekeeping as a consensual alternative to enforcement action by the Security Council under Chapter VII of the Charter. The basic principles of peacekeeping were developed by the much larger forces established in the Middle East following the Suez crisis of 1956, in the Congo in 1960 and in Cyprus in 1964. Despite a significant gap in the period 1967–73, when no new peacekeeping forces were authorized (after the expulsion of the Middle East force by President Nasser of Egypt, followed by the Six Day War of 1967), the growth of peacekeeping continued in the 1970s, with three further forces set up in the Middle East: between Egypt and Israel and on the Golan Heights following the Yom Kippur War of 1973, and in Lebanon in 1978 following the Israeli invasion of that country.[1]

The hardening of attitudes in the Cold War led to another hiatus in peacekeeping creation during the decade between 1978–88. However, the warming of relations between the superpowers in the late 1980s led to a vast increase in the use of peacekeeping, with forces being despatched to internal conflict zones that had previously been either in one or other of the superpower's spheres of interest (for example in Afghanistan and Nicaragua), or in an area of indirect conflict between them (for example in Angola and, less obviously, in Namibia). Peacekeeping has continued to expand geographically with the demise of the USSR in December 1991 and the emergence of the Russian Federation as successor to the Soviet Union's permanent seat on the Security Council in January 1992. Forces have been sent into what were previously thought of as intractable internal conflicts (Western Sahara, El Salvador, Cambodia and Mozambique), as well as to new intro-state wars (Yugoslavia and Somalia).

The lessening of political rivalries in the Security Council has enabled it to expand peacekeeping not only geographically, but in political and legal terms as well. As will be seen in Chapter 9, many of the new crop of peacekeeping forces are not simply maintaining the *status quo*, but are intimately involved in the settlement of conflicts by peaceful means. The UN's successes in Namibia and Nicaragua are illustrative of this integrated approach to peacekeeping. On the other hand, the peace process in Angola collapsed, while the warring parties in Bosnia and Somalia held out against a peaceful settlement.

The increase in activity by the Security Council has not only made 'blue helmets' commonplace throughout the world, but has also led to an increase in the use of enforcement (or 'Chapter VII') action in the form of mandatory economic sanctions and/or military response (Kuwait). The increase in enforcement action has sometimes led to measures being taken against one of the parties to a conflict in which a peacekeeping force is also present (for example the sanctions imposed against Serbia and Montenegro in 1992 despite the presence of the UN Protection Force between Serbia and Croatia as well as in Bosnia where both Serbia and Croatia were intervening). In other cases it has led to the peacekeeping force attempting to enforce a solution to the conflict, as in Somalia in June 1993 (see Chapter 10). The question must be asked whether such actions are really consonant with the traditions of peacekeeping; also, if these trends are maintained, whether the credibility of the UN as a neutral force for peace might be permanently undermined.

Principles

Before analysing the role of UN peacekeeping forces in internal conflicts, it is important to outline the legal principles governing any peacekeeping operation, whether one placed between states (the buffer or inter-state force) or between parts of states (the intra-state force).

Despite the fact that the concept of peacekeeping has developed in a piecemeal, *ad hoc* fashion, it is possible to provide a generic definition:

> As the United Nations practice has evolved over the years, a peacekeeping operation has come to be defined as an operation involving military personnel, but without enforcement powers, undertaken by the United Nations to help to maintain or restore international peace and security in areas of conflict. These operations are voluntary and

are based on consent and co-operation. While they involve the use of military personnel, they achieve their objectives not by force of arms, thus contrasting them with the 'enforcement action' of the United Nations. ...[2]

It is also clear that the authorization of such consensual, non-enforcement military activities is within the powers of the General Assembly as well as the Security Council. As the World Court explained in the *Expenses Case* , the Security Council has 'primary' but not exclusive competence under article 24(1) of the UN Charter to maintain or restore international peace and security.[3] Indeed, the first full-scale peacekeeping force in 1956, the First UN Emergency Force in the Middle East (UNEF I), was authorized by the General Assembly after UK and French vetoes had paralysed the Security Council. Politically, the peacekeeping function of the UN is now firmly in the control of the Security Council, though a great deal of organizational and logistical work is delegated to the Secretary General.[4]

Although the World Court in the *Expenses Case* emphasized that a clear line existed between peacekeeping and enforcement, and that both UNEF I and the UN Operation in the Congo (ONUC) were peacekeepers,[5] the constitutional basis of such forces can still be said to originate in Chapter VII. Article 40 of the Charter provides that 'in order to prevent an aggravation of the situation, the Security Council may ... call upon the parties concerned to comply with such provisional measures as it deems necessary or desirable...'. The Security Council has used this power not only to make mandatory demands that states cease firing or that foreign troops be withdrawn from the combat zone, but also to recommend such provisional measures. The power to call for provisional measures is also contained in article 40, with peacekeeping forces generally created to facilitate the observance of such measures when accepted by the parties to the conflict. Although peacekeeping is derived from article 40 of the UN Charter, its nature remains consensual and non-offensive, whether or not the call for provisional measures is mandatory.

Peacekeeping can occur after the parties to a conflict accept a cease-fire or a withdrawal, and then *consent* to the presence of a force on their soil. Normally consent is obtained from the legitimate governments concerned in inter-state conflict or from all the factions in an intra-state dispute. If the latter is not possible, consent is obtained only from the government which can lead to problems, as in southern Lebanon. If the consent of the government concerned is not given or is withdrawn, then the peacekeeping operation cannot remain on that state's territory. Theoretically, the UN could then change its mandate to one of enforcement although, given that states contribute to a peacekeeping force on a *voluntary* basis, they would have to give the UN permission for their troops to be used otherwise. Thus, contemplating a change in mandate is unlikely.

Not only is the consent of the host state necessary, but its continued *cooperation* with the peacekeeping force throughout the length of its stay is essential. *Impartiality* or *neutrality* is another of the essential features of peacekeeping, deriving from the non-prejudicial nature of provisional measures. Indeed, in the case of the 1500-strong UN Iraq–Kuwait Observation Mission (UNIKOM)), established by the Security Council by resolution 689 of 9 April 1991, the UN managed to maintain its neutrality in peacekeeping even after it had successfully prosecuted a war against one of the parties! Indeed, the Security Council imposed further conditions on Iraq after the war ended, including, *inter alia*, the settlement of the boundary between the two countries on the basis of the 1963 Agreement between Iraq and Kuwait.[6] It also sent a team of 500 UN guards to protect the camps established for the Kurds in the north in May 1991, again with Iraqi consent. The explanation perhaps lies in the fact that there is a clear legal distinction between the enforcement and peacekeeping functions of the UN, and also, on the political plane, by the fact that Iraq saw the use of force against it originating not from the UN but from the US and its Coalition partners.[7]

Another important aspect of peacekeeping, which clearly distinguishes it from enforcement, is that soldiers are authorized to use force only in *self-defence*. This limitation is more akin to an individual right of self-defence if shot at, rather than the much wider right of a state to self-defence, contained in article 51. Given that peacekeeping does not infringe the *sovereignty* of any state, it cannot be imbued with such a right. This severe limitation on the use of force by peacekeepers can present problems in intra-state situations when only the host government has consented to the force.

The problem is particularly acute in the case of the United Nations Interim Force in Lebanon (UNIFIL), established at the request of the Lebanese government in March 1978, following the partial withdrawal of Israel from Lebanon.[8] The Secretary General made it clear that UNIFIL would use force solely in the self-defence of troops and units, and would not undertake any of the responsibilities of the Lebanese government.[9] Unfortunately, UNIFIL is in a difficult situation, operating in a hostile environment in an area of Lebanon containing various armed factions not controlled to any degree by the Lebanese government, although in 1991 that government began to assert some authority in the south. Between 1978 and 1990, UNIFIL lost 130 soldiers from hostile acts. This has meant that UNIFIL has as yet been unable to fulfil either aspect of its mandate: to ensure the effective restoration of Lebanese sovereignty in the south or to supervise an Israeli withdrawal from the security zone it maintains south of the Litani river.

UN Peacekeeping in Civil Wars

The consensual, voluntary and essentially pacific nature of peace-keeping means that generally the force is restricted to observation and supervision of provisional measures accepted by the parties. More specifically the functions of a particular force depend on its mandate, usually located in the enabling resolutions of the Security Council or General Assembly, and in the reports of the Secretary General who is delegated the task of setting up the force. Usually the same model, derived from the principles governing UNEF I, is used (with slight variations) for every situation, although marked differences can be discerned between the mandates governing inter-state and intra-state peacekeeping forces.

Inter-state forces such as UNEF I are given the relatively clear tasks of supervising a cease-fire and a withdrawal to positions occupied before the conflict started, both of which have already been consented to by the parties. Inter-state forces have almost always proved successful within the limited objectives of their mandates.[10] The difficulties of peacekeeping in a civil war-type situation mean that the principles of peacekeeping (namely consent, neutrality and limited self-defence) are much harder to achieve, as the UN's experience in the Congo between 1960–64 illustrates.

The UN Operation in the Congo (ONUC) was initially sent under the authority of the Security Council at the request of the government of the Congo in July 1960, to provide assistance to that government until the Congolese security forces could ensure control, following the breakdown of order on Belgian decolonization.[11] When ONUC arrived it found itself in a precarious position: fighting was continuing, rival governments were being established, while secession of the Katanga region was being attempted with the active assistance of Belgian troops and mercenaries. A simple UNEF-type mandate and operation were clearly insufficient to prevent the collapse of the Congo altogether, although initially Secretary General Hammarskjöld seemed to take the opposite view.[12]

The increasing internationalization of the civil war led the General Assembly,[13] and then the Security Council, to adopt resolutions which seemed to authorize the use of force by the almost 20,000-strong contingent. In resolution 161 of 27 February 1961, the Council found that the situation in the Congo was a 'threat to international peace and security' and urged that ONUC 'take immediately all appropriate measures to prevent the occurrence of a civil war in the Congo, including arrangements for cease-fires, the halting of all military operations, the prevention of clashes, *and the use of force, if necessary, in the last resort*'. In resolution 169 of 24 November 1961, the Council further widened ONUC's mandate. The force was directed to maintain the territorial integrity and political independence of the Congo, to assist the central government to restore order, and to 'secure the immediate withdrawal and evacuation from the Congo of all foreign military ... personnel not under United Nations' command, and mercenaries'. In addition, it welcomed the restoration of the central government in August 1961 and rejected the Katangese claims to secession. To further these ends it authorized the use of force to expel foreign troops and mercenaries 'if necessary'.

Although ONUC, in the main, tried to keep within the principles of peacekeeping, particularly in the period before the adoption of resolution 161 – primarily by negotiating cease-fires and by not overtly siding with any one of the factions – it eventually had to use force to subdue the Katangese rebellion in April 1961, again in December 1961, and between December 1962 and January 1963.[14] It was very difficult to see ONUC as a true peacekeeping operation, in that it was authorized to use force beyond that necessary for strict self-defence, it was not impartial in the conflict and it received little cooperation. Although it did have the formal consent of the central government, for a period until August 1961 there was no real government in the Congo. On the other hand, ONUC was clearly not an enforcement contingent as undertaken by the UN force in Korea for instance, a view reinforced by the International Court in the *Expenses Case*.[15]

One acceptable explanation of the legal basis of ONUC is founded on article 40 of the Charter, the constitutional basis of most peacekeeping operations. Resolutions 161 and 169 could be said to contain a series of widely-drawn provisional measures designed to keep the Congo intact, as well as granting ONUC the authority to enforce those provisional measures if necessary.[16] The enforcement of provisional measures designed not to prejudice any of the parties could be said to fulfil the neutralist ideals of peacekeeping, but in effect it meant that ONUC was on the side of the central government against the secessionists. Nevertheless, the Security Council appeared to justify this by concentrating ONUC's use of force against foreign elements such as the mercenaries assisting the secessionists whose presence created the threat to international peace. The removal of foreign elements was designed to enable the factions to negotiate, and eventually resulted in the parties accepting a Plan of National Reconciliation.[17] The creation of conditions to facilitate such a reconciliation without foreign intervention could be said to fulfil the basic ideals of peacekeeping, although the extensive use of force needed to achieve this prevented such an operation from being mounted again during the Cold War. Instead the forces authorized by the Security Council in Cyprus in 1964 and in Lebanon in 1978 (among others) were clearly based on the inter-state concept; they were to act as buffers between the various factions, not to enforce the peace.

The end of the Cold War has seen the Security Council continue with traditional peacekeeping in internal conflicts, although it has increasingly veered towards allowing limited enforcement action if the parties are not willing to accept a peace plan. The quite extensive use of enforcement action by the UN Operation in Somalia (UNOSOM) will be reviewed in Chapter 10. In this chapter we will discuss the operation of the UN Protection Force in Yugoslavia, which as yet has not crossed the line from peacekeeping to enforcement.

The civil war between the various factions in Yugoslavia, most notably the Croatians and Serbians, commenced in June 1991, with the Security Council willingly ceding any attempt at brokerage or negotiation to the European Community. However, it did impose a mandatory arms embargo against the whole of Yugoslavia in resolution 713 on 25 September 1991, after determining that the continuation of the situation constituted a threat to international peace and security.

It was not until 27 November 1991 that the Security Council was eventually persuaded by international pressure to become involved in a possible peacekeeping operation. In resolution 721, it repeated its determination that the situation constituted a threat to international peace and security and requested that the Secretary General's envoy prepare a report on the feasibility of sending a peacekeeping force. The Council emphasized that this would be conditional on all parties complying with the cease-fire negotiated in Geneva on 23 November 1991.[18] The request for the force came from the Serbian-dominated Rump Yugoslav Collective State Presidency.[19] The Croatian authorities agreed to such a force on 28 November. The sticking points were principally the numerous cease-fire violations between the Serbian-dominated Yugoslav National Army and the Croatian forces, and the Federal request that the peacekeepers should be placed around the self-proclaimed Serbian autonomous regions within Croatia. Croatia denounced this second demand as an attempt to create a Greater Serbia and demanded that the force be positioned only on the officially recognized internal borders of the former Yugoslavia,[20] possibly in the hope that this would help create an international frontier,[21] bearing in mind the experiences of UNFICYP in Cyprus.

The cease-fire broke down in December 1991. In resolution 724 of 15 December, the Security Council agreed with the Secretary General[22] in stating that the conditions for establishing a force did not exist. Nevertheless, it agreed to send an advance team of 20 observers to prepare for the eventual deployment of a full force. Furthermore, it appealed to all states not to exacerbate the situation, a veiled and (as it turned out) unsuccessful attempt to persuade Germany and other states not to recognize any of the breakaway Republics.

The cease-fire between Croatia and the remnants of the Yugoslavian state (Serbia and Montenegro) began to take hold more effectively in January 1992, so that the Council was confident in sending another 50 observers specifically to supervise the cease-fire.[23]

With Croatia accepting that the Serbian-occupied areas of Croatia and the Serbian enclaves could be put under temporary UN control in so-called UN protected areas – a compromise agreed to by the Serbian leaders of these regions – the final blocks to the emplacement of the force were removed. Thus on 21 February 1992 in resolution 743, the Security Council unanimously authorized the sending of 14,400 peacekeeping troops to Yugoslavia, their mandate to oversee the cease-fire and to control the disputed areas until the parties, initially under European Community brokerage and then under joint EC/UN efforts, agreed to a final settlement.[24] This was a return to traditional-style peacekeeping, with UNPROFOR's mandate being in all respects a consensual and non-enforcement type.

In fact, the arrival of the first UN troops in Yugoslavia in March 1992 saw a further deterioration in the situation, with numerous and serious cease-fire violations occurring. There was also a deterioration in the central public of Bosnia-Herzegovina, with the Muslim and Croatian majority voting for independence, whilst Serbs in Bosnia committed themselves to remaining in the Yugoslavia Federation. Violence between the various communities in Bosnia broke out towards the end of March and was heightened in April 1992 with the announcement of a new Yugoslav state comprising the two remaining republics that had not sought independence, namely Serbia and Montenegro, to which Serbs in the other former republics, Croatia and Bosnia, claimed allegiance.[25]

With alleged outside involvement in the conflict in Bosnia in May 1992, principally from the new Yugoslav state in the shape of the remnants of the still powerful Yugoslav National Army (JNA), but also by the Croatian army, the Secretary General reported to the Security Council that UNPROFOR or any other peacekeeping force should not become involved in Bosnia, and that the UN plan for Croatia was in jeopardy because of the failure of the Serbian irregulars in Croatia to demobilize.[26] As a result the Security Council adopted resolution 752 on 15 May 1992 which, while recalling the provisions of Chapter VII of the Charter, demanded that the parties in Bosnia cease firing and cooperate with the European Community 'to bring about urgently a negotiated political solution respecting the principle that any change of borders by force is not acceptable'. It also demanded that the JNA and the Croatian army desist from interference and withdraw their forces immediately.

This apparently mandatory demand was not complied with, resulting in the Council adopting resolution 757 on 30 May 1992, in

which it condemned the JNA and the Croatian army. It then proceeded to impose sanctions on Serbia and Montenegro covering trade,
oil, sporting and air links, under Chapter VII of the Charter, after
determining 'that the situation in Bosnia and Herzegovina and in
other parts of the former Socialist Federal Republic of Yugoslavia
constitutes a threat to international peace and security'.

It appears that at this stage the UN lost its neutrality in the conflict
and could be seen to be siding against Serbia by taking mandatory
enforcement action against it. One cannot doubt that Serbia, or at
least the Serb militia, is the most guilty of the warring factions both
with its aggression against Bosnia and Croatia, and its policy of
ethnic cleansing. However, trying to keep the peace at the same time
as taking enforcement action is very difficult if not impossible, for
the UN. Despite remaining impartial, the blue berets are seen to be
the enemy by the Serbs.

Nevertheless, the Security Council, appalled by the suffering in
Bosnia, was gradually sucked into that conflict. On 8 June 1992, it
adopted resolution 758 authorizing the Secretary General to deploy
military observers to Sarajevo, the capital of Bosnia and scene of the
worst fighting, to supervise the withdrawal of heavy weapons from
around the airport. It also enlarged the mandate and strength of
UNPROFOR with 1,000 infantry; this was to allow for the delivery of
humanitarian supplies to the beleaguered city by securing the airport. The deployment of troops was conditional upon 'an effective
and durable cease-fire' being negotiated by the factions in Sarajevo,
apparently agreed to on 5 June 1992. In resolution 761 of 29 June
1992, following a report by the Secretary General,[27] the Security Council mandated 1,000 Canadian troops to secure the airport.

In resolution 770 of 13 August 192, the Security Council, 'acting
under Chapter VII of the Charter of the United Nations', called 'upon
States to take nationally or through regional agencies ... all measures
necessary to facilitate in coordination with the United Nations the
delivery by relevant United Nations humanitarian organizations and
others of humanitarian assistance to Sarajevo and wherever needed
in other parts of Bosnia...'. The phrase 'all measures necessary' has
been used in the past by the Security Council to authorize military
operations. Furthermore, the Council, in resolution 781 of 9 October
1992, imposed a no-fly zone over Bosnia. Authorization to enforce
this no-fly zone was granted by the Security Council in resolution
816 of 31 March 1993 to member states 'acting nationally or through
regional organizations or arrangements, to take, under the authority
of the Security Council and subject to close coordination with the
Secretary General and UNPROFOR, all necessary measures in the
airspace' of Bosnia in the event of further violations of the no-fly
zone. The first serious action taken under these resolutions was on 28

February 1994 when NATO jets shot down four Bosnian Serb war planes over the no-fly zone.

Safe areas under UNPROFOR were designated in resolutions 819 of 16 April 1993, 824 of 6 May 1993, 836 of 4 June 1993, and 844 of 22 June 1993, all adopted under Chapter VII of the UN Charter. Resolution 836 authorized UNPROFOR, in carrying out its mandate in the safe areas and 'acting in self-defence, to take the necessary measures, including the use of force, to reply to bombardments against the safe areas by any of the parties ...'. Limited use of air power by member states was also authorized by resolution 836 which decided that 'Member States, acting nationally or through regional organizations or arrangements, may take, under the authority of the Security Council and subject to close coordination under the Secretary General and UNPROFOR, all necessary measures, through the use of air power, in and around the safe areas in the Republic of Bosnia and Herzegovina, to support UNPROFOR in the performance of its mandate ...'. Until February 1994 no military action had been taken, either by UNPROFOR (except minor cases of self-defence) or by member states or other organizations, although the Security Council repeated its demands for a cease-fire in the whole of Bosnia under Chapter VII of the UN Charter, as well as reiterating the principles of international law upon which a settlement should be based.[28]

The large scale use of force is still being contemplated in Bosnia at the time of writing (February 1994) with much depending on the results of the latest peace negotiations between the three factions in Bosnia under EC/UN brokerage taking place in Geneva with the result that, in general, the UN is still relying on negotiation and consent to move humanitarian aid convoys as evidenced by a joint declaration by the three warring factions on 18 November 1993 allowing the unimpeded delivery of humanitarian aid. Despite the fact that Security Council resolutions have consistently reaffirmed the sovereignty and territorial integrity of Bosnia, as well as condemning the policy of ethnic cleansing operated by the Serbs and Croats in Bosnia and the acquisition of territory by the threat or use of force as unlawful,[29] the negotiations under EC/UN auspices seem to be, at the time of writing, contemplating some sort of three way division of Bosnia which seems contrary to all the principles of international law identified by the Security Council, although the latest truce between the Bosnian Croats and Muslims brokered by the United States on 23 February 1994 may change this approach. Nevertheless, it may be that if the negotiations are unsuccessful, the UN will be faced with the choice either of leaving Bosnia or crossing the line from peacekeeping to enforcement as it has done in Somalia. On the other hand, if the negotiations are successful, the Security Council has expressed its willingness to 'take all necessary measures to assist the parties in the effective implementation of the peace plan'.[30]

Indeed, the stakes were raised on 9 February 1994 when a mortar round killed 68 civilians in Sarajevo leading to NATO, operating under the Security Council mandate contained in resolution 836, threatening to use air strikes against Serb gunners in the hills around Sarajevo unless the guns were removed from the area or placed under UN control pursuant to a cease-fire agreement for Sarajevo, negotiated by UNPROFOR commander General Sir Michael Rose and the Secretary General's Special Representative Yasushi Akashi. The ten-day deadline was complied with, partially as a result of the NATO threat, but also as a result of Russian intervention in the form of 800 peacekeeping troops sent to reinforce UNPROFOR's policing of the cease-fire under a bilateral agreement made between the Bosnian Serbs and their traditional Russian allies. The relative success of the Sarajevo cease-fire plan has led to the possibility of a similar mechanism being used to ensure cease-fires in the other safe areas of Bihac, Srebenica, Gorazde, Tuzla, Zepa and perhaps beyond.

Peacekeeping by other International Organizations

If a peacekeeping operation conforms to the legal principles outlined above, then it can be lawfully undertaken either by a regional organization, or on an *ad hoc* collective basis, or indeed by individual states. Consensual, non-offensive operations do not breach the ban on the use of force contained in article 2(4) of the UN Charter, nor are they actions which require the authorization of the Security Council under article 53 which is confined to enforcement actions. An example of a true peacekeeping operation was that undertaken by the 2,500-strong *ad hoc* Multinational Force in the Sinai (MFO)). Although American dominated, this force has successfully undertaken observation of the requirements of the 1979 peace treaty between Egypt and Israel.

On the other hand, certain military operations have quite clearly not conformed to the principles of peacekeeping, even though the states concerned may use the term. As illustrated in Chapter 10, the Arab League/Syrian involvement in Lebanon since 1976 has at times had the consent of the various governments that have ineffectually attempted to rule a country in a state of civil war. Although thus gaining the appearance of consensuality necessary for a peacekeeping force, it is quite clear that the heavily armed force has acted aggressively against several of the factions in Lebanon on many occasions during its prolonged stay. Although its unlawful use of force may have eventually produced a more stable Lebanese government, Syria cannot excuse its unlawful action by bending the concept of peacekeeping.

It is clear from the operations in Lebanon, Liberia and the Dominican Republic (reviewed in Chapter 10 as enforcement actions), that the term 'peacekeeping', like so many legal concepts, is abused by states and international bodies operating outside the UN. The surest way of maintaining the integrity of any peacekeeping function is to keep it within UN auspices. Although it is not essential for peacekeeping operations mounted by regional bodies or individual states to have the authorization of the Security Council, proposers of such operations would be wise to seek advice from the UN and if possible to secure Security Council approval. Having said that, the analysis of the involvement of the Economic Community of West African States (ECOWAS) in Liberia contained in Chapter 10 will show the Security Council approving a peacekeeping operation which, in reality, amounted to an enforcement action.

Other examples of international organizations creating peacekeeping forces include an Arab League force placed in Kuwait in 1961; the Commonwealth Force in Southern Rhodesia pursuant to the Lancaster House Agreement of 1979; and an unsuccessful OAU force put into Chad to oversee a cease-fire in 1981. Although by no means a complete list, these three instances of peacekeeping by regional organizations illustrate principles and practice in this area. As regards peacekeeping in internal conflicts, only the Commonwealth force is strictly relevant as the other two involved outside states either threatening or using force (Iraq and Libya respectively). However, the OAU's involvement in Chad is relevant since it was designed not only to act as an inter-state force between Libya and Chad, but also for intra-state purposes.

On 19 June 1961, Kuwait finally achieved independence from the UK.[31] Six days later, Iraq reasserted its claim to sovereignty over Kuwait, with an implicit threat to use force. Thus, on 30 June, the rulers of Kuwait requested British and Saudi Arabian assistance under provisions of the agreement by which Kuwait had achieved independence. 6,000 British and Saudi troops arrived within a week. The British stated explicitly in the UN Security Council that the forces would be employed in a combat role only if Kuwait were attacked from across the border.[32]

On 20 July 1961, the Council of the Arab League adopted a resolution (in the absence of the Iraqis who had walked out in protest) which authorized members of the Arab League to assist Kuwait 'for the preservation of its independence' upon the withdrawal of British troops. The force consisted of troops from several Arab states and was expressly stated to be acting, first under the Arab League's Joint Defence and Economic Cooperation Treaty of 1950[33] (to which Kuwait had quickly adhered), which provides for collective self-defence in the face of aggression; as well as the Pact of the Arab League (to which Kuwait had been admitted, again in the absence of Iraq), which allows the Council to take measures necessary to combat aggression.[34] By the middle of October 1961 the Arab League force was in place and the British forces had been removed. By January 1963 the Iraqi threat had receded and the force's role was reduced to one of observation. A change in regime in Iraq in February 1963 led Kuwait to request the final withdrawal of League troops.

The precise basis of the Arab League Force in Kuwait remains unclear. As a self-defensive action, it did not require Security Council authorization under article 53 of the UN Charter. However, in many respects the force performed a peacekeeping role, with the consent of the government of Kuwait, if not of Iraq; but neither was it pitted against the Iraqis as a belligerent. It acted in many ways as a buffer force, observing a continuation of peace between the two countries. Although neither the Arab League Pact nor the later Defence Treaty explicitly envisaged the creation of a peacekeeping force by the Arab League, such a power could readily be implied for a regional organization concerned with peace and security, just as it has been established in practice by the UN. The successful performance of the Arab League in Kuwait in 1961, in what was essentially an inter-state conflict – where it complied with the requirements of its own treaties as well as the UN Charter – must be contrasted with the League's performance in the internecine conflict in the Lebanon starting in 1976 and reviewed in Chapter 10. This contrast highlights the difficulty of peacekeeping in internal conflicts.

The internecine conflict in Southern Rhodesia was brought to an end by the Lancaster House Agreement of 15 December 1979 which variously defined the terms of a constitution for an independent Republic of Zimbabwe; made arrangements for the immediate pre-independence period during which the country would return to the status of a British dependent territory under a Governor while elections were held; and finally, worked out the details of a cease-fire to end the fighting in the guerrilla war.

The cease-fire agreement entered into by the parties to the conflict stated that the British government was responsible for the establishment of a monitoring force, under the Command of the Governor's Military Adviser, 'to assess and monitor impartially all stages of the inception and maintenance of the cease-fire by the forces'. The Commanders of both the Rhodesian security forces and the Patriotic Front forces undertook to cooperate fully with the Commonwealth Force. The agreement also provided that 'members of the monitoring force will carry weapons for their personal protection and will be provided with vehicles and aircraft carrying a distinctive marking'.[35] In a statement accompanying the cease-fire agreement, the Chairman of the conference, Lord Carrington, stated that the force would be 1,200 strong and would contain troops from Australia, New Zealand, Kenya,

Figi and the UK. His statement also made it clear that the Commonwealth Force's role was one of peacekeeping, not enforcement:

> It is impossible for any external authority or force to guarantee that a cease-fire will be effective. Only the parties themselves can ensure this. The purpose of [the agreement] is to help the forces to initiate and maintain a cease-fire through arrangements by which they can be separated from their present inter-locked positions.... The task of a monitoring force is not and cannot be to compel either side to maintain a cease-fire, or in any sense to guard the forces of one side or the other. Its task is to observe and report on the manner in which the forces maintain the cease-fire agreement and thus to give an assurance that it will not be possible for any force to conduct any activities in breach of the cease-fire. ...[36]

The cease-fire became effective on 29 December 1979 and, despite breaches, was held sufficient for the election process to proceed, supervised by Rhodesian and British police as well as British election officials at the end of February 1980. A Commonwealth Observer Group (COG) and British election observers pronounced that, despite intimidation and irregularities, the election result, by which Robert Mugabe's ZANU party came to power, fairly reflected the wish of the Zimbabwean electorate. The Commonwealth Monitoring Force (CMF) withdrew in March 1980.[37]

The CMF was clearly a peacekeeping force. Despite the fact that the Commonwealth has no express power to create such a force, again it can be seen as a necessary implied power for an organization concerned with the peace and security of its members. The establishment of a stable, if undemocratic, Zimbabwe showed the positive aspect of a combination of peacekeeping and pacific settlement, an approach which has been widely used by the UN in recent years and which is reviewed in Chapter 9. It also shows the benefits of a combined approach over a simple traditional peacekeeping force such as UNIFIL in Lebanon or the OAU's force in Chad.

The OAU force in Chad in 1981–82[38] was again authorized by a regional organization not having specific competence to create a peacekeeping force but was accepted as coming within the implied powers of such a body. The Chairman of the OAU, President Moi of Kenya, specified two conditions before he would allow the OAU force to be sent to police the civil war in Chad: the invitation of the government of Chad, and the withdrawal of Libyan troops present in the country since 1980 at the request of the President of Chad.

The mandate of the OAU force was unclear. The enabling resolution of the Assembly of the OAU defined the function of the force as ensuring 'the defence and security of the country whilst awaiting the integration of Government Forces'. President Moi personally envisaged a far greater role, namely the supervision of free and fair elections in Chad. Both of these aims are within the ambit of peacekeeping; moreover, the emphasis throughout was on the neutrality and impartiality of the force. However, it appeared that the President of Chad saw the force simply as an additional arm of government, to be used in fighting against the rebels.

In addition, the OAU force was poorly organized, lacked logistical support and was not properly financed, the OAU having no experience in peacekeeping and limited resources. Six states originally volunteered to provide 10,000 troops, but after withdrawals, a force of only just over 3,000 arrived in Chad. Western financial help and a fund established by the Security Council[39] helped to pay for the operation.

It was clear that the rival Chadian forces were unwilling to negotiate a cease-fire (a normal precondition for the emplacement of a peacekeeping force), let alone a peaceful solution. In this atmosphere Nigeria withdrew half its contingent, leaving a force which increasingly, and inevitably, became involved in the fighting. When the Chadian capital fell to rebel forces in June 1982, the Chairman of the OAU ordered the withdrawal of the force by the end of the month.

The OAU operation in Chad was a failure not only because it was badly organized and poorly resourced, but also because of the inherent difficulty of peacekeeping in an internecine conflict where the parties had not yet agreed to a cease-fire. In such cases the peacekeeping force tends to be embroiled in the conflict, in effect, becoming an agent for enforcement, losing its neutrality and becoming the enemy of one or other of the factions. The involvement of the ECOWAS force in Liberia detailed in Chapter 10 further illustrates the problems of this type of operation.

The Laws of Armed Conflict and United Nations Forces

The application of the *jus in bello* (that part of the international laws of armed conflict governing the conduct of hostilities and the protection of victims of warfare) to the military operations of United Nations Forces, whether peacekeeping or enforcement, presents a number of conceptual and practical difficulties. In part this results from the failure to provide standing forces for UN service under article 43 of the Charter as was originally intended. In particular the failure to provide standing forces for UN service under article 43 of the Charter has meant that such forces have had to be constituted *ad hoc* on each occasion.[40] It has also meant that the intended role of the UN Military Staff Committee under article 47 has never been fully implemented.[41] These factors have been a practical obstacle to the development of any adequate formal clarification of the legal regime governing the operational conduct of UN Forces. However, even if the Chapter VII regime had been implemented in full, basic difficulties would remain. These lie firstly in determining to what extent, if any, the laws of armed conflict, which are expressed in terms of national armed forces, apply to UN Forces. Secondly, assuming they do, exactly which treaty provisions and what system of military discipline for their enforcement apply in a diversely constituted multinational force.

Jurisprudentially the basic question arises from the fact that, whether engaged in 'peacekeeping' or 'peacemaking', UN Forces are essentially conceived in a 'policing' role. Should they then be bound by the same restrictive rules which apply to belligerent states in the conduct of hostilities? Although it has international legal personality, the UN is not a state and does not participate in international relations as states do. Nor is its involvement in situations or armed conflict the same. It might be argued upon this basis that the *jus in bello* should not be applicable to the operations of UN Forces for the suppression of unlawful breaches or threats to peace.

Such a view would, however, rest upon deeply questionable assumptions. In the first place such an argument would tend towards the worst abuses of discredited *bellum justum* ('just war') concepts which Jean Pictet has described as follows:

> the well known and malignant doctrine of the 'just war, which … did nothing less than provide believers with a justification for war and all its infamy by offering a compromise between moral ideals and political necessities.[42]

This is a little unfair to the original proponents of the doctrine who, far from encouraging war and its brutalities, were admitting a limited exception to a prohibition upon war where yet worse evils threatened. The idea, with roots in ancient Roman practice, was developed by St Augustine of Hippo, especially in discussions in *Contra Faustem* and *De Civitate Dei*, and reached a mature form in the 13th century in the hands of St Thomas Aquinas in his *Summa Theologica*.[43] It was not part of the original intention that a 'just cause' should 'justify' common brutality. Indeed, St Thomas Aquinas explicitly urged that a 'just' cause might be rendered unjust when prosecuted by excessive means.[44] If the original theory merits exemption from Pictet's censure, later practice certainly did not. The late Professor-Colonel G.I.A.D. Draper remarked tellingly that

> the 'just war' doctrine proved a cover for great inhumanity and suffering in war. It came to be established by the subtlety of the canon lawyers that almost anything was justifiable in a 'just war'.[45]

This was not the original theory, but became an appalling reality.

Action under Chapter VII of the UN Charter cannot be argued to constitute a new *bellum justum* doctrine on behalf of the UN or any state. Indeed the Charter includes, in article 2(4), an explicit ban upon resort to force as a mode of international dispute resolution. However, this prescription does make provision of the 'justifiable' use of force in response to actual or threatened unlawful military action. There is in this a peril to be guarded against which may be seen as analogous with the historical abuse of the 'just war' doctrine. That this is more than arcane speculation has been shown by problems arising in some UN military operations in the 1990s. Using Chapter VII to condone a resort to force would have no foundation in the UN Charter itself and can be countered by arguments of both ethics and law.

At the ethical level, granted the basis of UN action in the amelioration and curtailment of military breaches and threats to the peace, it would seem perverse to suggest that humanitarian constraints should not apply to the UN's own operations. In the substantive laws of armed conflict, there is no doctrine of ends and means in the sense of a direct link between the legitimacy of resort to force and the mode of conduct of hostilities. So far as international armed conflicts between states are concerned, the point is made explicit by treaty provision. 1907 Hague Convention IV Respecting the Laws and Customs of War on Land states in its Preamble that

> ... these provisions, ... inspired by the desire to diminish the evils of war, ... are intended to serve as a general rule of conduct for the belligerents in their mutual relations and in their relations with inhabitants.

Common article 1 of the four 1949 Geneva Conventions states with yet greater clarity that

> the High Contracting Parties undertake to respect and to ensure respect for the present Convention in all circumstances.

There is no reason in principle to suggest that military 'policing' action in response to unlawful uses of armed force should *prima facie* be exempted from such constraints. D.W. Bowett remarks that

> ... there exists no rule of international law which, on the basis of the illegality of war ... alone, would compel the finding that the rules of law regulating [hostilities] ... do not apply to [lawful] ... belligerents to the same effect ... as was traditionally conceived ... it would appear to be ... unaccepted that United Nations Forces, absent other legal

considerations, are released from the ... law of war because of the legal status of its opponent.[46]

As a matter of principle this conclusion commends itself on grounds of both humanitarianism and pragmatism. There are, nonetheless, a number of 'other legal considerations' which are pertinent to all cases of UN or UN-authorized military action, nowhere more so than in non-international armed conflicts.

The most obvious point is clearly stated by Roberts and Guelff:

> The United Nations itself is not a party to any international agreements on the laws of war. Moreover, these agreements do not expressly provide for the application of the laws of war by U.N. Forces. However, it is widely held that the laws of war remain directly applicable to such Forces.[47]

Acting on the international plane, the UN must presumably be bound by relevant customary international law, in addition to such treaties as expressly or implicitly make provision for it. The UN's own existence rests upon the UN Charter which is a multilateral treaty. However, formal provision governing the application of the *jus in bello* to the operations of UN Forces would be beneficial, not least because the laws of armed conflict should not be allowed to rely on presumption and implication. Some attempts have been made to draft such an instrument, notably the 1971 Zagreb Resolution on Conditions of Application of Humanitarian Rules of Armed Conflict to Hostilities in which UN Forces may be Engaged, adopted by the Institute of International Law on 3 September 1971.[48] This Resolution states by article 2 that,

> The humanitarian rules of the law of armed conflict apply to the United Nations as of Right, and they must be complied with in all circumstances by United Nations Forces which are engaged in hostilities. ...

Though unequivocal, this is, of course, a draft declaration and not a legally binding provision. A closer approach to such a statement can be found in an exchange of correspondence in 1962 between UN Secretary General U Thant and the International Committee of the Red Cross in the context of the Congo crisis. U Thant assured the ICRC that

> U.N.O. [the United Nations Organization] insists on its armed forces in the field applying the principles of the 1949 Geneva Conventions as scrupulously as possible.[49]

Although this statement was made in the particular context of the 'Geneva' or international humanitarian sector of the *jus in bello*, which makes provision for protection of the victims of armed conflict,[50] it could also apply to the 'Hague' sector which regulates methods and means of warfare.[51] The qualifying clause 'as scrupulously as possible' simply implies that everything 'possible' will be done to secure and maintain compliance.[52]

The 1962 statement of principle is useful, although it still leaves open some vital issues. The most important question, inevitably, is *which* provision of the *jus in bello* applies to the operations of a given UN Force. This, in turn, raises questions about the constitution and mandate of each given Force and the nature of the situation to which it is despatched. The answer lies partly in the obligations of the UN itself and partly in those of contributing member states. If the UN is bound at least by customary public international law, a considerable part of the *jus in bello* which has attained customary status will apply to military operations by UN Forces.[53] As U Thant stated in 1962 (when the customary status of the Conventions was less certain than it now is), the 1949 Geneva Conventions will preponderantly apply to such operations, especially as the states contributing units are also bound by them. More debatable issues arise in connection with provisions of the *jus in bello* which have not yet, in whole or in part, attained customary status. The most important example at present would be any new provision in the two 1977 Protocols Additional to the 1949 Geneva Conventions. The Additional Protocols[54] do not explicitly apply to UN Forces; nor could it be contended that they should automatically do so. This issue can be resolved only by reference to the closely associated questions of the obligations of states contributing contingents for UN service and the military discipline of UN Forces.

A related issue arises in the context of the scope of military action permitted to UN Forces under their particular mandates, bearing in mind that the structure of Chapter VII of the UN Charter has not been implemented in the manner originally intended (see above). The juxtaposition of the complex political decision-making process in the Security Council with the shifting exigencies and requirements of military action on the ground can present many difficulties, as illustrated by UN military operations in former Yugoslavia.

The aim of the UNPROFOR Forces was originally to protect and facilitate humanitarian relief supplies to beleaguered populations and to assist in cease-fire arrangements. In the context of fighting between highly diverse forces – ranging from units of new national armed forces down to bandit gangs – such a mandate presented extreme difficulties; in trying to cope, the UN Forces were subjected to a barrage of criticism. For instance François Bouchet-Saulnier, the

Head of Legal Affairs of *Médecins sans Frontières*, was quoted as stating in November 1993 that

> No one knows on what legal basis they work. It is not possible to work with people taking on a mandate without fulfilling it.[55]

In principle this may have been so, but in the uncertainties of former Yugoslavia any efficacious UN action in terms of its mandate required a considerable degree of flexibility of response. The laws of armed conflict are clear enough, but in terms of negotiating aid convoys through a maze of conflicting authorities and unaccountable local 'warlords', absolute certainty of direction would be an unrealistic ideal. The difficulties of the task were tellingly illustrated by the rapid and successive departures of UN Commanders, including General Jean Cot, the Commander of UN Forces in former Yugoslavia, and General Briquement, the UN Commander in Sarajevo. In particular, policy arguments in relation to possible air strikes in support of UN operations in January 1994 suggested an uncertainty of policy direction which must have seriously undermined operational command.[56] A decision to authorize such strikes following the Market Square massacre in Sarajevo on 5 February 1994 led to communication with the Southern Command of NATO as a mode of practical implementation.[57] Such difficulties represent only part of the complex operational structure of UN Forces.

National Contingents in UN Forces and Applicable Law

The legal regulation and obligations of military units acting under UN authority will vary according to the circumstances in which they are placed. If the armed forces of a state, or states, are acting as national forces but under UN authorization, their position in terms of the *jus in bello* will be identical with that of any other national force engaged in armed conflict. Thus the Coalition Forces in the 1990–91 Gulf conflict were acting pursuant to a Security Council mandate, but all the states involved (Iraq, Kuwait and the Coalition powers) were equally bound by the *jus in bello* having customary force and by any other mutually binding obligations. As for any multinational force, the question arises as to what provisions (not yet having customary force) would apply where contributing states are not all party to the same treaties. This issue also arises in connection with UN 'blue beret' forces. UN Forces cannot be treated as legally identical, since they differ very considerably in both constitution and function, as D.W. Bowett has remarked:

> ... all Forces representing the United Nations are not engaged in performing functions which would invoke the application of the laws of

war. ... [E]ven those Forces whose mandate comprehends offensive 'combat or combat possibility' may not in all circumstances be called upon to exercise it.[58]

This is inevitable considering the widely differing situations in which UN Forces may be called to act. However, the comment made by General H.T. Alexander in relation to UN Forces in the Congo still retains relevance:

The orders to UN troops during the Congo operation included the direction that 'peaceful persuasion' was to be used as often as possible when coping with incidents, and implied that the offensive use of weapons was not to be resorted to. These directions caused many unfortunate incidents and casualties which could have been avoided. ... [59]

Even where 'combat' is not strictly intended, the use of armed force, may well become 'incidentally' necessary, as in Yugoslavia. Notwithstanding prior agreements for their safe passage UNPROFOR-protected convoys often came under attack, so that their basic aim of distributing relief could be achieved only with some display of force.[60] As General Alexander went on to state, this is an important issue in drafting orders for UN Forces but not in the application of the *jus in bello*. In the modern laws of armed conflict the criterion for the application of law is generally held to be the fact of international military hostilities, with appropriate variations in the case of non-international conflicts. Technical states of 'war' and other such considerations are no longer in practice considered,[61] although they retain importance in other areas including matters of international commercial law. It must, therefore, be accepted that where units of a UN Force *in fact* become involved in hostilities, as may often be anticipated, any applicable provisions of the *jus in bello* will become operative.

This leaves open the vital question of *what* provisions of the *jus in bello* would be applicable in a given case, a complex issue, especially in non-international conflicts. *Prima facie* distinct legal regimes apply to international and non-international armed conflicts.[62] So far as 'Geneva' law is concerned it will be recalled that a basic 'human rights' provision for non-international conflicts is made by common article 3 of the four 1949 Geneva Conventions with further, but still limited, provision in 1977 Protocol II Additional to those Conventions. However, these are treated as *minimum* prescriptions, with common article 3 providing that

the Parties to the conflict should further endeavour to bring into force, by means of special agreements, all or part of the other provisions of the present Convention.

As guardians of international legality, UN Forces should aim to achieve this outcome, not only in relation to 'Geneva' humanitarian law (to which the provision refers), as far as possible to 'Hague' law as well.

For provisions of the *jus in bello* which have not attained customary force (i.e. those which rest on the mutual assumption of express treaty obligations by the Parties in conflict, as for much of the two 1977 Protocols Additional to the 1949 Geneva Conventions) a problem could arise. Consider a UN Force comprising of some contingents from states which are party to the Additional Protocols and others which are not. Will the relevant Protocol then be applicable? The simplest response would be to assume the application of law binding upon all the Parties – those provisions having customary force. Provision for the application of additional elements of the *jus in bello* could then be made in the orders drafted for the UN Force in question. This, however, requires some caution in the light of the command organization and disciplinary regulation of UN Forces.

Command Structure and Disciplinary Regulation of UN Forces

The political sensitivities involved in the commitment of national forces to UN direction are most clearly shown in the treatment of the question of command of such Forces. Article 47(3) of the UN Charter provides that

> The Military Staff Committee shall be responsible under the Security Council for the strategic direction of any armed forces placed at the disposal of the Security Council. Questions relating to the command of such forces shall be worked out subsequently.

Leaving aside the point that this provision was drafted in the (unfulfilled) expectation that 'standing' forces would be set up under article 43 of the Charter, the reservation of tactical, as compared with strategic, direction speaks volumes. Although the submission of units of a state's armed forces to 'international' or foreign command is a matter of extreme political delicacy which can only be resolved *ad hoc* on each occasion, a UN Force manifestly requires an unequivocal command structure in order to be militarily effective. Historically, military field commanders have generally either been appointed outright by the Secretary General as the UN executive director or have been recommended for appointment by him. Some part has also been played by a Military Adviser to the Secretary General and to a greater or lesser extent by the Security Council. Practice has of course varied, but the basic patterns emerged early from experience with the UNEF force in the Middle East and the ONUC force in the Congo. In both cases the importance of clear lines of command authority and responsibility became very obvious. In particular the relation between the political requirements of the UN, the practical exigencies of military action and the, sometimes divergent, understandings of contributing Governments and national contingent commanders have always presented special difficulties, as J.M. Boyd has commented:

> Because of these dual [UN and national] lines of authority, one guiding principle must be accepted – the United Nations Force Commander must have the final word on operational matters. This has been generally recognized and accepted. There is also ... appreciation ... that the national commander has a responsibility ... to [ensure] that his unit is not used in a manner that would exceed the approved mandate or ... be inconsistent with [national] understanding. ...[63]

In practice a senior officer from one of the states contributing units to the Force in question will be appointed Commander of the Force. In the case of UNPROFOR, command was initially (1992–93) vested in the French General Morrieon. This command involved both military and diplomatic skills, the latter vital in dealing both with tensions between the national contingents within the UN forces and negotiations with the many elements of the diverse warring parties. For UNOSOM II in Somalia – another highly sensitive appointment – the Turkish Lieutenant-General Cevik Bir was appointed to command in February 1993.

In 1977, the UN Special Committee on Peacekeeping Operations attempted, in the 11th Report of a Working Group, to deal with the question of command organization. Article 8 of the Report read as follows:

> The command in the field will be exercised by a force commander appointed [on the proposal of the Secretary-General] [by the Secretary-General] [with the consent of] [by] the Security Council. The Commander will be given necessary authority over all the elements of the operation within the terms of the mandate and specific directives. The Commander shall co-operate [through appropriate channels] with subsidiary bodies which the Security Council may establish to assist the Council.[64]

The multiple alternatives included in this provision are, again, eloquent testimony of the political sensitivities involved. As with much of the practical operation of Chapter VII of the UN Charter, the procedures for command and control of UN Forces have inevitably developed from hard practical experience and in ways somewhat different from those originally intended or theoretically desirable. Considering all the associated political and military problems, the command of UN Forces has in most cases been commendable.

The Commander of a United Nations Force will, *inter alia*, have the duty of securing uniform conduct by the constituent units of the Force, although this cannot embrace the prior training of personnel (type of training; quality of training). Certain basic national obligations are laid down with regard to military training, as in article 47 of 1949 Geneva Convention I:[65]

> The High Contracting Parties undertake, in time of peace as in time of war, to disseminate the text of the present Convention as widely as possible ... and, in particular, to include the study thereof in their programmes of military ... instruction, so that the principles thereof may become known ... in particular to the armed fighting forces. ...

How, and how effectively, this is done will vary considerably. In addition, although all training should include customary obligations, other matters (such as important parts of the 1977 Additional Protocols) will largely depend upon the particular treaty obligations undertaken by individual states. The International Committee of the Red Cross felt it necessary, in the early 1960s, to draw attention to the matter of training, while expressing approval of the Secretary General's undertaking with regard to observance of international humanitarian law by UN Forces. The ICRC stated that

> ... each state is personally responsible for the application of [the Geneva] ... Conventions when supplying a contingent to the United Nations. It would therefore be highly desirable that such contingents receive, before leaving their own countries, instructions to conform to the provisions of the Geneva Conventions in the event of their finding themselves having to use force.[66]

This essentially reiterates what is anyway a national obligation, although drawing particular attention to the context of national contingents in UN Forces. The same point is made by article 4 of the 1971 Zagreb Resolution on Conditions of Application of Humanitarian Rules of Armed Conflict to Hostilities in which United Nations Forces may be Engaged of the International Law Association:[67]

> it is necessary that [members of] ... such Forces receive adequate and previous instruction on the law of armed conflict in its entirety, and especially on the meaning of the ... Geneva Conventions. ...

This again may be restating the obvious, but usefully and necessarily so in a specific context.

A final question relates to military discipline and breaches of the laws of armed conflict by members of UN Forces. Errors can always occur in the course of military action; for instance, a number of questions were raised about the Amirayah Bunker incident in the Gulf conflict, but no convincing evidence has been produced that this was the result of culpable misconduct as compared with tragic miscalculation. More stringent criticism has been levied at the treatment of civilians by the UNOSOM force in Somalia.[68] A specific evaluation of these criticisms is not relevant or possible here, but problems will inevitably arise and unlawful actions occur. This then raises the difficult questions of enforcement and disciplinary regulation.

There is no 'permanent' international criminal tribunal. Such international war crimes trials as have been conducted, primarily those in Nuremberg and Tokyo at the end of the Second World War, were set up on an *ad hoc* basis. The same is true of the war crimes Tribunal in relation to the conflict(s) in former Yugoslavia.[69]

Neither the UN as such nor its Military Staff Committee has any court martial jurisdiction or machinery; the only practical possibility must therefore be trial according to the military law of the respective member nation. This has been challenged at least once. In *Jennings* v *Markley*,[70] a US soldier serving with UN Forces in Korea was convicted by a US Court Martial of murder and assault with intent to do bodily harm. He claimed before the US District Court SD Indiana, Terre Haute Division, *inter alia* that the US Court Martial did not have jurisdiction over him as a soldier serving with the UN and that he should therefore have been tried by the UN Military Staff Committee, the International Court of Justice or by a Civil Court in the US. As stated, the Military Staff Committee has no court martial jurisdiction and the International Court of Jurisdiction has no criminal jurisdiction, most certainly not over individuals. Not surprisingly, the Court rejected these arguments:

> There is nothing in the Charter of the United Nations from which to conclude that a member of the armed forces of a member nation does not retain his status as a soldier in the army of the respective member nation. As a member of the United States Army, the petitioner, whether being led under the flag of the United States, or the United Nations, nevertheless remained subject to the immediate control and jurisdiction of the United States Army.[71]

It is difficult to consider any other conclusion. It is clearly the responsibility of each state to secure observance of the laws of armed conflict by its forces through its own military law and discipline.[72] In the event that a state contributing contingents to a UN Force proved unwilling, in breach of its obligations, to undertake any such necessary action, the matter would become one for process between the UN and the state in question or, possibly, between the victim state or entity and the state in question.

In the present condition of international relations and of the break-up of formerly established political units in the so-called 'New World Order', it seems likely that there will be a continuing and even increasing need for UN Military Forces to become involved in combat situations. In these circumstances, although the principles governing the application of the *jus in bello* to UN Forces may in practice be clear enough, a more formal clarification of the issue is highly desirable. In view of the inherent political, strategic and tactical ambiguities of action in striving for peace in non-international conflicts, the need is perhaps most pointed in such cases.

Notes

1   See, further, H. Wiseman, *Peacekeeping: Appraisals and Proposals* (Pergamon Press, 1983), chapter 2.
2   *The Blue Helmets: A Review of United Nations Peacekeeping* 2nd edn (UN Publication, 1991), p.4.
3   ICJ Rep. 1962, p.162.
4   E. Luard, *The United Nations* (Macmillan, 1979), pp.46–7.
5   ICJ Rep. 1962, p.166.
6   485 UNTS 321; SC Res. 687, 41 UN SCOR (1991).
7   However, UNIKOM's mandate has been upgraded to one of quasi-enforcement as a result of Iraqi violations; SC Res. 806, 28 UN S/PV (1993).
8   SC Res. 425, 33 UN SCOR (1978).
9   UN doc. S/12611 (1978).
10 N.D. White, *Keeping the Peace: The United Nations and the Maintenance of International Peace and Security* (Manchester University Press, 1993), chapter 9.
11 SC Res. 143, 15 UN SCOR (1960).
12 UN doc. S/4389 (1960).
13 GA Res. 1474, 4 UN GAOR ESS (1960). It could be said that this added nothing more to the mandate than indicated in previous Council resolutions; SC Res. 143, 146, 15 UN SCOR (1960).
14 UN doc. S/5240 (1963).
15 ICJ Rep. 1962, p.177.
16 G. Abi-Saab, *The United Nations Operation in the Congo* (OUP, 1978), p.105. But see D.W. Bowett, *United Nations Forces* (Stevens, 1964), p.180.
17 UN doc. S/5053/Add.13, Annex 1 (1962).
18 UN doc. S/23239 (1991).
19 UN doc. S/23240 (1991).
20 *Keesing's Record of World Events* (1991), p.38559.
21 The European Community's Arbitration Commission on Yugoslavia stated that the application of the principle of *uti possidetis* to the former Yugoslavia meant in fact that the internal boundaries between the republics became the international frontiers on disintegration (1992) 31 *ILM*, p.1499.
22 UN doc. S/23280 (1991).
23 DSC Res. 727, 46 UN SCOR (1991).
24 UN doc. S/23592 (1992).
25 *Keesing's* (1992), p.38848.
26 UN doc. S/23900 (1992).
27 UN doc. S/24075 (1992).

28 SC Res. 859, 43 UN S/PV (1993). See also SC Res. 871, 48 UN S/PV (1993).
29 See for example SC Res. 819, 48 UN S/PV (1993).
30 SC Res. 820, 48 UN S/PV (1993).
31 A full analysis of the situation is contained in H.A. Hassouna, *The League of Arab States and Regional Disputes* (Oceania, 1985), chapter 6.
32 SC 957 mtg, 16 UN SCOR (1961).
33 157 BFSP 669.
34 Article 6, 70 UNTS 238.
35 (1980) 19 *ILM* pp.401–3.
36 *Ibid.*, p.404.
37 *Keesing's* (1980), pp.30365–78.
38 G.J. Naldi, *The Organization of African Unity* (Mansell, 1989) pp.27–9.
39 SC Res. 504, 37 UN SCOR (1982).
40 See pp.235–8.
41 See p.238.
42 J. Pictet, *Development and Principles of International Humanitarian Law* (Martinus Nijhoff, 1985), p.13.
43 See St Thomas Aquinas, *Summa Theologica* 2a2ae. 40.
44 St Thomas Aquinas, op.cit., 2a2ae. 40, referring to St Augustine, *De Verbis Domini*.
45 G.I.A.D. Draper, 'The Christian and War', *International Relations* (1962) offprint, p.16.
46 D.W. Bowett, *United Nations Forces* (Stevens, 1964), p.496.
47 A. Roberts and R. Guelff, *Documents on the Laws of War*, 2nd edn (Oxford, 1989), p.371.
48 The text will be found in Roberts and Guelff, *op.cit.*, at pp.372–5.
49 The Secretary General's letter was published in the *International Review of the Red Cross*, January 1962. Reference to this undertaking is made by Roberts and Guelff, *op.cit.*, p.372.
50 For discussion of this law, see H. McCoubrey, *International Humanitarian Law* (Dartmouth, 1990).
51 The distinction between 'Geneva' and 'Hague' law is in some ways rather artificial, but it is nonetheless a convenient categorization. See H. McCoubrey and N.D. White, *International Law and Armed Conflict* (Dartmouth, 1992), pp.217–19.
52 As to 'impossibility' in this context, see J. Pictet, *op.cit.*, p.88. Also H. McCoubrey, 'The Laws of Armed Conflict and United Nations Forces: Regulating Military Action for Peace' (1993) 20 *Journal of Malaysian and Comparative Law*, pp.59–74.
53 This includes, for example, the preponderance of the provisions of the 1949 Geneva Conventions. As to the nature of customary law and the general sources of public international law, see I. Brownlie, *Principles of Public International Law*, 4th edn (Clarendon, 1990), chapter 1.
54 1977 Additional Protocol I makes further provision for international and, controversially, for certain 'internationalized' armed conflicts; 1977 Additional Protocol II makes additional provision for non-international armed conflicts.
55 *The Independent* (London), 23 November 1993.
56 *The Observer* (London), 23 January 1994.
57 The Secretary General, Dr Boutros Boutros-Ghali, requested the Secretary General of NATO to obtain a decision to this effect by the North Atlantic Council in a letter dated 6 February 1994. For discussion of the air strikes decision, see pp.182–3.
58 D.W. Bowett, *op.cit.*, p.499.
59 H.T. Alexander, 'U.N. Peace-Keeping Forces in Civil-War Situations' in E. Luard

(ed.), *The International Regulation of Civil Wars* (Thames and Hudson, 1972), at p.191.

60   British units serving with UNPROFOR were forced to respond to sniper attacks upon an aid convoy in June 1993.

61   See C. Greenwood, 'The Concept of War in Modern International Law' (1987) 36 *ICLQ* p.283.

62   See Chapter 5, pp.103–4.

63   J.M. Boyd, *United Nations Peace-Keeping Operations: A Military and Political Appraisal* (Praeger Publishers, 1971), pp.154–5.

64   UN doc. A/32/394 Annex II, Appendix I, 2–12–77. The text is set out in R.C.R. Siekmann, *Basic Documents on U.N. and Related Peace-Keeping Forces*, 2nd edn (Martinus Nijhoff, 1989), at p.264.

65   See also 1947 Geneva Convention II, article 48; 1947 Geneva Convention III, article 127; 1949 Geneva Convention IV, article 144; 1977 Additional Protocol I, article 83, all of which make exactly similar provision. 1977 Additional Protocol II, dealing specifically with non-international armed conflicts, provides simply, by article 19, that 'This Protocol shall be disseminated as widely as possible'.

66   Memorandum of the ICRC to Governments of States Party to the 1949 Geneva Conventions and Members of the UN on the Application of the Geneva Conventions by United Nations Forces. The text was published in the *International Review of the Red Cross* (1962) and is set out by R.C.R. Siekmann, *op.cit.*, p.282.

67   The text will be found conveniently in Roberts and Guelff, *op.cit.*, at p.374.

68   A very critical account was given by Karl Maier in *The Independent* (London), 14 August 1993.

69   For discussion of the Tribunal, see Chapter 11 at pp.274 ff.

70   [1961] 186 Federal Supplement, 611.

71   *Ibid.* at pp.612–13.

72   See 1949 Geneva Convention I, article 49; Convention II, article 50; Convention III, article 129, Convention IV, article 146; 1977 Additional Protocol I, articles 86 and 87.

9 Election Monitoring and other Methods of Conflict Settlement

The United Nations

Reference has already been made in Chapter 2 to the powers of the Security Council, the General Assembly and the Secretary General of the UN *vis-à-vis* the peaceful settlement of disputes. As shall be seen in this chapter, in practice the UN has utilized most of these powers in attempting solutions to civil wars. However, it must be emphasized that, as with peacekeeping, these powers are recommendatory in nature and so depend on the consent and cooperation of the belligerents concerned, whether states or factions.

The main efforts of the UN in this area usually take the form of the Secretary General or his representative performing 'good offices' in an attempt to help the parties to an internal conflict towards a cease-fire and a peaceful solution,[1] pursuant to a mandate from the General Assembly or the Security Council. In addition, it has been stated in Chapter 2 that the Secretary General himself has significant inherent powers in this area. On other occasions a peaceful solution may be agreed to by the parties to the internal conflict and, if necessary, by their 'backer' states. Such an agreement may include a request for UN assistance. Finally, an agreement may be reached at an international conference convened under UN auspices or on an *ad hoc* basis. Again, the UN may be requested to help finalize the agreement.

The UN's assistance towards a peaceful solution may take many forms, but the dominant trend is for the monitoring of free and fair elections within the country. However, this is only one of the options open to the parties and the UN which is covered in this chapter. The focus will be on the actual or attempted implementation of peaceful solutions to internal conflicts rather than on the various modes of settlement as listed in standard texts, namely negotiation, mediation,

201

inquiry, conciliation, arbitration and judicial settlement, except to give a brief description of each.[2]

Negotiation occurs directly between the parties to a dispute, either through diplomatic machinery or through summit diplomacy between heads of state or government or faction leaders. *Mediation* involves a third party in negotiations and is therefore relevant for international organizations. The third party may simply be used by the parties to facilitate communication (strictly speaking this is 'good offices') or it may be asked to propose solutions. *Inquiry* can also involve international organizations since the parties agree to the sending of a commission of inquiry to ascertain the facts of the dispute. The UN and regional organizations have made significant practical contributions in this respect, as reviewed in Chapter 4. *Conciliation* is really a combination of the elements of inquiry and mediation, but is more formal and thus closer in many ways to adjudication. The conciliation commission looks at the facts and is empowered to define the terms of settlement which must, however, be accepted by the parties. There is limited institutional practice in this area. Whereas negotiation, mediation, inquiry and conciliation are diplomatic methods of settling disputes and may not necessarily comply entirely with international law, *arbitration and judicial settlement* does accord with the dictates of international law by means of an arbitral or judicial tribunal at the request of the parties. Such judicial methods within the context of international organizations are not a practical means of approaching internal conflicts because their machinery is geared for the settlement of inter-state disputes.

Regional and Other Organizations

As we have seen in Chapter 2, regional organizations possess similar powers in this field. Article 3(3) of the Charter of the OAU provides that Member states should agree to the 'peaceful settlement of disputes by negotiation, mediation, conciliation or arbitration'. Unlike the UN, the OAU is a much more loosely knit organization, relying primarily on informal diplomacy and the good offices of the OAU's Secretary General, despite the fact that the OAU Charter deliberately restricts the Secretary General's role to that of an administrator.[3] On paper the OAU has, as one of its principal institutions, a Commission of Mediation, Conciliation and Arbitration, established by article 19 of the OAU Charter and in an additional protocol of 1964.[4] However, this organ has not become operational, reflecting the unwillingness of African states to submit to formal dispute resolution mechanisms and also the limited budget of the African organization.

The OAS is a much more developed regional organization and has as part of its treaty make-up the *Pact* of Bogata or American Treaty on Pacific Settlement of 1948.[5] This is concerned solely with the settlement of disputes by peaceful means, providing for procedures of good offices, mediation, conciliation, investigation and judicial settlement and arbitration. Again, however, there is a contrast between theory and practice.[6] In practice the OAS does not use this treaty but rather the organs of the OAS created by the *Charter* of Bogata of 1948. These organs are the Inter-American Conference, which 'has the authority to consider any matter relating to friendly relations among the American States';[7] the Meeting of Consultation of Ministers of Foreign Affairs, which considers urgent matters of peace and security; the Council, which is permanently in session and has as a subsidiary organ, the Inter-American Committee on Peaceful Settlement, whose mandate is to assist in the pacific settlement of disputes through recommendations, as well as mediation and inquiry;[8] and the Secretary General who has developed a good offices function like his UN counterpart. In 1985 he was also given the power to bring to the attention of the Council or the Assembly 'any matter which in his opinion might threaten the peace and security of the hemisphere'.[9]

Furthermore, dispute resolution mechanisms and procedures can be found in the leading defence organization's make-up. In 1956 the primary organ of NATO, the North Atlantic Council, made a clear commitment to the peaceful settlement of disputes among members by resolving that, when disputes cannot be settled by direct negotiation, they should be submitted to NATO's good offices procedure through its Secretary General.[10]

Finally, regional organizations may mount a peacekeeping operation in an internal conflict, as with the Commonwealth Force in Rhodesia and the OAU force in Chad (reviewed in Chapter 8), and the West African peacekeeping force in Liberia (reviewed in Chapter 10) which has subsequently been supplemented by a UN force. However, regional organizations are usually involved only in negotiating a peaceful solution and not directly in the peacekeeping component. For example, the Secretary General of the relevant organization may work alongside his UN counterpart, as with OAS involvement in the Central American peace process and in Haiti, and with the OAU in Western Sahara.

This reflects the inability or rather unwillingness of regional organizations to become involved in the internal affairs of their members, as Professor Merrills has pointed out:

External limitations on the influence of regional organisations are matched by an internal limitation of comparable importance – the inability to deal effectively with disputes *within* member states. Regional organisations are created to further cooperation *between* states, and only in special cases, such as the European human rights system or the EEC, are they given jurisdiction over internal affairs. In practice this consideration does not altogether rule out regional intervention over matters of internal government if regional neighbours become sufficiently alarmed. Often, however, revolutions, civil wars and other disruptive events within states will so divide the membership as to make regional initiatives politically impossible. It is therefore not surprising that the two organisations in which the problem has arisen most frequently, the OAU and the OAS, have shown a marked disinclination to become involved in domestic affairs.[11]

The attempted secession from Nigeria of the Biafran region in 1967 typifies the approach of regional organizations to internal conflicts. Unusually, the OAU did discuss the conflict at its Fourth Assembly meeting, but subject to the overall condition that it should not attempt to interfere in the internal affairs of Nigeria. Throughout the several years of conflict, the OAU repeated its support for the territorial integrity of Nigeria, although some of its members did dissent and recognize Biafra as an independent state.[12]

In recent years, the UN has shown a willingness to attempt to settle internal conflicts by peaceful means, and increasingly in combination with the relevant regional organization. In Africa, this has culminated in the overseeing of the Eritrean secession achieved, unlike in Biafra, with the consent of the host state. We now turn to the role of the UN in partnering these operations.

Good Offices

The Secretary General of the UN or other international organization may offer his good offices to the belligerents in an internal conflict at any stage. Sometimes this may occur prior to a cease-fire, as in Namibia, Nicaragua and many of the other examples reviewed below. On other occasions a cease-fire is established, either with or without a request for a peacekeeping presence, and then the parties negotiate with the help of the Secretary General or his representative. The difference in approach can lead to radically different results. In many of the cases reviewed below, the UN has helped to negotiate a whole 'package' – from cease-fire to the holding of a referendum or elections. Such an approach, which often combines peacekeeping in a traditional sense with peacemaking based on an agreed pacific settlement, is fraught with dangers (as the UN's experience in Angola shows), but if implemented by the parties, it can lead to peaceful solutions (witnessed by the UN's successes in Nicaragua and Namibia). On the other hand, the establishment of a cease-fire as a priority followed by negotiations has the short-term advantage of securing a cessation of hostilities but the long-term disadvantage of often failing to achieve an overall political settlement, as both parties are unwilling to shift from the *status quo* established by the cease-fire. In this section we will briefly review the latter method, which in UN terms is the more traditional approach to peacekeeping and peace-making.

In the case of Cyprus, Security Council resolution 186 of March 1964 established the UN Force in Cyprus (UNFICYP) to oversee a cease-fire agreed to by the parties; it also recommended that the Secretary General appoint a mediator to seek a peaceful solution through good offices. Peacekeeping and a peaceful solution were contained in the same resolution, but they were not linked in the sense that the government of Cyprus agreed to a specific peaceful solution as well as to UNFICYP. The limitations of this approach are shown by the fact that, although a cease-fire was established be-tween the Greek and Turkish communities in 1964, the presence of the UN peacekeeping force did not prevent a Turkish invasion of the northern third of the island in 1974.[13] Furthermore, there appears, as yet, no prospect of a permanent settlement on the island, with nego-tiations continuing unsuccessfully to the present day.[14]

With the end of the Cold War between the US and the Soviet Union in the late 1980s, a more dynamic approach to peacekeeping and peacemaking was attempted, whereby good offices and negotia-tions would lead to an integrated settlement combining the policing of a cease-fire with the resolution of the dispute by methods chosen by the parties in conflict. However, although the changed atmos-phere at the UN in the late 1980s provided opportunities for the greater use of an integrated approach, the first attempt at combining peacekeeping with peaceful solution was unfortunately unsuccess-ful. UN Under Secretary General Cordovez attempted to negotiate a complete settlement of the Afghan conflict under a General Assem-bly mandate of 1980.[15] This was to encompass not only non-interven-tion by the superpowers in Afghanistan, but also an internal political settlement between the Soviet-backed regime and the American and Pakistani-backed rebels. However, Soviet haste to withdraw its troops from the combat zone prompted the Geneva Accords of April 1988,[16] which provided for the withdrawal of Soviet troops, non-interven-tion and a small UN presence in the form of the UN Good Offices Mission in Afghanistan and Pakistan (UNGOMAP) to supervise the Soviet withdrawal. A peaceful solution to the internal Afghan con-flict was omitted; the Secretary General's Good Offices Mission con-tinues,[17] as does the war.

Referendum

Since the end of the Cold War, the method which best seems to encapsulate the development of the principles of peacekeeping – namely those of neutrality, cooperation and consent – without threatening the sovereignty of the state or states in question, seems to be when the UN has combined peacekeeping and pacific settlement. This has involved bringing pressure to bear on the parties not only to agree to a peacekeeping force as a buffer, but also to accept a recommendation for settlement either by the Security Council, the General Assembly, the Secretary General or by outside states, bodies or individuals. Thus the force not only performs traditional functions such as overseeing the cease-fire, but also supervises the implementation of the peaceful solution to the conflict. More precisely, two or three separate forces or one force with two or three distinct elements are normally involved: a traditional peacekeeping component, perhaps a civilian police element when necessary, and finally a civilian component, normally an election supervision division, to oversee the implementation of the agreed settlement process. Whilst the peacekeeping aspect is derived from article 40, the police and election elements, designed to help the parties towards the agreed solution, are more obviously derived from articles 36 and 37 of Chapter VI of the UN Charter.

The origins of this approach can be traced back to the Cold War period, when the Netherlands and Indonesia sought and were granted General Assembly approval for the creation of a UN Temporary Executive Authority (UNTEA) and a UN Security Force (UNSF) on West Irian in 1962, first to supervise a cease-fire between the belligerents, and then to assume temporary authority over the island pending the transference of sovereignty to Indonesia.[18] UNTEA and UNSF carried out these functions successfully and were withdrawn in 1963. However, the final aspect of the peaceful solution agreed to by the Netherlands and Indonesia[19] was not carried out when Indonesia refused to hold a plebiscite before 1970 as stipulated.

The idea of holding a referendum as a means of finalizing the status of a disputed territory was again proposed for the Western Sahara but has so far proved as unsuccessful as the West Irian experiment. The conflict between Popular Front for the Liberation of the Sanguia el-Harura and the Rio de Oro (POLISARIO) guerrillas and Moroccan troops, which started in earnest in 1976 when Spain withdrew from its former colony of Western Sahara, seemed to be another intractable problem in which the UN was marginalized. However, the Secretary General, alongside his opposite number from the OAU,[20] persisted in their good offices and made a significant breakthrough on 30 August 1988, when their settlement proposals were accepted by the parties. The Security Council then instructed the Secretary General's Special Representative to formulate a referendum plan.[21]

An acceptable referendum plan was not approved by the Security Council until 27 June 1990, when in resolution 658 it accepted the Secretary General's report in which he detailed the settlement process[22] whereby the Western Saharan people would choose between independence and integration with Morocco. The referendum was originally scheduled for January 1992, but has been postponed because of cease-fire violations and disagreements on the composition of the electorate in Western Sahara.

The UN Mission for the Referendum in Western Sahara, known by its French acronym MINURSO, was authorized by the Security Council on 29 April 1991 in resolution 690 and was emplaced in September 1991 following a cease-fire agreed to by both parties. Despite the consent of the factions, MINURSO is experiencing tremendous difficulties, not only in covering the vast territory with only 349 military observers, as well as police and civilian personnel, but mainly because the necessary cooperation from the parties has been lacking. Besides numerous cease-fire violations, the main problem concerns the census list of those entitled to vote in the referendum, with both sides disagreeing and with POLISARIO accusing the UN of favouring Morocco.[23]

In these circumstances, with two of the basic principles of peacekeeping in jeopardy – namely unconditional acceptance of the provisional measures by the parties and neutrality (not in this case in the UN's supervision of the cease-fire, but in the administration of the peace process) – serious doubts have been raised as to whether a successful outcome can ever be achieved to this long-running dispute. The Secretary General expressed these doubts in February 1992,[24] and although negotiations have been resumed periodically in the interim over the issue of voter eligibility, the referendum appears at the time of writing to be no nearer, despite the fact that, as early as December 1991, the Security Council commissioned a new report on voting criteria which continues to form a basis for discussion between the two parties.[25] The Security Council continues to renew MINURSO's mandate, while urging the parties to agree on a referendum before the end of 1994.[26]

Independence

The Western Saharan referendum could result in the independence of that territory. Such an outcome was successfully achieved in Namibia. During the period of détente in the late 1970s, there arose the false hope that a solution to the South African occupation of Namibia was at hand. In 1976, the Security Council declared that the Namibian people should be 'enabled freely to determine their own future' by means of free elections under UN supervision.[27] Indeed, optimism was so high, despite South Africa being non-committal, that Canada, West Germany, France, Britain and the US made a proposal for the settlement of the Namibian situation, detailing the electoral process they envisaged.[28] This led in 1978 to the appointment of a Special Representative to negotiate with the parties concerned over acceptance of the peace plan and a decision by the Security Council to establish the UN Transition Assistance Group in Namibia (UNTAG) in accordance with a report by the Secretary General 'to ensure the early independence of Namibia through free elections under the supervision and control of the United Nations'.[29]

The Secretary General's report of 1978 recognized the 'unique character' of the proposed operation in that it entailed not only peacekeeping in the true sense – supervising a cease-fire between the South West African Peoples Organization (SWAPO) and South African forces – but also supervision of free and fair elections leading to an independent state. This resulted in the Secretary General recommending a large military force of some 7,500, with a component of several hundred police and civilian administrators. The mandate of the military component was interpreted to include the monitoring of the cessation of hostile acts; the restriction of South African and SWAPO forces to base; the phased withdrawal of all except a specified number of South African forces; the prevention of infiltration, and the monitoring of the demobilization of civilian police forces.

As with any peacekeeping force, before UNTAG could be put in place it needed the consent of all the parties to the conflict. SWAPO had consistently accepted resolution 435, whereas South African consent was not forthcoming until 22 December 1988 when it signed, along with Cuba and Angola, a tripartite agreement consenting to the UN peace plan.[30] The plan was acceptable to the South Africans because the accord linked Cuban withdrawal from Angola with South African withdrawal from Namibia. The agreement was also the result of pressure by the US on South Africa and by the Soviet Union on Cuba and Angola. The agreement envisaged the independence process commencing on 1 April 1989. SWAPO and South Africa agreed to a cease-fire to commence on 1 April, so preparing the ground for UNTAG.

UNTAG's mandate was still based on the Security Council resolution of 1978 and the accompanying report by the Secretary General. The military component's task was to oversee the implementation of provisional measures necessary to the success of the independence process, which was to be monitored by the civilian component. UNTAG's mandate contained the possibility of its being able to enforce the peace, but it failed to do so when faced with a breakdown in the cease-fire. Indeed, both South Africa and the UN foresaw UNTAG as having only a neutral and impartial function.[31]

Although the Security Council resolved to implement its plan for Namibian independence in its original and definitive form, it eventually decided to reduce the size of UNTAG to 4,500. This followed intense pressure from the five permanent members who thought that the improved climate in southern Africa, in addition to financial constraints, meant that a smaller peacekeeping force was sufficient for the tasks in hand. The wrangling over the size of the force, combined perhaps with some complacency as to the anticipated success of the peace process, may have caused the inauspicious start to the UN plan when, on 1 April 1989, the cease-fire was breached. Several hundred SWAPO guerrillas infiltrating from Angola were met with force by South African troops purportedly acting under UNTAG authority (the UN had only 1,000 troops in Namibia, with very few in the border area).[32] Without doubt, the South African troops enforced the peace more harshly than the peacekeeping force was mandated to. On the other hand, SWAPO appeared to be in breach of the tripartite accord which confined the guerrillas to bases inside Angola. However, although SWAPO had consented to the UN plan as laid down in 1978, it was not a party to the agreement which finalized the details. The peacemakers seemed to have ignored the fact that all the parties to the dispute should have fully consented to all aspects of the peace agreement before the peacekeeping force was put in place.

During the fighting between SWAPO and the South African forces, the UN appeared helpless. It required a new agreement on 8 April between the original signatories to the tripartite accord – and this time consented to by SWAPO – before a new cease-fire could be made effective. The fresh agreement between South Africa, Angola and Cuba, with the US and the Soviet Union overseeing, provided for a cease-fire and a withdrawal of SWAPO fighters to north of the 16th parallel under UN supervision.

The shaky start to the UN plan gave rise to fears that the elections, scheduled for 1 November 1989, might be delayed. However, the Joint Monitoring Commission of Angola, South Africa and Cuba agreed on 14 May 1989 that the situation was sufficiently normalized for the plan to proceed on schedule. UNTAG then successfully ensured a free and fair election on 11 November 1989 at which 97 per cent of the electorate voted. Full independence was achieved on 21 March 1990.[33]

Elections

Although UNTAG's successful completion of its mandate was a cause for celebration, it must be borne in mind that the UN had been concerned with the question of South Africa's occupation of Namibia for over 40 years. Given the unique nature of the Namibian situation, it was questionable whether the UN would have another opportunity to try to combine peacekeeping with pacific settlement.

However, even before UNTAG had completed its task, the Secretary General, operating under a loose mandate from the Security Council and the General Assembly, was establishing a similar, if much smaller, operation in Central America. Although like UNTAG, it combined peacekeeping with pacific settlement, the Central American operation involved a further significant step in the legal and political development of peacekeeping. Whereas UNTAG was concerned with bringing about a state's independence, which could be seen as part of the UN's deep-rooted drive to end colonialism, the operation in Central America was concerned with the electoral process in an already independent state, namely Nicaragua.

Until the late 1980s, the UN had vetoed attempts by Nicaragua to have its complaints investigated by the Security Council.[34] The Reagan Administration viewed the blocking of any UN initiatives as part and parcel of its policy of removing the Sandinista government in Nicaragua. The Bush Administration decided to accept a peaceful solution to the problem by supporting the Central American peace process after the Guatemala Agreements were signed in August 1987 by Guatemala, El Salvador, Honduras, Nicaragua and Costa Rica.[35]

The Agreements were characterized by general pledges, which, *inter alia* called for national reconciliation; the cessation of hostilities within the countries concerned; democratization, which included commitments to freedom of the press, political pluralism and the ending of states of emergency; free elections in all five countries; the cessation of assistance to irregular forces and, finally, the non-use of territory for aggression against other states.

The agreement on free elections committed the five governments to involve the UN as well as the OAS in verifying the electoral processes in each state. Thus the UN could not claim credit for instituting the process of pacific settlement, the initiative having come from the parties to the various conflicts. However, it was certainly willing to assist the settlement process. In furtherance of the Guatemala Agreements, President Ortega agreed to hold elections in Nicaragua.[36] As part of this agreement, the Central American countries requested UN supervision of the electoral process, as well as announcing their agreement with the UN Secretary General that a multinational force should be placed in the area to help prevent cross-border attacks, weapons infiltration and any other kind of external interference with the electoral process.

The speed of UN reaction to this request was impressive, reflecting the fact that the UN Secretary General had kept very much abreast of the situation, pursuant to a very vague mandate initially granted in Security Council resolution 562 of 1985, which requested that he keep the Security Council aware of any developments in the Central American situation. After the initial request in February 1989, the Secretary General announced in July that a UN Observer Mission to Verify the Electoral Process in Nicaragua (ONUVEN) would be established to supervise elections.[37]

This was retrospectively endorsed by the Security Council in resolution 637 of 1989, which merely noted with 'appreciation the Secretary General's agreement with Nicaragua to deploy a United Nations elections observer mission in that country'. A similar approach was taken to the observer force, whose function it was to supervise a regional cease-fire. Again the Security Council appeared content to endorse the Secretary General's efforts when it adopted resolution 644 of 1989 formally authorizing the creation of ONUCA – the UN Observation Group in Central America.

The Secretary General's good offices mission in Central America derived from Security Council resolution 562 of 1985, but took on a much wider aspect. Resolution 562 merely accorded him a reporting function which is far removed from negotiating the emplacement of two UN forces. However, the Secretary General may have perceived his Central American mandate to be granted not only by the Security Council, but also by the unanimous support of the General Assembly expressed at its 42nd session in October 1987. Resolution 42/1 requested that the Secretary General afford the fullest support to the five Central American governments in their efforts to achieve peace, especially by granting the assistance requested in the setting up of verification machinery.[38]

ONUVEN, the electoral verification mission in Nicaragua, reported throughout the build-up to the election in Nicaragua; despite some irregularities, it was able to report, along with other observers, that a free and fair election took place in Nicaragua on 25 February 1990, which resulted in a surprising defeat for the Sandinista government. ONUCA successfully helped to maintain the peace in the region during the Nicaraguan elections[39] and was then redeployed by the Security Council, in resolution 650 of March 1990, to help in the demobilization of the Contras – the final step to a peaceful settlement of the internationalized civil war that has been waged on Nicaraguan soil for over a decade.

Despite the success of its election supervision in Nicaragua, the UN and regional organizations are by no means guaranteed against failure – as the situation in Angola amply illustrates. UNAVEM I was established after Cuba and Angola signed a bilateral accord on 22 December 1988,[40] providing for the withdrawal of Cuban troops from Angola. The bilateral accord provided that the 50,000 Cuban troops allegedly present in Angola, 'in accordance with Article 51 of the UN Charter', should be withdrawn by 1 July 1991, after phased withdrawal within Angola to the 15th and 13th parallels, providing that no flagrant violations of the tripartite agreement occurred. Angola and Cuba then requested that the Security Council verify 'the redeployment and the phased and total withdrawal of Cuban troops' from Angola. In anticipation of this agreement, on 20 December 1988, the Security Council decided to establish UNAVEM for a period of 31 months to carry out the mandate provided for in the agreement between Angola and Cuba.[41]

In fact the Cuban troop withdrawal was completed ahead of schedule, by the beginning of June 1991. However, UNAVEM did not become redundant in that, with the outside props removed (in the form of Cuban support for the Angolan government and South African support for UNITA), the two opponents in the civil war reached an agreement in Lisbon on 31 May 1991 on a cease-fire and the holding of elections by 30 November 1992. The parties requested UN supervision of the cease-fire and of the elections, leading to a revised mandate for UNAVEM, re-christened UNAVEM II, by Security Council resolution 696, unanimously adopted on 30 May 1991. UNAVEM thus became integral in the second stage of peacekeeping – the implementation of an agreed peaceful solution – involving not only such traditional peacekeeping functions as overseeing the cease-fire (to be carried out by the military component of the force), but also the supervision of the Angolan police force and of the elections (to be carried out by police and civilian elements).[42] To this end the size of the force was increased from 70 military observers to 350 military observers, 90 police observers and 71 civilian election observers.

The elections were held on 29 and 30 September 1992 under UNAVEM II's supervision and were declared generally free and fair by the Secretary General's Special Representative.[43] The governing party, the Popular Movement for the Liberation of Angola (MPLA), won the largest share of the vote; as a result, the National Union for the Total Independence of Angola (UNITA) challenged the validity of the elections. After a meeting of the Security Council on 6 October 1992, an *Ad Hoc* Commission was sent to Angola to support the implementation of the Peace Accords. The four-member Commission met with the leaders of the two factions and seemed assured that they would take every step possible to prevent violence in the country. The Council appeared satisfied with this when, on 19 October 1992, it made a statement welcoming the Commission's contribution to reducing tension and to finding a solution to the difficulties that had arisen since the elections. It called upon all the parties to abide by the commitments entered into by them, in particular with regard to the demobilization of their troops and the formation of the Unified Armed Forces, and to refrain from any action that would increase tension.

Nevertheless, in a later report the Secretary General recognized that, immediately after the election results were announced on 17 October 1992, UNITA had launched a nationwide operation to occupy municipalities in Angola by force; indeed, by 23 November 1992 it had control over two-thirds of the 164 municipalities in the country.[44] The fighting continued despite a demand for a cessation of hostilities by the Security Council on 30 October 1992 which was specifically directed at UNITA, effectively labelling it as the responsible party.[45] UNITA charges that UNAVEM II was guilty of colluding with the governing MPLA faction had been rejected as 'baseless' by the Security Council in a previous statement of 27 October 1992. Despite an apparent agreement by UNITA to accept the election results, despite a recommitment to the Peace Accords by both parties on 19 and 26 November, coupled with a further call for a cease-fire by the Council on 30 November, the fighting continued. Evidence that the Council's patience was wearing thin was found in the Presidential Statement of 22 December 1992 which called on the parties to agree on a 'realistic plan' for the implementation of the Accords. It also urged them to 'produce early evidence of their willingness and ability' to work together to implement the Accords 'so that the international community would feel encouraged to continue committing its scarce resources to the continuation of the United Nations operation in Angola on its present scale'.

Despite this veiled threat to withdraw UNAVEM II, the Security Council continues to renew the force's mandate, while demanding a cease-fire, compliance with election results and with the Peace Accords, as well as a resumption of UN-sponsored negotiations.[46] Although UNITA's complaint of UNAVEM II collusion with the government was without foundation, such allegations may well increase as the UN becomes involved in peacemaking and in organizing elections or referenda in which one side inevitably wins over the other. Thus the UN could endanger one of the founding principles of peacekeeping, that of neutrality.

Such dangers appeared even greater as regards the UN's involvement in the Cambodian peace process. As with Angola, the end of the Cold War signified a change in the attitude of the parties to the Cambodian conflict which had raged since the civil war of 1970–75. The Communists (the Khmer Rouge) won that war and then subjected the population of the country to genocidal outrages which cost about 2 million lives. The Vietnamese ousted the Khmer Rouge in 1979 and set up a puppet regime which waged war against the Khmer Rouge who were still supported by Communist China. When the Vietnamese pulled out in 1989, it appeared that the country might slip back into civil war. However, the UN-brokered peace talks, which started in earnest a few months before the Vietnamese troops withdrew in September, took hold in the post-Cold War climate, and Cambodia started taking some tentative but positive steps towards a peaceful solution to what had seemed to most observers an intractable conflict.

The four factions involved in the Cambodian conflict agreed to a cease-fire in May 1991 and signed the Paris Peace Accords six months later, on 23 October. This document contained several agreements detailing, *inter alia*, a comprehensive settlement of the Cambodian conflict which included the establishment of the UN Transition Assistance Authority in Cambodia (UNTAC) for an 18-month period, as well as a programme for elections and for the creation of a new Cambodian constitution.[47] The Security Council authorized the creation of UNTAC and the immediate despatch of a UN Advance Mission in Cambodia (UNAMIC) to deal with the initial supervision of the cease-fire and to assist in mine clearance.[48] The Secretary General was asked to prepare a plan for the full implementation of the peace process by creating and emplacing an effective UN peacekeeping force.

On 28 February 1992, the Security Council unanimously approved the Secretary General's implementation plan,[49] thus creating the largest and most ambitious UN peacekeeping operation in the Organization's history, with over 22,000 personnel (16,000 military personnel, 3,500 police monitors and over 1,500 civilian administrators) to be in position by May 1992. This would oversee the country's transition to a new regime after multi-party elections, scheduled for May 1993. The mandate of the force, derived from the Paris Peace Accords, covered a wide variety of matters, many beyond the core peacekeeping function of supervising a cease-fire.

The function of the military component of the force was to verify the withdrawal of all foreign forces, to monitor the cessation of outside military assistance, and to supervise the cease-fire and related measures such as the cantonment of the various armed bands and their subsequent disarmament and demobilization. The civilian administrators were to exercise direct control over existing institutions in Cambodia to ensure strict neutrality, whilst the civilian police monitors controlled the local police to ensure that law and order were maintained effectively and impartially. In addition to the election supervision, UNTAC has within it a human rights component along the lines of ONUSAL in El Salvador (see below).

It can readily be seen that UNTAC was in many respects the culmination of UN peacekeeping to date in that its mandate covered every aspect of traditional peacekeeping as well as the features of the new forces with integrated mandates. The concept behind the implementation plan, reflected in discussions in the Security Council at the adoption of resolution 745 and stated clearly by the Secretary General at the signing of the Final Act at the Paris Peace Conference, was 'to encourage the establishment of a neutral political environment in which the Cambodian people can freely determine their future'.[50]

As with the initial demobilization of SWAPO forces in Namibia, UNTAC ran into serious problems concerning the cantonment of the Khmer Rouge. The process envisaged that the emplacement of the peacekeeping force was to be followed by the demobilization and disarmament of the four factions, beginning on 13 June 1992. This would entail the collection of the arms of an estimated 200,000 troops from the various factions gathering in 95 UN-controlled regroupment areas. The Secretary General reported on 21 July to the Security Council that less than 5 per cent of this figure had been cantoned.[51] In addition the Khmer Rouge had stepped up its cease-fire violations. It spuriously used the excuse that the UN had not properly supervised the withdrawal of Vietnamese troops and that, by controlling the government administrators, it had conferred legitimacy on that government. The charge was obviously intended to undermine the UN's neutrality, a facet particularly essential to its success in this operation.

Despite these difficulties and the refusal of the Khmer Rouge to participate in the Supreme National Council (SNC) of Cambodia, established under the peace agreements as the country's temporary sovereign body, the UN, in consultation with the SNC, activated UNTAC's civil administration component on 1 July 1992, exercising control over foreign affairs, defence, finance, public security, information, health, education, agriculture, fishing, transport, postal distribution, energy, tourism and mines. In addition, the SNC agreed to the UN Electoral Law on 13 August, by which the elections were to be governed. The Security Council attempted once more to obtain Khmer Rouge compliance with the peace process when it adopted resolution 783 on 13 October but, with no evidence that its demands were being heeded, it changed tack. On 30 November 1992, it asked the Secretary General to consider the implications for the elections of the non-compliance of the Khmer Rouge, determining that they should proceed in May 1993 in all areas of Cambodia to which UNTAC had access. In addition, it suggested various types of embargoes that could be imposed against Khmer Rouge-held areas. Abandoning its policy of trying to encourage the Khmer Rouge to participate in the election process, it decided to proceed without them, despite the fact that only about 25 per cent of the troops of the four factions had by that time entered the cantonment sites, so creating the potential for conflict in an atmosphere of distrust and non-cooperation on the part of the Khmer Rouge.[52]

Cease-fire violation by all parties increased in the period leading up to the proposed election dates. In a report dated 3 May 1993 the Secretary General admitted that the elections would not be taking place in an environment as disarmed and politically neutral as was foreseen in the Paris Agreements. However, he stated that the elections would proceed, for any other course would mean giving in to unacceptable threats, particularly from the Khmer Rouge. In a later report to the Council on 15 May, the Secretary General said that UNTAC would be conducting 'the most impartial election possible in conditions that are not susceptible to its full control'. Despite these misgivings and the prospect of armed disruptions of voting by the Khmer Rouge, the elections were successfully carried out with a minimum of disruption in the period 25–28 May 1993 with a 90 per cent turnout.

Despite the euphoria that surrounded this somewhat unexpected success, there remains the possibility of a return to civil war similar to that in Angola, with the defeated government faction claiming election fraud by the victorious Front Uni National Pour un Cambodge Independent, Neutre, Pacifique et Cooperatif (FUNCINPEC). In resolution 840 adopted on 15 June 1993, the Security Council endorsed the results of the Cambodian election and called on all parties to comply with them. It welcomed Prince Sihanouk's efforts to promote national reconciliation under his leadership and fully supported to newly elected Constituent Assembly which had begun to draw up a constitution. The Security Council felt sufficiently confident to authorize the withdrawal of UNTAC in November 1993 after a new Cambodian government had been created.[53]

Difficulties for peacekeepers in Angola, Western Sahara and Cambodia have called into question the ambitious approach to peaceful settlement undertaken by the UN in recent years. This has been compounded by the re-emergence of unrest in Nicaragua in mid-1993 as well as in attempts to settle the conflict in Mozambique where, although the parties to the civil conflict agreed on 4 October 1992 to a peaceful settlement and to the emplacement of the UN Operation in Mozambique (ONUMOZ),[54] limited progress has been made on the ground.[55] The increased financial strain on the peace-keeping budget is another serious problem. It is questionable, as the Angolan experience is beginning to show, how long the world community will continue to finance what sometimes appear to be speculative settlement ventures, if the success rate, so encouraging in Namibia and Nicaragua, does not improve. Fortunately, the financial problems were not dramatically increased by the UN's limited involvement in the South African peace process where UN observers, initially despatched in August 1992,[56] monitored the successful election process held in April 1994.

Nevertheless, for the moment the Security Council has maintained the peacekeeping momentum, with forces authorized and emplaced in Haiti to help restore democracy, although the UN Mission in Haiti (UNMIH) is struggling to establish itself in the face of hostile factions;[57] in Georgia where the UN Mission (UNOMIG) is mandated with the task of supervising a fragile cease-fire;[58] in Liberia where the UN Observer Mission (UNOMIL) will supervise a cease-fire and elections to be held by March 1994 alongside the established Economic Community of West African States Military Observer Group (ECOMOG);[59] and in Rwanda where the UN Assistance Mission (UNAMIR)) will help implement a cease-fire and peace agreement between the government and the Rwandese Patriotic Front (RPF), leading to elections by December 1995.[60]

The strain on the UN's budget, the uncertainties about the success of election supervision, and the extent to which the world community sees such supervision as part of a wider acceptance of some sort of right to democracy[61] all call into question whether the UN's combined approach to peacekeeping and election supervision will continue, although current signs indicate that it will. However, question marks remain as to whether the UN will be on call as a neutral observer for any electoral process if so requested by a state or by factions within a state. Nevertheless, in October 1990, the General Assembly approved the establishment of the UN Observer Group for the Verification of Elections in Haiti (ONUVEH).[62] This operation did not have any military peacekeeping or observation component, consisting entirely of civilian observers whose function was to report on the electoral process taking place in that strife-torn country. Although peaceful elections took place on 16 December 1990, the elected government was ousted by a military coup in September 1991. It may tentatively be suggested that, without the stabilizing presence of a UN military component for at least one or two years, the chances of a stable government emerging from the electoral process in such a troubled country are much reduced. Further, the situation in Haiti is purely internal, unlike in Nicaragua, Namibia, El Salvador, Cambodia and Western Sahara, for instance, where international repercussions or implications were or continue to be a significant factor.

It may be in recognition of these limitations that the General Assembly, in accepting a recommendation of its Third Committee on Social, Humanitarian and Cultural Affairs, adopted a resolution on 17 December 1991 on the issue of periodic and genuine elections. The Assembly affirmed 'that electoral verification by the United Nations should remain an exceptional activity of the Organisation to be undertaken in well-defined circumstances, *inter alia*, primarily in situations with a clear international character'.

Despite this caveat, the Assembly stressed its conviction that 'periodic and genuine elections are a necessary and indispensable element of sustained efforts to protect the rights and interests of the governed and that ... the rights of everyone to take part in the government of his or her country is a crucial factor in the effective enjoyment of all of a wide range of other human rights and fundamental freedoms, embracing political, economic, social and cultural rights'. This referred to the significance of the Universal Declaration on Human Rights and the International Covenant on Civil and Political Rights, 'which establish that the authority to govern shall be based on the will of the people, as expressed in periodic and genuine elections'. Any requests for electoral assistance received by the Secretary General or the Electoral Assistance Unit at the UN, established in April 1992, should be notified to the 'competent organ' of the UN, which presumably means either the General Assembly or the Security Council,[63] for approval or not as the case may be. Between April 1992 and April 1993, the Electoral Assistance Unit provided electoral 'assistance' to 31 countries, although in the main this was simply advice, usually in the form of sending a consultant to the requesting country.[64] Only in Angola, Cambodia, El Salvador, Eritrea (see below) and Mozambique did the request result in an observer team whose purpose was to oversee the elections, although in other cases the UN consultants worked alongside observers from other countries or organizations. It appears that whilst General Assembly or Security Council consent has been sought for the establishment of observer teams, the Electoral Assistance Unit, under the supervision of the Under Secretary General for Political Affairs, can provide advice and send consultants without specific authorization from the Assembly or Council.

Human Rights

The continuation of the Central American peace process into El Salvador necessitated a further development of the integrated peacekeeping and peacemaking (in the form of pacific settlement) approach. Whereas the Nicaraguan operation required the supervision of a cease-fire and elections, the UN Observer Mission in El Salvador was initially set up to verify that the parties to the long-running civil war, namely the US-backed government and the left-wing Farabundo Marti National Liberation Front (FMLN) were complying with the human rights accord they signed at San José in July 1990.[65] Although not the usual type of provisional or interim measure that the UN undertakes, it can be seen that the observance of human rights by both parties to a particularly vicious civil war was an interim measure or a first step towards a lasting political settlement.

The Security Council, in establishing ONUSAL and outlining its initial mandate in resolution 693 on 20 May 1991, urged the parties to agree on a cease-fire and on a final pacific solution to the conflict. With these agreements as a foundation, ONUSAL would then become an integrated peacekeeping operation, verifying provisional measures as well as overseeing a final peaceful solution.

Such an approach illustrates the highly flexible and dynamic nature of peacekeeping and peaceful solution in the post-Cold War era. The major element of ONUSAL was formed from the disbanding of ONUCA which had effectively supervised the cease-fire necessary for the holding of elections in Nicaragua, illustrating how UN peacekeeping has been firmly built into the Central American peace process. The parties in El Salvador formally ended the civil war by agreements made on 31 December 1991 and on 16 January 1992, with the peaceful solution being detailed in the latter agreement and in negotiations lasting until June 1992.[66] The agreement contained a cease-fire commencing on 1 February 1992 and continuing for nine months until the FMLN's military structure was dismantled, with its members being integrated into the civil and political life of the country, including its institutions. Later negotiations revealed a new police force, a reformed electoral code to legalize the FMLN as a political party, as well as government purchase of land for peasants. The aim of the agreements was to address the social inequalities that led to the civil war – to create a 'revolution by negotiation' according to the Secretary General.[67] In order to service these agreements, the Security Council expanded ONUSAL's mandate by splitting the force into two, with a military division to verify cease-fire arrangements and a police division to monitor public order pending the formation of a new national police force.[68]

The formal ending of the civil war on 15 December 1992 was followed by a request from the government of El Salvador in January 1993 that the UN verify elections scheduled for March 1994.[69] However, the Security Council made it clear in a Presidential statement on 9 February 1993 that neither the government nor the FMLN had fully complied with the accords, in particular the government's obligations regarding its armed forces and the FMLN's duty to destroy its weapons under ONUSAL supervision. Despite these difficulties, the Security Council enlarged ONUSAL's mandate to include an electoral component to monitor and verify the elections in resolution 832 of 27 May 1993.[70] Peaceful elections were held on 20 March and 24 April 1994. ONUSAL's mandate has been extended until at least November 1994 to monitor continued compliance with the peace accords.

Secession

The UN's Electoral Assistance Unit was heavily involved in the referendum in the Ethiopian province of Eritrea in April 1993, which led to the secession of Eritrea from the rest of Ethiopia.

The Mengistu regime in Ethiopia, which held the country together by force, was finally overthrown in May 1991 by forces grouped under the Ethiopian Peoples Revolutionary Democratic Front, a close ally of the Eritrean Peoples Liberation Front (EPLF). The new provisional government of Ethiopia agreed that the EPLF could set up a separate interim administration in Eritrea, thus allowing the province to be separately administered until a referendum on independence was held in April 1993. In May 1992, the Eritrean Referendum Commission requested the UN to undertake the verification of this referendum, along with other international observers, particularly from the OAU. In response the Secretary General, after receiving reports from the Electoral Assistance Unit's consultants, requested that the General Assembly authorize the establishment of the UN Observer Mission to Verify the Referendum in Eritrea (UNOVER).[71] On 16 December 1992, the General Assembly acceded to this request.[72] A core team of 21 observers, headed by the Secretary General's Special Representative, arrived in January 1993, supplemented by an additional 86 observers in April.

In response to the question 'Do you wish Eritrea to be an independent country?' 99.8 per cent of the people who voted from 23–25 April 1993 (98.2 per cent of those eligible) responded affirmatively. ONUVER ensured the impartiality of the process by establishing a system of voter identification, observing the polling, guaranteeing that the EPLF fighters remained in barracks and making sure that those 300,000 of the 1.1 million registered voters who lived outside Eritrea were registered and could vote. The Secretary General's Special Representative stated that the vote was free and fair.[73] Eritrea made its formal declaration of independence on 24 May 1993, was recognized by Ethiopia as an independent country and was admitted to membership of the UN and OAU.

Conclusion

From this review of mainly UN practice, it can be seen that the role of international organizations in internal conflicts has increased dramatically with the end of the Cold War. Before that there was little attempt by the UN or by regional organizations to settle internal conflicts, but now a concerted effort is made by the UN to achieve peaceful settlements using peacekeeping where necessary and in tandem with the relevant regional organization when possible. The success of this new enterprise hangs in the balance as the international community weighs the advantages of settlement in cases such as Namibia, Nicaragua, Eritrea and (so far) Cambodia, with the apparent lack of success in Afghanistan, Angola, Haiti and Western Sahara. If the UN and its regional counterparts can eventually solve these conflicts and add to its list of successes settlements in Liberia, Mozambique and El Salvador, in which the process has not yet been completed, then there will be ample justification for claiming that the UN has helped to establish a viable means of settling internal conflicts – something that has always eluded the world community to date.

Notes

1   See further T.M. Frank and G. Nolte, 'The Good Offices Function of the UN Secretary General' in A. Roberts and B. Kingsbury, *United Nations, Divided World*, 2nd edn (Clarendon, 1993), pp.143–82.
2   See generally J.G. Merrills, *International Dispute Settlement*, 2nd edn (Grotius Publications, 191).
3   479 UNTS 39, articles 16–18.
4   (1964) 3 *ILM* p.1116. For discussion, see T. Maluwa, 'The Peaceful Settlement of Disputes among African States, 1963–1983: Some Conceptual Issues and Practical Trends' (1989) 38 *ICLQ* p.299.
5   30 UNTS 55.
6   See generally L.R. Scheman and J.W. Ford, 'The Organization of American States as Mediator' in S. Touval and I.W. Zartman (eds), *International Mediation in Theory and Practice* (Boulder, 1985).
7   119 UNTS 4, article 33.
8   See C. Sepulveda, 'The Reform of the Charter of American States' (1972) 137 *Hague Recueil* p.83.
9   See Merrills, *International Dispute Settlement*, p.210.
10 *Ibid.*, p.208.
11 *Ibid.*, p.219.
12 G.J. Naldi, *The Organization of African Unity* (Mansell, 1989), pp.37–8.
13 SC Res. 353, 29 UN SCOR (1974).
14 UN doc. S/25912 (1993). The fact that Greece and Turkey are both members of NATO meant that the lines of communication between the parties were kept open; Merrills, *International Dispute Settlement*, p.213.
15 GA Res. ES-6/2, 6 UN GAOR ESS (1980).
16 1988, 27 *ILM* p.577.
17 GA Res. 47/119, 47 UN A/PV (1992).
18 GA Res. 1752, 17 UN GAOR (1962).
19 274 UNTS 6311.
20 In August 1982 the issue of Western Sahara had split the OAU when the Saharan Democratic Republic was admitted to the organization, causing Morocco to leave. Despite this the Secretary General of the OAU continued with his good offices mission.
21 SC Res. 621, 43 UN SCOR (1988).

22 UN doc. S/21360 (1990).
23 *The Independent* (London), 6 February 1992.
24 UN doc. S/23662 (1992).
25 SC Res. 725, 46 UN SCOR (1991).
26 SC Res. 809, 48 UN S/PV (1993). Secretary General's report, 24 November 1993.
27 SC Res. 385, 31 UN SCOR (1976).
28 UN doc. S/12636 (1978).
29 SC Res. 435, 33 UN SCOR (1978).
30 UN doc. S/20346 (1988).
31 UN doc. S/20412/Add 1 (1989).
32 *Keesing's* (1989) p.36576.
33 UN doc. S/20967 (1990).
34 But see SC Res. 562, 40 UN SCOR (1985).
35 1987, 26 *ILM* p.1164.
36 *Keesing's* (1989) p.36460.
37 UN doc. S/20699 (1989).
38 GA Res. 42/1, 42 UN GAOR (1987). See also GA Res. 43/24, 43 UN GAOR (1988).
39 UN docs. S/20895, S/20979 (1989).
40 UN doc. S/20345 (1988).
41 SC Res. 626, 43 UN SCOR (1988).
42 UN doc. S/22627 Add 1 (1991).
43 (1992) 29(4) *UN Chronicle* p.9.
44 UN doc. S/24858 (1992).
45 SC Res. 785, 47 UN S/PV (1992).
46 SC Res. 804, 811, 823, 48 UN S/PV (1993). See also SC Res. 864, 48 UN S/PV (1993), imposing an arms and oil embargo over UNITA-held areas of Angola.
47 UN doc. S/23179 (1991).
48 SC Res. 717, 718, 46 UN SCOR (1991). Also SC Res. 728, 47 S/PV (1992).
49 SC Res. 745, 47 UN S/PV (1992); UN doc. S/23613 (1992).
50 UN Press Release, 23 October 1991; SC 3057 mtg, 47 S/PV (1992).
51 UN doc. S/24286 (1992).
52 UN doc. S/24800 (1992).
53 SC Res. 860, 48 UN S/PV (1993). But see SC Res. 879, 48 UN S/PV (1993).
54 See SC Res. 797, 47 UN S/PV (1992).
55 See SC Res. 818, 850, 882, 48 UN S/PV (1993).
56 SC Res. 765, 772, 47 UN S/PV (1992).
57 SC Res. 867, 873, 48 UN S/PV (1993).
58 SC Res. 858, 876, 48 UN S/PV (1993).
59 SC Res. 866, 48 UN S/PV (1993).
60 SC Res. 872, 48 UN S/PV (1993).
61 GA Res. 47/130, 47 UN A/PV (1992).
62 GA Res. 45/2, 45 UN GAOR (1990).
63 GA Res. 46/137, 46 UN GAOR (1991). But see GA Res. 47/138, 47 UN A/PV (1992).
64 UN Press Release GA/491, 16 April 1993.
65 UN doc. S/21541 (1990).
66 UN doc. S/23999 (1992).
67 (1992) 29(2) *UN Chronicle*, p.30.
68 SC Res. 729, 47 UN S/PV (1992).
69 UN doc. 26 January 1993.
70 See also SC Res. 888, 48 UN S/PV (1993). See further GA Res. 47/118, 47 UN A/PV (1992), which not only expressed support for the peace process in El Salvador, but also welcomed the agreement between the government of Guate-

mala and the URNG guerrillas, reached in Mexico City in April 1991 as a first step in ending the civil conflict in that country.

71   UN doc. A/47/544 (1992).
72   GA Res. 47/114, 47 UN A/PV (1992).
73   (1993) 30(3) *UN Chronicle*, p.39.

10 The Use of Coercion by International Organizations in Civil Wars

This chapter concentrates on the two principal forms of coercion used by international organizations to deal with internal conflicts, namely economic sanctions and the use of military measures other than peacekeeping.

Economic Coercion

The United Nations

Article 41 of the UN Charter reads as follows:

> The Security Council may decide what measures not involving the use of armed force are to be employed to give effect to its decisions and it may call upon the Members of the United Nations to apply such measures. These may include the complete or partial interruption of economic relations and of rail, sea, air, postal, telegraphic, radio, and other means of communication, and the severance of diplomatic relations.

The powers contained in article 41 were intended to allow for the imposition of mandatory enforcement measures following a threat to or breach of the peace under article 39. However, on many occasions, the Council has been unwilling to take mandatory action, calling instead for voluntary measures of sanctions. Such action can be viewed either as a reinterpretation of article 41 to allow for recommendations, or merely as a recommendation under Chapter VI, or a recommendation of enforcement action under article 39. Although the basis for such powers in the Charter is inconclusive, the Security Council has emphatically developed such power, the evolution of which lies in political compromise. In almost every case involving voluntary measures, the Western powers have objected to a finding under article 39 requiring mandatory sanctions. Voluntary sanctions, as the term implies, are breached with impunity and thus are relatively ineffective except as a symbolic statement. The General Assembly has developed a similar power under articles 10 and 14 of the Charter.

In the Rhodesian situation the Security Council called for an arms, oil and petroleum embargo to be imposed in 1965 following the Unilateral Declaration of Independence from the UK by the white minority regime.[1] The Western powers viewed this as a voluntary call, although others thought that it was 'only under Chapter VII that economic sanctions are mentioned'.[2] With at least two of the permanent members regarding the call as voluntary, the resolution was regarded as recommendatory.

International pressure sometimes has the effect of turning voluntary measures into mandatory ones. In the case of Rhodesia this happened relatively quickly: the Council first imposed selective mandatory sanctions in 1966 and then more comprehensive sanctions in 1968, with the aim of removing the white racist regime from power.[3] Nevertheless, with over two years elapsing before comprehensive mandatory measures were imposed, the effectiveness of the sanctions decreased for it allowed the Rhodesian economy time to prepare. The same can be said as regards the arms embargo placed on South Africa. This was originally a voluntary call made in 1963;[4] 14 years later it was made mandatory,[5] giving the South African government time to stockpile and to work out surreptitious supply routes.

Including Southern Rhodesia and South Africa, the Security Council has deployed the mandatory sanctions weapon on nine occasions, the others being as follows: comprehensive regimes against Iraq from 1990 and Yugoslavia (Serbia and Montenegro) in 1992; more selective regimes against Libya in 1992, Haiti in 1993 and UNITA-held areas of Angola in 1993; and arms embargoes against Somalia and Liberia in 1992. With the exception of Southern Rhodesia, all of the above sanctions regimes are still in place. It is clear from this list that during the Cold War until the end of the 1980s, the Council was very reluctant to use its full powers under article 41, but with the freeing of the Council from the chains of superpower control, it has used the power of this article quite frequently. Increasing use of its powers to impose mandatory sanctions indicates its faith in their effectiveness. The purpose here will be to review the use and efficacy of sanctions to combat and control internal conflicts, principally in Rhodesia, South Africa, Yugoslavia, Somalia, Liberia, Haiti and Angola.

There have been varying assessments of the effectiveness of the mandatory economic measures imposed against Rhodesia. The figures produced by the Security Council's Committee established to monitor reports on the effect of the sanctions regime suggest that, after struggling initially, from 1968 the Rhodesian economy improved.[6] This data would thus deny the effectiveness of economic measures.[7] Nevertheless, there is evidence to suggest that after 1974, with the combined effects of Mozambique's independence (Portugal, the colonial power, was a major sanctions breaker), the guerrilla war and the sanctions regime, the Rhodesian domestic situation as a whole began to decline. Although the application of sanctions did not immediately achieve the primary goals of the Security Council – either ending UDI by forcing Smith to negotiate, or ruining the Rhodesian economy and thus forcing internal change – it did help to achieve three subsidiary goals: the limitation of the conflict mainly to Rhodesian soil, the prevention of foreign military intervention to end UDI, and the inducement of the white regime to negotiate.

Nevertheless, in the Rhodesian case, sanctions were mandatory and so binding on member countries. The question remains as to why the Rhodesian economy was not affected more rapidly. One major reason for this was the poor timing of the imposition, whose effect Pokalas has summarized as follows:

> Such anticipatory actions as stockpiling materials, developing alternative supply sources to obviate over-dependence on any one source, diversifying domestic production, planting crops that were readily exportable, conserving key commodities and establishing new trade routes were utilised by Southern Rhodesia even prior to Security Council action.[8]

Comprehensive economic sanctions were imposed several years after the Unilateral Declaration of Independence by the Smith regime in 1965, which in UN terms was relatively quickly. However, it was six years since the UN had taken cognizance of the situation,[9] giving the regime ample time to prepare. For sanctions to have any chance of being effective, they must be immediate, mandatory and comprehensive. In the Rhodesian situation, sanctions were applied in a gradual crescendo of severity, creating many loopholes which the Security Council attempted to fill in a piecemeal fashion. Also, they did not have the full support of UN members, in particular the permanent members of the Security Council.

Furthermore, the sanctions in the Rhodesian situation were by no means watertight, and sanction breakers went unpunished in many instances.[10] Admittedly, in the case of Rhodesia, the two countries which openly defied sanctions, South Africa and Portugal, were at the time international pariahs and so outside the influence of the international community. Other prominent sanction breakers during the Rhodesian crisis were multinational corporations which proved most difficult to control because of their diverse locations and their economic and political power.

Another main sanction breaker was the US which in 1970 defied the Security Council by passing the Byrd Amendment enabling it to trade with Southern Rhodesia in strategic materials.[11] The Council, with the US abstaining, censored Washington in resolution 320 of 1972.[12] The Rhodesian economy could not but benefit from such illegal activities, as evidenced by its economy growing in proportion with the reported number of sanction violations. By 1968 there had been 13 violations; this had increased to 73 by 1970 and 346 by 1976. The US had committed 46 violations by 1978;[13] it had ignored a mandatory decision of the Security Council and had thereby abrogated its treaty obligations and breached Charter law. This cavalier attitude weakened the initial vigilance of other states, with the result that the mandatory measures were treated in a voluntary fashion, as a token gesture to be ignored with impunity.

Despite the weaknesses of the sanctions regime, the Smith government eventually negotiated majority rule, resulting in the Security Council lifting sanctions in 1979.[14] Sanctions had an effect, although Rhodesia was relatively strong in an economic sense. It was self-sufficient in agriculture, had abundant minerals (including gold) and a strong industrial base, but it still needed trade and investment. This is why the Council should have implemented a total embargo for, as Pokalas points out, 'had the embargo been properly implemented by States' legislation, strictly enforced by States' administration and judicial sectors, and diligently coordinated by the Committee, the Rhodesian economy would have floundered and ultimately collapsed'.[15]

Although evidence on the effectiveness of recent embargoes is preliminary, the sanctions experiences against Rhodesia and Iraq[16] seem to show that the only effective method of ensuring that the weaknesses of the target state's economy are exposed is to impose a comprehensive embargo. Limited embargoes are insufficient because, even if aimed at areas of weakness, other unsanctioned areas of the economy will develop to compensate.

The use of an arms embargo against South Africa was questionable because its strong economy and natural resource supply enabled it to produce its own weapons. However, an effectively policed arms embargo may be successful against a country like Somalia which is totally dependent on outside arms supplies. An arms embargo was thus imposed by the Council in resolution 733 of 23 January 1992. However, it contained no machinery for the monitoring of arms shipments, without which the Security Council has to rely on members' sense of obligation to implement a mandatory decision. Nevertheless, the fact that the Council did impose mandatory sanctions against one of the poorest nations in the world seems to have had some influence in leading the factions to negotiate. The Council's mandatory arms embargo against Liberia, imposed by resolution 788 of 19 November 1992, also seems to have had an impact on the peace process in that ravaged country, although by far the major factor may be the activities of the ECOWAS 'peacekeeping' force, which is exempted from the embargo. The effect of a mandatory oil and arms embargo against another extremely poor country, Haiti, by resolution 841 adopted on 17 June 1993, seems to have been even more dramatic, with the military regime agreeing on 2 July to the restoration of democracy under the deposed President, although the agreement was subsequently not implemented. The Security Council therefore reimposed the oil and arms embargo in October 1993, accompanied by the authorization to member states to stop suspected sanctions-breaking ships.[17]

These instances provide limited evidence that sanctions imposed to combat internal situations designated threats to the peace can be effective if the target state is very weak, and that a comprehensive embargo is not necessarily required to make these effective. Indeed, a comprehensive embargo against a state whose population is below the poverty line would seem inhumane in the extreme; as the sanctions regime against Iraq has shown, the UN ends up providing humanitarian assistance programmes to the country against which it has imposed an embargo. A slightly different approach has been taken as regards the civil war in Angola following the break-down in the peace process, with the Security Council imposing a mandatory arms and oil embargo only against UNITA-held areas of the country.[18] In this case sanctions are directed at the faction responsible for the continuation of the internal conflict. However, this more 'just' approach is only possible in a state which is not only divided politically or ethnically, but also geographically.

A more comprehensive embargo was imposed against the remnants of the war-torn state of Yugoslavia by resolution 757 of 30 May 1992. The Council condemned the continued intervention by Yugoslavia (Serbia and Montenegro) and Croatia in the former Yugoslav Republic and emerging state of Bosnia, and determined that the situation there constituted a threat to international peace and security. Despite the fact that both Serbia and Croatia were intervening in Bosnia in support of their respective factions, the Security Council implicitly blamed Serbia when it imposed mandatory sanctions against it on the import or export of commodities, except for 'supplies intended for medical purposes and foodstuffs' notified to the

Council's Committee on Sanctions against Yugoslavia, established by resolution 724 of 15 December 1991; it also froze financial and other transactions with Yugoslavia (Serbia and Montenegro).

This resolution built on the mandatory arms embargo imposed against the whole of Yugoslavia by resolution 713 of 25 September 1991. Clearly the aim of the arms embargo resolutions against Somalia, Haiti, Liberia and Yugoslavia is to prevent the escalation of the civil war which would be inevitable if outside states supplied arms to one faction or the other. One problem with this approach is that it leaves the most poorly armed faction, in this instance the Muslims in Bosnia, in a very vulnerable position. An attempt to lift the arms embargo to allow the Bosnian Muslims to receive arms was defeated on 29 June 1993 by a vote of six in favour to none against, with nine abstentions.

The aim of the more comprehensive sanctions regime against Serbia is to prevent its forces assisting the Bosnian Serbs in their struggle to gain more territory in Bosnia. Unlike the arms embargo, which is to prevent escalation, the aim of the regime against Serbia is to punish it for its intervention and support for the policy of ethnic cleansing, and to coerce it into withdrawing its military support for the Bosnian Serbs, as well as forcing that faction to agree (originally) to the Vance-Owen plan or to subsequent proposals for the peaceful settlement of the conflict in Bosnia.[19] The evidence is that the sanctions are having a dramatic effect in Serbia and Montenegro, with hyper-inflation, unemployment and many shortages being suffered as the embargo is tightened by those states surrounding Serbia and by the presence of NATO forces in the Mediterranean.

On 10 July 1992, NATO and the Western European Union (WEU), a regional defence pact established in 1954,[20] agreed to a policy of policing UN sanctions against Yugoslavia by means of an air and sea operation in the Adriatic, although without the authority to stop vessels suspected of breaking sanctions.[21] The UN resolution imposing sanctions, resolution 757, did not contain within it an express mandate to states to employ their navies to oversee sanctions. However, this was later remedied by resolution 787, adopted on 16 November 1992, in which the Council, 'acting under Chapters VII and VIII' of the UN Charter, called upon states, acting nationally or through regional agencies or arrangements, 'to use such measures commensurate with the specific circumstances as may be necessary under the authority of the Security Council to halt all inward and outward maritime shipping in order to inspect and verify their cargoes and destinations and to ensure strict implementation of the provisions of resolutions 713 (1991) and 757 (1992)'.

Other Organizations

It has been seen in Chapter 2 that articles 8 and 20 of the 1947 Rio Treaty seem to permit the Organization of American States to impose mandatory sanctions. One of the problems with this is whether such a power requires the authorization of the UN Security Council under article 53(1) of the Charter as a type of enforcement action.

Early practice of the OAS on this issue occurred when it imposed a limited sanctions regime against the Dominican Republic in 1960 for subversive activities against Venezuela, and in 1962 against Cuba for subversive activities against other Latin American countries. Although neither of these instances of institutional practice concerned an internal conflict, they did reveal the uncertainty that exists over the interpretation of article 53. Both cases were debated in the Security Council which divided between Eastern bloc states and their sympathizers (stating that mandatory sanctions were enforcement measures within the meaning of article 53 and so required Security Council authorization), whilst Western states and their supporters argued to the contrary (that only military measures could be so construed).[22]

There were other attempts in the early years of the OAS of member states requesting that it convoke a meeting of the Organ of Consultation of the Rio Treaty with a view to imposing sanctions or other measures. One such instance was the request by ten members on 28 June 1954 which expressed concern at the 'intervention of the international communist movement in the Republic of Guatemala and the danger which this involves for the peace and security of the Continent'. It requested that the Council of the OAS convoke a meeting of the Organ of Consultation under the Rio Treaty 'for the purpose of considering a danger to the peace and security of the Continent and to agree upon the measures which it is desirable to take'. The OAS Council did resolve to convoke a meeting of foreign ministers as the Organ of Consultation, but events in Guatemala meant that the meeting did not take place.[23]

Despite these early instances of the OAS using or considering using its sanctioning machinery, since the late 1960s when it ceased to be dominated by the US, the use of sanctions by the OAS has been strictly limited. However, the most striking use in recent times does suggest a change in approach. The imposition of sanctions against Haiti in 1991 suggests that, with the collapse of the Soviet Union and the demise of the Communist bloc, opposition to the imposition of economic sanctions without the prior authorization of the Security Council seems to have disappeared, or at least no state has overtly objected to it. The military coup in Haiti on 30 September 1991 was quickly followed by the imposition of sanctions under the Rio Treaty by an *ad hoc* Meeting of Ministers of Foreign Affairs of the OAS on 8

October. These consisted of a trade embargo, the freezing of Haitian government assets, the banning of arms sales and the diplomatic isolation of the military junta that had overthrown the democratically elected government of President Aristide.[24] Although the Security Council did not comment on the legality of the OAS action, the General Assembly unanimously approved the OAS resolution which imposed sanctions against the regime.[25]

When initially imposed, it was expected that sanctions would have an instant effect on the nation's poor economy which was heavily dependent on the US, one of the proposers of the resolution. However, the embargo failed to produce any concessions. Instead, it provided opportunities for the pro-coup elite and sections of the army to make profits by smuggling, although there was evidence of devastating effects on the welfare of the general population. In the light of this the OAS Foreign Ministers, acting again under the Rio Treaty, tightened the sanctions regime on 17 May 1992. The new sanctions barred ships from ports in the region from delivering oil and other commercial cargoes to Haiti, banned commercial air flights from transporting goods and ended the issuing of travel visas.[26] Again, this move was welcomed by the General Assembly in a resolution adopted by consensus.[27] Although the sanctions did not have immediate effect, eventually they forced the junta into an agreement negotiated under UN/OAS auspices, but only after the Security Council itself had imposed an oil and arms embargo on 17 June 1993. Unfortunately, at the time of writing (February 1994), the agreement remains to be implemented.

The OAS is one of the few international organizations whose constitution permits the imposition of binding sanctions. Its practice has been to impose sanctions against its own members, although article 28 of its 1948 Charter seems to envisage external sanctions, for instance if an American state is subjected to an armed attack.[28] Another organization that has the power to impose sanctions according to its treaty make-up is the European Community, now European Union (EC/EU). However, the EC has gone further, as shall be seen, by imposing sanctions against non-members in which a threat to the peace has arisen, namely South Africa and Yugoslavia. The rationale appears to be that the EC acts primarily as an economic organization with a common commercial policy, leading to decisions regulating external trade. Alongside this the EC is developing a common foreign policy[29] which enhances its ability to adopt sanctions against non-members. The OAS, on the other hand, not seeking to operate as an integrated economic unit, uses sanctions within its membership only for security purposes.

The European Community has acted collectively to impose sanctions only a few occasions. As with the OAS, the procedure is a curious combination of using institutional machinery along with an informal meeting of the Foreign Ministers of the EC/EU, known as the EPC (European Political Cooperation). Decisions reached in this forum do not give rise to enforceable obligations under Community law. In the case of sanctions, the EPC can simply agree on a common European position; on other occasions, the matter is taken on board by the Council of the EC/EU in the form of a binding regulation or decision. The treaty base for this power is article 113 of the Treaty of Rome which provides for a 'common commercial policy' covering external trade.[30] For example, a regulation was adopted following the Argentinian invasion of the Falklands in 1982 suspending the import of all products originating from Argentina.[31] A similar regulation was adopted following the Iraqi invasion of Kuwait in 1990.[32]

In the case of South Africa, the EPC met on 10 September 1985 in an attempt to draw up a list of economic sanctions covering arms, oil, military cooperation and sport, to try to bring an end to the state of emergency and widespread civil unrest in that country.[33] The UK opposed the sanctions. Although the other members agreed to the imposition of sanctions, without approval by the Council of Ministers and implementation in the form of a binding regulation under articles 113 and 189 of the Treaty of Rome,[34] the sanctions were not binding on the UK. Nevertheless, London appeared to accept a limited package of measures agreed to by the other states on 25 September 1985.[35] The EPC met again on 15–16 September 1986 and agreed on a more extensive package of measures against South Africa, consisting of a ban on the imports of South African iron, steel an gold coins and an end to new investment there. Germany refused to agree to a ban on South African coal imports; the then British Prime Minister Mrs Thatcher seemed to undermine the whole EPC agreement by stating that she had serious doubts about the value of sanctions.[36] At this stage the Council of the EC adopted regulations and decisions which made the ban (on investments, gold coins, and iron and steel) binding on all members of the EC.[37] The arms and sports boycotts were not enacted as binding community legislation, but it must be remembered that EC members were bound by the UN arms embargo until it was terminated by the UN Security Council resolution 919 of 25 May 1994.

With the South African government promising reform in 1990 and lifting the state of emergency in June of that year, the UK was the first to announce that it was revoking the EC's ban on new investments in February 1990. The Council lifted its investment ban on 25 February 1991,[38] after the South African government had repealed some of its apartheid legislation. Other binding sanctions covering iron and steel and gold coins were revoked on 15 April 1991 and 22 January 1992, as well as the voluntary embargoes on oil and sport, despite objections by the African National Congress (ANC).[39]

Other organizations or international arrangements adopted a purely voluntary approach towards sanctions against South Africa, not possessing, as the EC and the OAS do, the power to impose sanctions. The Commonwealth, formerly the British Commonwealth of Nations, is 'a voluntary association of independent sovereign states, each responsible for its own policies, consulting and cooperating in the common interests of their peoples and in the promotion of international understanding and world peace'. There is no formal constitution and most business in the field of international relations is carried on at biennial heads of government meetings.[40] The Commonwealth first agreed a package of sanctions in August 1986, but without that agreement constituting a treaty or other sort of binding commitment, the sanctions were only voluntary. Even these were lifted at the 28th biennial Commonwealth heads of government meeting in October 1991 when the process of reform in South Africa seemed to be irrevocably underway.[41]

In contrast the Organization of African Unity, established in 1963, has consistently supported the imposition of sanctions against South Africa by its members and the world community, although no such provision exists in its Charter. The aims of the OAU are simply to fulfil the purposes and principles of the OAU Charter, contained in articles 2 and 3 of that instrument. Amongst these are pledges to eradicate colonialism, promote respect for human rights, as well as respecting the principle of non-intervention.[42] However, without the treaty power to impose sanctions, the OAU has simply called for them to be applied against South Africa. Despite the reform process started in February 1990 with the release of ANC leader Nelson Mandela, the 27th Assembly of the heads of state or government of the OAU on 5 June 1991 called for the various voluntary sanctions regimes in place against South Africa to be maintained until 'positive, profound and irreversible changes towards the abolition of apartheid' were made.[43]

Despite the fact that the EC/EU sometimes simply agrees on sanctions without enacting them as binding regulations or (as in the case of South Africa) takes a mixed and incremental approach, it has the power to make them binding from the outset, as in the recent imposition of trade sanctions against Yugoslavia. Interestingly, the initiative for these sanctions (in the period before the Security Council adopted resolution 757 of 30 May 1992), came from a NATO summit of 8 November 1991 which itself decided to impose sanctions,[44] despite the fact that the NATO treaty, being simply a self-defence pact, does not grant this power. Article 2 does speak of developing economic collaboration between the state parties to the NATO treaty, but this is far removed from imposing economic sanctions against a state which is neither a member of NATO nor is attacking a member of NATO.

The formal decision by the Council of the EC on economic sanctions against Yugoslavia was made on 11 November 1991, thus also suspending any economic cooperation agreements between the EC and Yugoslavia.[45] The EPC was pushing for a complete and binding trade embargo against Serbia and Montenegro when the Security Council adopted resolution 757. The EC thereafter adopted its complete trade embargo[46] – a binding decision on all members of the EC.

The power to impose mandatory sanctions against states appears very limited in regional or defence organizations, the main examples being the OAS and the EC. In both organizations, however, evidence suggests that such power can be effective in relation to internal conflicts. In Haiti it has led to moves towards the restoration of democracy, and in Yugoslavia it has caused severe economic hardship in Serbia although it has not yet brought an end to the conflict in Bosnia. Furthermore, the 'carrot and stick' approach to sanctions against South Africa taken by the EC did seem to accelerate the reform process in that country. In all these instances the Security Council also imposed mandatory sanctions. Member states of the UN are bound to comply with Security Council resolutions imposed under article 41 of the UN Charter by means of articles 25 and 103. Although it is debatable whether the regional organizations themselves are bound by Security Council resolutions,[47] the point seems rather moot if the members of those organizations also belong to the UN, as they invariably do.

Military Measures

The United Nations

The UN's collective security role was premised, in 1945, on the ability of its primary organ, the Security Council, ultimately to use military measures to enforce the peace. The Council's ultimate weapon and deterrent was contained in article 42, which stated:

> Should the Security Council consider that measures provided for in Article 41 would be inadequate or have proved to be inadequate, it may take such action by air, sea, or land forces as may be necessary to maintain or restore international peace and security. Such action may include demonstrations, blockage, and other operations by air, sea, or land forces of Members of the United Nations.

Article 43 then details the mechanism whereby armed forces were to be made available, namely by 'special agreements' with members of the UN, describing the numbers, location and the state of readiness of such forces. These agreements were to be reached as soon as possible.

The agreements foreseen by article 43 were never arrived at because after 1945 the unity of the Allies soon collapsed into a bitter ideological struggle between East and West. Nevertheless, the Security Council did manage to instruct the Military Staff Committee, established under article 47 of the UN Charter and consisting of the Chiefs of Staff of the permanent members, to report to the Council by April 1947 on the basic principles that should govern the UN's armed forces.[48] The Committee's report did contain draft articles detailing such basic principles. Unfortunately, only half of these were accepted by all the permanent members.[49]

The major areas of agreement were that the initial contributions of armed forces should come from permanent members, with other members contributing at a later stage. It was also agreed that members' forces should be under the command of the contributing nation except when they were being utilized by the Security Council; in this case, they would come under the overall political control of the Security Council and under the operational and military command of the Military Staff Committee. Although these were indeed significant initiatives towards a collective security ideal in terms of the control of UN forces (which has been singularly lacking in UN military operations to date), there were disagreements on practical issues such as the size of the force and the contributions from each permanent member; the Soviet Union, for instance, expressed its preference for a small force with equal contributions.

Furthermore, the Soviet Union was of the opinion that the UN armed forces could not be used against any of the permanent members, an argument which, though undermining both the collective security ideal and the ideal of the rule of law, seemed to be supported by the following practical consideration: the voting system agreed upon by the permanent members at Yalta and embodied in article 27 of the Charter allowed any permanent member to veto a proposed military action, including, and especially, one aimed at itself. Yet the US, as well as preferring a much larger army, thought that the force could be used against a permanent member guilty of aggression. Furthermore, the UK stated that the problem of the veto could be avoided by meeting aggression committed by a permanent member by combining articles 43 and 51, not articles 42 and 43.[50] In other words, aggression could be met by the UN army (minus the aggressor state's troops) in an action of collective self-defence rather than as authorized by the Security Council. Indeed, in examining the handful of UN military operations to date, similar confusion concerning the right of collective self-defence and the concept of collective security remains apparent.

With no likelihood of consensus between the permanent members, at least during the Cold War, the idea of a standing army was shelved, although the Military Staff Committee continued its formal, if unproductive, meetings. It is generally thought that in the absence of agreements reached under article 43, the Security Council is unable to 'decide' on the use of military measures under article 42.[51] Articles 39 and 42 seem to envisage the Council having the power to make binding, mandatory decisions which would compel member states to take military action against a transgressor. Without the agreements under article 43, it would seem difficult for the Council to impose an obligation on member states to provide armed forces whenever it demanded them. A counter-argument would be to point to article 41, which empowers the Security Council to impose mandatory sanctions against a state, a decision binding on all member states without the requirement for any prior agreements between them and the UN beyond that contained in article 25. However, the rationale behind article 43 was the recognition that, to undertake military action, the Security Council would require a much higher degree of coordination and logistical organization. Without that, a mandatory demand that states provide military forces would appear vacuous. Furthermore, article 106 of the Charter permits the permanent members to make transitional arrangements for military action 'pending the coming into force of such special agreements referred to in Article 43 as in the opinion of the Security Council enable it to begin the exercise of its responsibilities under Article 42'. This implies that the agreements in article 43 are a prerequisite for the Security Council's use of article 42.[52]

However, no inextricable link exists between articles 42 and 43 in the sense that it would be a misuse of power for the Council to decide on the use of military measures under articles 39 and 42 without any *a priori* agreements under article 43. It would appear acceptable for the Council to use the power granted to it in article 42 without the mechanisms that were designed to make the imposition of military coercion a practical option. If an alternative practical option emerged, such as an *ad hoc* coalition prepared to act under UN authority, then that would appear to be *prima facie* lawful. During the Cold War the possibility of the Council acting under article 42 with or without agreements under article 43 was such a remote possibility that article 42 was effectively a dead letter. However, with the ending of the Cold War, the possibility again exists of the Security Council utilizing article 42. Furthermore, there have been suggestions of having at least a small UN force ready to take military action. At the special Security Council Summit of Heads of State on 31 January 1992, President Mitterand of France offered to make 1,000 troops available to the UN under the control of the Military Staff Committee.[53]

Although it may be argued that the agreements under article 43 are not necessary to make the Council's military option under article 42 a practicality, the Charter does strongly indicate that UN control of such military operations is an essential prerequisite for the legality of military action by the Security Council. This is indicated by articles 46 and 47(3) which provide that 'plans for the application of armed force shall be made by the Security Council with the assistance of the Military Staff Committee'; moreover, 'the Military Staff Committee shall be responsible under the Security Council for the strategic direction of any armed forces placed at the disposal of the Security Council...'. Strategic control by the Military Staff and overall political control by the Security Council appear necessary to achieve the collective security concept in that they embody the centralization of the collective use of force.

This argument can be used to criticize the Security Council's practice in the use of the military option, for instance when it has simply delegated authority and control to a state or group of states. A counter-argument would be that if the Security Council authorizes just one state to use force to achieve an objective within the ambit of the UN's security role, this is still a *collective* use of force in the sense that is exercising the collective will of the Security Council on behalf of the UN. All the more so when the Security Council authorizes a group of states to achieve a military objective. The question remains whether control by the Security Council and the Military Staff Committee is essential properly to fulfil the collective security function. It could be argued that the provisions of articles 46 and 47(3), as well as article 43, are simply formalities which, if in operation, would facilitate the use of the power contained in article 42. They can thus be seen as just one method of allowing the Council to fulfil its collective security role. As a prerequisite for the use of military enforcement action by the Security Council, these formalities would then be unnecessary.

What is required is a clear indication by the Security Council of the extent and nature of the armed force that it is requesting states to undertake. Problems of lack of continuous control can be overcome by a clear and unambiguous mandate at the outset. If states using force under this authority then wish to use more or less force, they must seek a change in mandate from the Security Council. This seems to be an acceptable compromise between complete delegation to states and unnecessary formalities and bureaucratic control by Committee. It may be unnecessary to place military operations under the complete control of the UN to achieve the centralization of force necessary to fulfil the concept of collective security if, at the outset, the Security Council effectively defines the *objectives* of the military operation, thereby preventing the use of military action for unauthorized purposes.

If the Security Council is dominated by a state or group of states which manages to persuade it to undertake military action that fulfils their as well as the UN's objectives, then as long as the Council has defined those purposes clearly (according to this interpretation of Charter law), then it, and not the state or group of states, is the initiator of the use of force. Use of centralized power to achieve the ends of a dominant individual or group is not necessarily unlawful if that power is channelled correctly through the relevant institutional structures. Current dominance by the West in the Security Council does not mean that, when it uses that organ to fulfil the collective security purposes of the UN as well as its own ends, it is automatically a misuse of power. The result – an erratic collective security system, stuttering into life only when the interests of the West are affected – may be better than none at all. Indeed, arguments of self-interest may embarrass the West into agreeing that the Council can be used to fulfil purposes beyond narrow Western interests, as evidenced by the West's reluctant proposal to use limited military measures to bring humanitarian relief to Bosnia, embodied in Council resolution 770 adopted on 13 August 1992, as well as the Council authorization for air strikes to protect safe areas in Bosnia in resolution 835 of 4 June 1993. This eventually led to NATO threats of air strikes against Bosnian Serbs surrounding Sarajevo on 9 February 1994. In addition, the Council authorized member states to enforce a no-fly zone over Bosnia in resolution 816 on 31 March 1993. Further evidence is provided by the Council's more grandiose authorization of a US-led force (UNITAF) in Somalia in December 1992.

Whether the development of the military option is implied from articles 39 or 42 (or both) is not of great import if that power is used to fulfil the purposes of the UN and is clearly formulated at the outset of any operation. To date, however, the Security Council has never 'decided' to use military force; it has simply recommended that states, on a voluntary basis, use force in particular situations and for particular purposes. The Council has simply recommended, for instance, that limited force be used to prevent cargoes from reaching the port of Beira in 1966, from leaving or reaching Iraq in 1990 and Yugoslavia in 1992. On these occasions the recommendations were intended to make a UN embargo more effective.

On 9 April 1966, the Council adopted resolution 221 which, *inter alia*, authorized Britain 'to prevent, by the use of force if necessary, the arrival at Beira of vessels reasonably believed to be carrying oil for Southern Rhodesia' which it considered a threat to the peace. In the absence of any article 42 agreement between Britain and the UN, this resolution can only be regarded as a recommendation to Britain, presumably under article 39, to take enforcement action. Although under no obligation to carry out the patrol, Britain, as the proposer of the resolution, willingly and effectively did so.

The Beira patrol was maintained successfully by Britain until 1975. Resolution 221 was itself the result of a threatened breach of the voluntary oil embargo against Rhodesia by two Greek-registered tankers. The *Joanna V* was already in Beira but, as a result of resolution 221, which also empowered the UK to arrest the ship on departure if she discharged her oil, it left with a full load. The *Manuela* was stopped by a British warship before entering the port, with the result that the captain changed the tanker's course.[54]

The Beira patrol was a limited measure aimed at facilitating the fulfilment of UN objectives as regards the internal situation in Southern Rhodesia. Similar measures are currently in force against Yugoslavia and Haiti. Full-scale military might has rarely been used by the Security Council, except against Korea and Iraq, and only the former can be categorized in some respects as an 'internal' conflict. The UN's response was set in motion when, on 25 June 1950, 100,000 North Korean troops crossed the 38th parallel that had divided the country since the Second World War. The Communist North Korean aim was to unite the country by force. The US requested a meeting of the Security Council; with the Soviet representative absent in protest at the continued presence of Nationalist China in the permanent seat, the Council adopted a US proposal. Resolution 82 of 25 June determined that the 'armed attack' by North Korea constituted a 'breach of the peace', and called for an immediate cessation of hostilities and a withdrawal of North Korean forces to the 38th parallel. North Korea ignored this demand, with the result that the US sent combat forces to South Korea.[55] Although not specified as an action of collective self-defence, the US move could only have been justified as such at this early stage in the war.[56]

However, the US sought to utilize the other exception to the ban on armed force – namely the use of force under the auspices of the Security Council – by proposing what was to become resolution 83 of 27 June 1950. This recommended 'that the Members of the United Nations furnish such assistance to the Republic of Korea as may be necessary to repel the armed attack and to restore international peace and security in the area'. Secretary General Lie wanted some form of central UN control over this force,[57] but the US refused. Instead the Council adopted a French and British proposal as resolution 84 on 7 July 1950: 'that all Members providing military forces ... make such forces available to a unified command under the United States of America'. The resolution also authorized the use of the UN flag concurrently with the flags of contributing states, and finally requested the US to provide the Security Council with regular reports 'on the course of action taken by the unified command'.

The British representative, Sir Gladwyn Jebb, explained the military action in Korea as coming under article 39 of the Charter on the basis that, in the absence of agreements under article 43, the Council could not 'decide' on military action within the terms of article 42, but could call on states to volunteer to help.[58] Nevertheless, authority should not be totally delegated to a single state without adequate safeguards to prevent its national interests from outstripping the collective security interests of the Security Council. Resolution 84 appeared simply to delegate or even abdicate responsibility to the US which supplied 90 per cent of the troops. The force was not controlled by the UN; instead its commander, General MacArthur, was appointed by the US and took his orders from the White House.

When ambassador Malik of the Soviet Union returned to his permanent seat at the end of July 1950, thereby preventing the US from adopting any further substantive resolutions on Korea, the American war effort was well under way and did not require any further enabling resolutions. Resolution 82, mandating the military action, was ambiguous: did it simply authorize the pushing back of North Korea, or did the elliptical phrase 'to restore international peace and security to the area' allow the US-led army to push into North Korea? In any event the Western-dominated General Assembly adopted a resolution on 7 October 1950 calling for stability throughout Korea and for steps to be taken for the establishment of a unified country. Furthermore the resolution stated that UN forces should stay in Korea until these objectives were fulfilled, implicitly authorizing the crossing of the 38th parallel.[59] This approach by the Assembly suggests that it was treating the Korean conflict as an intra- as opposed to an inter-state conflict.

Unfortunately the crossing of the parallel did not restore peace and security to Korea. Instead when the UN forces pushed towards the Chinese frontier, the People's Republic of China responded with massive force. The war then swung towards the Communists until, by July 1951, the UN forces eventually managed to hold them around the 38th parallel. Negotiations between the UN Command (in fact the US)[60] and a North Korean and Chinese delegation eventually produced an armistice in July 1953 dividing the country, an agreement which has lasted, uneasily, to the present day.

It can be strongly argued that the UN operation in Korea was an unconstitutional delegation of authority to the US, enabling it to use the Organization to exceed collective UN goals in order to fulfil the US national objective of fighting Communism. However, such an argument is difficult to prove, in that combating aggression is one of the prime aims of the Organization as embodied in article 1(1) of the Charter. Furthermore, if the Korean War were treated as essentially an internal conflict, a legitimate collective aim might have been the restoration of peace and security to the country as a whole.

Doubts about whether the objectives of the operation were sufficiently collective could have been allayed, either by greater control of the armed forces through a Committee established by the Security Council, or by more specifically defining the aims motivating the UN response. If the Council decides to authorize offensive action to maintain or restore international peace and security, then the resolution(s) should clearly state as much. If doubts exist, then the response should be limited to defensive action. In this respect the UN action is akin to that taken in collective self-defence although its legal basis remains distinct, deriving from article 39 (and possibly 42) rather than article 51 of the Charter. This argument signifies that the American decision to push into North Korea went too far, putting American war aims above those of the UN. However, the US did gain the somewhat ambiguous support of the General Assembly although it acted before the adoption of the Uniting for Peace Resolution explicitly granted the Assembly the power to recommend military measures.

Whatever the debates about the legality of the UN operation in Korea, it appeared largely to be considered an inter-state conflict, a case of 'aggression' rather than a 'threat to the peace'. Given that the Security Council's second attempt at using full-scale military force was also clearly an inter-state situation – reversing Iraq's invasion of Kuwait in August 1990 – no clear instances of full-scale military force in internal conflicts have occurred. However, the line between peacekeeping and military enforcement has been overstepped by the UN on several occasions, namely in the Congo, Somalia and Yugoslavia (see Chapter 8). The operation in Somalia, which clearly and explicitly crossed that threshold, will be examined here.

The overthrow of the regime of Siad Barre in January 1991 signified a further deterioration in the civil war to the point of anarchy. The Security Council somewhat belatedly acted to try to contain the conflict which was exacerbating the famine in the drought-stricken country. In resolution 733 of 23 January 1992, it imposed a mandatory arms embargo and demanded that the various armed factions observe a cease-fire. A cease-fire in Mogadishu was agreed by the two main warring factions on 3 March 1992, with provision for a small number of UN military observers (about 40) to monitor it. The leaders also agreed to develop a plan for the unimpeded delivery of humanitarian aid. The Security Council supported the sending of a limited number of observers in resolution 746, adopted on 17 March 1992.

Further negotiations led the Council to adopt resolution 751 on 24 April 1992, establishing the UN Operation in Somalia (UNOSOM), a team of 50 military observers to monitor the cease-fire agreed to on 3 March. The Security Council later authorized an expanded a force of 3,000 peacekeepers mandated as follows: to facilitate an immediate cessation of hostilities throughout Somalia and the maintenance of a permanent cease-fire; to provide urgent humanitarian assistance; to supervise the indigenous police force; and to promote national reconciliation and peaceful settlement.[61] As with UNPROFOR in Bosnia, one of UNOSOM's main tasks was to provide humanitarian assistance to the starving population. The Secretary General's plan to provide aid included the establishment of aid corridors and zones of peace, as well as the deployment of UNOSOM (which in part consisted of a security force) so that UN aid convoys would not have to hire local gunmen in highly dangerous operations.[62]

This immediately raised the possibility of UNOSOM's security arm needing to 'force' its way through the multitude of tribal armed bands in the country, bands which did not appear to be under any central command. In resolution 767 adopted on 27 July 1992, the Security Council did not exclude 'other measures' to deliver humanitarian assistance if the cooperation of factions was unforthcoming. It also supported the Secretary General's proposal to establish four operational zones in Somalia under UNOSOM supervision. The Secretary General stressed the need for the UN to adapt UNOSOM's involvement as appropriate, eventually enlarging the operation in an effort to bring about a sustained cease-fire throughout the country, while at the same time pressing for national reconciliation.

UNOSOM's severe problems in gaining the cooperation of the various warlords in Somalia meant that by September 1992 only 60 UN troops had arrived in Somalia to assist with humanitarian work, although another 440 had been agreed to.[63] The Security Council was urging the acceptance of another 750 armed security troops to escort relief convoys outside the capital.[64] The resolution also called on all parties and factions to cooperate with the UN in the deployment of security personnel. As with traditional peacekeeping, attempts to solve the conflict ran in parallel with the deployment of peacekeepers. Pursuant to a Council mandate,[65] Under Secretary General Eliasson met with clan leaders from 10–12 September 1992 and reached agreement that, during the next 100 days, free and safe access would be provided for the delivery of humanitarian assistance to affected populations.

However, the situation in Somalia deteriorated so that relief efforts were continually hampered in October and November 1992.[66] The 100-day programme achieved very limited success, with only a trickle of humanitarian aid reaching most parts of Somalia due to the theft and hijacking of relief convoys. In response to this, on 29 November 1992, the Secretary General outlined the options before the Council for creating conditions for uninterrupted delivery of relief supplies.[67] The final choice from these options vividly illustrates the changing nature of UN operations in civil conflicts, reflecting a move away from simple humanitarian provision towards some sort of enforcement. The options were, first, a continued deployment of UNOSOM under the existing principles of peacekeeping. The Secretary General stated that this option 'would not in present circumstances be an adequate response to the humanitarian crisis in Somalia'. Second, to abandon the use of international military personnel to protect humanitarian relief, withdraw UNOSOM's military elements and leave humanitarian agencies to negotiate with faction leaders. This option was favoured by some of the humanitarian agencies, but the Secretary General stated that he was 'more than ever convinced of the need for international military personnel to be deployed in Somalia'. Finally, that force should be used, either by UNOSOM in a limited area or country-wide, or by a group of states under Security Council authorization.

As regards the last option, while favouring the development of enforcement action under the command and control of the UN in the future, the Secretary General recognized that, at present, the UN did not have the capacity to mount such an operation within the time frame required. Dr Ghali concluded that the only option was to resort to Chapter VII of the Charter; a Council-authorized operation undertaken by member states would be acceptable as long as its aims were precisely defined and limited in time to facilitate post-conflict peacekeeping and peacemaking. The Secretary General advised that the US Secretary of State had informed him that, if the Council chose to authorize the use of force to ensure aid delivery, the US was willing to lead such an operation.[68]

On 3 December 1992, the Security Council unanimously adopted resolution 794 which recognized 'the unique character of the present situation in Somalia' requiring 'an immediate and exceptional response' in the form of action 'under Chapter VII'; namely the authorization of the 'Secretary General and Member states cooperating to implement the offer' by the US 'to use all necessary means to establish as soon as possible a secure environment for humanitarian relief operations in Somalia', after determining that the 'magnitude of the human tragedy caused by the conflict in Somalia, further exacerbated by the obstacles being created to the distribution of humanitarian assistance, constitutes a threat to international peace and security'. The Council demanded that the parties comply with a cease-fire and cooperate with the force to be established. It also expressed alarm at violations of international humanitarian law and at attacks on the Pakistani UNOSOM contingent in Mogadishu.

The resolution contained very little concerning the command and control of the force; indeed, it implicitly left this issue to the US by authorizing 'the Secretary General and the Member States concerned to make the necessary arrangements for the unified command and control of the forces involved, which will reflect' the US offer. However, it did request the establishment of mechanisms for coordination and liaison between UNOSOM and the new force, later known as the Unified Task Force (UNITAF). UNOSOM was to be expanded up to 3,500 at the Secretary General's discretion, perhaps in anticipation of its eventually replacing UNITAF. The resolution did not mention a time frame or specific tasks for UNITAF beyond the establishment of a 'secure environment for humanitarian relief operations in Somalia'. The resolution ended by simply inviting the Secretary General to continue his peaceful efforts to achieve a political settlement.

Under the initial phase of 'Operation Restore Hope', UNITAF was composed of 28,000 US personnel, later to be supplemented by 17,000 personnel from 20 other states. As a result of their operations, food distribution started to improve dramatically by January 1993. In his report the Secretary General suggested that UNITAF should also be neutralizing the heavy weapons of the various factions, inducing them to give up their small arms and beginning the task of clearing mines.[69]

On 18 December 1992, the General Assembly lent its support to the peace process when it welcomed the idea, proposed by various factions in a meeting with the UN, of convening an international peace conference on Somalia under the auspices of the UN and African organizations. The Assembly stated that a lasting peace could be achieved through a process of national reconciliation 'culminating in a final comprehensive, politically negotiated settlement among all the political entities and segments of the Somali people'. In particular it outlined the conditions necessary for the restoration of peace and stability on Somalia: 'strict observance of a cease-fire, full cooperation with the United Nations peacekeeping forces, national reconciliation, assistance to refugees, displaced persons and returnees, a constitution that guarantees democracy, freedom and justice, and free and fair elections'.[70]

UNITAF was emplaced on 9 December 1992 and immediately adopted a fairly aggressive stance towards disarming the various factions in the country and in opening up humanitarian aid routes. It was not afraid to use substantial force beyond that required for self-defence, as shown by the destruction of a weapons store which occasioned the deaths of 30 Somalis on 7 January 1993. Nevertheless, the US-led and dominated force did not attempt to impose a peaceful settlement on the Somali factions by the use of military force. Indeed, it appeared anxious to withdraw and be replaced by a new UN force. The US started to reduce its troop commitment in February 1993, even before the Security Council approved the Secretary General's proposal[71] for a 28,000-strong UN force (UNOSOM II) under Chapter VII of the Charter on 26 March 1993. Resolution 813 authorized the use of force, if necessary, to ensure the delivery of humanitarian assistance, but also stressed the need to restore peace, to disarm factions and to protect relief workers, suggesting the possible wider use of force. UNOSOM II would also be responsible for returning hundreds of thousands of refugees, clearing land mines, setting up a police force and helping to rebuild the economy.

UNITAF handed over responsibility, effectively for the policing of Somalia, on 4 May 1993. The new force was condemned by the leader of one of the most intransigent Somali factions – General Aydid – who stated that UNOSOM II should be confined to relief work and should cease 'interfering in the internal affairs' of Somalia.[72] Fighting on 5 June between UNOSOM II and Aydid's SNA (Somalia National Alliance) led to the death of 23 UN Pakistani soldiers, the largest UN troop loss in a single incident since the Congo. On 6 June, the Security Council adopted resolution 837 which condemned the unprovoked attack on the UN and called for the arrest and punishment of those responsible, including General Aydid. US forces, called back from the Gulf, joined UNOSOM II and launched a series of attacks between 12–16 June on SNA strongholds. Demonstrations against these attacks resulted in UN Pakistani troops shooting dead 20 civilians. By the end of June 1993 it was estimated that at least 31 UN soldiers had been killed, along with several hundred Somalis.[73] Although the situation subsequently improved, with disarmament of the various factions taking place in tandem with UN-brokered local agreements between clan leaders in certain parts of Somalia, clashes between UNOSOM II and Somali gunmen continue, most recently on 31 January 1994, resulting in the deaths of eight Somalis.[74]

Although the use of force in Somalia was not of the same order as that employed in the Gulf against Iraq in 1991, the level of force authorized and used by UNITAF and UNOSOM II extended well beyond that normally allowed for traditional peacekeeping operations, even those in dangerous intra-state conflicts such as experienced by UNIFIL in Lebanon. The new type of force, combining peacekeeping with enforcement where necessary, was envisaged by the Secretary General in his report entitled *Agenda for Peace*, adopted pursuant to the Summit Meeting of the Security Council on 31 January 1992, in which he proposed the establishment of peace enforcement units to be used in cases where a cease-fire has been agreed to but not yet complied with. The limited aim of these forces would be to secure a cease-fire, by the use of force if necessary. They would not undertake full enforcement measures under articles 42 and 43 (designed to meet and repulse outright aggression such as committed by Iraq against Kuwait), nor would they be peacekeeping forces depending upon the consent and cooperation of the parties concerned, at least not initially.[75] However, as the UN experience in the

Congo shows, the enforcement of provisional measures can amount to the virtual imposition of a settlement on a country, or at least to the creation of conditions under which a settlement can emerge.

Other Organizations

As has been pointed out in Chapters 1 and 2, a self-defence pact such as NATO or the former Warsaw Pact does not have the right, without UN authorization, to intervene in a civil war unless the relevant state is the subject of an indirect armed attack. This could be in the form of an outside state supporting insurgents so fully as to amount to indirect aggression within the meaning of article 3(g) of the General Assembly's Definition of Aggression on 1974.

Although not a civil war as such, the Soviet Union and some of its Warsaw Pact partners did intervene in the internal affairs of Czechoslovakia in August 1968. Although, in essence, the Soviet Union wanted to replace the reforming leadership that had recently and lawfully gained power in Czechoslovakia in order to preserve the Socialist bloc from capitalist contamination,[76] the Soviet representative on the Security Council justified the action as coming within article 51 of the Charter as 'collective self-defence' against a capitalist attack.[77]

However, even though the treaties establishing self-defence pacts seem to be based entirely on article 51, recent events have raised the possibility of such organizations being used by the Security Council to carry out enforcement operations in accordance with Chapters VII and VIII of the Charter. In resolution 770 of 13 August 1992, the Security Council, 'acting under Chapter VII of the Charter of the United Nations', called 'upon States to take nationally or through regional agencies ... all measures necessary to facilitate in coordination with the United Nations the delivery by relevant United Nations humanitarian organizations and others of humanitarian assistance to Sarajevo and wherever needed in other parts of Bosnia...'. The phrase 'all measures necessary' has been used in the past by the Security Council to authorize military operations. Furthermore, in resolution 781 of 9 October 1992, the Council imposed a no-fly zone over Bosnia. Authorization to enforce this zone was granted by the Security Council in resolution 816 of 31 March 1993. Safe havens were established by resolutions 819 of 16 April 1993, 624 of 6 May, 836 of 4 June, and 844 of 22 June under UNPROFOR protection, including the use of force if necessary. Limited use of air power by member states was also authorized by resolution 836. NATO commanders discussed with the Secretary General the use of NATO forces, both for the implementation of humanitarian aid packages as well as for air strikes, although no clear military action has been taken as yet. NATO, acting under

UN resolutions, threatened air strikes against the Bosnian Serbs surrounding Sarajevo on 9 February 1994. In the same month, on 28 February, NATO jets enforced the no-fly zone over Bosnia by shooting down four Bosnian Serb war planes. It appears from these precedents that the Security Council *can* use NATO – if NATO's members are willing – to carry out enforcement measures. NATO by itself, of course, could not initiate enforcement action, only action in collective self-defence.

Moving on to regional organizations, these are explicitly recognized in article 53 of the UN Charter as being capable of enforcement action under Security Council authorization. Despite this, very few regional organizations' constituent treaties seem to envisage the exercise of military measures. As has been seen in Chapter 2, the OAS does have this capacity in its constituent treaties and used it during the internal strife in the Dominican Republic in 1965.

The US originally claimed that its military intervention in the Dominican Republic in 1965 was motivated to protect American citizens in that strife-torn country.[78] The American army had established a neutral zone in the capital by the end of April 1965, by which time it had effectively altered the course of the civil war in favour of the right-wing faction. There was little doubt that the initial American intervention was contrary to article 2(4) of the UN Charter. However, the American force was then formally replaced by an OAS-negotiated Inter-American Force, although still mainly composed of US troops. The OAS force was mobilized after a cease-fire at the request of the various factions. It was intended to be neutral and to help the parties bring about the restoration of democracy;[79] in other words, a peace-keeping force in the truest sense.

The OAS operation in the Dominican Republic was lawful in that it was neither an enforcement action within the meaning of article 53, nor a use of force within the meaning of article 2(4) of the UN Charter. However, this could not retroactively legalize the initial unlawful intervention by the US.[80] Indeed, some members of the Security Council saw the OAS operation as merely a continuance of the initial unlawful intervention, whilst others thought that it was not a true peacekeeping force.[81]

One aspect of peacekeeping is that it requires the prior consent of the parties to the conflict. In the case of the military action in Grenada in 1983, the US relied on the argument that the decision to take collective action by the Organization of Eastern Caribbean States (OECS) did not require authorization by the Security Council under article 53 of the UN Charter since it was undertaken at the request of the lawful governmental authority in Grenada.[82] However, the action was not claimed by the US to be one of peacekeeping nor one of collective self-defence under article 51; instead it was said to be a military action to restore internal order. In fact, the Governor General who made the request did not have the constitutional authority to do so.[83] Besides which, a request for forcible intervention to restore order would appear to be a invitation for enforcement action, requiring authorization by the Security Council under article 53, even though the Governor General requested what he termed a 'peacekeeping' force for this purpose.[84] The US-dominated military action *forcibly* restored order on the island, rather than simply overseeing an agreement by the parties, and so could not be categorized as a peacekeeping operation. Besides being a breach of the UN Charter, the OECS action in Grenada seemed to be in breach of the treaty which established the organization in 1981,[85] article 8 of which may envisage military action, but only in collective self-defence against external aggression in accordance with article 51 of the UN Charter.

The misuse of regional organizations to further US policy may have come to an end with its military intervention in Panama in December 1989 which was not accompanied by the usual supposed justifications based on authorization by regional bodies. Indeed, the US has long since been unable to rely on the OAS to further its foreign policy. The principal legal argument used to justify its intervention in Panama was one of self-defence under article 51 of the UN Charter and article 21 of the OAS Charter. There was certainly no armed attack against the US from Panama, only alleged dangers to US servicemen, nationals and the Panama Canal which, despite American arguments to the contrary,[86] were not sufficient to justify invoking the right of self-defence. The Panamanian National Assembly had declared 'war' on the US before the latter's intervention, but after suffering a prolonged economic boycott, there was no evidence that this was anything more than empty rhetoric. It did, however, provide a convenient excuse for American intervention which was condemned not only by the UN General Assembly, but also by the OAS.[87]

Although the main examples of the use (or misuse) of regional organizations come from the Americas, other organizations have used military coercion, even though their charters do not appear to grant such powers and despite the fact that no Security Council authorization was secured under article 53 of the UN Charter. The establishment of a small symbolic Arab Security Force by the Arab League in June 1976, followed by the creation in October 1976 of a much larger Arab Deterrent Force (ADF) of 30,000 troops mainly from Syria in response to the civil war in Lebanon,[88] is another example of a regional organization attempting peacekeeping operations in an unsuitable environment, requiring escalation to military intervention or enforcement.

Although parts of the mandate of the ADF appeared to be based on a peacekeeping concept (supervision of a cease-fire, withdrawal of troops and the collection of weaponry belonging to parties to the internal conflict), other aspects seemed to grant the force much wider powers of enforcement (maintaining internal security and assisting the Lebanese authorities to take over public utilities).[89] Although it is possible to argue that the UN gave a similarly wide mandate to ONUC in the Congo, as we have seen in Chapter 8, that operation too became one of enforcement. In addition, if the performance of the Arab League Force is examined, it can be seen that it became increasingly ruthless in its actions and was not afraid to use military coercion beyond what was required in strict self-defence. Furthermore, even when the Lebanese government withdrew its consent from the ADF in 1982, the Force – which was by then composed entirely of Syrian troops – remained and increasingly aligned itself with the pro-Syrian factions in Lebanon.[90] The situation seemed to be a reverse of the Dominican Republic situation in 1965. In that case, the US military intervention was succeeded by an OAS 'peacekeeping' operation, whereas in the Lebanon in 1976, the initial Arab League initiative was gradually replaced with Syrian military intervention.

Neither the Pact of the Arab League of 1945[91] nor the Treaty of Joint Defence and Economic Cooperation of 1950,[92] drawn up by some of the members of the Arab League, contained any explicit reference to the creation of peacekeeping or coercive military operations. It may be possible to argue that the power to create peacekeeping forces is implicit in the provisions of a treaty creating a regional organization, one of whose purposes is to coordinate members' policies 'in order to achieve cooperation between them and to safeguard their independence and sovereignty'.[93] However, it is unlikely also to imply a power to undertake military enforcement action in an internal conflict. The Treaty of Joint Defence does not envisage military enforcement action, being based on article 51 of the UN Charter.[94] Even if it were possible to imply the power to take enforcement action from the wording of article 3 of the Treaty on Joint Defence (which provides that 'in the event of a threat of war or the existence of an international emergency, the Contracting States shall immediately proceed to unify their plans and defensive measures, as the situation may demand'), then the military action should still be authorized by the UN Security Council under articles 53 and 103 of the UN Charter.

The civil war in the West African state of Liberia started in 1989 when the National Patriotic Forces of Liberia (NPFL), led by Charles Taylor, rebelled against the corrupt and incompetent regime of Samuel Doe.

In July 1990, the Liberian government accepted a peace proposal put forward by the 16-member Economic Community of West African States (ECOWAS) consisting of a cease-fire, the deployment of a regional peacekeeping force, and the immediate formation of a government of national unity. Despite the fact that this proposal was rejected by the NPFL, on 25 August 1990 a 4,000-strong peacekeeping force known as the ECOWAS Monitoring Group (ECOMOG) arrived in Liberia. The NPFL saw this as military intervention on behalf of the beleaguered government. Although ECOMOG attempted to tread the neutral tightrope of a true peacekeeping force, it slowly became embroiled in the civil war, particularly after the death of President Doe in September 1990. At the time of Doe's death, the NPFL controlled 90 per cent of Liberia, although not the capital, Monrovia. It is arguable that, at that point, ECOWAS should have accepted the NPFL as the *de facto* government. Instead, ECOMOG started an offensive against the NPFL as well as increasing the already large Nigerian element of the force. The new Nigerian commander of the force was ordered by the Nigerian government to take offensive action against the rebels. Parallels can easily be drawn with the Syrian involvement in the ADF in Lebanon.

A series of cease-fires were agreed to by the various factions, culminating in the Yamoussoukra IV Accords of 30 October 1991,[95] which also detailed procedures for disarmament of the various factions, the restructuring of ECOMOG to make it less dominated by Nigeria, the surrendering of territory to ECOMOG by the NPFL, and the holding of elections. The cease-fire did not hold, Taylor being angered by ECOWAS' recognition of Amos Sawyer, an exiled politician, as interim President. This led to fighting between the expanded 9,000-strong ECOMOG force and other rebel factions against the NPFL during 1992.

At this stage the UN Security Council became involved, adopting resolution 788 on 19 November 1992, which imposed a mandatory arms embargo against the whole of Liberia, except for ECOMOG. The resolution also expressed support for the Yamoussoukra IV Accords, whilst recalling the provisions of Chapter VIII of the UN Charter and commending 'ECOWAS for its efforts to restore peace, security and stability in Liberia'. From January 1993, ECOMOG again went on the offensive against the NPFL, pushing them back from the capital with the help of an extra 5,000 troops. On 26 March the Security Council adopted resolution 812 which threatened further measures if the peace accords were not complied with. The parties finally agreed to the implementation of the Liberian Peace Agreement on 25 July, which contained provisions for the involvement of UN observers in the disarmament and elections processes. In resolution 856 of 10 August 1993, the Security Council agreed to despatch an advance team of 30 military observers to pave the way for the emplacement of a UN Observer Mission for Liberia (UNOMIL) to help implement the peace agreement.[96]

It can be seen from this account that, during its long involvement in Liberia, ECOMOG had overstepped the boundary between consensual and neutral peacekeeping and military enforcement action. Despite the fact that neither the treaty establishing ECOWAS nor the 1990 Protocol on Mutual Assistance in Defence Matters[97] clearly provides for military enforcement actions, the UN Security Council apparently retrospectively endorsed the action in resolution 788 as coming within the provisions of Chapter VIII of the UN Charter. Like NATO in Bosnia, the UN is prepared to sanction military action by a regional or defence organization, even though that body is apparently not acting within the powers of its own constituent treaty.

Notes

1   SC Res. 217, 20 UN SCOR (1965).
2   SC 1265 mtg, 20 UN SCOR (1965).
3   SC Res. 232, 21 UN SCOR (1966); SC Res. 253, 23 UN SCOR (1968).
4   SC Res. 181, 18 UN SCOR (1963).
5   SC Res. 418, 32 UN SCOR (1977).
6   See UN doc. S/12265 (1975).
7   J.A. Sigmon, 'Dispute Resolution in the United Nations: An Inefficient Forum?' (1984) 10 *Brooklyn Journal of International Law*, p.437 at p.450.
8   J. Pokalas, 'Economic Sanctions: An Effective Alternative to Military Coercion?' (1980) 6 *Brooklyn Journal of International Law*, p.289 at p.312.
9   See GA Res. 1747, 17 UN GAOR (1962).
10 See SC Res. 333, 28 UN SCOR (1973).
11 H.R. Strack, *Sanctions: The Case of Rhodesia* (Syracuse University Press, 1978), pp.162–4.
12 SC Res. 320, 27 UN SCOR (1972).
13 Pokolas, 'Economic Sanctions', p.314.
14 SC Res. 460, 34 UN SCOR (1979).
15 Pokalas, 'Economic Sanctions', p.306.
16 See generally D.L. Bethlehem (ed.), *The Kuwait Crisis: Sanctions and their Economic Consequences* (Grotius, 1991).
17 SC Res. 874, 875, 48 UN S/PV (1993).
18 SC Res. 873, 48 UN S/PV (1993).
19 See further Sc Res. 820, 48 UN S/PV (1993).
20 See further D.W. Bowett, *The Law of International Institutions*, 4th edn (Stevens, 1982), pp.185–9.
21 *Keesing's* (1992), p.39013.
22 See M. Akehurst, 'Enforcement Action by Regional Agencies with Special Reference to the O.A.S.' (1967) 45 *BYIL* p.175. at pp.188–92.
23 *Inter-American Treaty of Reciprocal Assistance: Applications Volume 1 1948–1959* (OAS publication), pp.165–9.
24 *Keesing's* (1991) p.38522. UN doc. S/23127 (1991). OAS doc. MRE/RES.2/91.
25 GA Res. 46/7, 46 UN GAOR (1991).
26 *Keesing's* (1992) p.38905. OAS doc. MRE/RES.3/92. (1992) 86 *AJIL* p.667.
27 GA Res. 47/20, 47 UN GAOR (1992).
28 See above, Chapter 2.
29 See Chapter 4.

30   298 UNTS 11.
31   EC Regulation 877/82, *OJ* 1982 L102/1/
32   EC Regulation 2340/90, *OJ* 1990 L213/1.
33   *Bull.EC* (1985/9) para.2.5.1.
34   S. Bohr, 'Sanctions by the United Nations Security Council and the European
     Community' (1993) 4 *EJIL* p.256 at p.266. Article 189 of the Treaty of Rome
     empowers the Council to adopt regulations, directives and decisions binding
     on member states. Such legislation under article 113 must be adopted by a
     qualified majority of 54 votes. The weighted voting mechanism of the Council
     unevenly distributes 76 votes amongst the 12 members.
35   *Bull.EC* (1985/9) para.2.3.30.
36   *Bull.EC* (1986/9) paras. 2.4.1., 2.4.2., 2.4.3.
37   EC Decision 86/459, *OJ* 1986 L268/1; EC Regulation 3302/86, *OJ* 1986 L 305/6.
38   EC Decision 91/114, *OJ* 1991 L59/18; *Bull.EC* (1991/1/2) para.1.3.32.
39   *Keesing's* (1985) p.33898; (1986) pp.34597–8; (1990) p.37234 and p.37910; (1991)
     p.38132.
40   J.G. Starke, *Introduction to International Law*, 10th edn (Butterworths, 1989),
     pp.116–18.
41   *Keesing's* (1991) p.38552.
42   479 UNTS 39.
43   *Keesing's* (1991) p.38279.
44   *Bull.EC* (1991/11) para.1.4.4.
45   EC Regulation 3300/91, *OJ* 1991 L 315/1.
46   EC Regulation 1432/92, *OJ* 1992 L 151/4.
47   See generally S. Bohr, *op. cit.*
48   SC 105 mtg, 2 UN SCOR (1947).
49   Special Supp. (No. 1) 2 UN SCOR (1947).
50   L.M. Goodrich, E. Hambro and P.S. Simons, *Charter of the United Nations*, 3rd
     edn (Columbia University Press, 1969), p.323.
51   J.P. Cot and A. Pellet, *La Charte des Nations Unies* (Economica, 1985), pp.709–11.
52   But see J. Quigley, 'The United States and the United Nations in the Persian
     Gulf War: New Order or Disorder?' (1992) 25 *Cornell International Law Journal*,
     p.1 at pp.33–7.
53   SC 3046 mtg, 47 UN S/PV (1992).
54   UN doc. S/7249 (1966).
55   See statement by President Truman, 27 June 1950, *United States Policy in the
     Korean Crisis*, 18 (1950).
56   But see the Secretary General's view, T. Lie, *In the Cause of Peace* (Macmillan,
     1954), p.322.
57   *Ibid.*, p.334.
58   SC 477 mtg, 5 UN SCOR (1950).
59   GA Res. 376, 5 UN GAOR (1950).
60   L. Goodrich, 'Korea: Collective Measures against Aggression' (1953) 494 *International Conciliation*, p.157 at p.178.
61   SC Res. 775, 47 UN SCOR (1992).
62   UN doc. S/24480 (1992).
63   UN docs. S/24452 and S/24451 (1992).
64   SC Res. 775, 47 UN SCOR (1992).
65   SC Res. 767, 47 UN SCOR (1992).
66   UN docs. A/47/553, S/24859 (1992).
67   UN doc. S/24868 (1992).
68   UN doc. S/24868 (1992).
69   UN doc. S/24992 (1992).
70   GA Res. 47/167, 47 UN A/PV (1992).

71 UN DOC. S/25168 (1993).
72 *Keesing's* (1993), P.39451.
73 *Keesing's* (1993), P.39499. See also SC Res. 865, 878, 885, 886, 48 UN S/PV (1993).
74 See further SC Res. 897, 49 UN S/PV (1994).
75 (1992) 31 *ILM* p.966.
76 See statement by Brezhnev, 1968, 20 *Current Digest of the Soviet Press*, No. 46, pp.3–4.
77 SC 1441 mtg, 23 UN SCOR (1968).
78 UN doc. S/6310 (1965).
79 SC 1020 mtg, 20 UN SCOR (1965).
80 M. Akehurst, 'Enforcement Action by Regional Agencies', p.213.
81 Cuba, USSR, Jordan, France, Uruguay; SC 1221 mtg, 20 UN SCOR (1965).
82 D.R. Robinson, 'Letter from the Legal Adviser' (1984) 18 *International Lawyer* p.382 at p.384.
83 W.C. Gilmore, *The Grenada Intervention* (Mansell Publishing, 1984), p.73.
84 *Ibid.*, p.65.
85 (1981) 20 *ILM* p.1166.
86 US State Department, *Panama: A Just Cause* (Bureau of Public Affairs, 1989), p.2.
87 *New York Times*, 23 December 1989.
88 For a thorough review, see I. Pogany, *The Arab League and Peacekeeping in the Lebanon* (Avebury, 1987).
89 *Ibid.*, appendix 3.
90 *Ibid.*, Chapter 8.
91 70 UNTS 238.
92 157 BFSP 669.
93 Article 2 of the Pact of the Arab League.
94 Article 2.
95 UN doc. S/24811 (1991).
96 *Keesing's* (1993), pp.39258 and 39306. See further SC Res. 866, 48 UN S/PV (1993).
97 (1975) 14 *ILM* p.1200.

11 Crimes, Breaches and Liabilities

War crimes play a somewhat disproportionate and even misleading role in the perception of the laws of armed conflict. The fundamental purpose of the *jus in bello*, in particular, is not the detection and punishment of war crimes, but the maintenance of certain basic standards of conduct in armed conflict. The question of 'war crimes' and the appropriate response thereto arise only in the light of failure in that basic objective. Nonetheless, as for any area of law, the linked questions of breach and enforcement are clearly significant. In an 'open-textured' international community, the means for coercive enforcement are manifestly far less than in almost any system of municipal law. Indeed much of the suasive 'sanction' of public international law, including the laws of armed conflict, lies in the expectations of the international community. It has been remarked elsewhere that,

> Any form of communal relations rests ultimately upon the shared assumptions of the members of the community; a member who seriously and/or repeatedly violates such assumptions in effect declares unwillingness to participate in the community concerned. This may render normal relations impossible and ... ostracism may be the ultimate sanction for violation of basic norms... .[1]

Where, despite such diffuse but not wholly ineffective suasion, serious breaches of the laws of armed conflict are perpetrated, the question of enforcement will obviously be important.

In the general area of 'war crimes', difficult questions of definition and jurisdiction arise even in the context of *international* armed conflicts. Where non-international armed conflicts are concerned, such problems are compounded.

In this context, the range both of jurisdictions and categories of offence may be considerable. Depending upon the context and the nature of the alleged offences, either (or both) national and/or international jurisdictions may be involved. The categories of possible

offences range across a spectrum of municipal criminal law to breaches
of the international laws of armed conflict, crimes against humanity
and crimes against peace, with some degree of overlap between
categories. Two basic questions underlie all of these offences, however: firstly, the definitions and types of criminal liability and, secondly, how and where defendants may be tried.

Municipal Criminal Liabilities

The treatment of civil war in municipal legal systems raises many
difficult questions. Potential criminal liabilities range from what might
be considered 'war crimes' to matters which are in any context the
stuff of daily crime statistics. At the municipal level some of the most
difficult questions perhaps arise in relation to liabilities for treason.
In the UK the law of treason still derives from the Treason Act 1351.
Treason includes waging war against the Sovereign in the realm and
adhering to, aiding or comforting the enemies of the Sovereign. The
medieval statute is phrased in personal terms by reference to the
King or Queen, which remains appropriate where assassination of
the head of state is concerned, but in other cases must now be taken
to refer to the constitutional sovereign, the Crown in Parliament.
Almost any system of municipal law would treat an attempt forcibly
to overthrow the established government as in some sense 'treasonable'. This seemingly simple assertion, however, conceals a number
of difficulties, the first and foremost being the definition of 'lawful'
authority.

The questions of authority and obligation are key issues in jurisprudence. Many criteria of identification have been advanced, ranging from coercive force,[2] through formalistic 'rule'-based analyses,[3]
to moral assessments.[4] There are many other approaches and vari-
ants which are not necessarily so mutually antagonistic as is often
claimed,[5] but the mere variety indicates the complexity of the issue.
Whatever theoretical view is taken, there remains a very practical
issue in the context of civil war. This has been put in various ways,
the best known perhaps being the 18th-century aphorism that treason never succeeds because, if it does, no-one dares to call it treason.[6]

The same broad issue was taken up by the ancient Chinese Confu-
cian scholar Mencius (Meng K'e) in response to a question from one
of his disciples about regicide. Mencius addressed the issue from the
point of view of a 'right to rule' rather than political pragmatism, but
the approaches manifestly overlap. When asked whether regicide
could be permissible, Mencius responded as follows:

A man who mutilates benevolence is a mutilator... . He ... is an 'outcast'. I have indeed heard of the punishment of the 'outcast Tchou', but I have not heard of any regicide.[7]

In a context of civil war there are, by definition, conflicting views of allegiance and authority, what is ultimately seen as 'treason' may in practice depend upon the outcome of armed conflict.

An early but telling example of these questions can be found in the aftermath of the 17th-century English Civil War. In the conflict be-tween King and Parliament, Charles I was defeated and in due course handed over to the Parliamentary Forces. Long and fruitless negotia-tions followed with a view to establishing a constitutional settle-ment, it having indeed been General Cromwell's original intention to preserve the monarchy if that might be. The negotiations failed be-cause, on the one hand, the King would not negotiate in good faith as a result of his genuine but extreme commitment to an ideology of royal 'divine right'; on the other hand, the extreme section of the Parliamentary Army would in any case not have believed in the King's good faith. Following the 'purge' of Parliament by Colonel Pride in December 1648, a Commission was set up to try Charles I, the charge against him being, in essence, treason in waging war against his own people. The assertion that he had originated the war and therefore bore sole responsibility for it is questionable. Perhaps inevitably, however, Charles I was convicted, condemned to death and finally executed on 30 January 1649.

Analysis of the event has been both various and sometimes per-verse. On the one hand Charles I has become a martyr; to this day, official constitutional theory contends that he was 'murdered'. The reign of Charles II is officially dated not from 1660, when – following the failure of the Commonwealth in the incompetent hands of its second Lord Protector – General Monk invited him to return from exile, but from 1649. A formalistic expression is found in the now somewhat antique view of G.M. Trevelyan:

> Unless the theoretic declaration of the omnipotence of the Lower House held good by 'the law of Nature', [the] ... Commission had no legal power. Furthermore, Charles had committed no legal crime. Law and pity would both plead on his side.[8]

Unlike Tsar Nicholas II, however, Charles I was *tried* and at least in theory had the right to answer his accusers – an opportunity which he disdained until it was too late. The root of the difference between the execution at Whitehall in 1649 and the shooting in the cellar of the Ipatiev House at Ekaterinaberg in 1918 is indicated by H.L.A. Hart in the context of the relationship of legal validity and efficacy:

> To insist on applying a system of rules which had ... been discarded
> ... would ... be as futile as to assess the progress of a game by refer-
> ence to a scoring rule which had been ... discarded ... [O]ne way of
> nursing hopes for the restoration of an old social order destroyed by
> revolution, and rejecting the new, is to cling to the criteria of legal
> validity of the old regime.[9]

Under the Commonwealth the defeated Royalists did precisely this.
Upon the Restoration in 1660 they were vindicated in theory, although not quite in fact: the throne to which Charles II was restored
was not identical to the one which his father had occupied.

After the Restoration those surviving regicides who were in the
hands of the government were tried and executed. Gruesome revenge was also taken upon the dead bodies of Oliver Cromwell and
others, who were exhumed to be hung, drawn and quartered. The
trial of the regicides followed the same pattern of political harshness
as had the trial of the King in 1649. In other cases a much greater
difficulty arose. Lord Campbell, in his 'Life' of Lord Chancellor
Clarendon, highlights the trial of Sir Harry Vane who was not a
regicide but was convicted for having acted under the authority of
Parliament after Charles's execution:

> No satisfactory answer could be given to the plea that the parliament
> was then *de facto* the supreme power of the state, and that it could be
> as little treason to act under its authority as under the authority of a
> usurper on the throne – which is expressly declared by the statute of
> Henry VII not to be treason.[10]

The real problem in all these cases is not so much the political fact of
the transformation of the legal order following the outcome(s) of
civil war as the *retroactive* imposition of a new or restored order.

As a political issue, this problem has particular relevance for modern non-international armed conflicts. Essential provision is made in
this regard by 1977 Protocol II Additional to the 1949 Geneva Conventions, article 6(5):

> At the end of hostilities, the authorities in power shall endeavour to
> grant the broadest possible amnesty to persons who have participated
> in the armed conflict, or those deprived of their liberty for reasons
> related to the armed conflict, whether they are interned or detained.

This provision has evident merit in seeking to facilitate both an ending of conflict and a viable process of 'reconstruction' thereafter. The
question nonetheless remains of determining what may be the 'broadest possible' amnesty in a given situation. The provision itself is
governed by a humanitarian imperative, with such an amnesty pre-

sumably including the bulk of 'political offences'. Its aim is to avert the criminalization of being on the losing side. At the same time many crimes and other violations may be committed in a civil conflict in respect of which no case for amnesty could be made out. Important guidance in this respect is afforded by the provisions of article 6(2) of 1977 Additional Protocol II for 'due process' in criminal trials in relation to non-international armed conflicts:[11]

> (b) no-one shall be convicted of an offence except on the basis of individual penal responsibility;
> (c) no-one shall be held guilty of any criminal offence on account of any act or omission which did not constitute a criminal offence, under the law, at the time when it was committed; ...

This would rule out the imposition of collective or generic penalties and the retrospective criminalization of actions. Actions criminal under existing municipal law would, however, be subject to prosecution. The terminology of 'political' offences is not used by 1977 Additional Protocol II, but a concept of exclusion similar to that is set out by the 1951 Convention Relating to the Status of Refugees, article 1E(b).[12] A potential 'refugee' is excluded from the provision of the 1951 Convention by article 1E(b) if 'he [or she] has committed a serious non-political crime outside the country of refuge prior to [her or] his admission to that country as a refugee'. The concept of 'serious non-political crime' would seem to set an acceptable criterion for evaluating the extent of amnesty in the present context. The issue may all too readily be illustrated by the experience of the conflict(s) in the early 1990s in former Yugoslavia.

A widely reported trial involved two Serbian fighters captured by Bosnian forces and charged with the massacre of civilians and rape of interned women. Both crimes may be considered as 'war crimes' and as offences under municipal law *stricto sensu*. However they are categorized, the trial of Borislav Herak and Sretko Damjanovic on serious criminal charges arising from a largely non-international armed conflict was significant. On 30 March 1993 both defendants were convicted and condemned to death by firing squad, subject to judicial appeal.[13] It seems that Herak confessed without wish to appeal, but Damjanovic claimed that he had been beaten into confessing. In this context it has been remarked elsewhere that '[t]here is no good reason to doubt that at the trial due process was observed but, as always, an opportunity is afforded for later criticism. ...'[14] The problem in such circumstances is to ensure that justice is both done and seen to be done. This inevitably raises the question of 'due process' and its practical demonstration.

The Problem of Due Process in Municipal Trials

'Due process' is by definition an issue of procedure rather than substance, though of course procedural propriety may to some extent
inhibit substantive abuses. Lon L. Fuller claims for his procedural
natural law that

> the internal morality of law [presents] ... a variety of natural law. It is,
> however, a procedural or institutional kind of natural law, though ...
> it affects and limits the substantive aims that can be achieved through
> law.[15]

However, Fuller himself admitted that there are limits to the extent
of this effect;[16] certainly, the observance of norms of due process is no
guarantee that the laws thus applied are unobjectionable. Presuming
that the substantive norms in question are acceptable, however, the
procedural propriety of their application becomes a vital issue.

Basic standards in this respect are set out by the proscription of
common article 3(1)(d) of the four 1949 Geneva Conventions of

> the passing of sentences and the carrying out of executions without
> previous judgment pronounced by a regularly constituted court, af-
> fording all the judicial guarantees which are recognized as indispen-
> sable by civilized peoples.

Whether this provision was limited to capital crimes, which it certainly includes, might be debated. In a modern context, however,
where capital punishment itself is at issue in 'human rights' terms, a
rather broader remit might be anticipated. Such a view is supported
by the expansion of this provision in 1977 Protocol II Additional to
the 1949 Geneva Conventions. In the trial of criminal offences committed in a non-international armed conflict, article 6(2) sets out a
general requirement in relation to judicial process:

> No sentence shall be passed and no penalty shall be executed on a
> person found guilty of an offence except pursuant to a conviction
> pronounced by a court offering the essential guarantees of independ-
> ence and impartiality. ...

Six particular requirements are then enumerated.[17] The accused must
be informed of the charges and afforded the right and means of
defence; conviction may only be upon the basis of personal responsibility; the act must have been criminal at the time of its commission
and there may be no retrospective imposition of harsher penalties,
although retrospective benefit of a lighter penalty must be granted;
innocence is to be presumed until guilt is proven according to law;

the accused has the right to be tried in his or her presence; and, finally, no-one may be compelled to testify against him or herself or to confess. Article 6(3) adds that a person convicted must be advised of any further judicial remedies (i.e. rights of appeal) and of any relevant time limits. Provision for capital sentences is made by article 6(4) which forbids the imposition of the death sentence upon persons aged under 18 at the time of the offence or upon pregnant women or mothers of young children. It may be taken that the reprieve is permanent in relation to the offence in question.

The observation of these requirements would clearly ensure adequate procedural guarantees but, even assuming the requisite intention and will, there remain significant potential difficulties in practical implementation. Two possible situations must be envisaged. Defendants might be tried within their 'home' jurisdiction or in that of the (or an) 'opposing' side. In either case there will be difficulty in the perception of justice being done. As Francoise Hampson has remarked,

> Just as trials by one's own side run the risk of appearing biased in favour of the accused, so trials by the other side may be seen as biased against the defendant. Such a trial looks like revenge by the party having custody. There is a risk of actual or apparent unfairness against the accused.[18]

This is a very real problem. Observation of the 'due process' requirements set out above will not preclude criticism, but may at least arm the proceedings against it. The only secure path to the conduct of proceedings which are *seen* to be just may be through some form of 'international' or at least trans-national tribunal. This raises other complex issues in the present context.[19]

In the context of municipal proceedings relating to non-international armed conflict, a vexed question arises in determining the applicable law. Apart from the questions of retroactivity and amnesty considered above, it may be assumed that the municipal criminal law of the territory concerned will be applicable. However, even if a new or emergent state decided to adopt a new legal order, this could not be retrospectively applied (for the reasons already considered). The former legal order would thus pertain, though not in such matters as 'treason'. In cases of serious crimes violating social taboos found in most systems of criminal law, this is unlikely to present major definitional problems.

War Crimes and Other Internationally Defined Liabilities

Where 'war crimes' in a strict sense are concerned, non-international armed conflicts present peculiar difficulties, the most obvious one being which provisions of the laws of armed conflict should apply. The minimum requirement is set by common article 3 of the 1949 Geneva Conventions, expanded by 1977 Additional Protocol II where applicable. Further agreements to cover a much broader regime are encouraged, but the question of the applicable law in a given conflict remains potentially complex.[20]

It must first be asked what constitutes a 'war crime'. In principle any violation of the laws of the armed conflict could satisfy this criterion. All law is intended to be obeyed, subject to 'defences' arising from 'impossibility[21] but, so far as fundamental humanitarian norms are concerned, the formulation, advanced by Jean Pictet, has much to commend it.[22] Nonetheless a practical distinction exists between minor or technical incongruences and gross violations – labelled 'grave breaches' in the context of *international* armed conflicts. A basic list of 'grave breaches' is set out by the 1949 Geneva Conventions (with further provision for particular categories of protected persons); these comprise

> wilful killing, torture or inhuman treatment, including biological experiments, wilfully causing great suffering or serious injury to body or health, and extensive destruction and appropriation of property not justified by military necessity and carried out unlawfully and wantonly.[23]

An extended list is set out, in the context of international conflicts, by 1977 Protocol I Additional to the 1949 Geneva Conventions.[24] The 1977 provisions include a significant body of material impinging upon the 'Hague' focus on methods and means of warfare:

> It seems reasonable to conclude that the modern concept of war crimes embraces a flexible grouping of 'serious' breaches of the laws and customs of warfare with the 'Geneva' (including major 'Hague' elements) category of 'grave breaches' as an irreducible core but not a comprehensive definition. ... [T]he real criterion of identification [is] ... perhaps the gravity of the *actus reus* and its consequences.[25]

All of this relates to international armed conflicts where the principles (if not the details) of implementation are fairly clear.[26]

In terms of non-international armed conflicts, wider variations exist so that treating each conflict as a case *sui generis* may be unavoidable. There are nonetheless some useful pointers, not least deriving from the very limited experience which exists of international trials.[27]

The issue may be further complicated when offences are defined by municipal provisions deriving from international obligations. This will particularly be the case where suspects are being tried by their own side. It is the obligation of each state to express the requirements of the laws of armed conflict, at least in relation to 'grave breaches' of 'Geneva' law, in the relevant provisions of its municipal military and civil law.[28] None of this impinges explicitly upon either common article 3 of the 1949 Geneva Conventions or 1977 Protocol II Additional thereto. However, such matters will be relevant where parties to a conflict have, as encouraged by common article 3 of the 1949 Geneva Conventions, agreed to the application of a broader spectrum of *jus in bello* provision, as in former Yugoslavia. Naturally, the 'minimum' requirements of both common article 3 and 1977 Additional Protocol II must assume *some* enforcement capability, otherwise they will be merely exhortatory.

'War crimes' are not the only internationally defined offences which pertain to non-international armed conflicts. Another commonly encountered problem is that of mercenarism. The involvement of foreign nationals unconnected with any of the parties in civil conflicts has a long history, a well-known instance being the large number of foreign sympathizers who fought with the Republican side in the International Brigade in the Spanish Civil War. Mercenaries, of course, fight only for financial reward. Apart from moral disapprobation, there is a strong practical objection to mercenary participation in combat: it is in the interests of mercenaries, not that conflicts should be resolved, but that they should be continued and exacerbated.

Modern international concern with mercenarism arose largely from the involvement of foreign 'soldiers of fortune' in liberation and post-liberation conflicts in Africa. In a broad range of insurrections from Congo to Angola, 'mercenaries' of various types played a significant and sinister part. Continuing concern with the issue of mercenarism is indicated by their alleged involvement in an attempted coup in the Seychelles in 1982 and in the conflicts in the early 1990s in former Yugoslavia. Not surprisingly, a lead in objecting to mercenarism was taken by the OAU whose position was founded partly upon general concern with the fact that mercenaries could exacerbate conflicts and partly upon disapprobation of the political (im)balance deriving from mercenary involvement. OAU statements condemning mercenary activity were made in 1967 and 1971, while on a number of occasions the General Assembly also expressed serious concern about the issue. A crisis was reached with the establishment of the People's Republic of Angola following the victory of the MPLA in its post-colonial conflict. Thirteen captured foreign fighters – all involved with defeated factions – were put on trial as 'mercenaries' in Luanda in June 1976. The trials were conducted on the basis that the defendants were not legitimate combatants and were guilty of criminal offences by virtue of being mercenaries. To prove their case, the prosecution cited OAU statements, a number of UN General Assembly Resolutions and the provisions relating to Crimes against Peace in the Charter of the International Military Tribunal at Nuremberg at the end of the Second World War.[29] That the persons tried were mercenaries, in terms of any of these definitions, seems highly probable. The difficulty in the case was essentially that of *nulla crimen sine lege* (no crime except as defined by law). Francoise Hampson has commented on the issue as follows:

> The trial itself appears to have been fair, procedurally speaking. Compliance with the presumption of innocence is, however, in doubt; ... The trial has been criticised for breaching the principle of *nulla crimen sine lege*. ... [T]here was at that time no internationally recognized criminal offence of unlawful participation in a conflict. There is also grave doubt as to whether it was an offence under Angolan criminal law.[30]

At the end of the trial very severe sentences were passed and implemented, with many of the defendants being executed. The Luanda trial may be held to illustrate two essential problems in the international response to mercenarism. Granted that there was no definitive proscription against the illegality of mercenarism at that time, it may be asked *why* the subject for so long remained in a legal 'grey area'. The answer to that can lie only in lack of political will, a situation which has subsequently been reversed to some extent. Another difficulty lies in the understanding of the problem and the definition of mercenarism, which has also since been specified.

The Luanda trial was observed by an International Commission which in due course produced the 1976 Luanda Draft Convention on the Prevention and Suppression of Mercenarism. This may be seen as a product of its particular context, but the issue of mercenarism had at last been firmly placed on the international political agenda. Three principal, and very similar, definitions of a 'mercenary' can now be considered.

The most effective modern definition of a 'mercenary' is set out, in the context of international armed conflict, by 1977 Protocol I Additional to the 1949 Geneva Conventions. Article 47(2) states that,

> A mercenary is any person who:
> (a) is specially recruited locally or abroad in order to fight in an armed conflict;
> (b) does, in fact, take a direct part in the hostilities;
> (c) is motivated to take part in the hostilities essentially by the desire for private gain and, in fact, is promised, by or on behalf of a Party to the conflict, material compensation substantially in excess of that prom-

ised or paid to combatants of similar ranks and functions in the armed forces of that Party;
(d) is neither a national of a party to the conflict nor a resident of territory controlled by a party to the conflict;
(e) is not a member of the armed forces of a Party to the conflict; and
(f) has not been sent by a State which is not a Party to the conflict on official duty as a member of its armed forces.

It will be noted that this list is cumulative; a mercenary will fall foul of all these criteria rather than just some of them. Thus, for example, fighters who are not nationals or residents of any party to a conflict but are motivated to participate by political sympathy will not 'qualify' as 'mercenaries'. Article 47 excludes such persons from 'prisoner of war' status if they are captured in an international armed conflict. Although this means that they would lose such status if, upon investigation (with guarantees of due process), they were found to be 'mercenaries', the provision is not a licence for summary execution upon suspicion.

Although article 47 denies mercenaries the status of legitimate combatants, it does not render the recruitment of mercenaries unlawful. A further definition is afforded by the 1989 UN Convention against the Recruitment, Use, Financing and Training of Mercenaries. This Convention was adopted on 4 December 1989 by the UN General Assembly after ten years' work by an *Ad Hoc* Drafting Committee, which in part pursued the advances made in this area by 1977 Additional Protocol I. By article 19(1), the 1989 Convention will come into force on the 30th day after the deposit of the 22nd instrument of ratification or accession with the UN Secretary General. It is a somewhat depressing comment upon the continuing lack of international political will in relation to this issue that, at the time of writing, this has not yet happened.[31]

By article 1(1), the 1989 Convention defines 'mercenaries' in much the same terms as article 47 of 1977 Protocol I Additional to the 1949 Geneva Conventions. Article 1(2), however, adds the following:

A mercenary is also any person who, in any other situation:
(a) Is specially recruited locally or abroad for the purpose of participating in a concerted act of violence aimed at:
(i) overthrowing a Government or otherwise undermining the constitutional order of a State; or
(ii) undermining the territorial integrity of a State;
(b) Is motivated to take part therein essentially by the desire for significant private gain and is prompted by the promise or payment of material compensation;
(c) Is neither a national nor a resident of the State against which such an act is directed.

States are forbidden to recruit or facilitate the training of such persons and are required to prohibit such activities by others.[32] The persons themselves are stated explicitly to commit an offence.[33] According to Article 13,

> The State Party in whose territory the alleged offender is found shall, if it does not extradite him [or her], be obliged, without exception whatsoever and whether or not the offence was committed in its territory, to submit the case to its competent authorities for the purpose of prosecution, through proceedings in accordance with the laws of that State. Those authorities shall take their decision in the same manner as in the case of any other offence of a grave nature under the law of that State.

It is interesting that no mention is made of 'due process' or the equivalent. The general 'human rights' expectation of such a standard must, however, be presumed.

The 1977 Convention for the Elimination of Mercenarism in Africa, which came into force on 22 April 1975[34] and is open to ratification or accession by members of the OAU,[35] adopts by article 1(1) a similar definition of a 'mercenary' to that set out by 1977 Protocol I Additional to the 1949 Geneva Conventions. Article 1(2) then continues:

> The crime of mercenarism is committed by the individual, group or association, representative of a State or the State itself who with the aim of opposing by armed violence a process of self-determination, stability or the territorial integrity of another State, practises any of the following acts:
> (a) Shelters, organizes, finances, assists, trains, supports or in any manner employs bands of mercenaries:
> (b) Enlists, enrols or tries to enrol in the said bands:
> (c) Allows the activities mentioned in paragraph (a) to be carried out in any territory under its jurisdiction or in any place under its control or affords facilities for transit, transport or other operations of the above mentioned forces.

This is a useful definition of involvement in mercenarism, as distinct from actually being a 'mercenary'. Certain interpretive difficulties may arise, e.g. in so far as the achievement of self-determination may by definition be contrary to the territorial integrity and stability of a state. This is especially the case now that the question of self-determination is addressed in a post-colonial rather than in a decolonizing context.[36] The practice of mercenarism is rendered unlawful in any event. According to article 2, assuming command over mercenaries is an aggravating factor. As to jurisdiction, article 8 requires a state party to take measures for the punishment of offenders found on its territory or to extradite them to the territory where the offence was committed.[37] This provision effectively provides for a 'universal' jurisdiction amongst states Party. When the 1989 UN Convention comes into force, it will have the same impact through article 12.

A number of issues are raised by these various proscriptive or limiting provisions. The extended definition of mercenaries given by the 1989 Convention would unequivocally include many instances of non-international armed conflict, as does the 1977 OAU Convention. In all these cases the careful and cumulative definition deriving ultimately from 1977 Protocol I Additional to the 1949 Geneva Conventions is a vitally important indicator of the nature of the international concern with mercenarism. The emphasis is very much upon the classical 'soldier of fortune' who fights not for allegiance, duty or other commitment, but simply for money. This is perhaps too specific an emphasis. In her analysis, Francoise Hampson highlights the general problem of 'foreign participation in conflicts'[38] and suggests that the proscription should cover 'the participation of individual foreigners in the use of force for political ends'.[39]

The problems of foreign troops in regular service with the armed forces of another state as well as foreign advisers clearly arise and are admitted; so too is that of the fighter of ideological commitment. Under modern definitions, neither the International Brigade nor the Condor Legion in the Spanish Civil War would be considered mercenaries and this seems totally appropriate. The central problem appears indeed to lie in the narrowly defined 'soldier of fortune' concept. Other questions of deployment are potentially serious, but fall for consideration in the area of the *jus ad bellum* rather than the *jus in bello*.

An example of the necessity for careful and extended drafting can be seen from a Security Council debate. In a consideration on 20 May 1982 of the role of suspected mercenaries in the attempted coup in the Seychelles, the Argentine representative suggested that the Gurkha regiments in the British army might be considered 'mercenaries'. The British representative responded as follows:

> The only internationally agreed definition of who is a mercenary is to be found in [1977 Additional] Protocol I.... That definition excludes anyone who is 'a member of the armed forces of a party to a conflict'. The Gurkhas comprise units of regular troops: they form a fully integrated part of the United Kingdom forces [in accordance with agreements openly and honourably arrived at with the Government of Nepal]. ...[40]

The bracketed words are taken from the preceding paragraph of the British representative's reply. The pitfalls to be avoided in a definition of mercenarism and the success in this respect of 1977 Protocol I and related provisions are amply demonstrated by this exchange.

The Issue of Genocide

A number of other criminal offences of international legal interest may arise in non-international armed conflicts, most of which would now fall within the general remit of Human Rights law. This would include abuses which are clearly unlawful but which are not necessarily associated with warfare. One matter which demands particular attention in the present context, however, is the crime of genocide.

Genocide was formally defined as a result of the experience of the policies of ethnic persecution and destruction adopted by the Third Reich between 1933 and 1945. By General Assembly (1946) Resolution 96(I), the UN affirmed the criminality of 'genocide' and initiated studies leading to the drafting of an appropriately worded treaty for its repression. The result is the 1948 UN Convention on the Prevention and Punishment of the Crime of Genocide (the Genocide Convention).

The Convention, by article II, defines genocide as,

> any of the following acts committed with intent to destroy, in whole or part, a national, ethnical, racial or religious group, as such:
> (a) Killing members of the group;
> (b) Causing serious bodily or mental harm to members of the group;
> (c) Deliberately inflicting on the group conditions of life calculated to bring about its physical destruction in whole or in part;
> (d) Imposing measures intended to prevent births within the group:
> (e) Forcibly transferring children of the group to another group.

It will be noticed that this definition includes the elements both of *mens rea* and *actus reus* (guilty mind and guilty act) in that there is an initial specification of *intention* followed up by *action*. The definition relates to the particular ethnocidal policies practised in the Third Reich (i.e. extermination), but has a considerably broader application. Some of the categories of action would not involve eradication as such; they might simply aim at precluding people from sustaining a group identity. This would particularly be the case in the circumstances envisaged by paragraphs (d) and (e).

Whether brutal repression meets the technical criteria of 'genocide' may not always be easily resolved. The forcible displacement of Bosnian Muslim people in the actions offensively termed 'ethnic cleansing' raised this question.[41] The UN Commission of Experts set up under Security Council Resolution 780 (1992) considered that some of these actions 'could' fall within the definition.[42] At the application of Bosnia-Herzegovina the International Court of Justice was also called upon to consider this issue and to give an indication of 'provisional measures'. On 3 April 1993 the Court claimed that the request did not require it to determine whether genocide had indeed been committed, but did require the government of Serbia and Montenegro to take all measures within its power to prevent the commission of the crime of genocide.[43] The fundamental problem may again lie not in the *actus reus* element of the criteria, but in the particular *mens rea*. Whether or not ethnic cleansing is considered genocidal, it is clearly a very serious violation of basic *jus in bello* principles, quite apart from its human rights implications.

The question then arises of what is to be done where genocide is perpetrated in civil wars. Brutality directed at members of defined ethnic, cultural or religious groups, potentially amounting to 'genocide' may justify forceful intervention which, however, is rarely taken:

> In [some] ... instances of alleged genocide there has been a military response, but neither the intervening state nor other states have sought to justify the action solely as a humanitarian intervention, thus reflecting the fact that there is little *opinio juris* amongst states for such a right.[44]

Beyond the issue of military intervention, there arises the question of jurisdiction over persons suspected of involvement in genocide. The 1948 Genocide Convention, by article III, lists as 'punishable', genocide, conspiracy to commit genocide, direct public incitement to genocide and complicity in genocide. Article VI then provides that

> Persons charged with genocide or any of the other acts enumerated in article II shall be tried by a competent tribunal of the State in the territory of which the act was committed, or by such international penal tribunal as may have jurisdiction with respect to those Contracting Parties which shall have accepted its jurisdiction.

It would seem from this that genocide is not a crime of universal jurisdiction, triable by any state in whose territory a suspect might be found, failing extradition to a directly concerned state. The question of jurisdiction in respect of crimes of genocide was raised most pointedly in the Eichmann case in 1961.[45] Adolf Eichmann, an officer serving in the Gestapo, was in charge of the 'final solution' programme – the Nazi extermination campaign against Jewish people. After the Second World War he escaped to South America and established himself in hiding in Argentina. There he was found by a group of (possibly official) Israeli investigators, abducted and taken for trial under the Israeli 1951 Nazi and Nazi Collaborators (Punishment) Law for an offence phrased in terms similar to those of the 1948 Genocide Convention. The jurisdiction exercised over Eichmann in Israel, rather than in Germany, was argued to be justified on three broad grounds. The first, resting simply upon the municipal validity of the 1951 Israeli legislation, is not of direct relevance. This, however, led to the question of the international standing of that municipal jurisdictional base. It was argued that the crimes with which Eichmann was charged were *delicta juris gentium*, i.e. contrary to the law of nations and thus, in the absence of an international criminal court, triable by all nations. Granted that article I of the 1948 Genocide Convention does 'confirm that genocide ... is a crime under international law ...', it was argued that the terms of article VI of the Genocide Convention did not limit the possibility of trial either in cases referring to events prior to its coming into force or by states other than those in whose territory the crimes were committed. It was also argued that the seemingly restrictive jurisdictional provisions of article VI referred not only to events by states Party without compromise to a general right and duty of trial affirmed by article I. This is a possible interpretation, although article I could be viewed more narrowly. In the *Eichmann case* an argument was also entertained that the protective principle of jurisdiction (i.e. vesting jurisdiction in the injured state) might apply retrospectively.

The *Eichmann case* raised the further question of whether the abduction of Eichmann from Argentina, amounting to a *prima facie* violation of Argentine sovereignty, invalidated subsequent municipal proceedings. It was concluded that it did not.

The interpretation of article VI of the Genocide Convention raises some questions today, in particular the territorial limitation which was no doubt reasonable in dealing with the particular (and perhaps unique) jurisdictional context of the 1940s. Its appropriateness in a situation where a genocidal government or other authority remains in power in the territory in question seems doubtful. This said, in many cases including 'civil war', acts which constitute or are equivalent to genocide may well fall within a much broader jurisdictional remit, whether as 'war crimes' or otherwise. This would not arise directly under common article 3 of the 1949 Geneva Conventions or 1977 Additional Protocol II, although the obligations thereby undertaken at least imply municipal enforcement. Where a broader segment of the *jus in bello* is admitted, then a more general potential jurisdiction may be vested in High Contracting Parties.[46]

International Criminal Jurisdiction

In a discussion of international institutions and breaches of the laws of armed conflict, either internationally or internally, the obvious 'missing link' is a 'permanent' international criminal court. None exists, although the idea has from time to time been canvassed.[47] When the General Assembly adopted the text of the 1948 Genocide Convention, it also called upon the International Law Commission to consider the possibilities for an international criminal court.[48] These endeavours did not bear fruit and, for a variety of reasons – especially the sovereign sensitivities of member states – it seems improbable that they will do so in any proximate time-scale. Such international criminal tribunals as have been constituted were all *ad hoc* in nature and related to very abnormal circumstances, the primary examples being the International Military Tribunals which sat at Nuremberg and Tokyo at the end of the Second World War. These tribunals do not relate directly to questions of non-international armed conflict but, as the major models for international criminal process, they require brief consideration.

At the end of the First World War there was a demand for international trials. An (Allied) Commission upon the Responsibility of the Authors of the War and the Enforcement of Penalties prepared a list of no less than 896 alleged 'war criminals' of whom at least the major figures were to be tried by an *ad hoc* international tribunal. This scheme was so tainted with vendetta that it may be considered fortunate that it never materialized, largely because the principal proposed defendants were not made available. Some trials did take place before German courts and these made a useful contribution to the jurisprudence of armed conflict.[49]

At the end of the Second World War, a very different situation obtained. The violations of international law were flagrant, well documented (not least by the perpetrators themselves) and, by reason of the military collapse of the governments in question, almost uniquely open to prosecutorial investigation. The Nuremberg and Tokyo Tribunals differed technically in that the government of the Third Reich was held to have been inherently criminal, whereas the Imperial Japanese Government was considered a legitimate authority misdirected by a criminal group. The Charter of the International Military Tribunal at Nuremberg played a significant part in modern international criminal jurisprudence, its emphasis upon due process, including acquittals, setting an important standard.

Amongst the many important issues that arose in connection with these trials, two retain significant resonance in the present context: (1) the question of *individual* responsibility for *international* crimes and (2) the application of the principle of *nulla crimen sine lege* where relevant municipal law does not embody applicable international obligations.

In general individuals lack *locus standi* in public international law where legal 'personality' is vested in states and certain international institutions. In consequence,

> The norms of the *jus ad bellum* and the *jus in bello* are *prima facie* addressed to States, which are thereby placed under ... obligation to require individuals acting under their authority to comply with such prescription. Thus, in principle the [individual] ... acting contrary to the *jus in bello* should face ... proceedings under municipal ... law for an offence created pursuant to the international obligations of the State.[50]

To hold individuals responsible before an 'international' forum for criminal actions undertaken in pursuance of state policy may seem odd. Some, including William V. O'Brien, have indeed argued that the Nuremberg and Tokyo trials were in this sense innovatory and possibly questionable:

> By any standard, absolute denial of the act of state defense and imposition of direct individual responsibility for violations of international law was a major innovation. ... [T]he ... effort to present it as well-established international law was ludicrous.[51]

The idea was not in fact new. The admittedly very flawed 1918 proposals involved the same concept, while more distant precedents can be traced back to the pre-history of modern international law in the 15th century.[52] Like much else associated with these trials, the questions of implementation may have been less one of principle than of opportunity. So far as principle is concerned, the International Military Tribunal at Nuremberg stated in judgment upon this point that,

> individuals have international duties that transcend ... national obligations.... . He who violates the laws of war cannot obtain immunity while acting [under] ... the authority of the State if the State ... moves outside its competence under international law.[53]

This implicitly raises a fundamental question about the nature of the 'legal personality' of states and other entities in public international law.[54]

States and international institutions, like companies or other corporations in municipal legal systems, are essentially 'artificial' persons. It is true that the legal 'personality' of a human being may vary according to conditions and is ultimately tested by the recognition of the courts; the 'natural' personality of the human individual is nevertheless the inevitable basis of his or her legal 'personality'. This is not the case for states, institutions, corporations or companies. The recognition of their 'corporate' entity is a convenient and necessary 'bracketing' of a vastly complex common activity without which normal dealing (in this case international relations) would be virtually impossible. Nonetheless, a state, like a company, cannot of itself 'do' anything; it can act and indeed conceive a will only through its human agents. Where the 'fiction' of state or institutional 'personality' becomes a mere cloak for the perpetration of acts fundamentally subversive of the order wherein that 'personality' exists, the 'bracket' may be dissolved and inner realities scrutinized. The equivalent in English company law is termed 'lifting the veil of incorporation'. L.C.B. Gower remarks of this process that,

> In cases where the veil is lifted, the law either goes behind the corporate personality to the individual members, or ignores the separate personality of each company in favour of the economic entity constituted by a group of associated companies.[55]

This may or may not be related to wrongdoing, but the point of looking behind the 'personality' of the company to the acts of its agents is evident. A similar purpose may be served where the state is being used as a cloak for gross violations of international law, including the laws of armed conflict.

Different issues are raised by the application of the principle *nulla crimen sine lege* (no crime except as defined by law). If the municipal law of a state flouts obligations imposed by international law, it must be asked whether it is reasonable to hold an individual responsible for choosing the former over the latter. Where the applicable international norms are clear, however, the central issue will be that of the level of responsibility of the defendant. In a context such as Nuremberg or Tokyo, the question did not seriously arise since members of an unlawfully acting government could not plead municipal regulations which they had conspired to introduce. Another argument is whether a *monist* or *dualist* (one system or two) view of the relation between international and municipal legal systems is to be adopted, but again the issue concerns the level at which responsibility is fixed. Even the most determined dualist could not deny that international obligation takes effect at some point.

This broad question also feeds into that of *respondeat superior* as a defence against violations of the laws of armed conflict. Can soldiers or equivalent personnel rely upon superior orders as a defence when charged with the commission of 'war crimes'? The issue here is a little more complex and ultimately turns on the interpretation of duty and anticipated legal knowledge.[56]

International Criminal Tribunals after Nuremberg

In view of the near unique circumstances obtaining at the end of the Second World War, it is perhaps not surprising that the record of 'international' or multinational criminal jurisdiction since 1945 has been extremely thin. International trials were proposed at the end of the 1990–91 Gulf conflict, but the idea proved to be wholly impractical, not least by reason of the unavailability of the majority of likely defendants.

More substantive steps were taken towards setting up an international tribune in relation to the conflict(s) in former Yugoslavia, the first time that proceedings of this type had been contemplated in the context of (largely) non-international armed conflict. The arguments for and against such proceedings can be presented starkly:

> The main argument against any such proceedings clearly lies in the impediment which ... might [be] put in the way of a peace settlement.... [C]ontinuing conflict and possibly atrocities, would be a very high price to pay for ... war crimes trials. The counter-argument is that to ignore, and in effect thereby to condone, very serious violations of the laws of armed conflict sends out a disastrous message to any other[s] ... who might have such practices in mind.[57]

At the time of writing the practicality, utility, and not least the availability of potential defendants remain an open question. However, substantive moves towards the setting up of an *ad hoc* tribunal under UN aegis have proceeded further than ever before since the end of the Second World War.

By Resolution 808 of 22 February 1993, paragraph 1, the Security Council resolved that an international tribunal should be set up 'for the prosecution of persons responsible for serious violations of international humanitarian law committed in the territory of former Yugoslavia since 1991'. The organization and jurisdiction of the tribunal was then considered in detail and a draft statute prepared which was finally approved by the Security Council through resolution 827 of 25 May 1993. It must first be asked what authority the Security Council or any other organ of the UN has to set up such a tribunal. The International Military Tribunal was established under the inter-Allied 1945 London Agreement which in effect was a treaty arrangement for the situation. Such a process in the case of former Yugoslavia would have seemed both cumbersome and dilatory. The basis for the establishment of a tribunal as stated in the Secretary General's Report upon the matter[58] was as an enforcement measure within the meaning of Chapter VII of the UN Charter. In other words, the tribunal was viewed as a means of restoring international peace and security and would function as a subsidiary, judicial organ under article 29 of the UN Charter. Article 29 is vast in its potential scope, providing simply that '[t]he Security Council may establish such subsidiary organs as it deems necessary for the performance of its functions'.

The equation of trials with 'measures' under Chapter VII of the Charter, in particular under article 41 dealing with 'measures not involving the use of armed force ... to be employed to give effect to [the Security Council's] ... decisions' may seem somewhat innovatory but by no means unsustainable. The question again arises as to how far the armed conflict itself could be construed as international. Perhaps the situation in former Yugoslavia could best be taken as one of a 'crystallization' of international law, in that principles of jurisdiction that had been implicit now found explicit expression. The argument demands caution but at least does not carry the taint of retrospection since the acts concerned were by any standards and upon the agreement of the Parties themselves, unlawful.

In terms of the purpose and jurisdiction of the tribunal, an immediate question of terminology arises in the definition of 'international humanitarian law'.[59] However, the drafting of the Charter of the tribunal makes it clear that the term is intended to cover a very broad spectrum of the laws of armed conflict, including the 'Hague' and 'Geneva' aspects of the *jus in bello* together with aspects of 'human rights' law and elements of the *jus ad bellum*. The general competence of the Statute of the Tribunal, as stated by article 1, essentially repeats the remit set out by paragraph 1 of Security Council Resolution 808 of 22 February 1933. Articles 2 to 5 then list the offences with which the Tribunal is concerned: grave breaches of the 1949 Geneva Conventions; other violations of the laws or customs of war;[60] genocide, defined in the same terms as in the 1948 Genocide Convention, and Crimes against Humanity. The latter, a category established by the Charter of the Nuremberg Tribunal, is stated by article 5 of the Statute of the Tribunal for former Yugoslavia to comprise acts of murder, extermination, enslavement, deportation, imprisonment, torture, rape, persecution and 'other inhumane acts'.

The jurisdiction over persons is set out by articles 6 and 7 of the Statute of the Tribunal. Article 6 provides simply for jurisdiction over 'natural persons', that is *people* responsible for violations whatever their municipal status. The fundamental issue is addressed by article 7 paragraphs (1) and (2). Article 7(1) provides for *individual criminal responsibility* in any person involved in or abetting any of the offences set out in articles 2 to 5 of the Statute. Article 7(2) then adds that the official position of a defendant neither relieves him or her of criminal responsibility nor acts in mitigation of punishment. This denial of an 'Act of State' defence follows directly from the jurisprudence of Nuremberg. It has the evident and commendable aim of seeking to avert a flood of trials of NCOs whilst ministers and generals retire in safety. Whether this will be achieved remains to be seen.

The administrative structure of the Tribunal is a matter of some importance, with the Statute providing for two trial chambers and one appellate chamber[61] served in total by eleven judges, three in each trial chamber and five in the appellate chamber.[62] Appointment of judges is through election by the General Assembly from a list submitted by the Security Council. The candidates are to be persons of high moral character eligible for judicial appointment in their own countries, the phrasing being based, though not verbatim, upon article 2 of the Statute of the International Court of Justice.[63] No two judges may be nationals of the same state.[64]

Careful provision is made for the maintenance of due process in proceedings before the Tribunal; the essential guarantees, including information as to charges, presumption of innocence and rights to defence, are set out by article 21 of the Statute of the Tribunal. In the event of convictions, important questions arise in relation to penal sanctions and the modes and places of their imposition. Issues requiring consideration include the possibility of capital sentences, which have been imposed by Bosnian courts in relevant contexts,[65] and the place where custodial sentences can safely and properly be served. In the latter respect, the need to avoid both undue harshness and undue leniency is an obvious issue. The Statute of the Tribunal provides by article 24 that the sentencing power of the trial chambers is limited to imprisonment, the terms to be served being guided by the practice of the courts of former Yugoslavia, by the gravity of the offence and the personal circumstances of the defendant. Orders for the restoration of property criminally acquired may also be made under article 24(3), a matter of special significance in the context of so-called 'ethnic cleansing'.

The question of place of imprisonment presents major difficulties. Apart from the significant expense of possibly long custodial sentences, the dangers of terrorism, either from friends or foes of the prisoner, would be major disincentives for any third state in considering acceptance of persons convicted by the tribunal into its prison system. One possibility was incarceration in the home jurisdiction of the offender, subject to appropriate international oversight,[66] but this was not the solution adopted. Article 27 provides that sentences will be served in a state selected by the Tribunal from a list of states which have agreed with the Security Council to act in this capacity. Imprisonment will be according to the terms of the local national law, subject to supervision by the Tribunal. It is to be hoped that an adequate number of states do so agree since the supervision arrangements for, e.g., a relatively young offender sentenced to life imprisonment might be very extended. The precedent of Rudolph Hess imprisoned in Spandau Prison by the Nuremberg Tribunal indicates something of the potential commitment. Where, under the law of the incarcerating state, a prisoner sentenced by the Tribunal is eligible for pardon or commution of sentence, the question will be referred to the Tribunal for decision in the interests of justice and 'general principles of law'.[67] This implies a long-term existence for the Tribunal, which might therefore also be found other tasks.

Appeals on issues of law or fact lie to the Appeals Chamber of the Tribunal. Upon hearing an appeal, the Chamber may affirm, reverse or revise the decisions of the trial chamber which heard the case.[68]

The Tribunal is to sit at the Hague.[69] It enjoys all the privileges and immunities necessary to the performance of its functions.[70]

The establishment of the Tribunal represents a major step in endeavours to maintain the laws of armed conflict in cases of major violations. It is a particularly significant step in the context of non-international armed conflicts, although the situation which gave rise to it was by no means typical of civil upheavals in either context or extent. What fruit this initiative will ultimately yield, both in particular and in general, cannot now be predicted, though the stakes are high. A successful process would add invaluably to the means of enforcement available in the context of law and armed conflict; failure could encourage aggressors to be even more reckless.

The Question of Superior Orders

In the immediate context matters such as 'necessity' are hardly relevant, granted the fundamental nature of the humanitarian norms in question.[71] One troublesome issue does merit attention, however. Any system of military (or equivalent) discipline is ultimately founded upon obedience to superior orders which immediately raises the question of the extent to which a subordinate acting in obedience to an *unlawful* order is thereby absolved from liability. The matter has arisen from time to time in a number of jurisdictions.[72] The classical position which emerges from this jurisprudence is an 'ought to know' doctrine: if the subordinate knew or ought to have known that the order was unlawful, then there will be no defence although, depending upon the circumstances, there may still be a substantial mitigating factor. If, however, the subordinate did not, and could not be expected to, know that the order was unlawful, then a defence might be possible. So the matter stood in 1939. However, according to article 8 of the Charter of the International Military Tribunal at Nuremberg:

The fact that the Defendant acted pursuant to orders of his government or of a superior shall not free him from responsibility, but may be considered in mitigation of punishment if the Tribunal determines that justice so demands.

This appears to represent a doctrine of strict liability, but remember that this provision concerned the trial of senior figures in government and military command who to a very large extent were the 'superiors' in question. The issue related back to the potential defence at Nuremberg founded upon a maximum regression of responsibility so that everything could be laid at the door of Adolf Hitler who was already dead. Interestingly in the *Peleus case*, concerning orders from a submarine commander to fire upon shipwrecked survivors from a sunken ship (heard before a British Military Tribunal in Hamburg), the Judge-Advocate remarked in judgment upon this point that '[if] it must have been obvious ... that it was not a lawful command [subordinates] ... are not to be excused'.[73] This appears to reflect the classical 'ought to know doctrine' in a case genuinely involving unlawful orders to subordinates.

Article 7(4) of the Statute of the Tribunal for former Yugoslavia adopted the 'Nuremberg' formulation without qualification, leaving superior orders as no more than a plea in mitigation in all circumstances. As in Nuremberg, of course, the offences before the tribunal were so substantial that no subordinate could hope to rely upon an 'ought to know' doctrine of superior orders, even if such were conceded to exist. Whether the same position would hold in more ambiguous circumstances must remain an open question, although an absolute doctrine of strict liability must be considered very harsh.

In the context of former Yugoslavia, the (often seemingly deliberate) vagueness of command structures and chains of responsibility clearly presented particular difficulties. This, coupled with the nature of the crimes under consideration, all tend to suggest that the stricter 'Nuremberg' formula had evident advantages. It may be added that whatever view of 'superior orders' is taken, the central issue is not the existence of liability but on whom it devolves. If a subordinate is excused, the superior who gave the unlawful order will yet remain liable. Interestingly, article 7(3) of the Statute of the Tribunal for former Yugoslavia emphasizes the liability of superiors who knew that a subordinate was about to act unlawfully within the scale of offences set by the Statute, and failed to take measures to prevent this or to punish the perpetrator thereafter.

The General Relevance of the Tribunal

The potential, for both good and ill, of the Tribunal set up to consider war crimes charges arising from the conflicts in former Yugoslavia is obviously considerable. In conclusion, it must be emphasized that the trial of offenders is, at most, a very poor second best. The primary aim of the laws of armed conflict – avoiding aggression altogether and mitigating its impact if it occurs – has by definition failed by this point. Greater emphasis must therefore be placed on securing compliance with international law and upon adequate processes of national training and dissemination including, where possible, to those fighting in dissident forces.

Notes

1   H. McCoubrey 'The Idea of War Crimes and Crimes against Peace since 1945', University of Nottingham Department of Law/Centre for International Defence Law Studies, *Research Papers in Law* No. 2 (June 1992), p.2.

2   Taken as the hallmark of the classical positivist analyses of Jeremy Bentham and John Austin, although this is a considerable over-simplification. See J. Bentham, *Of Laws in General, circa* 1782 (ed.) H.L.A. Hart (Athlone Press, 1970), Ch. 1, para. 1.

3   Especially that of H.L.A. Hart; see *The Concept of Law* (Oxford University Press, 1961; extended second edn 1994), Ch. 6. Rules-based analysis has been much criticized recently; see in particular R. Dworkin, *Taking Rights Seriously* (Duckworth, 1977), Chapters 2, 3 and 4; also *A Matter of Principle* (Oxford University Press, 1985), Chapters 1–4.

4   The central concern of Naturalist theories. This is found in a vast range of writings, including those of Plato, Aristotle, St Augustine of Hippo, St Thomas Aquinas, the 17th- and 18th-century Social Contractarians, Lon L. Fuller and John Finnis. For a modern view, see J. Finnis, *Natural Law and Natural Rights* (Oxford University Press, 1980), Ch. 9.

5   For brief discussion, see H. McCoubrey and N.D. White, *Textbook on Jurisprudence* (Blackstone Press, 1993), Ch. 1.

6   Treason may of course be variously defined, but at any given time the assumption will be made of allegiance to the authority then in power, except in cases of alien military occupation.

7   *Mencius*, I.B.8, trans. D.C. Lau (Penguin, 1970), p.68.

8   G.M. Trevelyan, *England under the Stuarts*, 1904 (Methuen, 1965), p.276.

9   H.L.A. Hart, *The Concept of Law* (Oxford University Press, 1961), pp.100–101.

10 Lord Campbell, *Lives of the Lord Chancellors* (John Murray, 1846), Vol. III, p.195.

11 As to trial processes, see pp.260 ff, below.

12 As to refugee status, see Chapter 7, pp.149 ff.

13 *The Daily Telegraph* (London), 31 March 1993.

14 H. McCoubrey, 'The Armed Conflict in Bosnia and Proposed War Crimes Trials', *International Relations* (1993) XI, p.411 at p.429.

15 Lon L Fuller, *The Morality of Law*, revised edn (Yale University Press, 1969), p.184.

16 See *ibid.*, p.153.

17 Article 6(2)(a)–(f).
18 F. Hampson, 'Violation of Fundamental Rights in the Former Yugoslavia, II. The Case for a War Crimes Tribunal', *The David Davies Memorial Institute of International Studies*, Occasional Paper no. 3 (February 1993), pp.6–7.
19 See below, pp.271–7.
20 As to the application of the laws of armed conflict in non-international conflicts, see Chapter 1 at pp.17 ff. For consideration of applicable 'Hague' Law, governing methods and means of conflict, see Chapter 5.
21 There is some debate over the extent of 'defences' in terms of 'military necessity'; see H. McCoubrey, 'The Nature of the Modern Doctrine of Military Necessity', *Revue de Droit Militaire et de Droit de la Guerre* (1991) XXX, pp.217–42.
22 See J. Pictet, *Development and Principles of International Humanitarian Law* (Martinus Nijhoff, 1985), p.88.
23 1949 Geneva Convention I, article 50; 1949 Geneva Convention II, article 51; similar provision is made by 1949 Geneva Convention III, article 130, with further provision for prisoners of war; 1949 Geneva Convention IV, article 147 also makes similar provision, with expanded reference to the protection of civilians.
24 In particular by article 85(3)(4).
25 H. McCoubrey, 'The Idea of War Crimes and Crimes against Peace since 1945', University of Nottingham Department of Law/Centre for International Defence Law Studies, *Research Papers in Law* No. 2 (June 1992), p.18.
26 For discussion, see H. McCoubrey and N.D. White, *International Law and Armed Conflict* (Dartmouth, 1992), Ch. 20. An extended analysis of the development of the criminal jurisprudence of international armed conflict prior to the 1977 developments will be found in G. Schwarzenberger, *International Law, Vol. II, Armed Conflict* (Stevens, 1968), pp.443–546. A useful and more recent analysis will be found in R.S. Clark and I.A. Lediakh, 'The Influence of the Nuremberg Trial on the Development of International Law', comprising Chapter IX in G. Ginsburgs and V.N. Kudriavtsev (eds), *The Nuremberg Trial in International Law* (Martinus Nijhoff, 1990), pp.249–83.
27 See pp.271 ff, below.
28 1949 Geneva Convention I, article 49; 1949 Geneva Convention II, article 50; 1949 Geneva Convention III, article 129; 1949 Geneva Convention IV, article 146. See also implicit reference in 1977 Additional Protocol I, article 85.
29 P.W. Mourning, 'Leashing the Dogs of War: Outlawing the Recruitment and Use of Mercenaries', *Virginia Journal of International Law* (1982) 22, p.589 at pp.602–3.
30 F. Hampson, 'Mercenaries: Diagnosis before Proscription', *Netherlands Yearbook of International Law* (1991) XXII, p.3 at p.27.
31 Bowman and Harris, *Multilateral Treaties: Index and Current Status*, Ninth Cumulative Supplement (University of Nottingham Treaty Centre, 1992), Treaty 955, p.84. This appeared to remain the case in early 1994.
32 1989 Convention, article 5. This is to say that they will be so constrained when the Convention comes into force.
33 *Ibid.*, article 4.
34 Bowman and Harris, *op.cit.*, Ninth Cumulative Supplement, Treaty 451, p.173.
35 Articles 13 and 14.
36 See pp.22 ff, above.
37 Article 7 of the Convention requires the application of the 'severest penalties' available under the laws of the state concerned, including capital punishment.
38 F. Hampson, *op.cit.*, at p.37.
39 *Ibid.*
40 (1982) LIII *British Yearbook of International Law*, p.418.

41   For discussion of so-called 'ethnic cleansing', see Chapter 7 at pp.155 ff, above.
42   UN doc. S/25274, p.16., See also p.157, above.
43   *Case concerning Application of the Convention on the Prevention and Punishment of the Crime of Genocide (Bosnia and Herzegovina v Yugoslavia)* (1993) ICJ Reps., 3.
44   H. McCoubrey and N.D. White, *International Law and Armed Conflict* (Dartmouth, 1992), p.117–18.
45   *Attorney-General of the Government of Israel v Eichmann* (1961) 36 *International Law Reports*, 5.
46   See in particular, 1949 Geneva Convention I, article 49; 1949 Geneva Convention II, article 50; 1949 Geneva Convention IV, article 146. See also 1977 Additional Protocol I, article 88.
47   For a detailed consideration of this question, see M. Cherif Bassiouni, *International Criminal Law, III, Enforcement* (Transnational Publishers, 1987), Chapters 1 and 2.
48   GA Res. 260 (III)B, 3 UN GAOR (1948).
49   E.g., the *Dover Castle* and *Llandovery Castle* cases concerning hospital ships; see (1922) 16 *American Journal of International law*, p.708.
50   H. McCoubrey, 'The Idea of War Crimes and Crimes against Peace since 1945', University of Nottingham Department of Law/Centre for International Defence Studies, *Research Papers in Law*, No. 2 (June 1992), pp.8–9.
51   W.V. O'Brien, 'The Nuremberg Precedent and the Gulf War' (1991) 31 *Virginia Journal of International Law*, p.391 at pp.393–4.
52   In particular the *Hagenbach case* in 1474. For discussion of this case see G. Schwarzenberger, *International Law, Vol. II, Armed Conflict* (Stevens, 1968), pp.462–6 and R.K. Worzel, *The Nuremberg Trials in Public International Law* (Stevens, 1962), pp.19–21.
53   'IMT Judgement and Sentences' (1947) 41 *American Journal of International Law*, p.172 at p.221.
54   As to the legal personality of international institutions, see pp. ...., above.
55   L.C.B. Bower, *Principles of Modern Company Law*, 5th edn (Sweet and Maxwell, 1992), p.108.
56   See below, pp.277–8.
57   H. McCoubrey, 'The Armed Conflict in Bosnia and Proposed War Crimes Trials' (1993) XI *International Relations*, p.411 at p.432.
58   UN doc. S/25704 (3 May 1993), paragraph 28.
59   As to definitions see p.103, above.
60   This category includes the rules and principles set out by 1907 Hague Convention IV and the Regulations respecting Land Warfare annexed thereto, as interpreted and applied by the International Military Tribunal at Nuremberg.
61   Article 11.
62   Article 12.
63   Statute of the Tribunal for former Yugoslavia, article 13.
64   Article 12.
65   See p.259, above.
66   See H. McCoubrey, *op.cit.*, at pp. 431–2.
67   Article 28 of the Statute.
68   Article 25.
69   Article 31.
70   Article 30.
71   For discussion, see H. McCoubrey and N.D. White, *International Law and Armed Conflict* (Dartmouth, 1992), at pp.339–43. See also, H. McCoubrey, 'The Nature of the Modern Doctrine of Military Necessity' (1991) XXX *Revue de Droit Militaire et de Droit de la Guerre*, pp.217–42.
72   See, e.g. *R v Thomas* (1816) 4 M&S, 41; *Riggs v State* (1866) 43 Tenn., 85; *R v*

Smith (1900) 17 SCR, 561; the *Llandovery Castle case* (1922) 16 *American Journal of International Law*, 704; The *Peleus case*, Vol. I, *War Crimes Trials* (William Hocky & Co., 1948); and *Military Prosecutor v Melinski* (1958/9) 17 Pesahim Mehojiins, 90. For extended discussion, see L.C. Green, *Superior Orders in National and International Law* (A.W. Sithoff, 1976).

73   Volume I, *War Crimes Trials* (William Hocky and Co., 1948).

Bibliography

Books

Abi-Saab, G., *The United Nations Operation in the Congo* (Oxford University Press, 1978).

Adams, V., *Chemical Warfare, Chemical Disarmament* (Macmillan, 1989).

Arend, A.C. and R.J. Beck, *International Law and the Use of Force* (Routledge, 1993).

Bassiouni, C., *International Criminal Law, III, Enforcement* (Transnational Publishers, 1987).

Beckett, W.E., *The North Atlantic Treaty, the Brussels Treaty and the Charter of the United Nations* (Stevens, 1950).

Bedjaoui, M. (ed.), *Modern Wars* (Zed Books, 1986).

Bethlehem, D.L. (ed.), *The Kuwait Crisis: Sanctions and their Economic Consequences* (Grotius, 1991).

Bowett, D.W., *The Law of International Institutions*, 4th edn (Stevens, 1982).

Bowett, D.W., *United Nations Forces* (Stevens, 1964).

Boyd, J.M. *United Nations Peace-Keeping Operations: A Military and Political Appraisal* (Praeger Publishers, 1971).

Brogan, P., *World Conflicts*, 2nd edn (Bloomsbury, 1992).

Brownlie, I., *Principles of Public International Law*, 4th edn (Clarendon Press, 1990).

Cassese, A. (ed.), *The Current Legal Regulation on the Use of Force* (Martinus Nijhoff, 1986).

Cot, J.P. and A. Pellet, *La Charte des Nations Unies* (Economica, 1985).

Delissen, A.J.M. and C.J. Tanja (eds), *Humanitarian Law of Armed Conflict Challenges Ahead: Essays in Honour of Frits Kalshoven* (Martinus Nijhoff, 1991).

Dinstein, Y., *War, Aggression and Self-Defence* (Grotius, 1988).

Dworkin, R., *A Matter of Principle* (Oxford University Press, 1985).

Dworkin, R., *Taking Rights Seriously* (Duckworth, 1977).

Farago, L., *Aftermath: Martin Borman and the Fourth Reich* (Simon and Schuster, 1974).

Finnis, J., *Natural Law and Natural Rights* (Oxford University Press, 1980).

Fox, H. and M. Meyer (eds), *Armed Conflict and the New Law, Vol. II, Effecting Compliance* (British Institute of International and Comparative Law, 1993).

Fuller, L.L., *The Morality of Law* (Yale University Press, 1969).

Gilmore, W.C., *The Grenada Intervention* (Mansell, 1984).

Ginsburg, G. and V.N. Kudriavtsev (eds), *The Nuremberg Trial in International law* (Martinus Nijhoff, 1990).

Goodrich, L.M., E. Hambro and P.S. Simons, *Charter of the United Nations*, 3rd edn (Columbia University Press, 1969).

Goodwin-Gill, G.S., *The Refugee in International Law* (Oxford University Press, 1983).

Gower, L.C.B., *Principles of Modern Company Law*, 5th edn (Sweet and Maxwell, 1992).

Green, L.C., *Superior Orders in National and International Law* (A.W. Sithoff, 1976).

Han H.H. (ed.), *Terrorism and Political Violence: Limits and Possibilities of Legal Control* (Oceania, 1993).

Harris, D.J., *Cases and Materials on International Law*, 4th edn (Sweet and Maxwell, 1991).

Hart, H.L.A., *The Concept of Law* (Oxford University Press, 1961).

Hassouna, H.A., *The League of Arab States and Regional Disputes* (Oceania, 1975).

Hathaway, J.C., *The Law of Refugee Status* (Butterworths Canada, 1991).

Henkin, L. (ed.), *Right v Might: International Law and the Use of Force* (Council of Foreign Relations Press, 1989).

Herczeg, G., *Development of International Humanitarian Law* (Akedemiai Kiado, Budapest, 1984).

Hobbes, T., *Leviathan* (1651, Pelican edn, 1968).

Jackson, B.S. and D. McGoldrick (eds), *Legal Visions of a New Europe* (Kluwer, 1993).

Jennings, R. and A. Watts, *Oppenheim's International Law* (Longman, 1991).

Kalshoven, F., *Assisting the Victims of Armed Conflicts and other Disasters* (Martinus Nijhoff, 1989).

Kalshoven, F., *Constraints upon the Waging of War*, 2nd edn (ICRC, 1991).

Lie, T., *In the Cause of Peace* (Macmillan, 1954).

Lillich, R. (ed.), *Humanitarian Intervention and the United Nations* (University Press of Virginia, 1973).

Luard, E., *A History of the United Nations: The Years of Western Domination 1945–1955*, vol. 1 (Macmillan, 1982).

Luard, E. (ed.), *The International Regulation of Civil Wars* (Thames and Hudson, 1972).

Luard, E., *The United Nations* (Macmillan, 1979).

H. McCoubrey, *International Humanitarian Law* (Dartmouth, 1990).

McCoubrey, H., *The Development of Naturalist Legal Theory* (Croom Helm, 1987).

McCoubrey, H. and N.D. White, *A Textbook on Jurisprudence* (Blackstone Press, 1993).

McCoubrey, H. and N.D. White, *International Law and Armed Conflict* (Dartmouth, 1992).

Meron, T., *Human Rights in Internal Strife: Their International Protection* (Grotius, 1987).

Merrills, J.G., *International Dispute Settlement*, 2nd edn (Grotius Publications, 1991).

Moore, J.B., *A Digest of International Law*, Vol. I (US Government Printing Office, 1906).

Moore, J.B., *International Arbitrations to which the United States has been a Party* (US Government Printing Office, 1898).

Moore, J.N. (ed.), *Law and Civil War in the Modern World* (John Hopkins University Press, 1974).

Moore, W., *Gas Attack* (Leo Cooper, 1987).

Naldi, G.J., *The Organization of African Unity* (Mansell, 1989).

Oppenheim, L., *International Law, Vol. I, Disputes, War and Neutrality*, 6th edn in H. Lauterpacht (ed.) (Longmans, 1940).

Padelford, N.J., *International Law and Diplomacy in the Spanish Civil Strife* (Macmillan, 1939).

Pictet, J., *Development and Principles of International Humanitarian Law* (Martinus Nijhoff, 1985).

Pogany, I., *The Arab League and Peacekeeping in the Lebanon* (Avebury, 1987).

Pomerance, M., *Self-Determination in Law and in Practice* (Martinus Nijhoff, 1982).

Roberts, A. and R. Guelff (eds), *Documents on the Laws of War*, 2nd edn (Oxford University Press, 1989).

Roberts, A. and B. Kingbury (eds), *United Nations, Divided World*, 2nd edn (Clarendon Press, 1993).

Ronzitti, N., *Rescuing Nationals Abroad through Military Coercion and Intervention on Grounds of Humanity* (Martinus Nijhoff, 1985).

Rowe, P. (ed.), *The Gulf War 1990–91 in International and English Law* (Routledge/Sweet and Maxwell, 1993).

Russell, R.M. and K.M. Muther, *A History of the United Nations Charter* (Brookings Institute, 1958).

Sandoz, Y., C. Swinarski and B. Zimmermann (eds), *Commentary on the Additional Protocols of 8 June 1977 to the Geneva Convention of 12 August 1949* (ICRC/Martinus Nijhoff, 1987).

Schwarzenberger, G., *International Law, Vol. II, Armed Conflict* (Stevens, 1968).

Shaw, M.N., *International Law*, 3rd edn (Grotius, 1991).

Sieghart, P., *The Lawful Rights of Mankind* (Oxford University Press, 1986).

Siekmann, R.C.R., *Basic Documents on U.N. and Related Peace-Keeping Forces*, 2nd edn (Martinus Nijhoff, 1989).

Speer, A., *Inside the Third Reich* (Sphere Books, 1971).

Spiers, E.M., *Chemical Warfare* (Macmillan, 1986), p.17.

Starke, J.G., *Introduction to International Law*, 10th edn (Butterworths, 1989).

Strack, H.R., *Sanctions: The Case of Rhodesia* (Syracuse University Press, 1978).

Swinarski, C. (ed.), *Studies and Essays in International Humanitarian Law and Red Cross Principles in Honour of Jean Pictet* (ICRC with Martinus Nijhoff, 1984).

Touval, S. and I.W. Zartman (eds), *International Mediation in Theory and Practice* (Boulder, 1985).

Trevelyan, G.M., *England under the Stuarts* (Methuen University Paperbacks, 1965).

White, N.D., *Keeping the Peace: The United Nations and the Maintenance of International Peace and Security*, 2nd edn (Manchester University Press, 1993).

Wiseman, H., *Peacekeeping: Appraisals and Proposals* (Pergamon Press, 1983).

Worzel, R.K., *The Nuremberg Trials in Public International Law* (Stevens, 1962).

Articles

Akehurst, M., 'Enforcement Action by Regional Agencies with Special Reference to the O.A.S.' (1967) 45 *BYIL* p.175.

Berberg, E., 'Regional Organisations: A United Nations Problem' (1955) 49 *AJIL* p.166.

Bohr, S., 'Sanctions by the United Nations Security Council and the European Community' (1993) 4 *EJIL* p.256.

Falk, R.A., 'The Shimoda Case: A Legal Appraisal of the Atomic Attacks upon Hiroshima and Nagasaki' (1965) 59 *AJIL* p.759.

Faundez, J., 'International Law and Wars of National Liberation' (1989) 1 *African Journal of International and Comparative Law*, p.85.

Fong, C., 'Some Legal Aspects of the Search for Admission into other States of Persons leaving the Indo-Chinese Peninsula in Small Boats' (1981) 52 *British Yearbook of International Law*, p.53.

Garner, J.W., 'Recognition of Belligerency' (1938) 31 *AJIL* p.398.

Gasser, H-P, 'A Measure of Humanity in Internal Disturbances and Tensions: Proposal for a Code of Conduct' (1988) January–February, *International Review of the Red Cross*, p.38.

Gilmour, D.R., 'The Meaning of "Intervene" within Article 2(7) of the United Nations Charter' (1967) 16 *ICLQ* p.330.

Goodhart, A.L., 'The North Atlantic Treaty of 1949' (1951) 79 *Hague Recueil*, p.187.

Goodrich, L., 'Korea: Collective Measures against Aggression' (1953) 494 *International Conciliation*, p.157.

Greenwood, C., 'The Concept of War in Modern International Law' (1987) 36 *ICLQ* p.283.

Hampson, F., 'Mercenaries: Diagnosis before Proscription' (1991) 22 *NILR* p.3.

Kelsen, H., 'Is the North Atlantic Treaty a Regional Arrangement?' (1951) 45 *AJIL* p.162.

Lavalle, R., 'The "Inherent" Powers of the UN Secretary General in the Political Sphere; A Legal Analysis' (1990) 37 *NILR* p.22.

McCoubrey, H., 'Protection of Creed and Opinion in the Laws of Armed Conflict', *University of Nottingham Research Papers in Law*, No. 7 (February 1993).

McCoubrey, H., 'The Armed Conflict in Bosnia and Proposed War Crimes Trials' (1993) 11 *International Relations*, p.411.

McCoubrey, H., 'The Idea of War Crimes and Crimes against Peace since 1945' *University of Nottingham Research Papers in Law*, No. 2 (June 1992).

McCoubrey, H., 'The Laws of Armed Conflict and United Nations Forces: Regulating Military Action for Peace' (1993), 20 *Journal of Malaysian and Comparative Law*, p.59.

McCoubrey, H., 'The Nature of the Modern Doctrine of Military Necessity' (1991) 30 *Revue de Droit Militaire et de Droit de la Guerre*, p.217.

McCoubrey, H., 'Yugoslavia at War: International Laws of Armed Conflict and the Yugoslav Crisis' (1992) 136 *Solicitors Journal*, p.914.

Meyer, M.A., 'Liability of Prisoners of War for Offences Committed Prior to Capture: The Astiz Affair' (1983) 32 *ICLQ* p.948.

Mourning, P.W., 'Leashing the Dogs of War: Outlawing the Recruitment and Use of Mercenaries' (1982) 22 *Virginia Journal of International Law*, p.589.

O'Brien, W.V., 'The Nuremberg Precedent and the Gulf War' (1991) 21 *Virginia Journal of International Law*, p.391.

Pokalas, J., 'Economic Sanctions: An Effective Alternative to Military Coercion? (1980) 6 *Brooklyn Journal of International Law*, p.289.

Quigley, J., 'The United States and the United Nations in the Persian Gulf War: New Order or Disorder?' (1992) 25 *Cornell International Law Journal*, p.1.

Rao, T., 'When does War Begin?' (1972) *IJIL* p.368.

Schachter, O., 'United Nations Law in the Gulf Conflict' (1991) 85 *AJIL* p.425.

Schlager, E.B., 'Does CSCE Spell Stability for Europe?' (1991) 21 *Cornell International Law Journal*, p.503.

Sepulveda, C., 'The Reform of the Charter of American States' (1972) 137 *Hague Recueil*, p.210.

Sigmon, J.A., 'Dispute Resolution in the United Nations: An Inefficient Forum?' (1984) 10 *Brooklyn Journal of International Law*, p.437.

Treverton, G.F., 'Elements of a New European Security Order' (1991) 45 *Journal of International Affairs*, p.91.

Westing, A.H., 'The Threat of Biological Warfare' (1985) 35 *Bioscience*, p.627.

Index